FOODI MULTI-COOKER COOKBOOK

515 Delicious Recipes for Air Fryer, Instant Pot, Pressure Cooker, Slow Cooker and More

MARK BRIAN

Table of Contents

FEARLESS FLAVOR RECIPES........ 202

INTRODUCTION

There is nothing like delicious and comforting home-cooked meals. If you are conscious regarding taste and health, you want to be sure about the level of quality of your foods. However, in the modern busy lifestyle, it often becomes difficult to maintain this healthy meal habit. The cooking time, nutritional value and also other necessary aspects related to home-cooking makes it very difficult for you to maintain the healthy lifestyle that you have always wanted.

The good thing is that there exists a solution to prepare home-cooked foods in a minimum amount of time required along with 90 % nutrient retention. As you probably guessed it. We are talking about the Mufti-cooker that is a panacea for modern-day cooking challenges.

The Foodi Multi-Cooker- is revolutionary! You can cook essentially anything in a Multicooker - from meats and main courses to rice, potatoes, vegetables of every description, dessert to even yogurt, Better yet. pressure cooking and air frying cooking lets you to cook foods up to 70 faster, and 75% less fat, on average, than conventional cooking methods, do, which means you save energy in addition to your precious time!

The Foodi Multi-Cooker has amazing features: The Frozen to Crispy, in as little as 20 minutes, pressure cook frozen meats to quickly defrost and Cook them at the same time. Then drop the Crisping lid to give meal a crispy finish; 360 Meals, Cook proteins, grains, and veggies at the same time to create flavorful, multi-textured meals in one pot; One-Pot Wonders, Elevate your favorite casseroles, stews, chilis, and desserts with a crispy or bubbly layer of your favorite topping. The Foodi Multi-cooker can also be used as an oven, steamer, roaster, dehydrator, and slow cooker.

This cookbook presents carefully hank-picked and delicious recipes that you can cook in your Foodi. Just pick the best recipes you like and Start Cooking with your Foodi Multi-Cooker now: with a collection Of 510 mouth-watering, delicious recipes to prepare using your Multi-cooker Foodi.

It is my belief that food is medicine, and what you put in your body has a direct impact on your overall quality of life. Let this cookbook be your guide to a healthier chapter in your family's life, and experience what cooking at home should be like -easy, delicious, & nutritious.

HOT HEARTY

CLASSIC

RECIPES

1.   Creamy Parmesan Spinach Dip

Ingredients

- 10 oz frozen chopped spinach, thawed and excess liquid squeezed out
- 1/2 cup light sour cream, full fat for Keto
- 5 tbsp light mayonnaise, full fat, check labels for Keto
- 1/3 cup Parmigiano Reggiano
- 1/4 cup scallion, chopped
- fresh pepper to taste

Instructions

1. Combine all the ingredients in a medium bowl.
2. Can be made one day in advance and stored in the refrigerator.
3. Remove from refrigerator 30 minutes before serving.

2.   Garlic Shrimp

Ingredients

- 1 lb large shrimp, peeled and deveined (weight after you peel them)
- 6 cloves garlic, sliced thin
- 1 tbsp Spanish olive oil
- crushed red pepper flakes
- pinch paprika
- salt
- 1/4 cup chopped fresh herbs like cilantro or parsley
- Lime wedges for serving

Instructions

1. In a large skillet, heat oil on medium heat and add the garlic and red pepper flakes.
2. Sauté until golden, about 2 minutes being careful not to burn.
3. Add shrimp and season with salt and paprika.
4. Cook 2-3 minutes until shrimp is cooked through.
5. Do not overcook or it will become tough and chewy.
6. Add chopped fresh herbs and divide equally in 3 plates.

3. Lamb Kofta Kebabs

Ingredients

- 1/2 pound ground grass-fed lamb
- 1/2 cup parsley
- 1/2 inch fresh turmeric, grated
- 1/4 teaspoon sea salt

Instructions

1. Gather 4 wooden kebab skewers. Soak skewers in water for 1 hour.
2. Preheat oven to 300 degrees.
3. In a food processor, add parsley and process for 30 seconds, or until finely chopped.
4. Add lamb and grated turmeric to the processor and run until evenly mixed.
5. Form lamb tightly around the kebab skewers. Salt the exterior of the meat.
6. Line a baking sheet with foil and place an oven-safe rack on top of it so there is at least one inch of space between the rack and the pan. You may use a cast iron grill pan to get grill marks instead.
7. Place kebabs on the grill and place in the upper third of your oven. Bake for 18-20 minutes, or until the internal temperature has reached 160 degrees.
8. Remove lamb kofta from oven and garnish with grated turmeric and parsley sprigs.

4. BBQ Pulled Beef Sando

Ingredients

- 3lbs Boneless Chuck Roast
- 2 tsp Pink Himalayan Salt
- 2 tsp garlic powder
- 1 tsp onion powder
- 1 tsp black pepper
- 1 tbsp. smoked paprika
- 2 tbsp. tomato paste
- 1/4 cup apple cider vinegar
- 2 tbsp. coconut aminos
- 1/2 cup bone broth
- 1/4 cup melted Kerrygold Butter

Instructions

1. Trim the fat off of the beef and cut in to two large pieces.
2. In a small bowl mix together the salt, garlic, onion, paprika and black pepper. Then rub it all over the beef. Place the beef in your slow cooker.
3. In another bowl melt the butter, whisk in the tomato paste, vinegar and coconut aminos. Pour it all over the beef. Then add the bone broth to the slow cooker, pouring it around the beef.
4. Set on low and cook for 10-12 hours. When done, remove the beef, set the slow cooker to high and let the sauce thicken. Shred the beef then add it back in to the slow cooker and toss with sauce. Serve!

5. Shrimp Zucchini Noodles

Ingredients

- 2 tablespoons unsalted butter
- 2 tablespoons olive oil
- 1 pound medium shrimp, peeled and deveined
- 1 shallot, minced
- 4 cloves garlic, minced
- 1/4 teaspoon red pepper flakes, or more, to taste
- Kosher salt and freshly ground black pepper, to taste
- 1/4 cup vegetable stock
- 2 tablespoons freshly squeezed lemon juice
- 1 teaspoon lemon zest
- 1 1/2 pounds (4 medium-sized) zucchini, spiralized
- 2 tablespoons freshly grated Parmesan

Instructions

1. Combine butter and olive oil in a large skillet over medium high heat. Add shrimp, shallot, garlic and red pepper flakes; season with salt and pepper, to taste. Cook, stirring occasionally, until pink, about 2-3 minutes.
2. Stir in vegetable stock, lemon juice and lemon zest; season with salt and pepper, to taste. Bring to a simmer; stir in zucchini noodles until heated through, about 1-2 minutes.
3. Place zucchini into meal prep containers, garnished with Parmesan, if desired.

6. Low Carb Chili

Ingredients

- 1/2 tbsp avocado oil
- 2 ribs celery, chopped
- 2 lbs. 85/15 ground beef
- 1 tsp ground chipotle chili powder
- 1 tbsp chili powder
- 2 tsp garlic powder
- 1 tbsp cumin
- 1 tsp salt
- 1 tsp black pepper
- 1 15 oz. can no salt added tomato sauce
- 1 16.2 oz. container Kettle & Fire Beef Bone Broth

Instructions

1. In a large pot, heat avocado oil over medium heat. Add chopped celery and cook until softened, about 3-4 minutes. Transfer celery to separate bowl and set aside.
2. In same pot, add beef and spices and brown beef until cooked throughout.
3. Lower heat to medium-low, add tomato sauce and beef bone broth to cooked beef, and simmer covered for 10 minutes, stirring occasionally.
4. Add celery back to pot and stir until well-incorporated.
5. Garnish, serve, and enjoy!

7. Soy Free Ahi Poke

Ingredients

- 1lb give or take of sashimi grade Ahi tuna
- 2 tbsp coconut aminos
- 1 tbsp + 1 tsp sesame oil
- 1/2 tsp salt
- 1–2 tbsp toasted sesame seeds
- 1–2 stalk green onion
- 1/2 lemon
- Cilantro (optional)
- Other options: chopped macadamia nuts, mango, pineapple, red onion, lemon zest, minced ginger

Instructions

1. With a sharp knife cut your ahi in to 1/4 inch cubes & set in a bowl.
2. Add in oil, aminos, salt & squeeze in lemon.
3. Gently toss with hands.
4. Add in sesame seeds & sliced green onion.
5. Gently toss again.
6. You can add the avocado directly to the tuna or serve it over it.
7. Up to you.

I like to serve it with guacamole or avocado mixed with kraut!

8. Quick and Easy Sloppy Joes Recipe

Ingredients

- 1 pound ground beef (80% lean)
- 1 pound medium stalk celery (diced)
- 1 small yellow onion (diced)
- 2 cloves minced garlic
- 3/4 cup beef broth
- 1/4 cup tomato paste
- 2 tablespoons So Nourished powdered erythritol
- 2 teaspoons Worcestershire sauce
- 1 teaspoon dijon mustard
- salt and pepper

Instructions

1. Cook the beef in a large skillet over medium-high heat until browned, breaking it up with a spoon.
2. Stir in the celery, onion, and garlic and cook for 5 to 6 minutes until tender.
3. Add the remaining ingredients and stir well to combine.
4. Reduce heat and simmer on low for 20 minutes until it starts to thicken.
5. Serve the sloppy joes on keto bread or in lettuce cups.

9. Beef Stir Fry

Ingredients

- 1/2 cup zucchini, spiralized into 6-inch noodles
- 1 bunch baby bok choy
- 1/4 cup organic broccoli florets
- 8 ounces grass-fed flank or skirt steak, sliced against the grain into thin strips
- One 1-inch knob of ginger, peeled and cut into thin strips
- 2 tablespoons avocado oil or grass-fed ghee, divided
- 2 teaspoons coconut aminos

Instructions

1. Chop the end of the stem off your bok choy and discard.
2. In an heated pan, add 1 tablespoon of oil or ghee and sear your steak on medium-high heat, 1-2 minutes on each side.
3. Reduce heat to medium. Add remaining ghee, broccoli, ginger and coconut aminos to the pan. Cook for one minute, stirring frequently.
4. Stir in Bok choy and cook for another minute.
5. Stir in zucchini and cook until the noodles are at your desired preference. Watch closely, because they cook quick!

10. Beef Barbacoa

Ingredients

- 3 pounds grass-fed chuck roast fat cut off and cut into large chunks
- 1 large onion, peeled and sliced
- 6 garlic cloves
- 2 4oz can of green chilis
- 1 tablespoon oregano
- 1 teaspoon salt
- 1 teaspoons pepper
- 3 dried chipotle peppers stems removed and broken into pieces
- juice of 3 limes
- 3 tablespoons coconut vinegar
- 1 tablespoon cumin
- 1/4 cup water

Instructions

Add all Ingredients to the Instant Pot and stir.

1. Place lid on, make sure vent is closed, and hit the "manual" button. Increase time to 60 minutes.
2. Once done, let naturally release or press "cancel" and release the pressure.
3. Remove lid, shred with a fork, and hit the "sauté" button. Stir regularly as the juices reduce. This may take up to 20-30 minutes to fully reduce.

11. Chicken Fajita Soup

Ingredients

- 2 lbs boneless skinless chicken breasts mine were frozen
- 2 cans of diced tomatoes 10 oz
- 2 cups of chicken broth
- 2 tablespoons of taco seasoning I used homemade taco seasoning
- 2 teaspoons of minced garlic
- 1/2 cup of onion chopped
- 1 green bell pepper chopped
- 1 red bell pepper chopped

Instructions

1. Combine all the ingredients in the Instant Pot.
2. Lock the lid on top and set the valve to sealing.
3. Set the timer for 30 minutes.
4. Do a quick release.
5. Remove the chicken and shred.
6. Return the chicken to the pot and Stir to combine the flavors.

12. Crunchy Chicken Wraps

Ingredients

- 8 ounces of canned chicken (low sodium)
- 1 medium-sized carrot
- 1 stalk celery
- 1/4 cup mayonnaise (low fat)
- 1/2 red bell pepper
- 2 whole wheat lavash
- 2 pita bread wraps
- 1/2 teaspoon powdered onion

Instructions

1. Cut up paprika, celery sticks, and carrots into little cubes and mix in a deep dish.
2. Get another deep dish and mix mayonnaise and onion powder in it.
3. Smear about 2 tablespoonfuls of the mayo mixture over each pita bread.
4. Measure about 4 ounces of chicken and place on one half of the pita bread and about half of the vegetables.
5. Fold the pita bread into a roll and cut diagonally into two halves. Hold fast with a toothpick.

13. Cucumber Salad

Ingredients

- 2 tbsp Italian or Caesar salad dressing
- 2 cups sliced fresh cucumber ¼-inch slices (you can peel if you so desire)
- Fresh ground black pepper to taste

Instructions

1. Using a deep dish, mix some salad dip and slices of cucumber.
2. Cover the dish with its lid and shake well.
3. Spritz some ground cayenne pepper and then put the covered dish in the fridge.
4. Serve chilled.

14. Mac in a Flash (Macaroni and cheese)

Ingredients

- 1/4 tsp dry ground mustard
- 3 cups water
- 1 cup uncooked noodles, any shape
- ½ tbsp unsalted butter
- 1/2 cup of grated cheddar cheese

Instructions

1. Pour noodles into boiling water and leave to simmer till it is soft for about 7 minutes, then drain.
2. Spritz the hot, cooked noodles with cheese, add ground mustard butter, and then stir.
3. Serve this dish hot.

15. Red Cabbage Casserole

Ingredients

- 1 cup chopped fresh onion
- 4 cups shredded fresh red cabbage
- ¼ cup red wine vinegar
- 3 cups of peeled, fresh apples (cored and sliced)
- 2 tbsp of brown sugar
- ¼ cup water
- 2 tbsp butter (unsalted)
- ¼ tsp ground black pepper

Instructions

1. Set the oven to a temperature of 300°F and leave to heat up.
2. Coat a big stew dish with vegetable oil or butter.
3. Get a deep dish and mix all the ingredients together. All except butter.
4. Pour the contents of the deep dish into the stew dish and smear with butter.
5. Cover the stew dish and leave to sauté for at least 2 and a half hours on high heat.

16. Roasted red pepper dip

Ingredients

- 1 cup red peppers (roasted)
- ½ tbsp juiced lemon
- 1 tbsp olive oil
- ½ tbsp cumin
- 1 clove garlic

Instructions

Put all the ingredients together in a food processor and serve it with baked pita chips.

17. Crispy Cauliflower Buffalo Wings

Ingredients

- Water (1 cup)
- Cauliflower (1 head)
- Chickpea flour (1 cup)
- Garlic powder (1 tsp.)
- Finely ground Himalayan salt (.5 tsp.)

Instructions

1. Warm up the oven to reach 450° Fahrenheit.
2. Whisk or sift the flour, water, garlic powder, and salt until well incorporated.
3. Chop or snap the cauliflower into bite-sized pieces. Roll the cauliflower through the mixture.
4. Bake for 15 to 20 minutes. Shuffle around halfway through the cooking cycle.
5. Combine the hot sauce with the butter or oil in a pan to melt and stir.
6. After 15 minutes; transfer the cauliflower from the oven, and toss in with the sauce to coat each piece.
7. Roast for another 20 minutes until crispy.

18. Foodi Sticky Wings

Ingredients

- 1 lb Chicken Wings
- 1 tsp sea salt divided
- 1/4 cup honey
- 1/2 cup rice vinegar
- 2 tsp red chili pepper paste see recipe to make your own or look for Gourmet Garden in your local grocery store
- 1 tsp ginger fresh and grated
- 1 small orange zest and juice

Instructions

1. Add 2 cups of water to the inner pot and place the rack in the low position inside the pot. Place wings on a single layer on the rack that came with your Ninja Foodi on the low position. Place the pressure lid on and turn the valve to seal. Set pressure on High and the time for 2 minutes. When the time is up, immediately release the pressure and remove the lid when all the pressure has been released.

2. In a bowl, combine rice vinegar, zest & juice from a small orange or tangelo, red pepper paste, freshly grated ginger, 1/2 tsp fine grind sea salt, honey.

3. Remove the chicken wings from the rack and place on paper towels. Pat dry until as much moisture has been removed as possible. Salt wings with remaining 1/2 tsp fine grind sea salt.

4. Put the Asian sauce in the inner pot of the Ninja Foodi. Place the rack in the low position into the inner pot. Put the dried wings in a single layer on the rack. Set the Tender Crisp function to 390° F. for 30 minutes. Flip the wings every 10 minutes until desired color is reached. See post for timing and color chart.

5. Dump wings into pot and stir to coat with sauce. Remove from pot and allow to cool slightly before eating. Enjoy!

19. Buffalo Chicken Wings

Ingredients

- 1/2 cup water
- 2 pounds frozen chicken wings, drums and flats separated
- 2 tablespoons canola oil
- 2 tablespoons Buffalo sauce
- 2 teaspoons kosher salt

Instructions

1. pressure build: 6 minutes

2. Pour water into pot. Place wings into the Cook & Crisp™ Basket and place basket in pot. Assemble the pressure lid, making sure the PRESSURE RELEASE valve is in the SEAL position.

3. Select PRESSURE and set HIGH. Set time to 5 minutes. Select START/STOP to begin.

4. When pressure cooking is complete, quick release the pressure by turning the PRESSURE RELEASE valve to the VENT position. Carefully remove lid when unit has finished releasing pressure.

5. Pat wings dry with paper towels and toss with 2 tablespoons oil in the basket.

6. Close crisping lid. Select AIR CRISP, set temperature to 390°F, and set time to 15 minutes. Select START/STOP to begin.

7. After 7 minutes, open lid, then lift basket and shake wings or toss them with silicone-tipped tongs. Lower basket back into pot and close lid to resume cooking.

8. While the wings are cooking, stir together Buffalo sauce and salt in a large mixing bowl.

9. When cooking is complete, transfer wings to the bowl with Buffalo sauce and toss to coat.

20. Lentil Orzo Soup

Ingredients

- 1 tablespoon vegetable oil
- 1 onion, diced
- 3 carrots, diced
- 5 cloves garlic, minced
- 2 cans (15 oz.) diced tomatoes
- 4 cups chicken broth
- 4 cups water
- 1 1/2 cups brown lentils, rinsed
- 2 teaspoons cumin
- 1 teaspoon garlic salt
- 1/4 teaspoon red pepper flakes
- 2 tablespoons dried parsley
- 1/2 teaspoon salt
- 1/2 teaspoon pepper
- 1/2 cup orzo
- 2 cups roughly chopped baby spinach

Instructions

1. Select sauté and add oil to cooking pot. When oil is hot, sauté onion and carrots until tender, about 8 minutes. Add garlic, cook for one minute. Add tomatoes, broth, water, lentils, cumin, garlic salt, red pepper flakes, parsley, salt and pepper.

2. Select high pressure and 10 minutes cook time. When beep sounds turn pressure cooker off, use a Quick Pressure Release to release the pressure.

3. When valve drops carefully remove lid, tilting away from you to allow steam to disperse.

4. Select Simmer and add orzo; simmer 10 minutes or until orzo and lentils are tender.

5. Add spinach and cook until spinach wilts.

6. Season to taste with additional salt and pepper if needed

21. Chili Spice Chicken & Chimichurri

Ingredients

- 2 teaspoons kosher salt
- 1 tablespoon ground paprika
- 1 tablespoon chili powder
- 1 tablespoon ground fennel
- 1 teaspoon fresh cracked black pepper
- 1 teaspoon onion powder

- 1 teaspoon garlic powder
- 1 teaspoon ground cumin
- 2 uncooked bone-in, skin-on chicken breasts (3/4–1 1/4 pounds each)
- 1 tablespoon canola oil

Chimichurri

- 1/4 cup olive oil
- 1/2 bunch fresh cilantro
- 1/2 bunch fresh parsley
- 1 shallot, peeled, cut in quarters

- 4 cloves garlic, peeled
- Zest and juice of 1 lemon
- 1 teaspoon kosher salt

Instructions

1. In a small mixing bowl, stir together all the dried spices.

2. Pat chicken breasts dry. Coat with canola oil, then season them liberally on all sides with the spice mixture.

3. Preheat unit by selecting AIR CRISP, setting the temperature to 375°F, and setting the time to 5 minutes. Select START/STOP to begin.

4. After 5 minutes, add chicken to Cook & Crisp™ Basket. Close crisping lid. Select AIR CRISP, set temperature to 375°F, and set time to 35 minutes.

5. While chicken is cooking, combine the chimichurri ingredients in the bowl of a food processor and process until finely minced, being careful not to over-blend.

6. After 25 minutes, check chicken for doneness. Cooking is complete when internal temperature reaches 165°F. Cook for up to 35 minutes. When cooking is complete, allow chicken to cool for 5 minutes, then serve with a generous amount of chimichurri.

22. Beef Jerky

Ingredients

- 1/4 cup soy sauce
- 2 tablespoons Worcestershire sauce
- 2 tablespoons dark brown sugar
- 1 teaspoon ground black pepper
- 1 teaspoon garlic powder

- 1 teaspoon onion powder
- 1 teaspoon paprika
- 2 teaspoons kosher salt
- 1 1/2 pounds (24 ounces) uncooked beef eye of round, cut in 1/4-inch slices

Instructions

1. Whisk together all ingredients, except beef. Place mixture into a large resealable plastic bag.

2. Place sliced beef in bag with seasonings and rub to coat. Marinate in refrigerator for at least 8 hours or overnight.

3. Strain meat; discard excess liquid.

4. Lay meat slices flat on the Ninja dehydrating rack or Ninja Cook & Crisp Layered Insert. Arrange them in a single layer, without any slices touching each another.

5. Place dehydrating rack or Cook & Crisp Layered Insert in Cook & Crisp Basket. Place basket in pot and close crisping lid.

6. Press DEHYDRATE, set temperature to 155°F, and set time to 7 hours. Select START/STOP to begin.

7. Jerky will be pliable and soft after 5 hours, continue cooking for up to 7 hours if crispier jerky is desired.

8. When cooking is complete, remove dehydrating rack or Cook & Crisp Layered Insert from pot. Transfer jerky to an airtight container.

23. Beef Chili & Cornbread Casserole

Ingredients

- 2 pounds uncooked ground beef
- 3 cans (14 ounces each) kidney beans, rinsed, drained
- 1 can (28 ounces) crushed tomatoes
- 1 cup beef stock
- 1 large white onion, peeled, diced
- 1 green bell pepper, diced
- 1 jalapeño pepper, diced, seeds removed
- 4 cloves garlic, peeled, minced

- 2 tablespoons kosher salt
- 1 tablespoon ground black pepper
- 2 tablespoons ground cumin
- 1 tablespoon onion powder
- 1 tablespoon garlic powder
- 2 cups Cheddar Corn Bread batter, uncooked
- 1 cup shredded Mexican cheese blend
- Sour cream, for serving

Instructions

1. Approx. Pressure Build: 8 Minutes

2. Place beef, beans, tomatoes, and stock into the pot, and breaking apart meat. Assemble pressure lid, making sure the PRESSURE RELEASE valve is in the SEAL position. Select PRESSURE and set to HIGH. Set time to 15 minutes. Select START/STOP to begin.

3. When pressure cooking is complete, quick release the pressure by moving the PRESSURE RELEASE valve to the VENT position. Carefully remove lid when unit has finished releasing pressure.

4. Select SEAR/SAUTÉ and set to MD. Select START/STOP. Add onion, green bell pepper, jalapeño pepper, garlic, and spices; stir to incorporate. Bring to a simmer and cook for 5 minutes, stirring occasionally.

5. Dollop corn bread batter evenly over the top of the chili.

6. Close crisping lid. Select BAKE/ROAST, set temperature to 360°F, and set time to 26 minutes. Select START/STOP to begin.

7. After 15 minutes, open lid and insert a wooden toothpick into the center of the corn bread. If toothpick comes out clean, skip to step 7. If corn bread is not done, close lid to resume cooking for another 8 minutes.

8. When corn bread is done, sprinkle it with cheese and close lid to resume cooking for 3 minutes, or until cheese is melted.

9. When cooking is complete, top with sour cream and serve.

24. Steak, Mashed Potatoes & Asparagus

Ingredients

- 5 Russet potatoes, peeled, cut in 1/2-inch pieces
- 1/2 cup water
- 1/4 cup butter, divided
- 1/2 cup heavy cream
- 1 cup shredded cheddar cheese
- 1 tablespoon olive oil
- 1 tablespoon plus 2 teaspoons kosher salt, divided
- 3 teaspoons ground black pepper, divided
- 2 frozen New York strip steaks (12 ounces each, 1 1/2 inches thick)
- 1 bunch asparagus, trimmed

Instructions

1. Approx. Pressure Build: 9 Minutes

2. Place potatoes and water into the pot.

3. Place the reversible rack in the pot over potatoes, making sure rack is in the higher position. Season steaks with 1 tablespoon salt and 1 teaspoon pepper, then place them on the rack.

4. Assemble pressure lid, making sure the PRESSURE RELEASE valve is in the SEAL position. Select PRESSURE and set to high (HI). Set time to 1 minute. Select START/STOP to begin.

5. While the unit is pressure cooking, toss the asparagus with olive oil, 1 teaspoon salt, and 1 teaspoon black pepper.

6. When pressure cooking is complete, quick release the pressure by moving the PRESSURE RELEASE valve to the VENT position. Carefully remove lid when unit has finished releasing pressure.

7. Remove rack with steaks from pot and pat steaks dry. Mash potatoes with 1/4 cup butter, cream, cheese, 1 teaspoon salt, and 1 teaspoon pepper, using a mashing utensil that won't scratch the nonstick surface of the pot.

8. Return rack with steaks to pot over mashed potatoes. Place asparagus on rack next to steaks. Close crisping lid. Select BROIL and set time to 8 minutes for medium steak or 12 minutes for well-done. Select START/STOP to begin.

9. When cooking is complete, remove steaks from rack and allow to rest for 5 minutes before serving with mashed potatoes and asparagus.

25. Shrimp & Grits

Ingredients

- 3 cups water, divided
- 1 cup grits (or coarse grind cornmeal)
- 3 teaspoons kosher salt, divided
- 16 frozen uncooked jumbo shrimp, peeled, deveined, patted dry
- Juice of 1 lemon
- 1 teaspoon olive oil
- 2 cloves garlic, peeled, minced
- 1 teaspoon chili powder
- 1 teaspoon garlic powder
- 1 teaspoon black pepper
- 1/4 cup butter, cut in 8 pieces
- 1/4 cup grated Parmesan cheese
- 2 tablespoons fresh parsley, chopped, for garnish
- 2 scallions, thinly sliced, for garnish

Instructions

1. Approx. Pressure Build: 6 Minutes

2. Pour 1/2 cup water into the pot.

3. Place grits, 2 teaspoons salt, and remaining 2 1/2 cups water into the Ninja® multi-purpose pan* (or an 8-inch baking pan). Stir to combine.

4. Place pan onto the reversible rack, making sure rack is in the lower position. Place rack with pan in pot. Assemble pressure lid, making sure the PRESSURE RELEASE valve is in the SEAL position.

5. Select PRESSURE and set to HIGH. Set time to 4 minutes. Select START/STOP to begin.

6. While grits are cooking, place shrimp in a medium bowl and toss them with lemon juice, olive oil, garlic, chili powder, garlic powder, pepper, and remaining salt. Coat thoroughly; set aside.

7. When pressure cooking is complete, allow pressure to natural release for 10 minutes. After 10 minutes, quick release remaining pressure by moving the PRESSURE RELEASE valve to the VENT position. Carefully remove lid when unit has finished releasing pressure.

8. Stir the butter and cheese into the grits until completely melted.

9. Lay shrimp on top of grits and close crisping lid.

10. Select BAKE/ROAST, set temperature to 375°F, and set time to 10 minutes. Select START/STOP to begin.

11. When cooking is complete, garnish with parsley and scallions and serve.

16

26. Buffalo Cauliflower Bites

Ingredients

- 2 heads cauliflower, trimmed, cut in 2-inch florets
- 1 1/2 cups water, divided
- 1 1/2 cups cornstarch
- 1/2 cup all-purpose flour
- 2 teaspoons baking powder
- 1 teaspoon garlic powder
- 1 teaspoon onion powder
- 1 teaspoon kosher salt
- 1 teaspoon black pepper
- 2 eggs
- 1/3 cup buffalo wing sauce

Instructions

1. Approx. Pressure Build: 6 Minutes

2. Pressure Release: Quick

3. Place cauliflower and 1/2 cup water into the pot. Assemble pressure lid, making sure the PRESSURE RELEASE valve is in the SEAL position.

4. Select PRESSURE and set to LOW. Set time to 2 minutes. Select START/STOP to begin.

5. When pressure cooking is complete, quick release the pressure by turning the PRESSURE RELEASE valve to the VENT position. Carefully remove lid when unit has finished releasing pressure. Drain cauliflower and chill in refrigerator until cooled, about 10 minutes.

6. Whisk together cornstarch, flour, baking powder, garlic powder, onion powder, salt, and pepper. Whisk in eggs and 1 cup water until batter is smooth. Add chilled cauliflower to bowl with batter and gently toss until well coated. Transfer coated cauliflower to baking sheet and chill in freezer for 20 minutes.

7. Close crisping lid. Preheat the unit by selecting AIR CRISP, setting the temperature to 360°F, and setting the time to 5 minutes.

8. Meanwhile, arrange half the cauliflower in an even layer in the bottom of the Cook & Crisp™ Basket. After 5 minutes, place basket into the pot.

9. Close crisping lid. Select AIR CRISP, set temperature to 360°F, and set time to 20 minutes. Select START/STOP to begin. When first batch of cauliflower is crisp and golden, transfer to a bowl. Repeat with remaining chilled cauliflower.

10. When cooking is complete, microwave hot sauce for 30 seconds, then toss with cooked cauliflower. Serve immediately.

27. Baked Macaroni & Cheese

Ingredients

- 1 tablespoon baking soda
- 1 tablespoon ground black pepper
- 1/2 cup lemon juice
- 1 tablespoon onion powder
- 5 cups water
- 1 tablespoon garlic powder
- 1 box (16 ounces) dry elbow pasta
- 1 teaspoon mustard powder
- 1 cup heavy cream
- 2 cups panko or Italian bread crumbs
- 1 bag (16 ounces) shredded cheese
- 1 stick (1/2 cup) butter, melted
- 2 tablespoons kosher salt

Instructions

1. Approx. pressure build: 7 minutes
2. Air crisp: 7 minutes
3. Place baking soda and lemon juice into the pot. Stir until dissolved and bubbling has stopped. Add the water and dry pasta, stirring to incorporate.
4. Assemble pressure lid, making sure the pressure release valve is in the SEAL position. Select PRESSURE and set to low (LO). Set time to 0 minutes (the time the unit takes to pressurize is long enough to cook the pasta). Select START/STOP to begin.
5. When pressure cooking is complete, allow pressure to natural release for 10 minutes. After 10 minutes, quick release remaining pressure by moving the pressure release valve to the VENT position. Carefully remove lid when unit has finished releasing pressure.
6. Add remaining ingredients, except bread crumbs and butter, to the pot.
7. Stir well to melt cheese and ensure all ingredients are combined.
8. In a bowl, stir together the bread crumbs and melted butter. Cover pasta evenly with the mixture.
9. Close the crisping lid. Select AIR CRISP, set the temperature to 360°F, and set the time to 7 minutes. Select START/STOP to begin.

When cooking is complete, serve immediately

28. White Chicken Chili

Ingredients

- 1.5 lb Chicken breast
- 2 cloves garlic
- 1 cup chopped onion
- 1 cup chopped celery
- 1 cup heavy cream
- 1 tablespoon Pablano pepper may use jalapeno pepper
- 3 cups Chicken broth
- 1 cup water
- 1 tbsp Cumin
- 1 tbsp Turmeric
- Salt and Pepper to taste
- Avaocodo oil, coconut or extra virgin olive oil

Instructions

1. First cook your chicken breast. I set mine on a trivet or in steamer basket. Add a cup of water to the pot and set on High Pressure for 12 minutes and let naturally release. Remove chicken and shred with a fork.

2. Add Avocodo oil (or coconut, or extra virgin olive oil) to the bottom of your pots liner. Hit saute and let heat up for a minute or so. Add diced onions, celery, pablano pepper and garlic. Saute all until onion is lightly brown.

3. Add in your broth, and water. Simmer for just a few minutes. Then Add chicken spices, and heavy cream. Mix well. Set Ninja on Pressure cook, add pressure cooking lid and set for 3 minutes. Once timer is up, do a slow release a little at a time so you don't get a splatter. You may even let naturally release but it may cause your celery to be a little softer. I liked the little bit of texture it added to the chili. ENJOY!

29. Pulled Pork

Ingredients

- 2.5 lb Boneless Pork Loin Roast frozen
- 1 cup Chicken bone broth I used Mushroom Chicken Bone Broth because that's what I had but regular chicken is awesome
- 2 tsp Sea salt
- 1 tsp Black pepper
- 1 tsp Smoked paprika
- 1 tsp Garlic powder
- 1/2 tsp Red pepper flakes
- 3/4 cup Sugar-Free BBQ sauce

Instructions

1. Add the frozen roast, bone broth and seasonings to the removable cooking pot

2. Close the Pressure Lid, turn the valve to "SEAL" and set the Ninja Foodi Pressure Cooker to "Pressure Cook". It'll take about 10 minutes to come to pressure since the meat is frozen.

3. Set the time to 120 minutes or 1 hour and 30 minutes and press "Start/Stop"

4. Set the valve to "Vent" for a quick release of the air. Once the steam finishes escaping. Open the pressure lid.

5. Remove the roast from the pressure cooker and shred the meat with meat claws or two forks

6. Turn the Ninja Foodi to "Sear/Saute" and allow the cooking broth to come to a rolling boil/bubble.

7. Mix in the BBQ sauce and allow it to reduce by half (~5 minutes).

8. Mix in the shredded meat to the cooker and turn the Ninja Foodi off.

30. Cola BBQ Ribs

Ingredients

- lbs pork baby back ribs about 2 racks of ribs
- 1 yellow onion sliced
- 1/3 cup spicy dry rub
- 1/2 cup AlternaSweets BBQ sauce
- 1/2 cup Zevia Cola

Instructions

1. MAY BE NECESSARY: Remove the thin membrane (if it's there) from the back of the rib racks (The tutorial I always use can be found here). I've found that the ribs that I get from Trader Joes do not have it attached.

2. Sprinkle spicy dry rub on the ribs. Allow the ribs to marinate overnight

3. The next day: heat the 4 QT Stainless Steel Stockpot to medium heat

4. Add the sliced onions to the pan, followed by the ribs

5. Optional: Brown the ribs

6. Add the Zevia and the bbq sauce to the stockpot. Use a tong to incorporate.

7. Add the lid to the stockpot and set it on the Slow Cooker Base.

8. Turn the Slow Cooker Base to 3 and cook for 4-5 hours

31. Brussels Sprouts

Ingredients

- 2 tablespoons of coconut oil
- 1/2 cup of onion (yellow, white or even a few shallots would work best), chopped
- 1.5 – 2 teaspoons of minced garlic
- 3 strips of bacon, chopped
- 1 lbs of Brussels spouts, outer leaves removed and cleaned (leave whole)
- 1/2 cup water
- Salt and Pepper to Taste
- Butter, optional

Instructions

1. Turn your Instant Pot on Sauté

2. Add your coconut oil to the pot

3. Add your chopped onion and minced garlic and sauté for a minute

4. Add in your chopped bacon

5. Sauté until your onions are translucent and bacon crisps up

6. Add your prepared, whole Brussels Sprouts with a 1/2 of water

7. Salt and Pepper to Taste

8. Give it a quick stir to incorporate everything

9. Put on your lid, making sure that your vent is closed

10. Set on Manual for 3 minutes on LOW PRESSURE

11. Once cooking is completed (listen for that beep) do a quick release

12. Open your lid when ready and drop in a bit of butter and stir (optional)

13. Drain out the liquid

14. Plate those bad boys up and try not to eat them all folks!

32. Chicken Enchilada Soup

Ingredients

Soup

- 1 tbsp extra virgin olive oil
- 1 large yellow onion, diced (150 g/ 5.3 oz)
- 3 cloves garlic, minced
- 1 large red bell pepper, diced (158 g/ 5.6 oz)
- 1 large jalapeño, minced (35 g/ 1.2 oz)
- 240 ml sugar-free tomato sauce (8 fl oz)
- 1 tbsp chili powder
- 1 tbsp chipotle pepper in adobo sauce (15 g/ 0.5 oz)
- 2 tsp ground cumin

- 1 tsp garlic powder
- 1 tsp onion powder
- 1 tsp white wine vinegar
- 1 tsp sea salt or pink Himalayan salt
- 1/2 tsp oregano
- 3 cups chicken broth (720 ml/ 3/4 quart)
- 1 lb chicken breasts (450 g)
- Optional toppings:
- diced avocado
- sliced jalapeno pepper
- sour cream
- minced cilantro

Instructions

1. Drizzle the olive oil into the Instant Pot and set to Sauté. Add in the onion, garlic, bell pepper, and jalapeño pepper. Cook 3-4 minutes until soft. Keto Instant Pot Chicken Enchilada Soup

2. In a small bowl, mix together the tomato sauce, vinegar, chipotle chili, and spices. Pour into the pot. Keto Instant Pot Chicken Enchilada Soup

3. Add in the broth and chicken and give it a stir. Put the lid on and reset to Manual high pressure for 20 minutes. At the end of 20 minutes, release the vent valve. Keto Instant Pot Chicken Enchilada Soup

4. Remove the chicken and shred, add it back to the pot and give it a stir. Keto Instant Pot Chicken Enchilada Soup

5. To serve, top with desired toppings. Keto Instant Pot Chicken Enchilada Soup

6. Enjoy hot or let it cool down and store covered in the refrigerator for up to 4 days.

33. Crispy Air Fried Potatoes

Ingredients

- 1.5 pounds Golden Potatoes
- 1 tbsp Avocado Oil
- 1 tsp Garlic Powder
- 1 tsp Paprika
- 2 tsp Salt
- 1 tsp Ground Black Pepper

Instructions

1. Dice your potatoes into 1/2 inch thick cubes. Try to make them similar in size so they all cook up evenly.

2. In a large bowl, toss your potatoes with avocado oil, salt, pepper, garlic powder and paprika until evenly coated.

3. Place in air fryer basket and set the timer to 20 minutes and the temperature to 400.

4. Half way through the cooking cycle, toss potatoes and rotate so they cook even.

5. Remove crispy roasted potatoes from the air fryer basket and serve

34. Mozzarella Sticks

Ingredients

Batter

- 1/2 cup water
- 1/4 cup all-purpose flour
- 5 tablespoons cornstarch
- 1 tablespoon cornmeal
- 1 teaspoon garlic powder
- 1/2 teaspoon salt

Coating

- 1 cup panko bread crumbs
- 1/2 teaspoon salt
- 1/2 teaspoon ground black pepper
- 1/2 teaspoon parsley flakes
- 1/2 teaspoon garlic powder
- 1/4 teaspoon onion powder
- 1/4 teaspoon dried oregano
- 1/4 teaspoon dried basil
- 5 ounces mozzarella cheese, cut into 1/2-inch strips
- 1 tablespoon all-purpose flour, or as needed
- cooking spray

Instructions

1. Place water, flour, cornstarch, cornmeal, garlic powder, and salt in a wide, shallow bowl; mix into a batter the consistency of pancake batter. Adjust ingredients if needed to get the right consistency.

2. Stir panko, salt, pepper, parsley, garlic powder, onion powder, oregano, and basil together in another wide, shallow bowl.

3. Lightly coat each mozzarella stick with flour. Dip each stick in the batter and toss in the panko mixture until fully coated. Place sticks in a single layer on a baking sheet. Freeze for at least 1 hour.

4. Heat an air fryer to 400 degrees F (200 degrees C) according to manufacturer's instructions. Place a row of mozzarella sticks in the fryer basket. Spray with a light coat of cooking spray. Cook sticks for 6 minutes. Open fryer and flip the sticks with tongs. Continue cooking until golden brown, 7 to 9 minutes.

35. French Toast Sticks

Ingredients

- 2 large eggs
- 1/3 cup milk
- 1 tablespoon butter, melted
- 1 teaspoon vanilla extract

- 1 teaspoon ground cinnamon
- 4 slices day-old bread, cut into thirds
- 1 teaspoon confectioners' sugar, or to taste

Instructions

1. Mix eggs, milk, butter, vanilla extract, and cinnamon together in a bowl.

2. Line an air fryer basket with parchment paper. Dip each piece of bread into the milk mixture and place in the basket. Make sure they are not touching; cook in batches if necessary.

3. Preheat the air fryer to 370 degrees F (188 degrees C). Add basket and cook bread for 6 minutes; flip and cook for 3 minutes more. Sprinkle each stick with confectioners' sugar.

36. Tortilla with Ground Beef and Salsa

Ingredients

Low-carb tortillas

- 2 eggs
- 2 egg whites
- 5 oz. cream cheese, softened

- ½ tsp salt
- 1½ tsp ground psyllium husk powder
- 1 tbsp coconut flour

Filling

- 2 tbsp olive oil

- 1 lb ground beef or ground lamb, at room temperature

- 2 tbsp Tex-Mex seasoning
- ½ cup water

Salsa

- 2 avocados, diced
- 1 tomato, diced
- 2 tbsp lime juice

- salt and pepper

- 1 tbsp olive oil
- ½ cup fresh cilantro, chopped
- salt and pepper

For serving

- 6 oz. shredded Mexican cheese

- 3 oz. shredded lettuce

Instructions

Tortillas

1. Preheat the oven to 400°F (200°C).

2. Using an electric mixer with the whisk attachment, whisk the eggs and egg whites until fluffy, preferably for a few minutes. In a separate big bowl, beat the cream cheese until smooth. Add the eggs to the cream cheese, and whisk until the eggs and cream cheese form a smooth batter.

3. Mix salt, psyllium husk and coconut flour in a small bowl. Add the flour mix one spoon at a time into the batter and continue to whisk some more. Let the batter sit for a few minutes, or until the batter is thick like an American pancake batter. How fast the batter will swell depends on the brand of psyllium husk – some trial and error might be needed.

4. Bring out two baking sheets and put parchment paper on each.

5. Bake on the top rack for about 5 minutes or more, until the tortilla turns a little brown around the edges. Carefully check the bottom side so that it does not burn.

Filling

1. Place a large frying pan over medium-high heat and heat up the oil. Add the ground beef and fry until cooked through.

2. Add the tex-mix seasoning and water and stir. Let simmer until most of the water is gone. Taste to see if it needs additional seasoning.

Salsa and serving

1. Make the salsa from avocado, tomatoes, lime juice, olive oil, and fresh cilantro. Salt and pepper to taste.

2. Serve beef mixture in a tortilla, with shredded cheese, salsa, and shredded leafy greens.

37. Shrimp and Artichoke Plate

Ingredients

- 4 eggs
- 10 oz. cooked and peeled shrimp
- 14 oz. canned artichokes
- 6 sun-dried tomatoes in oil
- ½ cup mayonnaise
- 1½ oz. baby spinach
- 4 tbsp olive oil
- salt and pepper

Instructions

1. Begin by cooking the eggs. Lower them carefully into boiling water and boil for 4-8 minutes depending on whether you like them soft or hard-boiled.
2. Cool the eggs in ice-cold water for 1-2 minutes when they're done; this will make it easier to remove the shell.
3. Set eggs, shrimp, artichokes, mayonnaise, sun-dried tomatoes, and spinach on a plate.
4. Drizzle olive oil over the spinach. Season to enjoy with salt and pepper and serve.

38. Healing and Nourishing Vegetable Soup

Ingredients

- 1 large onion (150g)
- 3 celery full-length stick (120g)
- 3 large carrots (200g)
- 5 garlic cloves
- 1 cup. fresh parsley
- 1 tsp. dried rosemary
- 1.25 tsp. yeast free vegetable stock powder
- 2 cups chopped cauliflower
- 3 cups chopped green beans
- ½ tsp. sea salt
- cracked pepper
- 2 L of pure water

Instructions

1. Roughly chop Ingredients into small pieces and then add everything into your pressure cooker.
2. cook for 30 minutes to enhance the flavor
3. Serve in a bowl with sprouted toast or long-grain basmati rice

39. High Protein Spinach and Rice Balls

Ingredients

To Make Part One:

- 4 1/2 cups spinach leaves
- 1/3 cup pitted Greek olives
- 1 tablespoon nutritional yeast
- 1 tablespoon lemon juice

- 1 teaspoon garlic powder
- 3/4 teaspoon salt

To Make Part Two:

- 1 1/4 cup cooked rice
- 1/2 cup chickpea flour
- 1/2 cup ground almonds

To Serve Over:

Cashew sour cream or coconut yogurt

Instructions

1. Preheat your oven to 360°F.
2. Add all ingredients of part 1 into a food processor and blend.
3. Then transfer the mixture into a large bowl and mix in the ingredients of part 2. Mix together well until you get a nice dough like texture. If it's too wet add a little bit more chickpea flour. Don't taste it now as uncooked chickpea flour is very bitter. Add pepper to taste as well if you like.
4. Create roughly 12 balls with your hands (it's a bit messy but fun) and place on a baking tray lined with baking paper. Put into the preheated oven and bake for 20 - 25 min (probably 20 min will do, you can check by tasting one of them, if there is no bitter taste to it then it's perfect).
5. Serve over cashew sour cream or coconut yogurt.

40. Traditional 'Beef' Stew

Ingredients

- 2 tablespoons olive oil
- 1 large yellow onion, diced
- 5 garlic cloves, minced
- 2 tablespoons tomato paste
- 1 tablespoon white wine vinegar
- 1 tablespoon balsamic vinegar
- 1/4 cup rice flour
- 4 cups veggie broth
- 2 large carrots, cut into 1 inch pieces
- 3 1/2 cups potatoes, cut into 1 inch chunks
- 3 stalks of celery, cut into 1/2 inch pieces
- 3 bay leaves
- 1 teaspoon black pepper
- 1 teaspoon thyme
- 1/4 cup parsley, chopped
- 1 1/2 packs beefless chunks

Instructions

1. In a large soup pot, heat the oil and saute the onions for 5 minutes on medium heat.
2. Add the garlic and tomato paste, stir and cook for 2 minutes.
3. Pour the vinegars in and briefly stir.

4. Add the flour, stir well and cook for 1 minute.

5. Add the broth, carrots, potatoes, celery, bay leaves, and black pepper and thyme.

6. Stir all Ingredients together, turn heat to medium/low and cook for 40 minutes.

7. Stir frequently so that veggies do not stick to the bottom of the pan.

8. After 40 minutes, add the parsley and the frozen beef and cook for an additional 2 minutes.

41. Savory Sweet Potato Breakfast Bowl

Ingredients

- 1/2 tablespoons olive oil
- 2 teaspoons minced garlic (about two cloves)
- 2 cups spinach
- 1 8-ounce can sweet potato puree or 1 cup mashed sweet potatoes
- 3 tablespoons pumpkin seeds
- 2 teaspoons sesame seeds

Instructions

1. In a medium skillet, heat oil over medium heat until glistening.

2. Add garlic and cook until fragrant, about 1 minute.

3. Add spinach and sautee until wilted, 1 minute more.

4. Scoop sweet potatoes into a bowl -- if you'd like these warmed, transfer to a small saute pan and heat for 30-60 seconds over medium heat until warmed through.

5. Top sweet potatoes with spinach, pumpkin seeds, sesame seeds and salt and pepper to taste.

42. Quinoa Burrito Bowl

Ingredients

- 1 cup quinoa (or brown rice)
- 2 15-oz cans of black or adzuki beans
- 4 green onions (scallions), sliced
- 2 limes, fresh juiced
- 4 garlic cloves, minced
- 1 heaping tsp. cumin
- 2 avocados, sliced
- small handful of cilantro, chopped

Instructions

1. Cook quinoa or rice. While cooking, warm beans over low heat.

2. Stir in onions, lime juice, garlic and cumin and let flavors combine for 10-15 minutes. When quinoa is done cooking, divide into individual serving bowls.

3. Top with beans, avocado and cilantro.

43. Green Goddess Bowl with Avocado Cumin Dressing

Ingredients

- 3 cups kale, chopped
- 1/2 cup broccoli florets, chopped
- 1 cup zucchini (make noodles with spiralizer)
- 1/3 cup cherry tomatoes, halved
- 2 Tbsp. hemp seeds

Avocado Cumin Dressing

- 1 Haas avocado
- 1 Tbsp. cumin powder
- 2 limes, fresh squeezed
- 1 cup filtered water
- 1/4 tsp. sea salt (Celtic Grey, Himalayan, or Redmond Real Salt)
- 1 Tbsp. extra virgin olive oil
- Dash cayenne pepper
- Optional: 1/4 tsp. smoked paprika

Tahini Lemon Dressing

- 1/4 cup tahini (sesame butter)
- 1/2 cup filtered water (more if you desire thinner, less for thicker)
- 1/2 lemon, fresh squeezed
- 1 clove garlic, minced
- 3/4 tsp. sea salt (Celtic Grey, Himalayan, or Redmond Real Salt)
- 1 Tbsp. extra virgin olive oil
- Black pepper to taste

Instructions

1. Lightly steam kale and broccoli (flash steam for 4 minutes at the most) and set aside.
2. Mix zucchini noodles, and toss them with a generous serving of Avocado Cumin Dressing. Add cherry tomatoes and toss again.
3. Plate the steamed kale and broccoli, and drizzle them with Lemon Tahini Dressing. Top kale and broccoli with the dressed noodles and tomatoes, and sprinkle the whole dish with hemp seeds.
4. Serve and enjoy!

44. Roasted Cauliflower & Turmeric with Coriander and Mint

Ingredients

- 1/2 cup coconut oil
- 1 tablespoon ground cumin
- 2 teaspoons ground turmeric (preferably organic)
- 1 large cauliflower, broken down into bitesized florets
- 1/4 cup pine nuts

- 2 tablespoons coriander/cilantro, chopped roughly
- 1 tablespoon mint, chopped roughly
- Himalayan salt to taste

Instructions

1. Preheat the oven to 425°/220°
2. Now it's time to get your hands dirty, so, in a large bowl, combine the coconut oil, cumin, turmeric, 1/2 teaspoon of salt and mix together with your hands (to warm the oil and properly combine everything)
3. Next, add in the cauliflower florets and mix it all through so everything gets covered and oily
4. Spread the cauliflower out onto a large baking tray and put into the preheated oven for around 15-20 minutes until the cauliflower softens and just starts to brown
5. And while this is cooking, chuck the pine nuts onto a little baking tray and put into the oven too for about a minute to toast them slightly.
6. To serve, transfer the cauliflower to a large serving bowl and sprinkle with the pine nuts, coriander/cilantro and mint and serve.

45. Chicken Bacon Ranch Casserole Recipe

Ingredients

- 1 pound broccoli (chopped well)
- 1 (8-ounce) package cream cheese (softened)
- 1 cup mayonnaise
- 1/2 cup sour cream
- 1 tablespoon fresh chopped parsley
- 2 teaspoons garlic powder
- salt and pepper
- 1 1/2 pounds cooked chicken thighs (chopped)
- 1/4 cup diced yellow onion
- 2 cups shredded cheddar cheese (divided)
- 4 slices cooked bacon (chopped)

Instructions

1. Preheat the oven to 350°F and lightly grease a 9x13-inch glass baking dish with cooking spray.
2. Fill a large saucepan with 1 inch of water then add a steamer insert.
3. Add the broccoli then bring the water to boil and cook for 7 to 8 minutes until just tender.
4. Drain the broccoli well and set it aside.
5. Combine the cream cheese, mayonnaise, and sour cream in a large mixing bowl.
6. Add the parsley, garlic powder, salt, and pepper then beat until smooth.
7. Stir in the broccoli, chicken, onion, and 1 ½ cups shredded cheese.
8. Fold in half the cooked bacon then spread it in the prepared baking dish.
9. Top with the remaining cheese and bacon then bake for 35 minutes until hot and bubbling.

46. Chicken Zucchini Enchilada

Ingredients

- 1 tablespoon extra virgin olive oil
- 1 large onion — chopped
- salt and black pepper to taste
- 2 cloves garlic — minced
- 1 teaspoon ground cumin
- 2 teaspoons chili powder
- 3 cups free-range organic shredded chicken
- 1? cups red enchilada sauce — divided
- 4 large zucchini — sliced with a mandolin or peeler
- 1 cup shredded Monterey Jack
- 1 cup shredded cheddar
- Sour cream — for drizzling
- Fresh cilantro leaves — for garnishing

Instructions

1. Preheat oven to 350°F.
2. In large skillet over medium heat, heat the oil. Add the onion and salt.
3. Cook until golden and brown, about 5 minutes. Add the garlic, cumin, chili powder, shredded chicken, and 1 cup enchilada sauce.
4. Stir well until combined.
5. Using a vegetable peeler or mandolin, make thin slices of zucchini. On a cutting board, lay out 4 zucchini slices slightly overlapping. Then, add 2 tablespoons of the chicken mixture on top. Roll up, and transfer carefully to a baking dish. Repeat with the remaining zucchini and chicken mixture.
6. After that, use the remaining enchilada sauce to top the zucchini enchiladas.
7. Sprinkle with the shredded Monterey Jack and cheddar cheese.
8. Bake for approximately 20 minutes, until the cheese is melted.
9. Garnish with sour cream and cilantro, and serve.

47. Chili Dog Casserole

Ingredients

- 8 all-beef hotdogs (sliced in half lengthwise)
- 1 pound ground beef (80% lean)
- 1 small red pepper (diced)
- 1 small yellow onion (diced)
- 2 cloves minced garlic
- 1 cup low carb tomato sauce
- 1 cup water
- 2 tablespoons tomato paste
- 1 teaspoon Worcestershire sauce
- 1 tablespoon chili powder
- 1 teaspoon ground cumin
- 1/2 teaspoon celery salt
- 1 cup shredded cheddar cheese
- salt and pepper

Instructions

1. Preheat the oven to 400°F and lightly grease a 7x9-inch glass baking dish with cooking spray.

2. Line the bottom of the baking dish with hotdogs then set aside.

3. Combine the ground beef, peppers, onions, and garlic in a large skillet over medium-high heat.

4. Cook until the beef is browned, breaking it up into chunks with a wooden spoon.

5. Stir in the tomato sauce, water, tomato paste, Worcestershire sauce, and seasonings.

6. Bring to a boil then reduce heat and simmer on medium-low for 30 minutes.

7. Spoon the chili over the hotdogs and sprinkle with cheese.

8. Bake for 15 to 20 minutes until the cheese is hot and bubbling.

9. Rest for 10 minutes before serving.

48. Spinach and Zucchini Lasagna

Ingredients

- 1 tablespoon extra virgin olive oil
- ½ onion — finely chopped
- 4 garlic cloves — crushed
- 2 tablespoons tomato paste
- 1 28-ounce can crushed tomatoes with the juice or 1¾ pounds of fresh tomatoes — peeled, seeded, and diced
- Salt and ground fresh black pepper to taste
- 1 tablespoon fresh basil — chopped
- 3 cups spinach
- 15 ounces part-skim ricotta
- 1 large egg
- ½ cup freshly grated Parmesan cheese
- 4 medium zucchini — sliced ?-inch thick
- 16 ounces part-skim mozzarella cheese — shredded
- ½ teaspoon parsley — chopped

Instructions

1. In a saucepan, heat the olive oil over medium heat.

2. Add the onions, and cook 4-5 minutes until they are soft and golden.

3. Add the garlic, and sauté, being careful not to burn the garlic.

4. Add the tomato paste and stir well. Add the chopped tomatoes, including the juice in case you are using canned tomatoes.

5. Add salt and ground fresh black pepper.

6. Bring to a low simmer, cover, and cook for 25-30 minutes.

7. Finally, remove from the heat, and add the fresh basil and spinach. Stir well.

8. Adjust the seasoning if necessary.

9. Arrange the zucchini slices in a single layer on a baking sheet coated with cooking oil spray. Broil for 5-8 minutes. Remove from the oven. Wait about 5 minutes to remove any excess moisture

with paper towels if necessary. (This part is very important to avoid the lasagna becoming too soupy.)

10. Preheat the oven to 375°F.

11. In a medium bowl, mix the ricotta cheese, Parmesan cheese, and egg. Stir well.

49. Asian Beef Zoodle Soup

Ingredients

- 1 tablespoon coconut oil
- 1 small onion, halved and thinly sliced
- 6 ounces fresh shiitake mushrooms, stemmed and sliced
- 2 cloves garlic, minced
- 2 teaspoons minced fresh ginger
- 5 cups Beef Bone Broth or Whole30-compliant beef broth

- 2 tablespoons coconut aminos
- 2 teaspoons Red Boat fish sauce
- 1 teaspoon kosher salt
- 2 medium zucchini
- 12 ounces boneless beef sirloin steak, thinly sliced across the grain (see Tip)

Toppings

- Fresh basil leaves
- Fresh cilantro leaves

- Sliced green onion Sliced jalapeño
- Lime wedges

Instructions

1. In an large pot, heat the coconut oil over medium heat. Add the onion and cook, stirring, until softened, about 2 minutes. Add the mushrooms and cook, stirring, for about 3 minutes. Add the garlic and ginger and cook, stirring, until fragrant, about 30 seconds. Add the broth, coconut aminos, fish sauce, and salt. Bring to a boil; reduce the heat to medium-low and simmer, uncovered, for 5 minutes.

2. Meanwhile, use a spiralizer (or julienne peeler) to cut the zucchini lengthwise into long, thin strands (or use a regular vegetable peeler to cut the zucchini lengthwise into thin ribbons). Add the zucchini noodles to the simmering soup and cook until just tender, about 1 1/2 minutes. Add the sliced steak and simmer until just cooked, 30 to 60 seconds. Ladle the soup into bowls and serve with the toppings of your choice.

50. Spaghetti Squash Tuna Casserole

Ingredients

- 2 5 oz Easy Open Cans Genova Albacore Tuna in Olive Oil, drained
- 1 tablespoon olive oil
- 1 15 oz can coconut milk (regular or lite)

- 1 large yellow onion, chopped
- 2 cloves garlic, minced
- 2 cups sliced baby bella mushrooms
- 1 1/2 teaspoon pepper

- 1 1/2 teaspoon sea salt
- 1 medium-large spaghetti squash
- 1 cup frozen peas, thawed
- 1/4 teaspoon cayenne pepper
- pinch of nutmeg
- 1/2 cup crushed sprouted seed or almond flour crackers
- parsley, for garnish

Instructions

1. Heat oven to 350°. Chop spaghetti squash in half length wise, scoop out seeds with a spoon. Coat the inside of each half with a tiny bit of olive oil. Place on a baking sheet, cut side down and bake for about 40-50 minutes or until you can easily pierce a fork through the squash.

2. While squash is baking, prepare your sauce by adding oil to a medium pot on medium-high heat. Add onion, garlic, salt, pepper, cayenne and nutmeg. Cook, stirring often, for about 10 minutes or until onion and garlic are aromatic and translucent.

3. Add mushrooms and cook until onions are browning a bit and mushrooms are soft.

4. Add in coconut milk and cook on medium high until sauce has reduced in half, to the thickness of gravy. Be sure to stir the sauce often so that it doesn't stick. This should take about 15-20 minutes. Once reduced, remove sauce from heat, add in thawed frozen peas and tuna. Stir to combine.

5. By this time your squash should be fully cooked, or close to it. Remove squash from oven and let cool for 5-10 minutes before scraping the inside of the squash with a fork to remove the spaghetti-like strands.

6. The cooked spaghetti squash may seem liquidy. If so, place in a fine-mesh colander to remove access liquid. Press strands down with a fork or spatula to really press it all out.

7. Add drained spaghetti squash strands into the sauce mixture and toss to combine.

8. Spoon spaghetti squash tuna mixture into the bottom of each squash half. Top each with 1/4 cup cracker crumbs.

9. Bump oven temp to 375° and bake for 10 minutes, or until casserole is heated through and crackers are a little golden.

10. Remove from oven, sprinkle with fresh parsley and enjoy!

51. Chicken and Shrimp Laap

Ingredients

- 1 teaspoon coconut flour
- 1 teaspoon oil
- 1 small shallot, thinly sliced
- 1 pound ground chicken thighs
- ½ pound large shrimp, peeled and chopped coarsely
- 2 tablespoons Asian fish sauce
- 2 tablespoons fresh lime juice
- ½ teaspoon cayenne pepper
- 2 scallions, thinly sliced
- ¼ cup chopped cilantro

- ¼ cup minced fresh mint leaves
- 1 head butter lettuce, washed and spun dry, and separated into leaves

Instructions

1. On a parchment-lined baking tray, toast the coconut flour in a 300°F oven for 5 to 7 minutes or until the flour turns golden brown. (You can also toast the coconut flour in a dry pan over low heat instead.) Set aside.
2. In the meantime, heat the oil in a large skillet over medium-high heat. Add the sliced shallot and sauté for 2 to 3 minutes or until softened.
3. Add the ground chicken, and break it up with a spatula. Cook, stirring, for 3 to 5 minutes until no longer pink.
4. Add the shrimp and stir-fry for another 2 to 3 minutes or until the shrimp is cooked through.
5. Remove the pan from the heat and add the fish sauce, lime juice, toasted coconut flour, and cayenne pepper. Adjust the seasoning to taste.
6. Sprinkle the chopped herbs on top. To eat, wrap a 1/3 cup of laap in a lettuce leaf and devour.

52. Instant Pot Chicken Noodle Soup

Ingredients

- 1 whole chicken skin removed
- 1 carrot peeled
- 1 large onion peeled, split in half
- 2 celery stalks
- 1 bay leaf
- 1 tbsp kosher salt
- 1 tsp peppercorns
- water
- 2 cups egg noodles
- chopped parsley

Instructions

1. Remove the skin from your chicken.
2. Place the whole chicken, 1 carrot, 1 onion, 3 stalks of celery, 1 bay leaf, 1 tbsp kosher salt and 1 tsp peppercorns into the Instant Pot.
3. Pour water over the top. Seal lid and let cook for 1 hour on high pressure, then do a quick release.
4. Remove the chicken from the pot, shred the meat, and discard the bones.
5. Using a skimmer to collect impurities, vegetables, peppercorns, and bay leaves and discard everything but the carrots.
6. Slice carrots into small cubes.
7. Add 2 cups of thin egg noodles to the broth and cook until al dente.
8. Season the soup with salt and pepper. Add chicken and carrots back to the Instant Pot, then hit the simmer button to bring the soup to a boil. Turn off the heat.
9. Add chopped parsley and serve.

53. Ribs Recipe – fall-off-the-bone tender!

Ingredients

- 2 lb pork baby back ribs or spareribs 1 rack*(see recipe notes)
- Dry Rub
- 2 Tbsp dry ranch powder/seasoning (with no salt added)
- 1 tsp garlic powder
- 1/2 Tbsp ground pepper
- tsp kosher salt (use fewer if using table salt)
- 1 Tbsp smoked paprika (regular, not hot)
- 1/4 tsp cayenne pepper
- 2 Tbsp mayonnaise or oil
- 1 Tbsp Dijon mustard
- 1/4 cup BBQ sauce
- Steaming Liquid
- 1/2 cup red wine
- 1/2 cup apple cider vinegar

Instructions

1. Make the rub by combining 2 tbsp unsalted dry ranch seasoning, 1 tsp garlic powder, 1/2 tsp black ground pepper, 1 tbsp kosher salt, 1 tsp smoked paprika, 1/4 tsp cayenne pepper, 2 tbsp mayonnaise or oil and 1 tbsp grain mustard or Dijon mustard, set aside.

2. Remove membrane: Flip the ribs meat side down, then insert a butterknife under the shiny thin, shiny membrane and wiggle it to loosen. With a paper towel grip the membrane and pull it off to remove. Cut ribs between each bone.

3. Massage the spices in: Add the ribs and the spice mixture and massage the spices into the meat. Set aside.

4. Make the steaming liquid by combining 1/2 cup of red wine and 1/2 cup of apple cider vinegar.

5. Fill the pot: Place the steam rack insert inside the Instant Pot insert, and pour in the prepared liquid, then place the ribs on top of the rack.

6. Cook: Set the pressure cooker to high pressure at 45 minutes. Once the time expires, preheat your oven to 350°Fdegrees with the baking rack in the middle. Alternatively, you can also use a grill heated to 425°F degrees.

7. Turn the steam valve on the Instant Pot to vent, and release the pressure.

8. Brush with BBQ sauce: Remove the ribs to a lined with parchment paper or foil baking sheet and brush the ribs with 1/4 cup of homemade bbq, or your favorite store brand of bbq sauce.

9. Bake: Bake the ribs in the oven for about 10-15 minutes until the sauce is well caramelized. Brush with BBQ sauce once more right before serving

54. Brown Rice Recipe

Ingredients

- 1 cup brown rice
- 1/2 tsp salt
- 1 1/3 cup chicken broth

- Optional Ingredients
- 1 sprinkle chopped parsley or cilantro
- 1 tbsp butter

Instructions

1. Measure 1 cup of brown rice and rinse 1-2 times until the water is clear.
2. Add rice, ½ tsp of salt and 1 ⅓ cup of chicken broth to the Instant Pot.
3. Place lid and make sure the valve is set to seal.
4. Set on manual then select high pressure at 30 minutes.
5. Once the countdown has finished, allow the rice to naturally release pressure for 20 minutes.
6. Open lid, fluff rice with a fork. Sprinkle the rice with chopped parsley or cilantro along with 1 tbsp of butter before serving if you would like.

55. Korean Beef and Rice

Ingredients

Korean Beef Ingredients

3 lb beef chuck roast, slice into 1-inch cubes

Korean Beef Sauce

- 1/2 cup broth
- 1/3 cup reduced-sodium soy sauce
- 1/3 cup brown sugar
- 6 cloves garlic, minced
- 1.5 tbsp rice wine vinegar
- 1 tsp onion powder

- 1 tsp dry ground ginger (1 tsp dry ground ginger = 1 Tbsp pure grated ginger)
- 1 Tbsp Sriracha Sauce (less or more, to taste)
- 1 tsp black pepper

Cornstarch Slurry

- 3 tbsp cornstarch or flour
- 3 tbsp water
- Also
- 4 green onions, thinly sliced
- 1 Tbsp sesame seeds

- White Rice
- 2 cups white long grain rice
- 3 1/3 cups broth or water
- 1 tsp salt

How to cook Korean Beef

1. Add all ingredients for the Korean Beef Sauce to a 6 qt Instant Pot (pressure cooker) and whisk until combined. Add the cubed beef and stir.

2. Cover with lid and set the pressure release valve to "SEALING". Cook on "Manual", "High" pressure and fix the timer to 30 min. Once the timer goes off, turn the pressure cooker off and allow the pressure to be released naturally for about 15 minutes, then turn the pressure release valve to "venting". Once the pot is depressurized, open the lid.

3. Combine the ingredients for the cornstarch slurry in a little bowl, then pour into the cooked beef and immediately stir. Turn the Instant Pot to "Saute" on the "High" setting and allow it to cook for 2-3 minutes or until the sauce is thickened.

4. Serve over rice, rice noodles, quinoa, or mashed potatoes. For this quantity of beef, you will need to cook about 2 cups of grains (rice or quinoa).

5. Garnish with green onions and sesame seeds, if desired.

To Cook Rice at the identical time as the Beef:

1. Fill a stainless steel pan like this one with 2 cups rice, 3 1/3 cups boiling water or broth, and 1 tsp salt.

2. 15 minutes into cooking time (for beef), turn the pressure release valve to "venting" and allow the pressure to be released. Then open the lid.

3. Place a trivet like this one over the beef. Set the processed pot with rice and water on top.

4. Close the lid, set the pressure release to "sealing", then pressure cook on "High" pressure for the remaining 15 minutes, followed by NPR (Natural Pressure Release) for another 15 minutes. After 15 minutes, turn the pressure release valve to "venting" allow to depressurize, and open the lid.

5. Remove the pot with the rice and fluff with the fork, cover with lid to keep warm. Remove the trivet.

6. Combine the starch and water with a whisk, add into the beef, stir and cook for 2-3 minutes until thickened.

7. Serve by spooning the beef over the rice.

56. Beef Rice Pilaf

Ingredients

For Beef Rice

- 1 1/2 lb beef, chuck, cubed to 1 inch, fat clipped
- 2 tbsp oil
- 1 1/2 cup short-grain rice, rinsed until the water runs clear, well-drained

- 1 large onion, diced
- 2 carrot, medium size, cut to 1/2 inch
- 1/2 cup tomato sauce
- 1 1/2 cups beef broth (could be replaced with water)

Seasoning

- 1 tsp black ground pepper
- 1 tsp garlic powder
- 1/2 tsp smoked paprika
- 1 tsp beef seasoning

- 1 bay leaf
- 2 tsp salt
- 1 head garlic, cut in half horizontally
- 1/4 cup chopped parsley

Instructions

1. Turn the Instant Pot to "Saute" function (30 min). When the display says "Hot" add 2 tbsp of oil and the 1 large diced onion and saute until lightly golden in color, about 5 minutes. Then add 2 cut up carrots, 1.5 lb of cubed beef and also add stir.

2. Next, add 1 tsp of ground pepper, 1 tsp garlic powder, 1/2 tsp smoked paprika, 1 tsp beef seasoning (if using), 2 tsp salt, 1/2 cup tomato sauce, and 1 bay leaf and 1.5 cups of beef stock.

3. Cover the Instant Pot with a lid, turn the steam valve to "sealing". Turn the pressure cooker to "Manual" and "High" heat for 45 minutes. Then once the time expires, cover the steam valve with a kitchen towel and turn it to "venting" to release pressure. Open the lid when the pressure is down.

4. Remove the bay leaf.Sprinkle 1.5 cups of rice over the top (do not stir) and spread it evenly with a spoon (so all rice is covered with liquid).

5. Press halved garlic head, cut side into the rice. Cover with lid, turn the steam valve to "sealing". Turn the Instant pot to "Manual" on "High" heat and set the timer to 15 minutes.

6. After the time expires turn the Instant Pot off and allow to depressurize naturally for 15-20 minutes (this step is important).

7. Next, turn the steam valve to "venting" and allow the rest of the steam to escape. Now open the lid, remove the garlic and squeeze it back into the rice (optional), add the parsley and gently fluff the rice with a fork for the ingredients to be evenly distributed.

57. Salmon Asparagus Foil Packets

Ingredients

- 1 lb asparagus tough ends trimmed
- 4 6-8 oz skinless salmon fillets
- 2 Tbsp olive oil
- 2 tsp kosher salt
- 1/4 tsp black ground pepper
- 1/2 tsp smoked paprika
- 1/3 tsp dry garlic powder or 2 cloves pressed garlic
- Also:
- 4 14-inch square foil pieces

Instructions

1. Place 1/4 lb of the asparagus in the center of each foil square. Sprinkle with about 1 tsp of salt and 1/2 tsp of black ground pepper. Drizzle with olive oil. Toss to coat.

2. Then put the salmon fillets on top of the asparagus. Sprinkle with kosher salt, black ground pepper, 1/2 tsp smoked paprika, and dry garlic or freshly pressed garlic. Drizzle with olive oil.

3. If planning to grill or roast right away, partially close the foil to expose the top of the salmon, or if you like the salmon to be steamed inside, close the foil all the way.

4. To grill - throw on the grill for about 15 minutes on a preheated to about 400F grill, the time will depend on the thickness of the salmon fillet. You are looking for the salmon to be opaque in the center.

5. To oven roast - place the packets on a baking sheet and bake in a preheated to 450F oven for about 15-20 minutes, depending on the thickness of the salmon fillet. You are looking for the salmon to be opaque in the center.

6. Once the salmon is prepared through, serve right away with a lemon wedge, if you want.

58. Kabob Style Pork and Vegetables

Ingredients

For the Pork:

- 1 Smithfield Marinated Roasted Garlic
- 1 Cracked Black Pepper Pork Tenderloin
- 2 tablespoons mayonnaise
- 1 tsp smoked paprika
- 1 tsp kosher salt
- For the Vegetables:
- 3 cups diced to 1-inch pieces bell pepper assorted color
- 1 cup Brussel sprouts large ones cut in half
- 1 1/2 cups asparagus cut to 2-3 inch pieces
- 2 tbsp oil
- 1/2 tsp Smoked Paprika
- 1/2 tsp crushed black pepper
- 1 tsp kosher salt

Instructions

1. Preheat oven to 450F. Line a baking pan with foil or parchment paper to prevent sticking.

2. Cut the tenderloin into 3 long pieces lengthwise, then cut across into 1+ inch cubes.

3. To the bowl, add the cut up tenderloin pieces, 2 tablespoons mayonnaise, 1 teaspoon paprika, and 1 teaspoon kosher salt. Toss everything to coat evenly.

4. Spread pieces of pork across the baking pan and bake in preheated, to 450F, oven for 10 minutes.

5. Now use the same bowl to add 3 cups cut up bell pepper, 1 cup brussel sprouts, 1 1/2 cups cut up asparagus, 2 tablespoons oil, 1/2 teaspoons smoked paprika, 1/2 teaspoons crushed black pepper and 1 teaspoon kosher salt. Toss everything together to coat.

6. After 10 minutes remove the baking pan with the pork and move the meat to one side. Add the vegetables to the other side of the baking sheet and spread around. Return to the oven and bake for another 10-13 minutes. If you like your vegetables charred a little, bake for just 5-6 minutes, then turn on the broil setting of the oven and broil for another 4-5 minutes or until the vegetables are done to your liking. Observe the oven, as it will go from done to charcoal very quickly if left unattended while broiling.

7. Transfer the meat and the vegetables to a serving dish and serve while hot.

59. Leftover Turkey Pasta

Ingredients

- 1 lb bow-tie pasta prepared according to package instructions
- 1 medium onion
- 3 cups leftover turkey pulsed in the food processor or ground
- 1 cup chopped or sliced bell peppers
- 1 cup cheese cheddar/mozzarella or any cheese you like
- 1/2 cup chicken stock
- 1/2 cup heavy whipping cream
- oil for frying the onion
- 1 cup sliced cherry tomato

Instructions

1. Heat couple tablespoons of oil over medium heat in a skillet, add onion and stirring often golden up the onion.

2. Put the turkey meat through a grinder, or use a food processor to pulse it until fine.

3. Combine the sautéed onion, cooked pasta, ground turkey meat, pepper, and cheese.

4. Add the stock and the heavy cream.

5. Mix everything together and heat through until the cheese is melted and the liquid is absorbed by the pasta. Season with salt and pepper, mix again. Serve hot with some tomatoes sprinkled on top.

60. Chicken and Squash Dinner

Ingredients

- 1 butternut squash
- 8 chicken thighs fat trimmed
- 10 cloves garlic peeled
- 3 Tbsp olive oil
- 3/4 Tbsp kosher salt
- 1 tsp ground black pepper
- 1 tsp paprika
- 1/2 tsp crushed chili peppers optional
- 2-3 twigs fresh thyme optional
- 1/4 cup finely chopped parsley for garnish (optional)

Instructions

1. Preheat oven to 375F with the baking rack in the center. Then Line a jelly roll baking sheet with parchment paper.
2. Combine all ingredients in a bowl
3. Toss everything together until all ingredients are coated fairly.
4. Distribute everything in the jelly roll pan. Bake in a preheated to 375F oven till 1 hour. Raise heat to 425 and bake for another 10-20 minutes until the chicken is golden in color.
5. Remove from the oven and serve 2 chicken legs with about 8 pieces of squash per serving. Sprinkle with chopped parsley as garnish if desired.

61. Cheesy Parmesan Crusted Salmon Bake

Ingredients

- 1 lb salmon fillet
- 1 cup of grated cheese mozzarella, Mexican, cheddar, gouda etc
- 2 cloves garlic peeled & pressed
- 2-3 Tbsp mayonnaise
- 1 tsp mustard powder
- 1/2 tsp paprika
- 1/2 tsp freshly ground black pepper
- 1/2 tsp salt
- Small bunch of flat-leaf parsley 1/4 cup chopped
- Parmesan Crust
- 1/2 Cup Panko Crumbs
- 1/4 – 1/3 cup grated parmesan cheese
- 1 Tbsp melted butter unsalted

Instructions

Make the Parmesan Panko Crust

1. Combine the Panko crumbs, grated parmesan cheese, and butter together in a pan. Stir until the butter coats the crumbs evenly. Set aside.
2. Chop the parsley

3. Thoroughly wash the parsley under running water and use a paper towel to dry the leaves. Cut off the stems, then finely chop the leaves. Set aside.

4. Continue with recipe

5. Rinse Salmon fillet under running water and pat dry with a paper towel. Cut into 1-inch cubes.

6. Stir the spices together.

7. Combine spices, parsley, pressed garlic, mayonnaise, and 1/2 the cheese to the salmon cubes. Stir to distribute the ingredients evenly.

8. Preheat oven to 425F with the baking rack in the center.

9. Transfer the mixture to an ovenproof baking dish (I used a 9"x6") and flatten the salmon mixture. Spray the top evenly with cheese, then breadcrumb mix.

10. Allow to bake for 5-7 minutes uncovered, then once the breadcrumbs are golden in color loosely cover with foil and bake for another 9-10 minutes or until the salmon is baked through in the middle of the dish. Remove from the oven and serve with steamed vegetables or a side dish of choice.

62. Cheesy Chicken & Rice

Ingredients

- 1 chicken breast cubed to 1-inch pieces
- 1 cup rice wassed under running water until the water runs clear
- 1/2 medium sized onion diced

- 1/2 medium sized carrot shredded
- 3 cloves garlic minced or pressed
- Olive Oil
- 2 Tbsp unsalted butter

Stir together and add:

- 3 cups hot chicken broth or 3 cups hot water + 1 Tbsp chicken bullion base
- 1/2 cup heavy cream
- Add at the end:
- 1/2 – 1 cup shredded cheese Mozzarella, Gouda, Cheddar or any other good melting cheese you like

- 1 tsp salt
- 1 tsp freshly ground pepper
- 2-3 Tbsp chopped parsley and/or chives

Instructions

1. Heat couple tablespoons of olive oil in a non-stick pan over immense heat and brown the chicken pieces on all sides. Add the butter, onions, and carrots and cook stirring often till the onion is translucent. Reduce heat to low-medium and add the rice, minced garlic, and stir.

2. Combine the chicken broth or combination of boiling water and the chicken bullion base with heavy cream and salt. Stir until dissolved.

3. Pour the mixture over rice, cover with a lid and cook for about 15 minutes or until the rice is cooked through.

4. Remove from heat and stir in grated cheese, freshly ground pepper and chopped parsley and/or chives. Taste and adjust the amount of seasoning. Serve hot right away.

63. Crispy Parmesan Little Potatoes

Ingredients

- 3 lb baby potatoes skin on, wassed clean
- Olive oil for sauteing
- Salt
- Pepper
- 3-4 cloves garlic or 1 – 1 1/2 tsp powdered garlic
- 1/2 cup grated Parmesan cheese
- 1/4-1/3 cup white wine Chardonnay

Instructions

1. Place the potatoes into a pot, cover with water and boil for about 10-15 minutes in well-salted water. Drain the water.

2. Heat skillet over high heat with some olive oil, add the potatoes, salt, and white wine. Keep tossing and cooking the potatoes with the wine until it dissolves. Continue searing the well-salted, tossing them from time to time to sear from all sides, about 5-8 minutes. For a more pronounced fresh garlic flavor add pressed garlic, parsley, pepper together, stir to coat evenly turn off the heat and transfer the potatoes to a serving dish. If you don't want the fresh garlic taste, add the garlic first, then saute for 2-4 minutes before combining the parsley and garlic.

3. Transfer potatoes to a serving dish, grate some good quality Parmesan cheese on top and serve warm.

64. Grill Pan Flat Iron Steak with Chimichurri Sauce

Ingredients

- Steak & Dry Rub
- 1 lb Skirt Steak
- 1 1/2 tsp Kosher Salt
- 1/3 tsp Paprika
- 2 Tbsp Olive Oil
- 1-2 Tbsp Steak Seasoning with no salt added
- 1 Tbsp Mesquite Seasoning with no salt added

Instructions

1. Make the Flat Iron Steak

2. Clean the steak with olive oil, then sprinkle with salt and spices. Press the seasoning in with your hand. Flip the meat and repeat.

3. If using a grill pan, heat it over medium-high heat until smoking (on my induction top cooking stove I heated the pan to 465F). If using a skillet, heat it over huge heat with a tablespoon or two of olive oil until lightly smoking. Place the meat diagonally to the grill marks and cook for around 3-4 minutes (for medium-rare) per side. If you're cooking inside, you will want to close the doors to all your rooms and probably turn off your smoke alarm until it's done the cooking. Otherwise, it WILL set off the alarms.

4. Halfway through, rotate the meat and put it diagonal to the grill marks but in the opposite direction to the first one. (For medium doneness cook for about 5 minutes per side. For average-well doneness cook about 6 minutes per side. For well-done cook for 7 minutes per side.)

5. When the first side is roasted or seared, flip the steak with tongs

6. Press something heavy on top and allow to cook on this side, rotating the meat halfway through the cooking to achieve the crisp-cross grill marks as explained above.

7. Once the steak is cooked to the desired doneness remove it to a warm plate, cover with foil and allow to rest for about 10 minutes. This will allow the juices to settle and not seep out as you cut the steak. Meanwhile, prepare the Chimichurri Sauce by following the recipe below.

8. Transfer the steak to the cutting board.

9. Cut the skirt steak with a cutting knife across the grain. Top with the Chimichurri Sauce and serve.

65. Stuffed Crepe & Egg Casserole

Ingredients

- 4 crepes made following this crepe recipe
- 1/2 cup chopped mushrooms
- 1/2 cup diced ham
- 1/2 cup cheese or a variety of cheeses

- 2-3 Tbsp chopped chives or scallions
- 3 eggs
- 2 Tbsp cream or milk
- Salt Pepper & Garlic Powder to taste
- 2-3 Tbsp chopped parsley *optional*

Instructions

1. Sauté mushrooms in a tablespoon of olive oil over huge heat until slightly golden. Transfer to a bowl and set aside.

2. Whisk the eggs, salt, pepper, garlic powder, and cream together in a pot. Set aside.

3. Lay the crepes down on a working surface, more browned side up, overlapping them slightly. Sprinkle the diced choice of meat, followed by mushrooms, 2/3 of the cheese, and scallions closer to the edge of the crepes.

4. Roll the crepes around the filling into a lengthy snake-like tube. Form a spiral with the rolled tube and fix it into a buttered or nonstick sprayed baking dish (oval 9"x5").

5. Pour the egg mix over the rolled crepes. Poke the crepes with a fork all over and then press to submerge in the egg mix. Sprinkle with remaining cheese.

6. Cover with plastic wrap and refrigerate if not planning to bake and serve right away.

7. Place on the middle rack in preheated to 350F oven for about 25 minutes or until the egg in the center is cooked and not runny.

8. Sprinkle with chives or parsley and serve right away with a choice of pickles, tomatoes or a dollop of sour cream.

66. Chicken Noodle Soup

Ingredients

- 8-9 drumsticks or 3 chicken breasts
- 2 average carrots or 1 cup of baby carrots
- 1 large onion peeled, split in half
- 2 celery stalks optional
- 1 1/2 Tbsp kosher salt
- 1 tsp peppercorns
- 1/2 Tbsp dry garlic flakes or 3 garlic cloves peeled
- 1 bay leaf
- 3 Qt water or broth
- 2 1/2 cups egg noodles

Instructions

1. Place the chicken, carrots, onion, celery (optional) and spices into the Crockpot. Cover with 3 Qts water or broth, then join peppercorns, garlic flakes, bay leaf, and salt. Cover with lid. Fixed to cook on 'High' for 4.5 hours or on 'low' for 6-8 hours.

2. Cook noodles according to package instructions. Drain. Add 1/2 tablespoon olive oil to noodles to keep them from sticking. Stir to coat. Refrigerate until ready to use.

3. After the 4.5 hours of cooking, the broth will need to be clarified. Line a sieve with 2-3 layers of paper towel and fix it over a soup pot (4-5 qts). Drain the broth through the paper towel-lined sieve discarding the onion & celery stalks, but keeping the carrots and the drumsticks. Rinse drumsticks and carrots from the impurities that are stuck to it.

4. Shred the chicken meat into as small of pieces as you desire, discarding the skin and bones. Slice carrots into small pieces.

5. Heat the noodles before adding to the soup. Add the shredded chicken, carrots and chopped parsley. Stir. Taste and adjust the seasoning amount.

67. Baked Chicken and Potatoes

Ingredients

- 8 chicken drumsticks, extra fat/skin trimmed
- 6-8 large potatoes cut in quarters
- 5-6 carrots cut in 1-2 inch pieces
- Kosher salt
- Black ground pepper
- 4 tsp dried garlic powder or 5 cloves garlic, crushed

- ½ tsp paprika optional
- 3-4 Tbsp olive oil.

Instructions

1. Preheat oven to 375F. Line a baking sheet with foil or equal better, parchment paper.
2. Thoroughly clean the potatoes & carrots with a scrubber and cut them in smaller pieces. Pat dry with a paper towel.
3. Pat dry chicken with paper towels to separate extra moisture.
4. Combine chicken, potatoes, and carrots to a parchment paper-lined 16"x21" baking pan and sprinkle with salt, ground pepper, and garlic. Drizzle with olive oil. Toss everything to coat.
5. Place in the oven and bake for 1 hour 15 minutes. Review for doneness, if the potatoes and chicken drums are soft and easily pierced with the fork they are ready.
6. If the chicken and potatoes have not browned up as much as you would want, turn the broil setting on the oven and broil for 5 minutes. Watch carefully, or they will burn.
7. Remove from the oven and serve right away in the baking dish or transfer to a hot serving plate.

68. Duck Confit

Ingredients

- 4 duck legs or 2 duck legs and 2 duck breasts
- 2 cups duck fat *optional. See note in the instructions
- salt
- ground black pepper
- 1 Tbsp garlic minced
- 1 large onion sliced
- 1/2 tsp oregano
- 1 tsp thyme

Instructions

1. Score the skin of the duck with a cutting knife, taking care not to go through the meat.
2. Sprinkle both sides with salt, pepper, oregano, thyme, and either dry or minced garlic. Place in a ziplock bag, add sliced onions and shake. Let sit in the fridge for 24-48 hours.
3. Preheat oven to 375F. Shake off excess seasoning and onion.
4. Place into an ovenproof baking dish small enough to snuggly fit the amount of duck you have.
5. Pour the 2 cups of duck fat on the roof
6. Then Place in the oven and roast for around 25 minutes.
7. Lower temperature to 275F – 290F, cover with foil and roast for another 2+ hours. Check to make sure that it's soft enough to fall off the bone.
8. Remove foil, increase the temperature to 375F and crisp the top of the skin, about 20-30 minutes.

69. Savory Apple-Chicken Sausage

Ingredients

- 1 large tart apple, peeled and diced
- 2 teaspoons poultry seasoning
- 1 teaspoon salt
- 1/4 teaspoon pepper
- 1 pound ground chicken

Instructions

1. In a large bowl, combine the apple, poultry seasoning, salt and pepper. Crumble chicken over mixture and mix well. Shape into eight 3-in. patties.

2. In a large, greased cast-iron or other heavy skillet, cook patties over medium heat until no longer pink, 5-6 minutes on each side. Drain if necessary.

70. Roasted Spaghetti Squash

Ingredients

- 1 large ripe spaghetti squash
- salt and fresh pepper

Instructions

1. Preheat oven to 350°.

2. Cut the squash in half lengthwise, scoop out the seeds and fibers with a spoon.

3. Place on a baking sheet, cut side up and sprinkle with salt and pepper.

4. Bake at 350° about an hour or until the skin gives easily under pressure and the inside is tender. Remove from oven and let it cool 10 minutes.

5. Using a fork, scrape out the squash flesh a little at a time. It will separate into spaghetti-like strands.

6. Place in a serving dish and serve hot.

NEW

EXPLORATION

RECIPES

71. Baked Garlic Lemon Tilapia

Ingredients

- 6 6 oz each tilapia filets
- 4 cloves garlic, crushed
- 2 tbsp butter
- 2 tbsp fresh lemon juice
- 4 tsp fresh parsley
- salt and pepper
- cooking spray

Instructions

1. Preheat oven to 400°.
2. Melt butter on a low flame in a small sauce pan. Add garlic and saute on low for about 1 minute. Add the lemon juice and shut off flame.
3. Spray the bottom of a baking dish lightly with cooking spray.
4. Place the fish on top and season with salt and pepper. Pour the lemon butter mixture on the fish and top with fresh parsley.
5. Bake at 400° until cooked, about 15 minutes.

72. Lighter Chicken Salad

Ingredients

- 2 pieces 1 lb boneless, skinless chicken breasts
- 1 chicken bouillon
- 1/4 onion, chopped
- 2 tbsp parsley chopped
- 2 celery stalks, finely chopped
- 3 tbsp Hellmann's Lite Mayonnaise, regular for Keto

Instructions

1. In a medium sauce pan, place chicken, half the celery, half the onion, parsley and cover with water.
2. Add bullion and cook on medium flame, covered for about 15-20 minutes, until chicken is cooked through.
3. Once cooked, remove chicken and let cool. Reserve chicken broth.
4. Cut chicken into small pieces and place in a bowl. Add onions, celery and mayonnaise, 1/8 cup reserved chicken broth and mix well. If looks dry add 1/8 cup more.
5. Serve on a bed of lettuce, in a lettuce wrap or on your favorite bread.

73. Denver Omelet Salad

Ingredients

- 8 cups fresh baby spinach
- 1 cup chopped tomatoes
- 2 tablespoons olive oil, divided
- 1-1/2 cups chopped fully cooked ham
- 1 small onion, chopped
- 1 small green pepper, chopped
- 4 large eggs
- Salt and pepper to taste

Instructions

1. Arrange spinach and tomatoes on a platter; set aside. In a large skillet, heat 1 tablespoon olive oil over medium-high heat. Add ham, onion and green pepper; saute until ham is heated through and vegetables are tender, 5-7 minutes. Spoon over spinach and tomatoes.

2. In same skillet, heat remaining olive oil over medium heat. Break eggs, one at a time, into a small cup, then gently slide into skillet. Immediately reduce heat to low; season with salt and pepper. To prepare sunny-side up eggs, cover pan and cook until whites are completely set and yolks thicken but are not hard. Top salad with fried eggs.

74. Stuffed Cabbage Rolls

Ingredients

For the Rice:

- 3 cups round rice
- 3 cups of water
- 1 Tbsp Better than Bouillion

For the stuffing:

- 2 medium-sized heads of cabbage
- 2 lbs ground beef/turkey/chicken
- 2 cups diced onion
- 1.5 cups shredded carrots
- 1 Tbsp ground mustard
- 2 Tbsp chopped dill
- 1 tsp dry garlic
- 1 Tbsp dry green onion OR 3-4 stems of green onion chopped
- 2 Tbsp Johny's Garlic Spread Seasoning optional
- Olive Oil
- 1 Tbsp kosher salt
- 2 tsp black ground pepper

Ingredients for Cooking Liquid

- 3 cups broth or 3 cups hot water + 1 tbsp Better than Bullion
- 4 Tbsp tomato paste
- 1 tsp salt

Instructions

Prepare the Cabbage

1. Remove a couple of outer leaves from the head of cabbage and discard; cut out the stem with a long knife; wrap the cabbage with plastic wrap and microwave for about 3-4 minutes. You want the leaves to be softened but not cooked through.
2. Remove the plastic wrap and remove the softened outer leaves. Keep removing until you get to the raw/uncooked leaves, then wrap the cabbage again and cook for another couple minutes until you're able to remove all leaves.
3. Cut out the tough middle part of the stem from the large leaves
4. Cut the large leaves in half, and then each half into halves again. Giving you 4 pieces. Each piece should be no bigger than the size of your palm. Prepare all the leaves and set aside

Partially Cook the Rice:

1. Rinse 3 cups of round rice in a sieve under cold running water until the water runs clear.
2. Add the rice to an average-sized pot, cover with 3 cups of hot boiling chicken broth or 1 tablespoon of Better than Bouillion combined with 3 cups hot boiling water. Cover with lid and cook on low heat until all water has evaporated about 10 minutes. Open the lid, fluff with a fork and allow to cool as you work on other ingredients.

Saute Vegetables:

1. Dice the onion and saute in a skillet with 1/4 cup of oil over medium heat until golden in color, about 10 minutes.
2. Add 2 shredded carrots, stir, cover with a lid and over low heat continue cooking, mixing several times throughout, for about 10 minutes. Allow to slightly cool.

75. Multi-Cooker Farmer's Cheese

Ingredients

- 1¾ gallons of whole milk
- 1 cup sour cream/ buttermilk

Also

- Multi-cooker or a pot
- Wooden Spoon
- Cheese cloth

Instructions

1. Fill the 8-quart bowl of the Multi-Cooker with 1¾ gallons of whole milk. Insert a probe thermometer into the pot and heat on the saute setting until 170F.
2. Allow the milk to cool to 110F.
3. In a separate container mix 1 cup of sour cream or buttermilk and 1 cup of heated (to 110F) milk.

4. Pour the sour cream mixture into the heated milk and whisk for about 1 full minute to incorporate it into the milk and cover with a lid.

5. Locked your multi-cooker to a yogurt setting for 8-12 hours. Loosely cover with a lid. Do not disturb the pot while it is setting (no moving, no bumping and no stirring).

6. When the milk has thickened, this can take between 5 and 12 hours depending on the milk and sour cream brand, cut it into squares with a long knife.

7. Now, heat mixture over low heat to about 120F-140 F. Stir the curds gently with a spoon. When they're about pea size, stop stirring. You want to catch the mixture when the curds are still soft and not hard and rubbery. If you overheat the mixture, the curds will lose too much moisture and you will get very rubbery cheese.

8. Pour into a cheesecloth-lined pot. Hang the cheesecloth with the curds until the whey stops dripping, about 5-8 hours.

9. Refrigerate the cheesecloth with the cheese overnight before trying to remove the cheesecloth if you want the cheese to stay in one whole round piece.

10. If not, you can transfer the cheese to plastic containers and keep in the fridge for up to 2 weeks.

76. Oatmeal

Ingredients

- 10 cups whole milk or water
- 3 cups quick-cooking steel-cut oats
- ½ cups granulated sugar or brown sugar
- 2 Tbsp vanilla extract

Instructions

1. Fill a pot with 10 cups of whole milk

2. Add 3 cups of sharp-cooking steel-cut oats, 1 cup of granulated sugar and give a quick stir.

3. Cook on the "Pressure Cooker" setting to 30 minutes. Allow the pressure to naturally decrease until you're able to open the pressure valve with no splattering, about 30 minutes.

4. Open lid, add 2 tbsp of vanilla extract and stir without scratching the bottom.

5. Serve hot as is, or with a dollop of jam, butter, fruits, berries or nuts.

77. Cuban Picadillo

Ingredients

- 1/2 large chopped onion
- 2 cloves garlic, minced
- 1 to mato, chopped
- 1/2 pepper, finely chopped
- 2 tbsp cilantro
- 1-1/2 lb 93% lean ground beef
- 4 oz 1/2 can tomato sauce (I like Goya, check label for Keto)

- kosher salt
- fresh ground pepper
- 1 tsp ground cumin
- 1-2 bay leaf
- 2 tbsp alcaparrado, capers or green olives would work too

Instructions

1. Brown meat on high heat in large sauté pan and season with salt and pepper. Use a wooden spoon to break the meat up into small pieces. When meat is no longer pink, drain all juice from pan.
2. Meanwhile, while meat is cooking, chop onion, garlic, pepper, tomato and cilantro.
3. Add to the meat and continue cooking on a low flame. Add alcaparrado and about 2 tbsp of the brine (the juice from the olives, this adds great flavor) cumin, bay leaf, and more salt if needed. Add tomato sauce and 1/4 cup of water and mix well. Reduce heat and simmer covered about 20 minutes.

78. Eggs with Scallions and Tomatoes

Ingredients

- 2 large eggs
- 3 large egg whites
- 4 diced scallions

- 1 large diced tomato
- 1 tsp olive oil
- salt and pepper

Instructions

1. Heat olive oil in a frying pan on a medium-low flame and add scallions and tomatoes.
2. Mix eggs in a bowl and season with salt and pepper.
3. Add the eggs to the frying pan and stir as they cook 2-3 minutes.

79. Pan Seared Shrimp

Ingredients

- 2 tsp vegetable oil
- 1 1/2 lbs shrimp, peeled and deveined (weight after peeled)
- 1/4 tsp salt
- 1/4 tsp ground black pepper
- 1/4 tsp crushed red pepper
- 2 tbsp dry parsley
- lemon wedges

Instructions

1. Heat 1 tsp oil in 12 inch skillet over high heat until smoking.
2. Meanwhile, toss shrimp with salt, pepper, parsley and crushed red pepper.
3. Add half of the shrimp to the pan in single layer and cook until edges turn pink, about 1 minute.
4. Remove pan from heat, flip shrimp using tongs and let it stand about 30 seconds until all of the shrimp is opaque except for the center.
5. Transfer to a plate and repeat with the second batch and the remaining teaspoon of oil.
6. After second batch has stood off the heat, add the first batch to the pan and toss to combine.
7. Cover skillet and let shrimp stand for 1 - 2 minutes.
8. Shrimp will now be cooked through.
9. Serve immediately with lemon wedges.

80. Shiitake and Manchego Scramble

Ingredients

- 2 tablespoons extra virgin olive oil, divided
- 1/2 cup diced onion
- 1/2 cup diced sweet red pepper
- 2 cups thinly sliced fresh shiitake mushrooms (about 4 ounces)
- 1 teaspoon prepared horseradish
- 8 large eggs, beaten
- 1 cup heavy whipping cream
- 1 cup shredded Manchego cheese
- 1 teaspoon kosher salt
- 1 teaspoon coarsely ground pepper

Instructions

1. In a large nonstick skillet, heat 1 tablespoon olive oil over medium heat. Add onion and red pepper; cook and stir until crisp-tender, 2-3 minutes. Add mushrooms; cook and stir until tender, 3-4 minutes. Stir in horseradish; cook 2 minutes more.
2. In a small bowl, whisk together remaining ingredients and remaining olive oil. Pour into skillet; cook and stir until eggs are thickened and no liquid egg remains.

81. Carne Bistec - Colombian Steak with Onions and Tomatoes

Ingredients

- 1-1/2 lbs grass fed sirloin tip steak, sliced very thin
- salt to taste
- garlic powder to taste
- cumin to taste
- 4 tsp olive oil
- 1 medium onion, sliced thin or chopped
- 1 very large tomato or 2 medium tomatoes, sliced thin or chopped

Instructions

1. Season steak with salt and garlic powder.
2. Heat a large frying pan until VERY HOT.
3. Add 2 tsp of oil then half of the steak and cook less than a minute on each side.
4. Set steak aside, add another teaspoon of oil and cook remaining steak.
5. Set aside.
6. Reduce heat to medium, add another teaspoon of oil and add the onions.
7. Cook 2 minutes, then add the tomatoes.
8. Season with salt, pepper and cumin and reduce heat to medium-low.
9. Add about 1/4 cup of water and simmer a few minutes to create a sauce, add more water if needed and taste adjust seasoning as needed.
10. Return the steak to the pan along with the drippings, combine well and remove from heat.
11. Serve over rice or for a low carb option with a sunny-side up egg on top.

82. Sauteed Collard Greens with Bacon

Ingredients

- 1 tbsp olive oil
- 1 slice bacon, chopped
- 3 cloves garlic, chopped
- 1 bunch collard greens, washed and dried
- salt

Instructions

1. Remove the tough stems that run down the center of the leaf.
2. Stack an few leaves, roll and slice into thin strips.
3. In an large saute pan, heat bacon on low heat.
4. When bacon fat melts, add oil and garlic, saute until golden, about a minute.
5. Add chopped collards to the pan, season with salt and cover.
6. Simmer covered until tender, about 10 minutes, stirring occasionally.

83. Shrimp Salad on Cucumber Slices

Ingredients

- 3/4 lb cooked shrimp, peeled (weight after peeled)
- 2 celery stalks, chopped
- 1 tbsp red onion, chopped
- 2 tbsp light mayonnaise, I used Hellmann's, check label for Keto
- chopped chives for garnish
- 1 tbsp fat free Greek yogurt, full fat for Keto
- Seasoning salt or adobo seasoning
- salt and fresh ground pepper
- 30 thin slices cucumber, about 1 large

Instructions

1. Combine shrimp, celery, onion, mayonnaise, yogurt, and season to taste with seasoning salt or adobo and pepper.

2. Arrange cucumbers on a platter, season with salt and top each slice with a heaping tablespoon of shrimp salad.

3. Top with chopped chives for garnish.

84. Skinny Tzatziki

Ingredients

- 8 oz fat-free Greek yogurt, I used Fage, use full fat for Keto
- 1 small cucumber, peeled and seeded (1 cup grated and squeezed dry)
- 1 clove garlic, crushed
- 1 tsp lemon juice
- 1 tbsp fresh dill, chopped
- 1 tbsp fresh chives, chopped
- kosher salt and fresh pepper

Instructions

1. Strain the yogurt using a metal strainer or a coffee filter for an few hours to remove as much liquid as possible. Set aside.

2. Scoop seeds out of the cucumber with a small spoon. Place cucumber in a mini food processor or grate with a box cheese grater. Drain the liquid from the cucumber in a metal strainer and sprinkle with a little salt (this helps release the liquid). You may want to use the back of a spoon to help squeeze out any excess liquid.

3. Combine strained cucumber, garlic, yogurt, salt, pepper, lemon juice, dill, chives and refrigerate at least 1 hour before serving.

4. Makes about 2 cups. Store in refrigerator for about a week.

85. Spaghetti Squash Pesto with Tomatoes

Ingredients

- 1 small spaghetti squash
- 15 large basil leaves
- 1 small clove garlic
- 1/4 cup olive oil
- 3 tbsp Parmigiano-Reggiano
- salt and fresh pepper
- 1 tomato, diced

Instructions

1. Cut squash in half lengthwise, scoop out seeds and fibers.
2. Place in a microwave safe dish and cover.
3. Microwave 8-9 minutes.
4. Remove from the microwave and scoop out flesh with a fork into a large bowl.
5. In a small blender combine basil, garlic, olive oil, parmesan cheese, salt a pepper and puree until smooth.
6. Combine pesto with two cups spaghetti squash (save any remaining squash for another recipe).
7. Add tomatoes and season with additional salt and pepper.

86. Roasted Broccoli Rabe with Garlic

Ingredients

- 1 large bunch broccoli rabe, rapini, tough stems removed
- 4-5 cloves garlic, smashed
- 2 tbsp olive oil
- salt and fresh pepper
- pinch crushed red pepper flakes, optional

Instructions

1. Heat oven to 400°.
2. Bring a large pot of salted water to a boil.
3. When water boils, add broccoli rabe and blanch one minute.
4. Remove from water and DRAIN WELL in a colander.
5. Add to a baking dish and mix with garlic, oil, salt, pepper, crushed red pepper flakes.
6. Roast 15-20 minutes.

87. Broiled or Grilled Pollo Sabroso

Ingredients

- 6 medium chicken thighs, with bone and skin
- 1 tbsp vinegar
- 2 teaspoons soy sauce, coconut aminos for whole30
- 1 packet Sazon, in Spanish aisle, I prefer Badia brand with no MSG
- 1 teaspoon Adobo, in Spanish aisle
- 1/2 teaspoon garlic powder
- 1/2 teaspoon dried oregano

Instructions

1. Season chicken with vinegar and soy sauce.
2. Add sazon, 1 teaspoon of adobo, garlic powder, oregano and adobo and mix well. (Don't use your hands or they will turn orange)
3. Let chicken marinate at least 15 minutes.
4. Broil or grill on low until chicken is cooked through, turning halfway, careful not to burn, about 30 minutes. Enjoy with rice and salad.

88. Pork Chops with Mushrooms and Shallots

Ingredients

- 1 tsp butter or ghee
- 4 pork loin chops, bone-in, trimmed or 1 lb (boneless)
- 1/2 tsp kosher salt
- fresh black pepper
- 1/4 cup chopped shallots
- 1 cup low sodium chicken stock
- 10 oz sliced baby bella mushrooms
- 1 tbsp Dijon mustard
- 2 tbsp chopped, fresh parsley

Instructions

1. In a large frying pan heat the butter over moderately low heat.
2. Season pork with salt and pepper.
3. Raise heat to medium and add the chops to the pan and sauté for 7 minutes.
4. Turn and cook until chops are browned and done to medium, about 7-8 minutes longer or until the pork reads 160F in the center.
5. Remove the chops and put in a warm spot.
6. Add shallots to the pan and cook, stirring, until soft, about 3 minutes.
7. Add the stock to deglaze the pan, stir in the mustard, 1 tbsp parsley, then add mushrooms, season with fresh pepper and cook about 3 minutes, or until mushrooms are done.
8. Put the chops on a platter and pour the mushroom sauce over the meat, top with remaining parsley.

89. Grilled Chicken with Spinach and Melted Mozzarella

Ingredients

- 24 oz 3 large chicken breasts sliced in half lengthwise to make 6
- kosher salt and pepper to taste
- 1 tsp olive oil
- 3 cloves garlic, crushed
- 10 oz frozen spinach, drained
- 3 oz shredded part skim mozzarella
- 1/2 cup roasted red pepper, sliced in strips (packed in water)
- olive oil spray

Instructions

1. Preheat oven to 400°F. Season chicken with salt and pepper. Lightly spray a grill or grill pan with oil. Cook chicken until no longer pink, about 2 to 3 minutes per side.

2. Heat a skillet over medium heat. Add oil and garlic, sauté a 30 seconds, add spinach, salt and pepper. Cook until heated through, 2 to 3 minutes.

3. Place chicken on a baking sheet, divide spinach evenly between the 6 pieces and place on top. Top each with 1/2 oz mozzarella, roasted peppers and bake until melted, about 3 minutes.

90. Pepper and Fresh Herb Frittata

Ingredients

- 12 large eggs
- 2 tablespoons minced fresh chives
- 2 tablespoons minced fresh parsley
- 2 teaspoons minced fresh basil or 1/2 teaspoon dried basil
- 2 teaspoons minced fresh oregano or 1/2 teaspoon dried oregano
- 1 teaspoon salt
- 1/4 teaspoon pepper
- 3 tablespoons olive oil
- 1/2 cup sliced pickled peppers
- 1/2 cup crumbled goat cheese

Instructions

1. Preheat broiler. In a large bowl, whisk eggs, herbs, salt and pepper until blended.

2. In a 10-in. broiler-safe skillet, heat oil over medium-low heat. Pour in egg mixture. Cook, covered, 10-12 minutes or until nearly set. Top with pickled peppers and cheese.

3. Broil 4-5 in. from heat 3-4 minute's or until eggs are completely set. Let stand 5 minutes. Cut into wedges.

91. Basil Green Goddess Dressing Recipe

Ingredients

- 1/2 cup light mayonnaise, such as Hellman's (regular for Keto)
- 1/2 cup scallions, chopped
- 1/2 cup chopped fresh basil, packed
- 1/8 cup fresh squeezed lemon juice, 1 lemon
- 1 clove garlic, chopped
- 1 tsp kosher salt
- 1/2 tsp freshly ground black pepper
- 1 tsp anchovy paste
- 1/2 cup light sour cream, full fat for Keto

Instructions

1. Place all ingredients except for sour cream in a blender and blend until smooth.
2. Add sour cream and process until blended.
3. Keep refrigerated until serving.

92. Broiled Salmon with Rosemary

Ingredients

- 24 oz or 4 pieces of salmon
- olive oil spray
- 2 tsp fresh lemon juice
- 2 tsp fresh, chopped rosemary
- 2 cloves garlic, minced
- salt and fresh pepper to taste

Instructions

1. Combine lemon juice, rosemary, salt, pepper and garlic. Brush mixture onto fish.
2. Spray the rack of a broiler pan with olive oil spray and arrange the fish on it.
3. Broil 4 inches from the heat until fish flakes easily when tested with a fork, approx. 4-6 minutes per 1/2 of thickness.
4. If fish is more than 1" thick, gently turn it halfway through broiling.

93. Filipino BBQ Pork Skewers

Ingredients

2.5 lb pork country style ribs, all fat trimmed, cut into 1" x 1" cubes

For the marinade:

- 6 oz 7-up
- 1/2 cup soy sauce
- 1/2 cup white vinegar
- 1 lemon, juice of

- 1/3 cup brown sugar
- 6 cloves garlic, crushed
- 1 tsp black pepper
- crushed red pepper flakes, optional

Instructions

1. Mix all Ingredients in a large non-reactive bowl and marinate the meat overnight.
2. If using wooden skewers, soak in water at least an hour so they don't burn on the grill.
3. Thread the meat onto skewers and grill.
4. Discard unused marinade.
5. Enjoy!

94. Corned Beef and Cabbage

Ingredients

- 2.5 lbs corned beef brisket in brine, fat trimmed off
- 1 cup baby carrots, peeled

- 1 small head cabbage, cut into 4 wedges
- 2 bay leaves

For the Horseradish Cream (Optional)

- 1 tbsp prepared grated horseradish
- 1/4 cup fat free sour cream, full fat for Keto

- 1/4 tsp dijon mustard
- salt and pepper

Instructions

1. In a large pot, place brisket, bay leaves and enough water to cover.
2. Simmer, covered for about an hour per pound.
3. When meat is tender add carrots.
4. Boil for about 10 minutes, then add cabbage.
5. Cook another 15- 20 minutes, until tender.
6. Remove the meat and place on a cutting board.
7. Slice the meat across the grain into thin slices.
8. Serve with vegetables and ladle some broth on top.

95. Chicken Broth

Ingredients

- 3 chicken breast halves
- 1 onion, quartered
- 1 tomato, quartered
- 1 cup carrots
- 2 celery stalks
- 2 cloves garlic
- 2-3 sprigs thyme
- 3 bay leaves
- fresh herbs like cilantro or parsley, I used cilantro
- whole peppercorns
- kosher salt

Instructions

1. Place all Ingredients into crock pot and fill with water.
2. Cover and cook on high for 4 hours or low for 8 hours.
3. When it's done, throw out all the vegetables, strain the liquid and remove the chicken for other recipes, like chicken salad, or anything that calls for shredded chicken.
4. If you're not using the stock right away you can store it in containers and refrigerate for up to 2 days or freeze for several months.
5. When the stock is chilled, the fat will rise to the top and harden and you can easily remove it.

96. Cheesy Broccoli and Chicken Casserole

Ingredients

- 2 heads broccoli, cut into florets
- 1 large rotisserie chicken, meat pulled and shredded
- 1 cup mayonnaise
- 1/2 cup heavy whipping cream
- 1 tablespoon chicken soup base
- 1 tablespoon dried dill weed
- 1 teaspoon ground black pepper
- 2 cups shredded Cheddar cheese
- cooking spray

Instructions

1. Preheat oven to 350 degrees F (175 degrees C).
2. Place broccoli florets in a 9x13-inch baking dish. Layer shredded chicken on top; press down onto broccoli.
3. Combine mayonnaise, heavy cream, chicken soup base, dill, and pepper in a bowl; mix well. Spread evenly over chicken and top with Cheddar cheese. Grease a piece of aluminum foil with cooking spray and cover baking dish with greased-side down.
4. Bake covered in the preheated oven, about 45 minutes. Remove aluminum foil and bake until golden brown, about 15 minutes. Remove from oven and let stand for 10 to 20 minutes before serving.

97. Caveman Chili

Ingredients

- 2 pounds ground pork
- 8 thick slices bacon, chopped
- 1 (14.5 ounce) can diced tomatoes, drained
- 1 onion, chopped
- 3 small green bell peppers, chopped
- 1 (6 ounce) can tomato paste
- 1 (1.25 ounce) package chili seasoning (such as McCormick)
- 1 pinch garlic powder, or more to taste
- 1 pinch onion powder, or more to taste
- salt and ground black pepper to taste
- 1 pinch ground cayenne pepper, or more to taste

Instructions

1. Place pork in a skillet over medium heat; season with salt and pepper. Cook and stir until browned and crumbly, 5 to 7 minutes. Drain and discard grease. Transfer pork to a slow cooker.
2. Place bacon in the hot skillet and cook over medium-high heat until evenly browned, about 10 minutes. Drain and discard grease. Transfer bacon to the slow cooker.
3. Combine drained tomatoes, onion, green bell pepper, and tomato paste into the slow cooker. Add seasoning packet, garlic powder, onion powder, and salt, pepper, cayenne pepper; stir to combine.
4. Cook on Low until flavors have combined, about 6 hours.

98. Creamy Taco Soup with Ground Beef

Ingredients

- 1 pound ground beef
- 1/2 cup chopped onion
- 2 cloves garlic, minced
- 1 tablespoon ground cumin
- 1 teaspoon chili powder
- 1 (8 ounce) package cream cheese, softened
- 2 (14.5 ounce) cans beef broth
- 2 (10 ounce) cans diced tomatoes and green chiles (such as RO*TEL)
- 1/2 cup heavy cream
- 2 teaspoons salt, or to taste

Instructions

1. Combine ground beef with onion and garlic in a large soup pot over medium-high heat. Cook and stir until beef is browned and crumbly, 5 to 7 minutes. Drain and discard grease. Add cumin and chili powder; cook 2 minutes more.
2. Drop cream cheese into the pot by bits and mash it into the beef with a big spoon until no white spots remain, 3 to 5 minutes. Stir in broth, diced tomatoes, heavy cream, and salt. Cook until heated through, about 10 minutes more.

63

99. Spicy Butternut Squash Soup

Ingredients

- 1 tablespoon olive oil
- 1 onion, diced
- 2 cloves garlic
- 1 pound butternut squash - peeled, seeded, and cut into 1-inch pieces
- 5 cups vegetable broth
- 1 tablespoon brown sugar
- 1 teaspoon salt
- 1/2 teaspoon ground black pepper
- 1/2 teaspoon ground ginger
- 1/2 teaspoon curry powder (optional)
- 1 cup heavy whipping cream

Instructions

1. Turn on a multi-functional pressure cooker (such as Instant Pot(R)) and select Saute function. Heat olive oil and add onion; cook until translucent, about 7 minutes. Add garlic and cook for 1 minute more.

2. Combine butternut squash, vegetable broth, brown sugar, salt, ground black pepper, ginger, and curry powder in the pot. Close and lock the lid. Select high pressure according to manufacturer's Instructions; set timer for 10 minutes. Allow 10 to 15 minutes for pressure to build.

3. Release pressure carefully using the quick-release method according to manufacturer's instructions, about 5 minutes. Unlock and remove lid. Blend with an immersion blender until creamy.

4. Stir in heavy whipping cream.

100. Garlic Tuscan Chicken

Ingredients

- 2 tablespoons olive oil
- 1 1/2 pounds skinless, boneless chicken breasts, thinly sliced
- 1 cup heavy cream
- 1/2 cup chicken broth
- 1/2 cup grated Parmesan cheese
- 1 teaspoon garlic powder
- 1 teaspoon Italian seasoning
- 1 cup spinach, chopped
- 1/2 cup chopped sun-dried tomatoes

Instructions

1. Heat olive oil in a large skillet over medium-high heat. Cook chicken until browned and no longer pink in the center, 3 to 5 minutes per side. Remove chicken and set aside on a plate.

2. Add heavy cream, chicken broth, Parmesan cheese, garlic powder, and Italian seasoning to the skillet. Whisk sauce over medium-high heat until starting to thicken, about 5 minutes. Add spinach and sun-dried tomatoes; simmer until spinach starts to wilt, about 1 minute. Return chicken to the skillet and cook until heated through, 2 to 3 minutes.

101. Halibut and Shellfish Soup

Ingredients

- 1 tsp olive oil
- 2 chopped shallots
- 2 cloves of garlic
- 3 medium diced tomatoes
- 4 oz dry white wine
- 1 cup clam juice
- 2 cups vegetable stock
- 3/4 lb halibut filet, skin removed cut into large pieces
- 1 lb shrimp, peeled deveined fresh shrimp
- 1 dozen littleneck clams
- pinch of saffron
- 1/4 cup fresh chopped parsley
- crusty bread for serving on the side, optional

Instructions

1. Add olive oil to a large heavy pot; over medium heat sautée shallots and garlic until translucent.
2. Add the tomatoes, wine, clam juice and the bone from the halibut if you have one.
3. Add vegetable stock, saffron, fresh thyme and stir.
4. Add the clams; cover and cook 2 minutes, add the shrimp and fish and cook and additional 3 to 5 minutes, or until the shrimp turns pink and the clams open.
5. Remove bone and serve with a crusty bread to dip into the juice.

102. Grilled Tuna over Arugula with Lemon Vinaigrette

Ingredients

- 5 oz sashimi tuna, sushi grade
- 1 tsp extra virgin olive oil
- 1 tsp fresh lemon juice
- 2 cups baby arugula
- 1 tsp capers
- kosher salt and fresh pepper

Instructions

1. Season tuna with kosher salt and fresh cracked pepper.
2. Place arugula and capers on a plate.
3. Combine oil and lemon juice, salt and pepper.
4. Heat your grill to high heat and clean grate well.
5. When grill is hot, spray grate with oil to prevent sticking then place tuna on the grill; cook one minute without moving.
6. Turn over and cook an additional minute; remove from heat and set aside on a plate.
7. Slice tuna on the diagonal and place on top of salad.
8. Top with lemon vinaigrette and eat immediately

103. Lemon Rotisserie Chicken

Ingredients

- 1 (2.5 pound) whole chicken
- 1 lemon, cut into 4 wedges
- 2 tablespoons olive oil
- 1 1/2 teaspoons salt
- 1 teaspoon garlic powder
- 1 teaspoon paprika
- 1/2 teaspoon ground black pepper
- 1 cup chicken broth

Instructions

1. Rinse chicken and pat dry. Insert lemon wedges inside the cavity.

2. Turn on a multi-functional pressure cooker (such as Instant Pot(R)) and select Saute function. Mix olive oil, salt, garlic powder, paprika, and pepper in a bowl. Rub top part of chicken with 1/2 of the spice mixture. Place the chicken, breast side down, and cook until crispy, 3 to 4 minutes.

3. Rub remaining spice mixture on the bottom side of the chicken. Flip chicken over with tongs and cook for 1 minute more.

4. Remove chicken from the pot. Place trivet inside the pot; place chicken back in the pot, breast side down on the trivet, and pour in chicken broth. Close and lock the lid. Select high pressure according to manufacturer's Instructions; set timer for 20 minutes. Allow 10 to 15 minutes for pressure to build. Release pressure using the natural-release method according to manufacturer's instructions, 10 to 40 minutes.

104. Parmesan Zucchini Fries

Ingredients

- cooking spray
- 2 eggs
- 3/4 cup grated Parmesan cheese
- 1 tablespoon dried mixed herbs
- 1 1/2 teaspoons garlic powder
- 1 teaspoon paprika
- 1/2 teaspoon ground black pepper
- 2 pounds zucchinis, cut into 1/2-inch French fry strips

Instructions

1. Preheat oven to 425 degrees F (220 degrees C). Line a baking sheet with aluminum foil and spray with cooking spray.

2. Whisk eggs in a shallow bowl. Combine Parmesan cheese, mixed herbs, garlic powder, paprika, and pepper in a separate shallow bowl; mix well.

3. Dip zucchini fries into beaten eggs, in batches; shake to remove excess, and roll in Parmesan mixture until fully coated. Place on the prepared baking sheet.

4. Bake in the preheated oven, turning once, until golden and crispy, 30 to 35 minutes.

105. Cinnamon Granola

Ingredients

1. 1/2 cup coarsely chopped walnuts
2. 1/2 cup coarsely chopped pecans
3. 1/2 cup unsweetened shredded coconut
4. 1/3 cup sliced almonds
5. 1 teaspoon ground cinnamon
6. 2 teaspoons granulated erythritol sweetener (such as Swerve)
7. 1 (1 gram) packet granular sucrolose sweetener (such as Splenda), or more to taste (optional)
8. 2 tablespoons butter, melted

Instructions

1. Preheat oven to 375 degrees F (190 degrees C).
2. Mix walnuts, pecans, coconut, and almonds together in a bowl.
3. Stir cinnamon, erythritol, and sucralose into melted butter; pour over nut mixture and stir to coat. Spread granola in a single layer on a baking sheet.
4. Bake in the preheated oven until crunchy, 8 to 10 minutes. Remove from oven; stir and allow to cool.

106. Loaded Chicken Salad

Ingredients

- 1 boneless chicken breast (about 300g, with or without skin)
- 1 tbsp extra virgin olive oil
- 1/4 tsp Himalayan salt
- 1/4 tsp black pepper
- 1 avocado
- 100 g mozzarella balls
- 1 large tomato (any colour)
- 1 har artichoke hearts (my jar was 170g)
- 1/2 red onion
- 5 asparagus
- 20 leaves basil
- 4 cups baby spinach (I used about 200g)

Dressing

- 2 tbsp extra virgin olive oil
- 1 1/2 tbsp balsamic vinegar
- 1 tsp dijon mustard
- 1 clove garlic
- pinch Himalayan salt
- pinch black pepper

Instructions

1. Peel and dice the avocado. Slice the red onion. Dice the tomato. Pile the basil leaves together, roll them up and slice. Cut the stems off the asparagus and slice in half. Mince the garlic.
2. Slice the chicken breast in half lengthwise. Sprinkle the 1/4 tsp of salt and pepper on each sides. Heat the 1 tbsp of olive oil in a cast iron skillet and place the chicken breasts in. Fry on each side, about 3 minutes each side, until they have a nice golden brown colour and cooked through. Add

the asparagus beside the chicken breasts and cook a few minutes until soft and grilled. Take out the chicken and slice.

3. In a small bowl, combine the minced garlic, olive oil, balsamic vinegar, dijon, and salt & peper.

4. Add the baby spinach to a large bowl or plate. Cover with the grilled chicken, avocado, mozzarella, tomatoes, artichoke, red onions, asparagus and basil leaves. Pour the dressing over and enjoy!

107. Chicken Enchilada Bowl

Ingredients

- 2 tablespoons coconut oil (for searing chicken)
- 1 pound of boneless, skinless chicken thighs
- 3/4 cup red enchilada sauce (recipe from Low Carb Maven)

- 1/4 cup water
- 1/4 cup chopped onion
- 1– 4 oz can diced green chiles

Toppings (feel free to customize)

- 1 whole avocado, diced
- 1 cup shredded cheese 1/4 cup chopped pickled jalapenos

- 1/2 cup sour cream
- 1 roma tomato, chopped

Optional: serve over plain cauliflower rice (or mexican cauliflower rice) for a more complete meal!

Instructions

1. In a pot or dutch oven over medium heat melt the coconut oil. Once hot, sear chicken thighs until lightly brown.

2. Pour in enchilada sauce and water then add onion and green chiles. Reduce heat to a simmer and cover. Cook chicken for 17-25 minutes or until chicken is tender and fully cooked through to at least 165 degrees internal temperature.

3. Careully remove the chicken and place onto a work surface. Chop or shred chicken (your preference) then add it back into the pot. Let the chicken simmer uncovered for an additional 10 minutes to absorb flavor and allow the sauce to reduce a little.

4. To Serve, top with avocado, cheese, jalapeno, sour cream, tomato, and any other desired toppings. Feel free to customize these to your preference. Serve alone or over cauliflower rice if desired just be sure to update your personal nutrition info as needed.

108. Chicken Philly Cheesesteak

Ingredients

- 10 oz boneless chicken breasts (about 2)
- 2 Tbsp worcestershire sauce
- 1/2 tsp onion powder
- 1/2 tsp garlic powder
- 1 dash ground pepper
- 2 tsp olive oil, divided
- 1/2 cup diced onion fresh or frozen
- 1/2 cup diced bell pepper fresh or frozen
- 1/2 tsp minced garlic
- 3 slices provolone cheese or queso melting cheese

Instructions

1. Slice chicken breasts into very thin pieces (freeze slightly if desired to make this easier) and place in a medium bowl. Add next 4 ingredients (worcestershire through ground pepper) and stir to coat chicken.

2. Heat 1 teaspoon olive oil in a large oven proof skillet. Add chicken pieces and cook until browned -about 5 minutes. Turn pieces over and cook about 2-3 minutes more or until brown. Remove from skillet.

3. Add remaining 1 teaspoon olive oil to warm skillet. Then add onions, bell pepper and garlic. Cook and stir to heated and tender- 2-3 minutes.

4. Turn heat off and add chicken back to skillet and stir with veggies to combine. Place sliced cheese over all and cover 2-3 minutes to melt.

109. Asiago Cauliflower Rice

Ingredients

- 3 cups cauliflower riced
- 1 cup Asiago cheese shredded
- 3/4 cup heavy cream

Instructions

1. In a large saute pan, add the riced cauliflower and 2 tablespoons of water. Cover and cook for 5 minutes.

2. Add the cream and cheese and mix until cheese is melted.

3. Taste to see if the cauliflower is done.

4. Take off the heat and serve.

110. Spinach-Mozzarella

Ingredients

- 1½ lbs ground chuck
- 1 teaspoon salt
- ¾ teaspoon ground black pepper
- 2 cups fresh spinach, firmly packed
- ½ cup shredded mozzarella cheese (about 4 oz)
- 2 tablespoons grated Parmesan cheese

Instructions

1. In a medium bowl, combine ground beef, salt, and pepper.
2. Scoop about cup of mixture and with dampened hands shape into 8 patties about ½-inch thick. Place in the refrigerator.
3. Place spinach in saucepan over medium-high heat. Cover and cook for 2 minutes, until wilted.
4. Drain and let cool. With your hands squeeze the spinach to extract as much liquid as possible.
5. Transfer to a cutting board, chop the spinach, and place in a bowl.
6. Stir in mozzarella cheese and Parmesan.
7. Scoop about ¼ cup of stuffing and mound in the center of 4 patties,
8. Cover with remaining 4 patties, and seal the edges by pressing firmly together.
9. Cup each patty with your hands to round out the edges, and press on the top to flatten slightly into a single thick patty.
10. Heat a grill or a grill pan to medium-high (if you're using an outdoor grill lightly oil the grill grates).
11. Grill burgers for 5 to 6 minutes on each side.

111. Chicken Noodle Soup

Ingredients

- drumsticks or chicken breasts
- medium carrots or baby carrots
- large onion, peeled, split in half
- celery stalks (optional)
- kosher salt
- peppercorns
- dry garlic flakes or garlic cloves, peeled
- bay leaf
- water or broth
- egg noodles
- chopped parsley

Instructions

1. Place the chicken, carrots, onion, celery (optional) and spices into the Crockpot. Cover with 3 Qts water or broth, then attach peppercorns, garlic flakes, bay leaf, and salt. Cover with lid. Set to make on 'High' for 4.5 hours or on 'low' for 6-8 hours.

2. Cook noodles according to package instructions. Drain. Add 1/2 tablespoon olive oil to noodles to keep them from sticking. Stir to coat. Refrigerate until ready to use.

3. After the 4.5 hours of cooking, the broth will need to be clarified. Line a sieve with 2-3 layers of paper towel and insert it over a soup pot (4-5 qts). Drain the broth through the paper towel-lined sieve discarding the onion & celery stalks, but keeping the carrots and the drumsticks. Rinse drumsticks and carrots from the impurities that are stuck to it.

4. Shred the chicken meat into as small of pieces as you want, discarding the skin and bones. Slice carrots into small pieces.

5. Heat the noodles before adding to the soup. Add the shredded chicken, carrots and chopped parsley. Stir. Taste and adjust the seasoning amount

112. Perfectly Simple Pot Roast

Ingredients

- 4 lb chuck roast
- 1 cup carrots baby carrots or 2 normal peeled carrots cut into 1-inch chunks
- 1 large onion cut into 8 pieces
- 1 head garlic peeled
- 2 cups water or broth
- 2 tsp kosher salt
- 1 tsp ground black pepper
- 1 tsp garlic powder
- 1 tsp pickling spice
- For Gravy:
- 2 Tbsp unsalted butter
- 4 Tbsp flour
- leftover liquid from pot roast

Instructions

1. Mix water, salt, ground black pepper, garlic powder, and pickling spice and stir until salt is dissolved.

2. If you want, brown all sides of the roast on a super hot skillet with a tablespoon oil. Otherwise, place the meat into the crockpot as is, surrounded by carrots, onions, and garlic, and then pour the water with the spices on top. Close with the lid and set it on "high" for 7 hours.

3. After 7 hours, skim the fat with a spoon (or do this after you have removed the meat and drained the liquid through a sieve)

4. Remove the meat to a separate dish and stay warm.

5. Set a sieve over a bowl. Pour the resting liquid and veggies through the sieve. Discard the solids and hold on to the liquid.

6. In a saucepan, melt butter over medium heat, then add the flour and cook it for several minutes until it's golden in color, all the while stirring to prevent it from burning. Slowly pour in the liquid and keep stirring with a whisk until the gravy is slightly thickened.

7. Now shred the meat with two forks into small pieces. You can serve it over mashed potatoes, rice, another grain or pasta, and pour some gravy on top.

8. Alternatively, you can slice the roast and serve it by slices, pouring the gravy atop it

113. Crock Pot Pepper Chicken

Ingredients

- 3 chicken breasts boneless, skinless
- 1 cup chicken stock
- 1 tsp mustard seeds
- 1 tsp garlic powder or 1 clove garlic crushed
- Sautee 30 minutes before the chicken is done the cooking

- 1 medium onion peeled and diced
- 2 bell peppers cut in thin strips
- 1-2 Tbsp olive oil
- Add at the end
- Salt & Pepper to taste
- 1/4 cup Garlic Sweet Sauce or Teriyaki Sauce

Instructions

1. Put the chicken breasts on the bottom of the crockpot. Pour the chicken stock on top. Add mustard seeds and garlic powder.

2. Set the timer to 6 hours and the temperature to "high". Set the breasts over about 2 times throughout the cooking, doing it for the first time 3 hours into the cooking process.

3. Around 20 minutes before the chicken is ready, sauté the onions in a skillet with 1 to 2 tablespoons of oil, until slightly golden.

4. Add strips of bell pepper and sautee some more until the pepper has taken on some color and shifted tender.

5. Once the chicken is ready, shred it with two forks. Do not remove the leftover liquid, it will support to keep chicken moist.

6. Add sautéed onion & pepper & the sauce of your choice. Season with freshly ground black pepper, sriracha & salt to taste.

7. Serve hot on a toasted bun.

114. Chicken Zoodles with Tomatoes & Spiced Cashews

Ingredients

- ½ tsp coconut butter
- 1 medium diced onion
- 450- 500 g chicken fillets
- 1 minced garlic
- Two medium zucchinis
- 400 g crushed tomatoes

- 7-10 cherry tomatoes (chop half)
- 100 g raw cashews* (for seasoning: turmeric, paprika, and salt)
- For seasoning: salt, pepper, dry oregano & basil

Special equipment: vegetable spiralizer

Instructions

1. Heat a large pan over medium/high heat. Add coconut butter and diced onions. Cook for 30 seconds to 1 minute. Be careful not to burn the onions.

2. Dice the chicken into 2 cm pieces.

3. Add chicken and minced garlic on a pan. Season with basil, oregano salt & pepper. Cook chicken for 5-6 minutes or until golden.

4. While the chicken is cooking, spiralize the zucchini. Cut them shorter when needed. If you don't have special spiralizer, then just use your vegetable peeler and make ribbons out of zucchini.

5. Add crushed tomatoes and let it simmer for 3-5 minutes.

6. Roast the cashews in another pan (or oven) until golden. Season with paprika, turmeric, and salt.

7. Finally add spiralized zoodles, cherry tomatoes and season with extra salt when needed. Cook for another 1 minute then turn off heat.

8. Serve the chicken zoodles with spiced cashews and fresh basil. Enjoy!

115. Beberé Enchilada Style Stuffed Peppers

Ingredients

- 2lb 85% lean pastured ground beef
- 1 cup organic frozen cauliflower rice
- 3 tbsp Kerry Gold butter
- 1/2 maui onion
- 1 large carrot
- 2 cloves garlic

- 2 tsp smoked sea salt
- 2 tsp beberé
- 5 large bell peppers
- 5 dollops organic, lactose free sour cream

Instructions

1. Heat a large skillet on medium heat. In the meantime dice your carrot, onion and garlic.

2. Add the butter to the skillet; once it's melted add in the diced veggies.

3. Sauté, stirring occasionally until tender, about 8 minutes.

4. Add in the beef, salt and bebere, stir well, breaking up the beef until crumbly and browned. Mix in the cauliflower rice. Stir until well incorporated. Remove the skillet from the heat.

5. Pre-heat the oven to 400F. While the oven heats cut the tops off of your peppers, remove the core and seeds. Then spoon the beef mixture into them. Arrange the peppers in a casserole dish.

6. Top each one with a dollop of sour cream. Sprinkle a little extra spice mix on top.

7. Bake for 40 minutes! Serve hot!

116. Creamy Tuscan Garlic Chicken

Ingredients

- 1½ pounds boneless skinless chicken breasts, thinly sliced
- 2 Tablespoons olive oil
- 1 cup heavy cream
- ½ cup chicken broth

- 1 teaspoon garlic powder
- 1 teaspoon italian seasoning
- ½ cup parmesan cheese
- 1 cup spinach, chopped
- ½ cup sun dried tomatoes

Instructions

1. In a large skillet add olive oil and cook the chicken on medium high heat for 3-5 minutes on each side or until brown on each side and cooked until no longer pink in center. Remove chicken and set aside on a plate.

2. Add the heavy cream, chicken broth, garlic powder, italian seasoning, and parmesan cheese. Whisk over medium high heat until it starts to thicken. Add the spinach and sundried tomatoes and let it simmer until the spinach starts to wilt. Add the chicken back to the pan and serve over pasta if desired.

117. Delicious Lemon Herb Low Carb Meatloaf

Ingredients

- 2 pounds 85% lean grass fed ground beef
- 1/2 tablespoon fine Himalayan salt
- 1 teaspoon black pepper
- 1/4 cup Nutrition Infoal Yeast
- 2 large eggs
- 2 tablespoons avocado oil
- 1 tablespoon lemon zest
- 1/4 cup chopped parsley
- 1/4 cup chopped fresh oregano
- 4 cloves garlic

Instructions

1. Pre-heat oven to 400F.
2. In a large bowl mix the ground beef, salt, black pepper and Nutrition Infoal yeast.
3. In a blender or food processor mix the eggs, oil, herbs and garlic. Blend until the eggs are froth and the herbs, lemon and garlic are minced and mixed.
4. Add the egg blend to the beef and mix to combine.
5. Add the beef to a small, 8×4 loaf pan. Smooth and flatten out.
6. Set in the oven, middle rack for 50-60 minutes.
7. Carefully remove from the oven and tilt the loaf pan over the sink to drain the fluid. Let it cool for 5-10 minutes before slicing into.
8. Garnish with fresh lemon and enjoy!

118. BBQ Pulled Beef Sando

Ingredients

- 3lbs Boneless Chuck Roast
- 2 tsp Pink Himalayan Salt
- 2 tsp garlic powder
- 1 tsp onion powder
- 1 tsp black pepper
- 1 tbsp. smoked paprika
- 2 tbsp. tomato paste
- 1/4 cup apple cider vinegar
- 2 tbsp. coconut aminos
- 1/2 cup bone broth
- 1/4 cup melted Kerrygold Butter

Instructions

1. Trim the fat off of the beef and cut in to two large picccs.
2. In a small bowl mix together the salt, garlic, onion, paprika and black pepper. Then rub it all over the beef. Place the beef in your slow cooker.
3. In another bowl melt the butter, whisk in the tomato paste, vinegar and coconut aminos. Pour it all over the beef. Then add the bone broth to the slow cooker, pouring it around the beef.

4. Set on low and cook for 10-12 hours. When done, remove the beef, set the slow cooker to high and let the sauce thicken. Shred the beef then add it back in to the slow cooker and toss with sauce. Serve!

119. Beef and Broccoli Bowls with Sunshine Sauce

Ingredients

For the Beef

- 1 tablespoon cooking fat
- 1 pound 85% lean grass fed ground beef
- 1 teaspoon fine salt
- 1 teaspoon granulated garlic
- 1 tablespoon coconut aminos

For the broccoli

- 4 broccoli crowns cut into florets
- 1 tablespoon avocado oil
- 1/2 teaspoon fine salt

For the Sunshine Sauce

- 1 tablespoon cooking fat
- 2 tablespoons sun flower seed butter o
- 1/4 cup bone broth
- 1 teaspoon ground ginger
- 1/2 of fine salt
- 2 teaspoon coconut aminos
- juice of one lemon
- 1 green onion, minced

To assemble

4 cups baby spinach (optional)

Instructions

1. Pre-heat the oven to 400F.
2. Toss the broccoli with fat and salt on a sheet pan massaging the fat into the florets, them spread them out on the sheet pan so they are not crowded.
3. Put the sheet pan while it pre-heats, once it comes to temperature set a time for 20 minutes.
4. In the meantime heat a large skillet over medium heat, when it comes to temperature add in the fat.
5. Crumble the ground beef into the skillet and add in the salt and garlic. Stir, breaking up with a whisk until browned and crumbly. Add in the coconut aminos and bring the heat up to high.
6. Cook, stirring occasionally until dark brown and crispy.
7. While that cook set a small sauce pot over medium heat.
8. Melt the fat then the sunflower seed butter, stirring until smooth.
9. Add in the bone broth, salt, aminos and ground ginger, stir until well combined and a dark tan.

10. Remove from the heat and stir in the lemon juice and stir until it's smooth again.

11. Mix in the green onion. Set aside.

12. To assemble the bowls make a bed of baby spinach in 4 large bowls. Spoon ground beef into each of the bowls. Add in the broccoli florets and spoon the sauce over everything. Dig in!

120. Fried Rice with Pork

Ingredients

- 1/2 head of medium cauliflower
- 2 large eggs
- 2 cloves garlic, chopped
- 100g pork belly
- 2 mini green capsicums
- 2 spring onions
- 1 tablespoon soy sauce
- 1 tsp black sesame seeds
- 1 tsp pickled ginger

Instructions

Prepare the caulirice

1. Chop the cauliflower into florets.

2. Place in a food processor and pulse until it forms rice sized granules. Don't go too far or you'll end up with cauliflower mash instead!

3. Heat some oil in a frying pan (or wok) add the cauliflower and saute over a medium heat for about 5 minutes, until cooked. Remove from pan and set aside.

Prepare the fried rice

1. Next, prepare your omelette by beating the eggs and adding to your frying pan. Swirl the mixture around to create a thin omelette. When cooked through, flip and cook an additional minute. Remove from pan and set aside.

2. Add your garlic to the frying pan and once fragrant, add the pork belly. While it's cooking, slice your omelette into small cubes.

3. Once the pork belly is cooked through, add the capsicum, half the spring onion and cook for an additional minute.

4. Next, add the cauliflower and egg back into the pan. Add in the soy sauce and stir thoroughly.

5. Cook over a high heat, until well combined and serve steaming hot.

6. Garnish with the remaining spring onions, sesame seeds and pickled ginger. Enjoy!

121. Asparagus Stuffed Chicken Parmesan

Ingredients

- 3 Chicken Breasts
- 1 teaspoon Garlic paste
- 12 stalks Asparagus (stalks removed)
- 1/2 cup Cream Cheese

- 1 tablespoon Butter
- 1 teaspoon Olive Oil
- 3/4 cup Marinara Sauce

- 1 cup shredded Mozzarella
- Salt and Pepper to taste

Instructions

1. To start prepping the chicken, butterfly the chicken (or slice it in half without slicing it all the way through. The chicken breast should open out like a butterfly with one end still intact in the middle). Remove the hardy stalks of the asparagus and set aside.

2. Rub salt, pepper and garlic paste all over the chicken breasts (inside and outside). Divide cream cheese between the chicken breasts and spread it on the inside. Place four stalks of asparagus and then fold one side of the breast over the other, tucking it in place with a toothpick to make sure it doesn't come open.

3. Asparagus Stuffed Chicken Parmesan is a easy, healthy dinner recipe that combines two of our favourites. Topped with marinara sauce and stuffed with cream cheese and asparagus, it's keto friendly, low carb, gluten free and ready in 30 minutes.

4. Preheat the oven, and set it to broiler. Add butter and olive oil to a hot skillet and place the chicken breasts in it. Cook the breasts on each side for 6-7 minutes (total time will be 14-15 minutes depending on the size of the breast) till the chicken is almost cooked through.

5. Top each breast with 1/4 cup marinara sauce, and divide the shredded mozzarella on top. Place in the oven and broil for 5 minutes till the cheese melts.

122. Roasted Chicken Stacks

Ingredients

- 5 small chicken breasts or chicken breast cutlets
- 1 head of savoy cabbage
- 5 slices of prosciutto
- 3 tbsp. coconut flour

- 2 tsp salt, more to taste
- 1 tsp black pepper
- 2 tsp Italian herb blend
- 1/2 cup bone broth
- 1/4 cup avocado oil

Instructions

1. Pre-heat oven to 400F.

2. Combine the chicken breast, salt, pepper, herbs and coconut flour in a gallon sized plastic bag. Shake to evenly coat the chicken, yes, like shake and bake!

3. Drizzle a tbsp. of the oil on the sheet pan.

4. Shred the savoy cabbage and make 5 little piles of shredded cabbage on the sheet pan. Sprinkle with a little salt. Drizzle a little oil on them. Place a coated chicken breast over each one. Lastly, top each chicken piece with a slice of prosciutto. Drizzle with remaining oil.

5. Roast at 400F for 30 minutes

6. Pour the broth into the sheet pan. Roast for another 10 minutes.

7. Remove from the oven and serve hot.

8. Use a spatula to scoop up one stack at a time.

123. Lettuce Wraps

Ingredients

- 1/4 cup full-fat Greek yogurt
- 1/3-1/2 cup blue cheese crumbles
- juice of 1/2 lemon
- 2 cooked chicken breasts, shredded (feel free to use chicken thighs or rotisserie chicken instead)
- 8 large, sturdy romaine lettuce leaves
- 2-3 tablespoons walnuts, toasted and crumbled
- 8 raspberries, split in half
- 2 teaspoon chives, sliced into 1/4-inch pieces

Instructions

1. In a large bowl, combine yogurt and blue cheese. Season with lemon juice to taste. Stir in chicken until fully coated.

2. Adjust with more yogurt, blue cheese, and/or lemon if needed.Spoon shredded chicken onto center ribs of romaine lettuce leaves, dividing meat equally between them.

3. Place on a cutting board or rimmed baking sheet. Set them upright next to each other to prevent leaves from falling over.

4. Evenly sprinkle walnut pieces, raspberry halves, and chives between lettuce leaves. Serve immediately.

124. Curry Chicken Lettuce Wraps

Ingredients

- 1 lb boneless skinless chicken thighs
- 1/4 cup minced onion
- 2 garlic cloves, minced
- 2 tsp Curry Powder
- 1.5 tsp pink Himalayan salt
- 1 tsp black pepper
- 3 tbsp. ghee
- 1 cup cauliflower rice
- 6-8 small lettuce leaves
- 1/4 cup Lactose free sour cream or plain, unsweetened coconut milk yogurt

Instructions

1. Prepare your vegetables and set aside.

2. Cut your chicken thighs into 1 inch pieces.

3. Heat a large skillet on medium heat. When it comes to temperature add in 2 tbsp. of ghee and then the onion. Stir often until browned.

4. Add in the chicken, garlic and salt. Stir well.

5. Cook the chicken, stirring often until browned, about 8 minutes.

6. Add in the third tablespoon of ghee, the curry and the cauliflower rice. Sauté until well combined.

7. Lay out your lettuce leaves, and spoon the curry chicken mix into each one.

8. Top with a dollop of cream!

DINNERTIME

SUCCESS

RECIPES

---

125. Butter Chicken

Ingredients

- 1.5 lbs chicken breast
- 2 tablespoons garam masala
- 3 teaspoons fresh ginger, grated
- 3 teaspoons minced garlic
- 4 oz plain yogurt
- 1 tablespoon coconut oil

Sauce:

- 2 tablespoons ghee or butter
- 1 onion
- 2 teaspoons fresh ginger, grated
- 2 teaspoons minced garlic
- oz crushed tomatoes
- 1 tablespoon ground coriander
- ½ tablespoon garam masala
- 2 teaspoons cumin
- 1 teaspoon chili powder
- ½ cup heavy cream
- Salt, to taste

Optional:

- cilantro
- cauliflower rice

Instructions

1. Cut chicken into 2 inch pieces and place in a large bowl with 2 tablespoons garam masala, 1 teaspoon grated ginger, and 1 teaspoon minced garlic. Add in the yogurt, stir to combine. Chill at least 30 minutes.

2. For the sauce, place the onion, ginger, garlic, crushed tomatoes and spices in a blender, and blend until smooth. Set aside.

3. Heat 1 tablespoon of oil in a large skillet over medium high heat. Place the chicken along with the marinade in the skillet, browning 3 to 4 minutes per side. Once browned pour in the sauce cook 5 to 6 minutes longer.

4. Stir in the heavy cream and ghee, continue to cook another minute. Taste for salt and add additional if needed. Top with cilantro and serve with cauliflower rice if desired.

126. Ground Beef and Cabbage Stir Fry

Ingredients

- 1 pound extra lean ground beef
- 9 ounce bag cole slaw mix or mix of green cabbage, purple cabbage, shredded carrots
- 2 scallions thinly sliced

- 1 tablespoon freshly grated ginger
- 2 tablespoons low-sodium soy sauce
- 1 tablespoon sriracha
- 1 tablespoon canola oil
- black sesame seeds for garnish

Instructions

1. Combine soy sauce and sriracha in a small mixing bowl and stir until smooth. Set aside.
2. Heat a 3 quart or larger pan over medium-high heat. Add canola oil and tilt the pan to spread the oil. Add ground beef and cook until browned, about 5 minutes, stirring frequently and breaking the meat apart.
3. Add cole slaw mix to the pan and stir with the beef. Cook until cabbage is wilted and tender, about 5 minutes, stirring frequently.
4. Reduce heat to medium-low. Pour sauce over the pan, and add ginger. Stir until everything is well-mixed. Add salt to taste, if needed.
5. Remove pan from heat. Stir in sliced scallions, and garnish with sesame seeds. Serve while hot.

127. Sheet Pan Hibachi Beef and Vegetables

Ingredients

For the marinade:

- 1 tablespoon minced fresh ginger
- 1 tablespoon minced fresh garlic
- 1/4 cup gluten free soy sauce (aka. tamari)

- 1 tablespoon sesame oil
- 1 tablespoon granulated erythritol sweetener (I used Swerve)

For the beef and vegetables:

- 1 pound beef tenderloin or boneless ribeye, cut into 1 inch pieces.
- 2 slices of peeled onion, 1/2 inch thick
- 2 cups chopped zucchini
- 1 cup white mushrooms, cut into quarters

- 1/2 cup chopped red bell pepper
- 2 tablespoons avocado or other light tasting oil
- 1/2 teaspoon kosher salt
- 1/4 teaspoon ground black pepper

Instructions

1. Preheat the oven to 425 degrees F.

2. Combine all of the marinade Ingredients in a medium sized bowl.

3. Add the pieces of beef (or other protein) to the marinade, and stir to coat.

4. Separate the onion rings and form into two cones on a large baking sheet. (OR just toss the rings with the other vegetables before roasting.)

5. Combine the remaining vegetables on the same baking sheet.

6. Add the oil, salt, and pepper and stir to coat the vegetables.

7. Spread the vegetables out on the sheet and place in the oven. Bake for 20 minutes.

8. Remove the pan from the oven and move the vegetables to one side to make room for the beef.

9. Add the beef to the pan, making sure the pieces are separated. Pour the marinade over the beef.

10. Return the pan to the oven and roast for another 8 minutes, or until the meat is cooked to your liking. Don't overcook or it will become dry and chewy.

11. Remove from the oven and stir the beef and vegetables together with the sauce.

12. Serve immediately over cooked cauliflower rice if desired.

128. Tomato Feta Soup Recipe

Ingredients

- 2 tbsp olive oil or butter
- 1/4 cup chopped onion
- 2 cloves garlic
- 1/2 tsp salt
- 1/8 tsp black pepper
- 1 tsp pesto sauce — optional
- 1/2 tsp dried oregano
- 1 tsp dried basil

- 1 tbsp tomato paste — optional
- 10 tomatoes, skinned, seeded and chopped — or two 14.5 oz cans of peeled tomatoes
- 1 tsp honey, sugar or erythritol — optional
- 3 cups water
- 1/3 cup heavy cream
- 2/3 cup feta cheese — crumbled

Instructions

1. Heat olive oil (butter) over medium heat in a large pot (Dutch Oven). Add the onion and cook for 2 minutes, stirring frequently. Add the garlic and cook for 1 minute. Add tomatoes, salt, pepper, pesto (optional), oregano, basil, tomato paste and water. Bring to a boil, then reduce to a simmer. Add sweetener.

2. Cook on medium heat for 20 minutes, until the tomatoes are tender and cooker. Using an immersion blender, blend until smooth. Add the cream and feta cheese. Cook for 1 more minute.

3. Add more salt if needed. Serve warm.

129. Brunch Spread

Ingredients

- 4 large eggs
- 24 asparagus spears
- 12 slices of pastured, sugar free bacon

Instructions

1. Pre-heat your oven to 400F.
2. Trim your asparagus about an inch from the bottoms. Then in pairs, wrap them with one slice of bacon. Hold your spears firmly and close together with one hand as you wind the slice of bacon starting from the bottom, to the top of the spear. Gently pull the bacon as you wind it, so it wraps tightly. Place it on a sheet pan.
3. Repeat with the remaining asparagus, so you have 12 pairs wrapped in bacon.
4. Place in the oven, set the timer for 20 minutes.
5. In this time, bring a small pot of water to a rapid boil. Gently place 4 large eggs in the boiling water. Set another time for 6 minutes.
6. Prepare a bowl with ice water. When the 6 minutes are up, use a slotted spoon or tongs to quickly transfer your eggs to the ice bath. Let them sit for 2 minutes before peeling the tops off.
7. Gently crack the top of the egg on a hard surface and peel away shell to reveal the tip of the egg.
8. When the asparagus are ready, serve on a tray or cutting board. If you don't have an egg holder use espresso cups to hold your eggs up.
9. With a small spoon scoop out the tops of the soft boiled eggs to reveal a perfectly runny yolk.
10. Dip your asparagus spears into your eggs. Feast, enjoy!

130. Cheesy Pizza Chicken in a Skillet

Ingredients

- 1 tablespoon olive oil
- 6 bone-in chicken thighs
- 1 cup low carb tomato sauce
- 3 ounces sliced pepperoni
- 1 1/2 cups shredded mozzarella cheese
- salt and pepper

Instructions

1. Preheat the oven to 350°F.
2. Heat the oil in a 12-inch cast-iron skillet over medium heat.
3. Season the chicken with salt and pepper then add to the skillet.
4. Cook for 3 to 4 minutes on each side until browned.
5. Pour the low-carb tomato sauce over the chicken and spread it evenly.
6. Top the chicken with pepperoni slices and sprinkle with mozzarella.
7. Bake for 25 minutes until the cheese is melted then place under a broiler to brown the cheese.
8. Remove from heat and let rest for 5 minutes before serving.

131. Salmon & Avocado Nori Rolls

Ingredients

- 3 square nori sheets (seaweed wrappers)
- 150-180 g / 5-6 oz cooked salmon or tinned salmon
- ½ red pepper, sliced into thin strips
- ½ avocado, sliced into strips
- ½ small cucumber, sliced into strips
- 1 spring onion/scallion, cut into 2-3" pieces
- 2 tablespoons mayonnaise
- 1 tablespoon hot sauce or Sriracha sauce
- 1 teaspoon black or white sesame seeds
- Coconut aminos for dipping, optional

Instructions

1. Place the nori sheet on a flat surface, such as a cutting board, shiny side down. Look at the fibres of the wrapper to see which way it needs to be rolled.

2. Add a third of the salmon to the right or left third of the nori sheet and top with two strips of pepper, cucumber and avocado. Add some green onion and a drizzle of mayonnaise and hot sauce. You can sprinkle with sesame seeds now or at a later stage, once the rolls are cut.

3. Lightly wet the top part of the nori sheet (the side you are rolling towards), just 1-2 cm of the wrapper. Pick up the opposite outer edge of the roll and start wrapping it over the Ingredients, using your fingers to keep it nice and tight. This can take a bit of practice, but don't worry if your roll doesn't look perfect. Roll it until the top edge of the wrapper overlaps the roll and press it tightly to stick. Place the roll on the cutting board with the seam facing down and then cut into bite-size pieces.

4. Serve right away with some coconut aminos or extra mayo for dipping, or pack in a container to take for lunch or keep as a snack in the fridge.

132. Beef Bourguignon

Ingredients

- 1.5 - 2 pounds beef chuck roast cut into 3/4-inch cubes
- 5 strips bacon diced
- 1 small onion chopped
- 10 ounces cremini mushrooms quartered
- 2 carrots chopped
- 5 cloves garlic minced
- 3 bay leaves
- 3/4 cup dry red wine
- 3/4 teaspoon xanthan gum (or corn starch, read post for Instructions)
- 1 tablespoon tomato paste
- 1 teaspoon dried thyme
- salt & pepper

Instructions

1. Generously season beef chunks with salt and pepper, and set aside. Select the saute mode on the pressure cooker for medium heat. When the display reads HOT, add diced bacon and cook for about 5 minutes until crispy, stirring frequently. Transfer the bacon to a paper towel lined plate.

2. Add the beef to the pot in a single layer and cook for a few minutes to brown, then flip and repeat for the other side. Transfer to a plate when done.

3. Add onions and garlic. Cook for a few minutes to soften, stirring frequently. Add red wine and tomato paste, using a wooden spoon to briefly scrape up flavorful brown bits stuck to the bottom of the pot. Stir to check that the tomato paste is dissolved. Turn off the saute mode.

4. Transfer the beef back to the pot. Add mushrooms, carrots, and thyme, stirring together. Top with bay leaves. Secure and seal the lid. Cook at high pressure for 40 minutes, followed by a manual pressure release.

5. Uncover and select the saute mode. Remove bay leaves. Evenly sprinkle xanthan gum over the pot and stir together. Let the stew boil for a minute to thicken while stirring. Turn off the saute mode. Serve into bowls and top with crispy bacon.

133. Chicken Enchilada Bowl

Ingredients

- 2 tablespoons coconut oil (for searing chicken)
- 1 pound of boneless, skinless chicken thighs
- 3/4 cup red enchilada sauce (recipe from Low Carb Maven)
- 1/4 cup water
- 1/4 cup chopped onion
- 4 oz can diced green chiles

Toppings (feel free to customize)

- 1 whole avocado, diced
- 1 cup shredded cheese (I used mild cheddar)
- 1/4 cup chopped pickled jalapenos
- 1/2 cup sour cream
- 1 roma tomato, chopped

Optional: serve over plain cauliflower rice (or mexican cauliflower rice) for a more complete meal!

Instructions

1. In a pot or Dutch oven over medium heat melt the coconut oil. Once hot, sear chicken thighs until lightly brown.

2. Pour in enchilada sauce and water then add onion and green chiles. Reduce heat to a simmer and cover. Cook chicken for 17-25 minutes or until chicken is tender and fully cooked through to at least 165 degrees internal temperature.

3. Careully remove the chicken and place onto a work surface. Chop or shred chicken (your preference) then add it back into the pot. Let the chicken simmer uncovered for an additional 10 minutes to absorb flavor and allow the sauce to reduce a little.

4. To Serve, top with avocado, cheese, jalapeno, sour cream, tomato, and any other desired toppings. Feel free to customize these to your preference. Serve alone or over cauliflower rice if desired just be sure to update your personal nutrition info as needed.

134. Crab Stuffed Mushrooms with Cream Cheese

Ingredients

- 20 ounces cremini (baby bella) mushrooms (20-25 individual mushrooms)
- 2 tablespoons finely grated parmesan cheese
- 1 tablespoon chopped fresh parsley
- salt

Filling

- 4 ounces cream cheese softened to room temperature
- 4 ounces crab meat finely chopped
- 5 cloves garlic minced
- 1 teaspoon dried oregano
- 1/2 teaspoon paprika
- 1/2 teaspoon black pepper
- 1/4 teaspoon salt

Instructions

1. Preheat the oven to 400 F. Prepare a baking sheet lined with parchment paper.

2. Snap stems from mushrooms, discarding the stems and placing the mushroom caps on the baking sheet 1 inch apart from each other. Season the mushroom caps with salt.

3. In a large mixing bowl, combine all filling Ingredients and stir until well-mixed without any lumps of cream cheese. Stuff the mushroom caps with the mixture. Evenly sprinkle parmesan cheese on top of the stuffed mushrooms.

4. Bake at 400 F until the mushrooms are very tender and the stuffing is nicely browned on top, about 30 minutes. Top with parsley and serve while hot.

135. Bacon and Spinach Frittata

Ingredients

- 6 duck eggs or 8 hen eggs
- 1 tablespoon grass-fed ghee
- 4 ounces pasture-raised bacon, cut in 1/2-inch pieces
- 1 1/2 cups green beans, cooked and cut in half
- 2 cups of spinach or collard greens, steamed and roughly chopped

- 4 ounces cherry tomatoes, sliced in half (optional)
- 1 rosemary sprig, finely chopped

1. Preheat convection oven to 350 F
2. In an oven-proof wide saucepan (I used a 12-inch pan) over medium heat, add the ghee, bacon and rosemary. Cook for 3 minutes until the bacon is slightly crisp.
3. To the same pan, add the green vegetables and tomatoes to heat up and soften.
4. Whisk the eggs in a bowl and then add to the pan, making sure they cover and reach all corners of the pan. Leave to cook for 5 minutes to set on the base and sides.
5. Transfer the pan to the oven and allow to cook for another 5 minutes until the top of the frittata has set. Remove and allow to cool.
6. Slice into 3 portions and serve with salad.

136. Lemon Butter Sauce for Fish

Ingredients

Lemon Butter Sauce

- 60 g / 4 tbsp unsalted butter , cut into pieces
- 1 tbsp fresh lemon juice
- Salt and finely ground pepper

Crispy Pan Fried Fish

- 2 x thin white fish fillets (120-150g / 4-5oz each), skinless boneless (I used Bream, Note 1)
- Salt and pepper
- 2 tbsp white flour
- 2 tbsp oil (I use canola)

Serving

- Lemon wedges
- Finely chopped parsley, optional

Instructions

1. Place the butter in a light coloured saucepan or small skillet over medium heat.
2. Melt butter then leave on the stove, whisking / stirring very now and then. When the butter turns golden brown and it smells nutty - about 3 minutes, remove from stove immediately and pour into small bowl.
3. Add lemon juice and a pinch of salt and pepper. Stir then taste when it has cooled slightly. Adjust lemon/salt to taste.
4. Set aside - it will stay pourable for 20 - 30 minutes. See Note 3 for storing.

Crispy Pan Fried Fish:

1. Pat fish dry using paper towels. Sprinkle with salt & pepper, then flour. Use fingers to spread flour. Turn and repeat. Shake excess flour off well, slapping between hands if necessary.

2. Heat oil in a non stick skillet over high heat. When the oil is shimmering and there are faint wisps of smoke, add fish. Cook for 1 1/2 minutes until golden and crispy on the edges, then turn and cook the other side for 1 1/2 minutes (cook longer if you have thicker fillets).

3. Remove immediately onto serving plates. Drizzle each with about 1 tbsp of Sauce (avoid dark specks settled at the bottom of the bowl), garnish with parsley and serve with lemon on the side. Pictured in post with Kale and Quinoa Salad.

137. Chicken Pot Pie

Ingredients

For the Chicken Pot Pie Filling:

- 2 tablespoons of butter
- 1/2 cup mixed veggies could also substitute green beans or broccoli
- 1/4 small onion diced
- 1/4 tsp pink salt
- 1/4 tsp pepper
- 2 garlic cloves minced
- 3/4 cup heavy whipping cream
- 1 cup chicken broth
- 1 tsp poultry seasoning
- 1/4 tsp rosemary
- pinch thyme
- 2 1/2 cups cooked chicken diced
- 1/4 tsp Xanthan Gum

For the crust:

- 4 1/2 tablespoons of butter melted and cooled
- 1/3 cup coconut flour
- 2 tablespoons full fat sour cream
- 4 eggs
- 1/4 teaspoon salt
- 1/4 teaspoon baking powder
- 1 1/3 cup sharp shredded cheddar cheese or mozzarella shredded

Instructions

1. Cook 1 to 1 1/2 lbs chicken in the slow cooker for 3 hours on high or 6 hours on low.

2. Preheat oven to 400 degrees.

3. Sautee onion, mixed veggies, garlic cloves, salt, and pepper in 2 tablespoons butter in an oven safe skillet for approx 5 min or until onions are translucent.

4. Add heavy whipping cream, chicken broth, poultry seasoning, thyme, and rosemary.

5. Sprinkle Xanthan Gum on top and simmer for 5 minutes so that the sauce thickens. Make sure to simmer covered as the liquid will evaporate otherwise. You need a lot of liquid for this recipe, otherwise, it will be dry.

6. Add diced chicken.

7. Make the breading by combining melted butter (I cool mine by popping the bowl in the fridge for 5 min), eggs, salt, and sour cream in a bowl then whisk together.

8. Add coconut flour and baking powder to the mixture and stir until combined.

9. Stir in cheese.

10. Drop batter by dollops on top of the chicken pot pie. Do not spread it out, as the coconut flour will absorb too much of the liquid.

11. Bake in a 400-degree oven for 15-20 min.

12. Set oven to broil and move chicken pot pie to top shelf. Broil for 1-2 minutes until bread topping is nicely browned.

138. Low Carb Lasagna

Ingredients

- 1 tablespoon butter, ghee, coconut oil, or lard
- 1/2lb spicy Italian sausage or sweet Italian sausage
- 15oz ricotta cheese
- 2 tablespoons coconut flour
- medium-high large whole egg
- 1 1/2 teaspoon salt
- 1/2 teaspoon pepper
- 1 teaspoon garlic powder
- a large clove garlic (finely chopped)

- 1 1/2 cup mozzarella cheese
- 1/3 cup parmesan cheese
- 4 large zucchini's
- 16oz Rao's marinara sauce
- 1 tablespoon mixed Italian herb seasoning
- 1/4 to 1/2 tsp red pepper flake (depending on how spicy you want this dish)
- 1/4 cup basil

Instructions

1. Slice the zucchini then sprinkle generously with sea salt. Place your salted zucchini on a paper towel for 30 minutes. Once 30 minutes is up, wring the zucchini noodles with a paper towel one last time to extract any moisture.

2. Heat 1 tablespoon of butter or fat of choice in a large skillet over medium-high heat. Crumble and brown Italian sausage. Remove from heat and let cool.

3. Preheat oven to 375 degrees and coat a 9×9 baking dish with cooking spray or butter.

4. Add ricotta cheese, 1 cup of mozzarella cheese, 2 tablespoons of parmesan cheese, 1 egg, coconut flour, salt, garlic, garlic powder, and pepper to a small bowl and mix until smooth. Set aside. Add Italian seasoning and red pepper flakes to a jar of marinara, stir well. Set aside.

5. Add a layer of sliced zucchini to the bottom of greased dish. Spread 1/4 cup of cheese mixture over zucchini, sprinkle with 1/4 of the Italian sausage and then add a layer of sauce. Repeat process 3-4 times until ingredients are all gone, ending with a layer of sauce. Add remaining mozzarella cheese and sprinkle with remaining parmesan cheese.

6. Cover with foil and bake for 30 minutes. Remove foil and bake for an additional 15 minutes until golden brown. Remove from oven and let sit for 5-10 minutes before serving. Sprinkle with fresh basil if desired.

139. Pigs in a Blanket

Ingredients

- 2 cups shredded mozzarella
- 2 ounces cream cheese (softened)
- 1/2 cup coconut flour
- 1 teaspoon dried oregano
- 3/4 teaspoon onion powder
- 1/2 teaspoon garlic powder
- 1/2 teaspoon baking powder
- 2 large eggs (whisked)
- 12 all-beef hotdogs
- 1 teaspoon sesame seeds

Instructions

1. Preheat the oven to 400°F and line a baking sheet with parchment.
2. Combine the mozzarella and cream cheese in a microwave-safe bowl and heat until melted then stir smooth and set aside.
3. Combine the coconut flour, oregano, onion powder, garlic powder, baking powder, and eggs in a mixing bowl then stir in the melted cheese until a dough forms – wet your hands because it will be sticky.
4. Divide the dough into 12 pieces and roll into balls.
5. Roll out each dough ball between two pieces of parchment into 8-inch circles.
6. Wrap each dough circle around a hotdog and place on the baking sheet.
7. Sprinkle with sesame seeds then bake for 15 to 20 minutes until browned.

140. Quiche Recipe

Ingredients

- 3 tablespoons coconut oil 45 ml, to cook with
- 6 slices bacon 168 g, diced
- 2 medium bell peppers 240 g, diced
- 1 medium onion 110 g, diced
- 4 cups spinach 120 g, chopped
- 2 small tomatoes 180 g, diced
- 12 medium eggs whisked
- 15 olives 45 g, diced
- 1/4 cup fresh basil leaves 8 g, chopped

- 3 cloves garlic 9 g, minced or finely diced
- 3/4 cup coconut cream (from the top of 1 refrigerated can of coconut milk) 180 ml
- Salt and pepper to taste

Instructions

1. Preheat oven to 350 F (175 C).

2. In a large skillet, melt the coconut oil over medium-high heat. Add the bacon and sauté until crispy, about 3 to 4 minutes. Remove the bacon with a slotted spoon and set aside.

3. In the same skillet, add the bell pepper and onion to the bacon fat and sauté for 5 minutes.

4. Add the spinach to the skillet and saute until wilted, about 1 to 2 minutes. Remove from the heat and let cool.

5. In a large bowl, combine the tomato, eggs, olives, basil, garlic, coconut cream, bacon, and spinach mixture. Season with salt and pepper. Pour the egg mixture into a 9-inch by 9-inch (23-cm by 23-cm) square baking dish.

6. Place in the oven and bake for 30 minutes until the eggs are soft but set.

141. One-Pan Chicken Stir-Fry

Ingredients

- 1/3 cup soy sauce
- 2 tablespoon rice vinegar
- 2 tablespoons So Nourished granulated erythritol
- 1 tablespoon sesame oil
- 1 teaspoon garlic powder
- 1 pound boneless chicken thighs
- 2 medium red peppers (cored and chopped)
- 2 cups green beans (sliced)
- 1 cup cauliflower florets
- 1 1/2 tablespoons olive oil
- 2 tablespoons sesame seeds

Instructions

1. Whisk together the soy sauce, rice vinegar, granulated erythritol, sesame oil, and garlic powder in a small bowl.

2. Chop the chicken into 1-inch pieces and place them in a zippered freezer bag.

3. Pour in the sauce and shake to coat then chill for at least 4 hours.

4. Preheat the oven to 425°F and line a large baking sheet with foil.

5. Drain the chicken and spread it on the baking sheet and bake for 8 minutes.

6. Toss the veggies with the olive oil and sprinkle onto the baking sheet with the chicken.

7. Bake for another 12 to 15 minutes until the chicken is done then sprinkle with sesame seeds to serve.

142. Delicious Lemon Herb Meatloaf

Ingredients

- 2 pounds 85% lean grass fed ground beef
- 1/2 tablespoon fine Himalayan salt
- 1 teaspoon black pepper
- 1/4 cup Nutritional Yeast
- 2 large eggs
- 2 tablespoons avocado oil
- 1 tablespoon lemon zest
- 1/4 cup chopped parsley
- 1/4 cup chopped fresh oregano
- 4 cloves garlic

Instructions

1. Pre-heat oven to 400F.
2. In a large bowl mix the ground beef, salt, black pepper and nutritional yeast.
3. In a blender or food processor mix the eggs, oil, herbs and garlic. Blend until the eggs are froth and the herbs, lemon and garlic are minced and mixed.
4. Add the egg blend to the beef and mix to combine.
5. Add the beef to a small, 8×4 loaf pan. Smooth and flatten out.
6. Set in the oven, middle rack for 50-60 minutes.
7. Carefully remove from the oven and tilt the loaf pan over the sink to drain the fluid. Let it cool for 5-10 minutes before slicing into.
8. Garnish with fresh lemon and enjoy!

143. Honey Mustard Salmon

Ingredients

For the keto honey mustard sauce:

- 1/4 cup Dijon mustard
- 1/4 cup allulose or 3 TBSP erythritol or xylitol
- 2 tablespoons white wine vinegar
- 1/4 cup avocado oil
- 1 clove garlic ran through a press, optional
- 1 tablespoon fresh dill optional

For the salmon sheet pan dinner:

- 4 salmon fillets (I like ButcherBox's Wild Alaskan!) skin on preferably
- 1 batch our roasted radishes lightly toasted
- 1 head broccoli trimmed

Instructions

For the keto honey mustard sauce:

1. In a medium bowl whisk together mustard, sweetener and vinegar.

2. Emulsify the oil into the vinegar mixture: pour in the oil very slowly into the vinegar mixture while whisking rapidly (feel free to use an electric whisk). Begin drop by drop and slowly increase speed into a stream. It should take about 2 minutes to incorporate all the oil. Adding in the garlic and dill is totally optional, but a very nice touch for salmon. Note: the sauce will still work great even if your emulsification fails, just won't be as smooth!

3. Set aside or refrigerate for 3-5 days.

4. For the salmon sheet pan dinner:

5. Preheat oven to 450°F/230°C. If roasting radishes, pop them in 30-45 minutes before the salmon (depending on size and how well you like them done, see roasted radish recipe for insight).

6. Rinse the salmon fillets and pat dry. Arrange fillets, skin sides down, in parchment or foil. Liberally brush the salmon with the honey mustard glaze. Allow to rest at room temperature for 15 minutes.

7. Take the radishes out of the oven roughly 10 minutes before they're done. Add in the broccoli florets, drizzle with extra virgin olive oil and season with salt and freshly ground black pepper. Place the marinated salmon fillets on the tray and bake for 10-12 minutes, or until just cooked through. Serve right away with plenty of sauce!

144. Superfood Meatballs

Ingredients

- 3lbs 85% lean grass fed ground beef
- 1lb pastured chicken livers
- 1 large shallot
- 4 medium carrots
- 3 garlic cloves
- 2 tbsp. grass fed butter
- 1 tsp dried oregano
- 2 tbsp. coconut aminos (separated)
- 3 tsp salt (separated)
- 2 tsp black pepper
- 1 tbsp. dried thyme (dried)
- 1 tbsp. garlic powder
- Olive oil

Instructions

1. Heat a large cast iron skillet on medium heat. While it heats, mince the shallots, carrots and garlic until fine. When the skillet comes to temperature add in the vegetables and sauté until aromatic and tender, about 8 minutes, stir often.

2. Add in the chicken livers along with 1 tsp salt and dried oregano. Cook, stirring often, until the livers are browned all over. Add in the 1 tbsp. coconut aminos and 1 tbsp. apple cider vinegar and cook until reduced and livers are cooked.

3. Remove from heat, and let cool a few minutes. Transfer to a food processor and pulse until it looks like ground beef. Then transfer to a large bowl, to cool to room temp.

95

4. Pre-heat oven to 425F. Add the ground beef to the bowl with the remaining salt and the rest of the seasoning. Mix well. Shape 1 ½ inch balls, will make aprx 30.

5. Drizzle olive oil all over the sheet pan. With oiled hands, coat each meatball in a little olive oil and you handle it to place it on the sheet pan. Then lightly drizzle them with the remaining coconut aminos.

6. Place in the oven, roast at 425F for 5 minutes. Then turn the temperature down to 350F and roast another 20 minutes before removing from the oven.

7. These meatballs are perfect for meal prep or feeding a crowd. Dunk them in ranch, pile on some guac or drizzle with lemon tahini sauce for some extra fats!

145. Cheesy Taco Pie Recipe

Ingredients

- 1 pound ground beef (80% lean)
- 1 tablespoon chili powder
- 1 tablespoon ground cumin
- 1 tablespoon garlic powder
- 1 cup heavy cream
- 6 large eggs
- 1 cup shredded cheddar cheese
- salt and pepper
- sour cream (to serve)
- Diced Avocado (to serve)

Instructions

1. Preheat the oven to 350°F and grease a 9-inch glass pie plate with cooking spray.
2. Cook the beef in a large skillet over medium heat until browned, breaking it up into chunks with a wooden spoon.
3. Stir in the chili powder, cumin, garlic powder, salt, and pepper then reduce heat and cook on medium-low for 5 minutes to thicken.
4. Spoon the beef mixture into the pie plate and set aside.
5. Whisk together the heavy cream and eggs then pour over the beef.
6. Sprinkle with cheese and bake for 30 minutes until the cheese is melted and browned.
7. Remove from the oven and let rest for 5 minutes.
8. Cut into wedges then serve with sour cream and diced avocado, if desired.

146. Zucchini pizza lasagna

Ingredients

For the zoodles:

- 3 Large zucchinis
- 1 Tbsp Salt

For the lasagna:

- 2 Tbsps Olive oil
- 1 lb Ground 99% fat-free Turkey
- 1 Cup Onion diced (1 small onion)
- 1 1/2 Tbsps Fresh garlic diced
- 1 tsp Salt
- pepper

- 1 15 oz Container of light or fat-free ricotta cheese
- 1 Large egg
- 1 14 oz Jar of pizza sauce
- 2 Cups Turkey Pepperoni slices 48 pepperonis to be exact
- 8 oz Light Mozzarella cheese grated
- 1/2 A Large green pepper, chopped
- 1/4 cup Slivered black olives
- 2 Tbsps Parmesan Cheese, finely grated

Instructions

1. Preheat the oven to 350 degrees.
2. Using a mandolin, slice the zucchini into thin slices, about 1/8 inch thick, Lay them out flat onto a cookie sheet and sprinkle with 1 Tbsp salt.
3. Bake them for 10-15 minutes, until just lightly beginning to brown, to get all the moisture out. Set aside.
4. In a large pan, heat the olive oil over medium/high heat. Add in the ground turkey, diced onion, diced garlic, 1 tsp of salt, and a pinch of pepper. Cook until the onion is soft and the turkey is browned.
5. While the turkey cooks, beat together the ricotta cheese, egg and another pinch of pepper. Set aside.
6. Once the turkey is done, it's time to assemble the lasagna!
7. Spray a 9x13 inch baking dish with cooking spray.
8. Start by pouring half the jar of pizza sauce on the bottom, followed by half the turkey, then layer half the zucchini noodles, half the ricotta mixture, half the pepperoni slices,and finish with half the grated mozzarella cheese.
9. Repeat the layers once more, except add the chopped pepper and olives on top of the last layer of mozzarella. Sprinkle with 2 Tbsp Parmesan cheese.
10. Turn the oven up to 375 and cover the lasagna with tin foil.
11. For the lasagna:
12. Bake, covered, for 45 minutes. Uncover and bake another 10 minutes.
13. Turn the broiler up to HIGH and broil for 2-3 minutes more, until the top is golden brown and bubbly!
14. Devour!

147. Steak Cobb Salad with Cilantro-Lime Vinaigrette

Ingredients

- 3 ounces grass-fed hanger steak
- 1 teaspoon avocado oil
- 1 pasture-raised egg
- 1 slice pasture raised bacon
- 1 cup riced cauliflower
- 1/2 avocado
- 1 cup arugula
- 1 cup mixed greens

- 2 tablespoons olive oil
- 1 teaspoon Brain Octane Oil or MCT oil
- ½ teaspoon lime juice
- 1 teaspoon apple cider vinegar
- ¼ teaspoon sea salt
- ¼ cup diced cilantro

Instructions

Bacon Cauliflower Rice

1. Add minced bacon to a pan over medium heat, cook until no longer translucent
2. Add cauliflower rice to the pan and cook for 4 minutes

Grass-Fed Hanger Steak

1. Pat the steak dry and salt both sides generously
2. Add avocado oil to pan over medium heat
3. Add steak to the pan and cook for 4 minutes a side
4. Let the steak rest for 5 minutes and then slice against the grain

Soft-Boiled Egg

1. Bring 6 cups of water to rolling boil
2. Set eggs into the water, cover and cook for 7 minutes

Cilantro-Lime Dressing

1. Add lime juice, apple cider vinegar, sea salt, cilantro, brain octane and olive oil in a food processor and blend until there are no more large chunks of cilantro.
2. Salad
3. Add mixed greens, arugula and all toppings in a bowl and toss

148. Miracle Noodle Broccoli Alfredo Recipe

Ingredients

- 2 ounces cream cheese (softened)
- 1 ounce butter
- 1/4 cup heavy cream
- 1/4 cup grated parmesan cheese
- 1/4 teaspoon garlic powder
- 1 teaspoon olive oil
- 1 1/2 cups broccoli florets
- 2 packages Miracle Noodles (fettuccini style)
- salt and pepper

Instructions

1. Combine the cream cheese and butter in a small saucepan over low heat.
2. When the butter and cream cheese are melted, whisk in the heavy cream and parmesan cheese until smooth and well combined.
3. Add the garlic powder, salt, and pepper then remove from heat.

4. Heat the oil in a large skillet over medium heat and add the broccoli.

5. Season the broccoli with salt and pepper and stir-fry for about 3 to 4 minutes until bright green.

6. Rinse the Miracle Noodles in cool water then pat dry.

7. Add the noodles to the skillet with the broccoli and cook for about 5 minutes, stirring often.

8. Pour the sauce over the noodles and broccoli then cook until heated through. Serve hot.

149. Beberé Enchilada Style Stuffed Peppers

Ingredients

- 2lb 85% lean pastured ground beef
- 1 cup organic frozen cauliflower rice
- 3 tbsp Kerry Gold butter
- 1/2 maui onion
- 1 large carrot
- 2 cloves garlic
- 2 tsp smoked sea salt
- 2 tsp beberé
- 5 large bell peppers
- 5 dollops organic, lactose free sour cream

Instructions

1. Heat a large skillet on medium heat. In the meantime dice your carrot, onion and garlic.

2. Add the butter to the skillet; once it's melted add in the diced veggies.

3. Sauté, stirring occasionally until tender, about 8 minutes.

4. Add in the beef, salt and bebere, stir well, breaking up the beef until crumbly and browned. Mix in the cauliflower rice. Stir until well incorporated. Remove the skillet from the heat.

5. Pre-heat the oven to 400F. While the oven heats cut the tops off of your peppers, remove the core and seeds. Then spoon the beef mixture into them. Arrange the peppers in a casserole dish.

6. Top each one with a dollop of sour cream. Sprinkle a little extra spice mix on top.

7. Bake for 40 minutes! Serve hot!

Notes

- Spice Mix: you can also use your favorite taco seasoning or hot curry
- Sour Cream recommendation: Green Valley

150. Shrimp & Bacon Chowder

Ingredients

- 6 slices bacon chopped
- 1 medium turnip cut into ½-inch cubes
- ½ cup chopped onion
- 2 cloves garlic minced
- 2 cups chicken broth
- 1 cup heavy whipping cream
- 1 pound shrimp peeled and deveined, tails on or off

- ½ teaspoon Cajun seasoning
- Salt and pepper
- Chopped parsley for garnish

Instructions

1. In an large pot or Dutch oven over medium heat, cook the bacon until crisp. Using a slotted spoon, transfer to a paper towel-lined plate to drain, reserving the bacon fat in the pan.

2. Add the turnip and onion to the pan and saute until the onion is tender, about 5 minutes. Stir in the garlic and cook until fragrant, another minute or so. Pour in the chicken broth and simmer until the turnip is tender, about 10 minutes.

3. Stir in the cream and the shrimp and simmer until the shrimp is pink and cooked through, another 3 minutes or so. Add the Cajun seasoning and season to taste with salt and pepper.

4. Garnish with the bacon and chopped parsley upon serving.

151. Kale & Mushroom Sausage Patties

Ingredients

- 1 lb ground pork
- 6 oz fresh mushrooms, chopped
- 1 bunch of kale, thinly sliced
- 2 T coconut oil
- 2 garlic cloves, minced
- ½ t salt
- ½ t garlic powder
- ½ t onion powder
- ¼ t fennel seed
- Pinch of ground ginger
- Pinch of nutmeg

Instructions

1. In a large skillet, melt one tablespoon of coconut oil.

2. Add the kale, mushrooms, and garlic and sauté until the veggies are cooked.

3. Place the ground pork in a mixing bowl and add the veggies and spices. Mix well and form into 10 patties.

4. Melt one tablespoon of coconut oil over medium heat and add half the sausage patties; cook until golden brown on each side and cooked in the middle. Repeat with the other half.

152. Taco Salad

Ingredients

Taco Seasoning

- 2 Tablespoons Chili powder
- 2 Teaspoons Ground cumin
- 2 Teaspoons Garlic powder
- 1/2 Teaspoon Onion powder

- 1/2 Teaspoon Dried oregano
- 1/4 Teaspoon Paprika
- 1 Teaspoon Sea salt
- 1/2 Teaspoon Cayenne pepper

Taco Salad

- 16 Ounces Ground Beef (80-20 Blend)
- 1 Head Green leaf lettuce (chopped)
- 2 Tablespoons Taco seasoning (recipe above)
- 8 Ounces Grape tomatoes (halved)

- 8 Ounces Cheddar cheese (shredded)
- 1 Medium Avocado (cubed)
- 8 Ounces Red onion (chopped)
- 1/3 Cup Mexican cream
- 2 Tablespoons Cilantro (chopped)

Instructions

Taco Seasoning

- Mix all of the ingredients together in a canning jar, make sure the lid is tight and shake until well combined.

Taco Salad

- Add the ground beef to a skillet on medium-high. Stir fry and separate the beef using a wooden spatula for about 10 minutes, until browned.
- Drain the beef of any excess grease and then stir in 2 Tablespoons of taco seasoning and combine well. About 5 minutes.
- Combine the rest of the Ingredients in a bowl. Add the ground beef mixture and top with Mexican cream and cilantro.

Notes

You can add black olives and salsa if you prefer. Guacamole can be substituted for the avocado chunks and sour cream can be used instead of Mexican cream.

153. Bacon Cheddar Chicken Calzones Recipe

Ingredients

- 2 cups shredded chicken
- 1 cup shredded cheddar cheese
- 4 slices bacon (cooked and crumbled)
- 2 tablespoons sour cream
- 2 tablespoons mayonnaise
- 8 ounces shredded mozzarella cheese
- 2 ounces cream cheese (softned)
- 1 large egg (whisked)
- 6 tablespoons almond flour
- 6 tablespoons coconut flour
- 6 tablespoons ground flaxseed
- 1 egg white (whisked)

Instructions

1. Preheat the oven to 350°F and line a baking sheet with parchment paper.
2. Stir together the shredded chicken, cheddar cheese, bacon, sour cream, and mayonnaise in a mixing bowl until well combined then set aside.
3. Combine the mozzarella and cream cheese in a microwave-safe bowl and heat on high heat for 60 seconds.
4. Stir the mixture and heat at 30-second intervals, stirring between each, until melted.
5. Add the egg, almond flour, coconut flour, and ground flaxseed and stir until fully incorporated – you can also use a stand mixer with the dough hook attachment.
6. Turn out the dough onto a piece of parchment and roll into a large rectangle then cut into three pieces.
7. Roll each piece of dough into a rectangle about ¼-inch thick then spread the chicken filling over them.
8. Fold up the ends and sides of each piece of dough around the fillings and press closed.
9. Brush the calzones with egg white and sprinkle with parmesan then bake for 45 to 50 minutes until golden brown.

154. Keto Banana Nut Muffins

Ingredients

Muffin Batter

- 1 1/4 Cup almond flour (I use this)
- 1/2 Cup powdered erythritol (I use this)
- 2 tablespoons ground flax (feel free to omit if you don't have it...it just adds a bit more depth to the flavors)
- 2 teaspoons baking powder
- 1/2 teaspoons ground cinnamon
- 5 tablespoon butter, melted
- 2 1/2 teaspoons banana extract
- 1 teaspoon vanilla extract
- 1/4 cup unsweetened almond milk
- 1/4 cup sour cream
- 2 eggs

Walnut Crumble

- 3/4 cup chopped walnuts
- 1 tablespoon butter, cold and cut in 4 pieces
- 1 tablespoon almond flour
- 1 tablespoon powdered erythritol

Instructions

1. Preheat oven to 350
2. Prepare muffin tin with 10 paper liners, and set aside
3. In a large bowl, mix almond flour, erythritol (or preferred sweetener) flax, baking powder and cinnamon
4. Stir in butter, banana extract, vanilla extract, almond milk, and sour cream.
5. Add eggs to mixture and gently stir until fully combined.
6. Fill muffin tins about 1/2-3/4 full with mixture.
7. *If you need more accurate measurements, weigh the batter on a food scale and divide by 10. That will give you the grams of batter per cup.

Crumble Topping

1. Add walnuts, butter, and almond flour to food processor.
2. Pulse a few times until nuts are chopped into small pieces. If mixture seems too dry (sometimes some walnuts are softer than others) feel free to add another tablespoon of butter.
3. Sprinkle bits of the mixture evenly over batter and gently press down.
4. Sprinkle erythritol on top of crumble mixture.
5. Bake for 20 minutes or until golden and toothpick comes out clean. Let cool for at least 30 minutes, an hour or more if possible. This lets them firm up.

If they seem to be cooking faster, take them out sooner to avoid burning. Alternatively, if they are still wet looking, return them to the oven for a few minutes keeping a close eye on them.

155. Spinach, Feta Bacon Burgers

Ingredients

- 1 lb. Ground Beef
- 6 Slices Maple Bacon – Cooked Crisp and Crumbled
- 1 Cup Baby Spinach – Rough Chopped
- ¼ Cup Sun-Dried Tomatoes
- ¼ Cup Parmesan Cheese – Shredded
- ¼ Cup Feta Cheese – Crumbled
- 2 Tbs. Garlic – Minced
- 1 tsp. Sea Salt
- 1 tsp. Black Pepper
- 1 ½ oz. Sweet Onion

Instructions

1. In a large mixing bowl, combine ground beef, bacon, spinach, sun-dried tomatoes, Parmesan cheese, feta cheese, garlic, sea salt and pepper.

2. Using a microplane grater, grate the onion into the meat mixture. Mix until all ingredients are well incorporated.

3. Form the mixture into 4 equal sized patties.

4. In a large skillet, over medium-high heat, sear the burgers 4-5 minutes on each side or until burgers have reached desired level of doneness.

5. Garnish with any extra spinach, sun-dried tomatoes or feta.

156. Loaded Cauliflower Bake

Ingredients

- 1 large head cauliflower, cut into florets
- 2 tbsp. butter
- 1 cup heavy cream
- 2 oz. cream cheese
- 1 1/4 cup shredded sharp cheddar cheese, separated
- Salt and pepper to taste
- 6 slices bacon, cooked and crumbled
- 1/4 cup chopped green onions

Instructions

1. Preheat oven to 350 degrees.

2. In a large pot of boiling water, blanch cauliflower florets for 2 minutes. Drain cauliflower.

3. In a medium pot, melt together butter, heavy cream, cream cheese, 1 cup of shredded cheddar cheese, salt, and pepper until well-combined.

4. In a baking dish, add cauliflower florets, cheese sauce, all but 1 tbsp. crumbled bacon, and all but 1 tbsp. green onions. Stir together.

5. Top with remaining shredded cheddar cheese, crumbled bacon, and green onions.

6. Bake until cheese is bubbly and golden and cauliflower is soft, about 30 minutes.

7. Serve immediately and enjoy!

157. Steak Fajita Roll-Ups

Ingredients

- Homemade Fajitas Seasoning Mix
- 1 pound thinly sliced sirloin tip steak (carne asada)*
- 1 tablespoon olive oil, divided
- 3 colored bell peppers cut into thin strips
- 1 large yellow onion , sliced
- 1 lime , juiced
- chopped fresh parsley or cilantro
- prepared Guacamole for serving , optional

Instructions

1. Prepare the fajitas seasoning mix and set aside.
2. Cut the steak into 2-inch wide by 6-inch long strips.
3. Rub the steak strips with some of the prepared seasoning mix and set aside.**
4. Heat olive oil in a grill pan over medium-high heat and add pepper strips and sliced onions to the grill pan; season with salt, pepper, and a sprinkle of the fajitas seasoning mix.
5. Cook for about 4 to 5 minutes, or until tender.
6. Remove from heat and let cool for a minute.
7. Top each slice of steak with the vegetables; roll up and secure with a toothpick.
8. Add remaining olive oil to the grill pan; heat it up and add the roll-ups to the pan.
9. Cook until browned, about 2 to 3 minutes per side.
10. Remove from heat, remove toothpicks, and transfer to a serving plate.
11. Squeeze lime juice over the roll ups and garnish with chopped parsley or cilantro.
12. Serve with prepared guacamole.

158. Shaved Brussels Sprouts Salad with Lemon Thyme Vinaigrette

Ingredients

- 1 lb of fresh organic brussels sprouts, shaved
- 1/4 cup good quality olive oil
- 1 tablespoon apple cider vinegar
- 1/4 teaspoon dijon mustard
- 1/4 teaspoon whole grain mustard
- 1/2 organic lemon, juiced
- 4 sprigs fresh organic thyme, leaves only
- Sea salt to taste

Instructions

1. Fill an large saucepan with water and bring to a gentle boil.
2. Place shaved brussels sprouts in water and allow to simmer for approximately 7-10 minutes or until crisp tender.

3. While your brussels sprouts are cooking, prepare your vinaigrette by placing the remaining Ingredients except sea salt in a small bowl and whisking together. Set aside.

4. When brussels sprouts are ready, drain them and immediately place them in an ice bath to stop the cooking process and preserve their bold green color. Allow to cool for 1-2 minutes in the ice bath and then drain them again.

5. Place drained brussels sprouts in a bowl and pour vinaigrette over. Toss to coat and add sea salt to taste.

159. Loaded Chicken Salad

Ingredients

- 1 boneless chicken breast (about 300g, with or without skin)
- 1 tbsp extra virgin olive oil
- 1/4 tsp Himalayan salt
- 1/4 tsp black pepper
- 1 avocado
- 100 g mozzarella balls

- 1 large tomato (any colour)
- 1 har artichoke hearts (my jar was 170g)
- 1/2 red onion
- 5 asparagus
- 20 leaves basil
- 4 cups baby spinach (I used about 200g)

Dressing

- 2 tbsp extra virgin olive oil
- 1 1/2 tbsp balsamic vinegar
- 1 tsp dijon mustard

- 1 clove garlic
- pinch Himalayan salt
- pinch black pepper

Instructions

1. Peel and dice the avocado. Slice the red onion. Dice the tomato. Pile the basil leaves together, roll them up and slice. Cut the stems off the asparagus and slice in half. Mince the garlic.

2. Slice the chicken breast in half lengthwise. Sprinkle the 1/4 tsp of salt and pepper on each sides. Heat the 1 tbsp of olive oil in a cast iron skillet and place the chicken breasts in. Fry on each side, about 3 minutes each side, until they have a nice golden brown colour and cooked through. Add the asparagus beside the chicken breasts and cook a few minutes until soft and grilled. Take out the chicken and slice.

3. In a small bowl, combine the minced garlic, olive oil, balsamic vinegar, dijon, and salt & peper.

4. Add the baby spinach to a large bowl or plate. Cover with the grilled chicken, avocado, mozzarella, tomatoes, artichoke, red onions, asparagus and basil leaves. Pour the dressing over and enjoy!

BUTCHER

&

BEAST

RECIPES

---

160. Spinach Artichoke Stuffed Chicken Breast Recipe

Ingredients

- 1 ½ lbs chicken breasts 6 4-oz. portions
- 2 tablespoons olive oil
- 4 ounces cream cheese softened
- ¼ cup Greek yogurt
- ½ cup Mozzarella cheese shredded
- ½ cup artichoke hearts thinly sliced
- ¼ cup frozen spinach drained, and tightly packed
- ½ tsp. salt divided
- ¼ tsp. pepper divided

Instructions

1. Pound chicken breast to 1-inch thick. Using a sharp knife cut each chicken breast down the middle, being careful not to cut all of the way through, to make a pocket for the spinach artichoke filling. Sprinkle chicken breasts with ¼ teaspoon salt and 1/8 teaspoon pepper.

2. In a medium-sized bowl combine the cream cheese, Greek yogurt, Mozzarella cheese, artichoke hearts, drained spinach, ¼ teaspoon salt and 1/8 teaspoon pepper. Mix until thoroughly combined.

3. Carefully fill each chicken breast with equal amounts of the spinach artichoke filling. If you have extra filling, set it aside until the chicken is almost done cooking.

4. In a large skillet over medium heat add olive oil and stuffed chicken breasts. Cover skillet and cook for 7-8 minutes on each side, or until chicken reaches 165 degrees with a meat thermometer.

5. During the last few minutes of cooking, add additional filling to the skillet to heat it up. Serve chicken with cauliflower rice, regular rice, mashed cauliflower, or mashed potatoes and enjoy!

161. Lemon Balsamic Chicken

Ingredients

- 8 boneless skinless chicken thighs (about 2 lbs)
- 3 tbsp. pastured butter
- 1 cup sliced onion
- 1 cup shredded purple cabbage
- 2 tbsp. minced lemon rind
- 2 bay leaves
- 2 tsp pink Himalayan salt
- 1 tsp dried Italian herb blend
- 1 tsp coarse black pepper
- 1.5 tbsp. balsamic vinegar
- 5 tbsp. olive oil

Instructions

1. Heat your electric pressure cooker on sauté mode. Add in 2 tbsp. of butter.
2. While it melts, peel and slice your onion. Go ahead and prep your lemon rind and your cabbage, too!
3. Add the onion, cabbage and lemon to the pressure. Sauté, stirring often until tender.

4. Add in the chicken thighs, seasonings and bay leaves. Stir well and cook, browning the chicken for a 2-3 minutes.

5. Pour in the vinegar. Cancel the sauté function. Close the lid, select pressure cook. Set it to poultry or high for 20 minutes.

6. Once it has finished, let the pressure releases naturally. Open the lid, stir the chicken to shred. Mix in the last tablespoon of butter.

7. Spoon this delicious saucy chicken all over your zoodles, drizzle with olive oil or avocado oil! Enjoy!

162. Shrimp & Cauliflower Rice Salad

Ingredients

For the salad:

- 4 cups riced cauliflower
- 2 cups cooked shrimp, sliced in half lengthwise
- 1 cup chopped red cabbage
- 1/4 cup chopped fresh basil
- 2 tablespoons grated pink grapefruit zest

For the vinaigrette:

- 1/4 cup fresh pink grapefruit juice
- 3 tablespoons avocado oil (or other light tasting oil)
- 2 tablespoons apple cider vinegar
- 3 tablespoons granulated erythritol (omit if Whole 30)
- 1/2 teaspoon ground black pepper
- 1 teaspoon kosher salt

Instructions

1. Combine the salad ingredients in a medium-sized bowl.

2. Place the vinaigrette ingredients in a small blender or magic bullet and blend until smooth.

3. Pour the vinaigrette over the salad and toss to coat.

4. Serve chilled or at room temperature.

5. Store leftovers in an airtight container in the refrigerator for up to 5 days. Do not freeze.

163. Mexican Shredded Beef

Ingredients

- 3 1/2 pounds pastured beef short ribs or beef shank
- 2 teaspoons ground turmeric
- 1 teaspoon salt
- 1/2 teaspoon pepper
- 2 teaspoons ground cumin
- 2 teaspoons ground coriander
- 1/2 cup water
- 1 cup cilantro stems, coarsley chopped
- Optional: 4 cloves of garlic (crushed), 1 teaspoon chipotle powder and 2 teaspoons paprika

Instructions

1. In a small bowl, combine dry ingredients.
2. Add short ribs to slow cooker and lightly coat each piece in the spice mix.
3. Sprinkle cilantro stems and optional garlic over the ribs. Carefully add water without rinsing spices off the meat.
4. Cook on low for 6-7 hours, or until it is falling apart. Check the meat at 6 hours and cook longer if it is not tender enough.
5. If desired, drain cooking liquid into a small saucepan and reduce for 10-15 minutes over medium heat.
6. Return liquid to the crock pot. Using two forks, pull the meat apart and shred the beef.
7. Serve hot with bulletproof guacamole, silverbeet leaves as a taco, roasted pumpkin, cucumbers, green beans and fresh cilantro.

164. Creamy Chicken Soup

Ingredients

- 2 liters filtered water (about 8 1/2 cups)
- 1 whole chicken (pastured and organic preferred)
- 2 tablespoons apple cider vinegar
- 3 1/2 cups cubed fresh pumpkin (or two 15-ounce cans of canned pumpkin, BPA-free)
- Juice from 1 lime
- 2 tablespoons finely chopped ginger
- 2 medium zucchinis
- 1/2 cup fresh parsley, finely chopped
- 1/2 cup fresh cilantro, finely chopped
- 2 teaspoons ground turmeric
- 1 cup coconut cream
- 2 teaspoons salt
- 2 shallots (optional)
- 4 cloves of garlic (optional)
- 1 teaspoon chili flakes (optional)
- Black pepper, to taste

Instructions

1. In a slow cooker or stock pot, add chicken and cover with water and apple cider vinegar. (Chicken may remain partially uncovered.)

2. Heat the pot or slow cooker on low heat and simmer for 4 hours, or until chicken can be pulled apart.

3. Carefully remove the chicken from the pot and set aside. Strain bone or skin fragments and reserve the remaining stock. Return stock to the pot and add pumpkin, zucchinis, and ginger. Simmer on low heat for about 15 minutes. Add zucchini and simmer a additional 15 minutes, or until pumpkin and zucchini are tender.

4. While vegetables cook, pull the meat off your chicken and set aside.

5. Once the pumpkin has softened, add the parsley, cilantro, shallots, lime juice, and coconut cream and chicken to warm through.

6. Taste the mix and ensure the salt, lime juice and spices are adjusted to your liking.

7. Serve hot, garnished with extra fresh herbs.

165. Beef Bourguignon

Ingredients

- 1.5 - 2 pounds beef chuck roast cut into 3/4-inch cubes
- 5 strips bacon diced
- 1 small onion chopped
- 10 ounces cremini mushrooms quartered
- 2 carrots chopped
- 5 cloves garlic minced
- 3 bay leaves
- 3/4 cup dry red wine
- 3/4 teaspoon xanthan gum (or corn starch, read post for instructions)
- 1 tablespoon tomato paste
- 1 teaspoon dried thyme
- salt & pepper

Instructions

1. Generously season beef chunks with salt and pepper, and set aside. Select the saute mode on the pressure cooker for medium heat. When the display reads HOT, add diced bacon and cook for about 5 minutes until crispy, stirring frequently. Transfer the bacon to a paper towel lined plate.

2. Add the beef to the pot in a single layer and cook for a few minutes to brown, then flip and repeat for the other side. Transfer to a plate when done.

3. Add onions and garlic. Cook for a few minutes to soften, stirring frequently. Add red wine and tomato paste, using a wooden spoon to briefly scrape up flavorful brown bits stuck to the bottom of the pot. Stir to check that the tomato paste is dissolved. Turn off the saute mode.

4. Transfer the beef back to the pot. Add mushrooms, carrots, and thyme, stirring together. Top with bay leaves. Secure and seal the lid. Cook at high pressure for 40 minutes, followed by a manual pressure release.

5. Uncover and select the saute mode. Remove bay leaves. Evenly sprinkle xanthan gum over the pot and stir together. Let the stew boil for a minute to thicken while stirring. Turn off the saute mode. Serve into bowls and top with crispy bacon.

166. Chicken with Roasted Red Pepper Cream Sauce

Ingredients

- 1 tablespoon clarified butter or avocado oil
- 4 chicken thighs or 2 thighs and 2 drumsticks
- 1/4 small yellow onion thinly sliced
- 2 large cloves garlic crushed
- 1/2 cup water

- 1/4 teaspoon salt
- 1/4 teaspoon black pepper
- 4 oz cream cheese
- 2 tablespoons roasted red bell pepper minced
- 1/2 teaspoon dried Italian herb seasoning

Instructions

1. Turn pressure cooker on, press "Sauté", and wait 2 minutes for the pot to heat up. Add the ghee or oil and the chicken thighs (skin down), and cook until browned, about 2 minutes per side. Press "Cancel" to stop sautéing.

2. Add the onion, garlic, water, salt, and black pepper to the pot. Turn the pot on Manual, High Pressure for 15 minutes and then do a quick release.

3. Use thongs to transfer the pieces of chicken to a plate; let them cool slightly, and then remove the skin (unless you don't mind soggy skin).

4. Press "Sauté", and whisk in the cream cheese, roasted red bell pepper, and dried Italian herb mix. Continue whisking until the sauce is smooth and thickened slightly, about 4 to 5 minutes. Return the chicken back to the sauce.

5. Serve along with cauliflower mash, cauliflower rice, or something else to soak up the sauce.

167. Pressure Cooker Pot Roast

Ingredients

- 2 to 3 pound roast
- 1 tsp salt
- 1 tsp pepper
- 2 cloves garlic
- 2 tbsp. worstershire

- 16 ounces radishes
- 1 medium onion
- 8 ounces mushrooms
- 1 cup beef stock
- 2 tbsp. avocado oil

Instructions

1. Slice mushrooms and cut radishes in half.
2. Quarter onions. Set aside
3. Place a tbsp of avocado oil into instant pot and set to saute.
4. Add vegetables to the Instant Pot. Cook until onions have caramelized. Radishes will not be fully cooked though.
5. Remove veggies and set aside
6. Add remaining tbsp of oil.
7. Salt and Pepper roast on both sides
8. Place roast on saute and brown roast on both sides
9. Pour in beef broth and Worcestershire sauce. Hit Manual high pressure for 45 minutes.
10. Allow Instant Pot to depressurize naturally then add back your veggies.
11. Hit manual. Change time to 1 minute high pressure. Once timer goes off, use quick pressure release.
12. Let roast and veggies sit in Instant Pot for ~5 minutes before eating.

168. Grilled Swordfish Skewers with Pesto Mayo

Ingredients

- 1 lb swordfish, cut into 1 inch cubes
- 16 cherry tomatoes
- salt and pepper

- 1 tsp olive oil to coat
- 1/4 cup pesto
- 1/4 cup mayonnaise

Instructions

1. Divide the swordfish cubes into four equal portions.
2. Alternate the swordfish with the cherry tomatoes on your skewers.
3. Brush with olive oil and season with salt and pepper.
4. Preheat the grill for at least 5 minutes, then carefully place your skewers on the hot grill.

5. Cook for about 1 minute per (four) sides of your cubes – a little longer if your swordfish pieces are really thick.

6. Serve warm or chilled with a salad.

7. Combine the pesto and mayonnaise in a small bowl and stir well. Serve with the skewers.

169. Thai Shrimp Soup

Ingredients

- 2 tbsp unsalted butter or ghee, divided in half
- ½lb (225g) medium uncooked shrimp, peeled and deveined
- ½ yellow onion, diced
- 2 cloves garlic, minced
- 4 cups chicken broth
- 2 tbsp fresh lime juice
- 2 tbsp fish sauce, this brand is whole30 compliant
- 2½ tsp red curry paste, like this one
- 1 tbsp coconut aminos (paleo whole30) or can use 1 tbsp tamari sauce for low carb
- 1 stalk lemongrass, bruised (smashed) and finely chopped
- 1 cup sliced fresh white mushrooms
- 1 tbsp grated fresh ginger root
- 1 tsp sea salt
- ½ tsp freshly ground black pepper
- 1 (13.66-ounce) can unsweetened, full-fat coconut milk (this brand is whole30 compliant)
- 3 tbsp chopped fresh cilantro

Instructions

1. Press the Sauté button once. Once the inner pot becomes hot, add 1 tbsp butter. Once butter is melted, add the shrimp and stir until shrimp turns pink and begins to curl. Immediately transfer shrimp to a medium bowl. Set aside.

2. Add remaining 1 tbsp butter to the inner pot. Once butter is melted, add onions and garlic and sauté until garlic is fragrant and onions become translucent. Press Cancel to turn off the heat.

3. Add chicken broth, lime juice, fish sauce, red curry paste, coconut aminos or tamari sauce, lemongrass, mushrooms, grated ginger root, sea salt, and black pepper. Stir to combine.

4. Cover, lock the lid and flip the steam release handle to the Sealing position. Select Pressure Cook on high, and set the cooking time for 5 minutes. When the cook time is complete, allow the pressure to release Naturally for 5 minutes (Don't touch the pot for 5 minutes), and then

carefully quick release the remaining pressure by flipping the steam release handle to "Venting". Press Cancel to turn off the heat.

5. Remove the lid. Add shrimp and coconut milk to the pot, and stir.

6. Press the Sauté button twice ("more or high" setting will light up), and let the soup come to a boil. Once boiling Press Cancel to turn off the heat. Let soup rest for 2 minutes in the pot.

7. Ladle the soup into bowls, sprinkle cilantro over the top to garnish and serve.

170. Bacon Cheddar Egg Bites

Ingredients

- 9-10 eggs
- 1/2 cup heavy cream (Sub coconut milk if preferred)
- 1 cup bacon, cooked and chopped or crumbled (about 6-8 slices)
- 1/2 cup cheddar cheese, shredded
- 1 tsp dried basil
- 1 tsp salt
- 1/4 tsp black pepper

Instructions

1. Spray silicone molds or 4 oz jelly jars liberally with non-stick cooking spray. Set aside.

2. Crack eggs into medium-sized bowl and gently whisk to scramble.

Mix in remaining Ingredients.

3. Pour egg mixture into silicone molds or jelly jars, distributing evenly.

4. Cover molds or jars loosely with aluminum foil.

5. Place trivet in bottom of Instant Pot cooking pot. Add recommended minimum amount of water.

6. Gently lower first silicone mold into pot to rest on top of trivet. (If using jelly jars, place first layer of jars on trivet, leaving about an inch between jars.)

7. Carefully lower second silicone mold and lay it to rest on top of the first mold. Be sure to rotate the mold so the cups are offset (make sure the bottom of the cups on the top mold rest on the spaces between the cups of the bottom mold). If using jelly jars, place second layer of jars, making sure to offset them from the first layer.

8. Close lid, seal vent, and set Instant Pot to cook on HIGH for 14 minutes.

9. Once cook time has ended, allow the Instant Pot to release pressure naturally for 5 minutes, then quick release the remaining pressure.

10. Remove lid and carefully take out molds or jars. You may need to use tongs or chopsticks if space is tight.

11. Place a plate on top of a mold, and holding the plate and mold together, invert, so that the plate is on bottom and the mold is upside-down on top. This should pop egg bites out of the mold. If not, gently press on the top of the mold cups to release.

To freeze

1. Place egg bites, not touching, on parchment-lined baking sheet and place in freezer for minimum of 1 hour, up to 4 hours.

2. Once frozen, remove egg bites from tray and place into freezer storage bag.

3. Label and date, then place bag back into freezer.

4. To reheat:

5. From thawed, microwave for 30 seconds.

6. From frozen, microwave for 1 1/2 to 2 minutes.

171. Ropa Vieja

Ingredients

- 1 (3 – 3 ½) pound chuck roast
- 1 onion, sliced
- 4 teaspoons minced garlic
- 2 ½ teaspoons dried oregano
- 2 teaspoons cumin
- 2 teaspoons paprika
- 2 teaspoons salt
- 1 teaspoon smoked paprika
- ½ teaspoon black pepper
- ½ teaspoon ground cloves
- 1 (14.5 ounce) can diced tomatoes
- 2 bay leaves

Add Later:

- 3 bell peppers (I use a combo of green, red and yellow), sliced
- Green olives with pimentos, garnish

Instructions

1. Add all of the Ingredients (except the ones listed under add later) to an Instant Pot.

2. Secure the lid, close the valve and cook for 90 minutes.

3. Naturally release pressure.

4. Shred the beef using two forks.

5. Press the sauté button, add the bell peppers and cook for 4-5 minutes, or until tender.

6. Stir in the green olives.

172. Beef Brisket Pho

Ingredients

- 1.75 - 2 lbs Beef brisket
- 1-1.25 lbs beef shank soup bones, , beef knuckle bones, or a combination
- 1 ¼ cups dry shiitake mushrooms*, (rehydrate overnight in room temperature water)
- 3 loose carrots, , roughly chopped*

- 1 medium size yellow onion, , peeled but not sliced (leave it as a whole)
- 1 large size leek, , roughly diced into segments
- Water

Pho Aroma Combo:

- 2 fat thumb size ginger, (scrub clean, no need to peel)
- 4 star anise
- 2 cinnamon sticks

- 2 ½ tsp fine sea salt*
- 1 tbsp Red Boat fish sauce
- 1 tsp five spice powder, (optional)
- Tea bags or cheese cloth

- 8 green cardamom
- 3 medium size shallots
- 4-5 cilantro roots, (alt. 1 ½ tsp coriander seeds)

Garnish:

- Lime wedges
- Baby bok choy
- Bean sprouts
- Red or green fresno chili peppers

- Mint leaves
- Asian/Thai basil, (optional)
- Cilantro, (optional)
- Hot chili pepper sauce, (optional)

Instructions

Pre-Cooking:

1. Soak the dry shiitake mushrooms overnight in room temperature water. If rush on time, soak in warm temperature water until the mushrooms are soft and tender.

2. Pre-boil the bones and brisket: add the bones and brisket to a large stockpot and cover with water. Bring the water to boil over high heat, then reduce to medium and simmer for 10 more minutes. Rinse the bones and meat over room temperature tap water. Set aside. Discard the broth.

3. Grill the Ingredients under "Pho Aroma Combo" in a cast iron over medium heat. No oil added. Rotate and flip the Ingredients frequently until you can smell a nice and lovely fragrant. Be careful not to burn the aroma combo. Slightly charred outer surface is okay but not burnt.

4. Slice the mushrooms. Save the mushroom water. Roughly dice leek. Add aroma combo and leeks to large tea bags or cheesecloth tied with a string.

Instant Pot Cooking:

1. In a 6-quart size instant pot, add beef bones, brisket (fatty side up), diced carrots, aroma combo and leeks (in tea bags). Strain the mushroom water as you add the liquid to the pot. Fill the pot with more tap water until it reaches the 4 liter mark. Close the lid in Sealing position - Press Soup - Adjust to 40 minutes/High pressure/More.

2. Allow the instant pot come to natural pressure release (valve dropped), discard the whole onion and aroma combo in tea bags.

3. Remove the brisket and soak it in cold water for at least 10 minutes. This will prevent the meat from turning dark color. Discard aroma & leek tea bags, yellow onion, and beef bones. Season the broth with 2 ½ tsp fine sea salt, 1 tbsp fish sauce, and 1 tsp five spice powder (optional).

4. Thin slice the brisket in 45 degree angle and against the grain. Ladle the broth over bean sprouts, carrots, mushrooms, mint leaves, Asian basil, chili peppers, and sliced brisket. Serve hot with lime wedges.

173. Chicken Breast Recipe

Ingredients

- 4 lb Chicken breast
- 1 tbsp Italian seasoning (or any spices you like)
- 1/2 tsp Sea salt
- 1/2 tsp Black pepper
- 1 cup Chicken broth (or use homemade)

Instructions

1. Place the chicken into the pressure cooker. Season with Italian seasoning, sea salt, and black pepper (or any other spices you like). Pour the chicken broth around the sides of the chicken.

2. Close the lid and select the either the "Poultry" or "Manual" setting. Set the time to 8 minutes for fresh chicken breast, or 13 minutes for frozen chicken breast. (These times are for typical 6-8 ounce chicken breasts. If yours are larger, add a couple of minutes.)

3. When done, let the pressure naturally release for at least 5 minutes. After that, you can turn the valve to "vent" for quick release if you're in a hurry, or continue natural release for the most tender texture.

Unplug the pressure cooker and use two forks to shred the chicken. (I prefer to do this right in the pressure cooker, mixing with the juices.) Drain if serving right away, or store with the broth to retain moisture.

174. Chorizo Chili

Ingredients

- 1 1/2 tablespoons olive oil or coconut oil
- 1 large brown onion, roughely chopped
- 1 medium carrot (or 2 small ones), peeled and diced into small cubes
- 1 celery stick, diced into small cubes
- 7 oz / 200 g chorizo sausage, peeled and diced
- 1 long red chilli, finely diced
- 2.2 lb / 1 kg ground beef (grass-fed, if possible)
- 3 cloves garlic, finely diced
- 2 teaspoons ground cumin
- 2 teaspoons ground coriander seed
- 2 cups / about 400 g tinned chopped tomatoes
- 4 tablespoons tomato paste

- 1 tablespoon Tamari or soy sauce (coconut aminos for those on Whole30/paleo)
- 2 teaspoons salt

- 2 bay leaves
- 3 tablespoons of port or fortified red wine (optional but adds lots of depth)

To serve: flash pan-fried zucchini or cooked white rice, chopped avocado and cilantro.

Instructions

1. Turn the Instant Pot on and press the Sauté function key (it should say High, 30 mins). Add the oil, onion, carrot, celery, chorizo and chili and cook together for 3-4 minutes.

2. Add the beef, garlic, spices and stir. Add the tinned tomatoes and paste and stir. Add the rest of the Ingredients and stir together. Press Keep Warm/Cancel.

3. Place and lock the lid, make sure the steam releasing handle is pointing to Sealing. Press MANUAL (High Pressure) and set to 15 minutes. After 3 beeps the pressure cooker will start going.

4. Once the time is up, let the pressure release naturally for 5 minutes, then use the quick release to let off the rest of the steam.

5. If storing in the freezer, make sure to cool down the chili first.

175. Beef Tongue into Delicious CRISPY BEEF

Ingredients

- 1 beef tongue
- 3 cups water
- 2-3 Tablespoons lard or other traditional fat
- 2-3 teaspoons sea salt

- freshly ground black pepper to taste (omit for AIP)
- 1 teaspoon garlic powder optional
- 1 teaspoon cumin optional (omit for AIP)

Instructions

1. Place whole tongue and water into Instant Pot. (See Recipe Notes below if you don't have an IP.) Seal lid and close valve. Select Stew setting. IP will cook for 35 minutes. Allow pressure to release naturally for 30 minutes, then put dish towel over valve and release pressure.

2. Using tongs, remove tongue to cutting board to cool slightly. When cool enough to handle, peel tongue, making a cut through the skin to begin. (See photo.)

3. Slice tongue starting at the tip, in 1/2" slices, at a slight angle to get larger pieces at the tip.

4. beef tongue into crispy beef- slicing before frying

5. Heat large cast iron skillet or other pan over medium-high heat. Add 1 Tablespoon fat to pan, spreading it around. Place meat slices closely together. Sprinkle with 1 tsp. Sea salt, freshly ground pepper, to taste, and optional spices. Cook for 5 minutes, then reduce heat to medium

for an additional 3 minutes. Check the surface that's frying. When it's crispy flip each piece. beef tongue into crispy beef- frying

6. Lightly salt second side of meat. Fry on second side until crispy. Remove first batch and start second batch of meat frying: repeat frying steps with any meat that remains, using lard, sea salt and spices as you did with the first batch.

7. Remove meat to a cutting board and cut into thin strips, as desired. Serve in Mexican food settings, such as tacos, big salads, and over eggs with green chilies, inside soft tortillas etc. With accompaniments: fresh cilantro, sweet onions, salsa, avocado, sour cream, cheese, fresh radishes etc.

176. Green Chile Chicken Burrito Bowl

Ingredients

Green Chile Chicken Ingredients

- 4 boneless, skinless chicken breasts, trimmed and cut into strips
- 1 cup green chile salsa (Look for a green chile salsa without much sugar, see notes for what we used.)
- 1 can (4 oz.) diced green chiles (Anaheim chiles, not jalapenos!)

Tomato-Avocado Salsa Ingredients:

- 2 avocados, diced and tossed with 1 T lime juice
- 1 1/2 cups diced tomato or cherry tomatoes cut in half
- 2 green onions, thinly sliced
- 1 T olive oil
- 3 T fresh lime juice (1 T is for tossing with avocado and the rest is for the salsa. See note about the lime juice I used.)
- salt to taste

Cauliflower Rice Ingredients:

- About 6 cups frozen cauliflower rice (We used two 12 oz. packages, but if you have the big package from Costco, just measure out 6 cups.)
- 2 T olive oil
- 1 onion, chopped small
- 1 large Poblano chile pepper, seeds and stem removed and finely diced (These are often called Pasilla Peppers in U.S. grocery stores.)
- 1 tsp ground cumin
- salt and fresh-ground black pepper to taste

- 2 T fresh lime juice to toss with the cooked rice (optional)

Instructions

1. Measure out about 6 cups frozen cauliflower rice, break apart lumps, and let it thaw on the counter.

2. Trim chicken breasts and cut each one lengthwise into 2 or 3 strips (so you'll have shorter pieces of chicken when you shred the cooked chicken apart.)

3. Put chicken into the Instant Pot with the Salsa Verde and diced green chiles.

4. Lock the lid and set Instant Pot to MANUAL, HIGH PRESSURE, 8 minutes.

5. When the cooking time is up, use NATURAL RELEASE for 10 minutes, then release the rest of the pressure manually.

6. Remove chicken to a cutting board to cool while you turn the Instant Pot to SAUTE, MEDIUM HEAT and cook the sauce to reduce it, about 8-10 minutes.

7. When it's cool, shred shred chicken apart and put it back into the Instant Pot to mix with the flavorful green chile sauce. You can use the pressure cooker to keep it warm if needed.

8. While chicken cooks, dice avocados and toss with 1 T lime juice, dice tomatoes, and slice green onions. Toss the diced avocado, diced tomato, and sliced green onion with the olive oil, other 2 T fresh lime juice, and a little salt to make the salsa. (If you're doing Weekend Food Prep, I would only make half the salsa and make the rest when you eat the leftovers.)

9. Chop the onion and cut out seeds and stem from the Poblano chile and finely chop the chile.

10. Heat 2 T olive oil in a large non-stick frying pan over medium high heat; add the chopped onion and cook 2-3 minutes. Add the finely diced poblano and cooker 2-3 minutes more. The add the ground cumin and cook about a minute more.

11. Add the cauliflower rice and cook, stirring frequently, until all the liquid has evaporated, the rice is hot, and it's cooked through. This will take about 6-8 minutes, depending on how thawed the cauliflower is, but start to check after about 5 minutes. Season the cooked cauliflower rice with salt and fresh-ground black pepper to taste, and stir in the lime juice if you like the idea of an extra touch of lime.

12. To assemble the finished bowl meal, put a generous amount of cauliflower rice into a bowl, top with a generous scoop of the green chile chicken with sauce, and top with Tomato-Avocado salsa.

13. If you're making this for Weekend Food Prep, I would only make half the amount of salsa when you eat this the first time. Refrigerate the leftover shredded chicken and cooked cauliflower rice separately. When you're ready to eat leftovers, make the rest of the salsa and heat the chicken and cauliflower rice in the microwave or in a pan on the stove.

177. Taco Meat

Ingredients

- 2 pounds ground beef
- 4 tablespoons oil
- 2 red onions, diced
- 3 green bell peppers, diced
- 5 garlic cloves, minced
- 2 teaspoons chili powder
- 2 teaspoons oregano
- 1 teaspoon salt
- 1 teaspoon dried basil
- ½ teaspoon turmeric
- ½ teaspoon black pepper
- 1 teaspoon paprika
- 1 teaspoon cumin
- ½ teaspoon cayenne
- ½ teaspoon chipotle powder
- Cilantro, garnish

Instructions

Add all of the Ingredients to the Instant Pot except for the ground beef.

1. Press the "sauté" button and stir-fry for 5-6 minutes.
2. Then add the ground beef to the pot and cook until mostly brown.
3. Secure the lid, close the pressure valve and cook for 10 minutes at high pressure.
4. Naturally release pressure (or you can quick release too if you're in a hurry).
5. Open the lid, and if the meat released any liquid then press the sauté button to boil it off.
6. Garnish with cilantro and serve.

178. Balsamic Beef Pot Roast

Ingredients

- One boneless chuck roast, approximately 3 lbs.
- 1 Tbsp kosher salt
- 1 tsp black ground pepper
- 1 tsp garlic powder
- 1/4 cup of balsamic vinegar
- 2 cups water
- 1/2 cup onion, chopped
- 1/4 tsp xanthan gum
- Fresh parsley, chopped to garnish

Instructions

1. Cut your chuck roast in half so you have two pieces. Season the roast with the salt, pepper, and garlic powder on all sides. Using the saute feature on the instant pot, brown the roast pieces on both sides.
2. Add 1/4 cup of balsamic vinegar, 1 cup water, and 1/2 cup onion to the meat. Cover and seal, then using the manual button set the timer for 40 minutes. When the timer runs out, release the pressure by moving the lever to the "venting" setting. Once all the pressure is released, uncover the pot.

3. Carefully remove the meat from the pan to a large bowl. Break carefully into chunks and remove any large pieces of fat or other refuse.

4. Use the saute function to bring the remaining liquid to a boil in the pot, and simmer for 10 minutes to reduce.

5. Whisk in the xanthan gum, then add the meat back to the pan and stir gently.

6. Turn off the heat and serve hot over cauliflower puree, garnished with lots of fresh chopped parsley.

179. Lemon Garlic Chicken

Ingredients

- 6-8 boneless chicken thighs skinless or with skin*
- sea salt and pepper to taste
- 1/2 teaspoon garlic powder
- 2 tablespoons olive oil
- 3 tablespoons butter
- 1/4 cup chopped onion
- 4 garlic cloves , sliced or minced
- 2 - 4 teaspoons Italian seasoning (I actually usually use 1 - 1 1/2 tablespoon but feel free to adjust to your liking)

- zest of half a lemon
- Juice of one lemon
- 1/3 cup 1/3 cup homemade or low sodium chicken broth **PLEASE SEE NOTES BELOW
- Chopped fresh parsley and lemon slices for garnish if desired
- 2 tablespoons heavy cream
- Instant Pot (I have the 6 Quart DUO)
- OR Cast Iron Skillet

Instructions

1. Season the chicken with salt, pepper, garlic powder and chili flakes.

2. Press the Sauté function (Normal setting) on the Instant Pot and add the olive oil to the pot. (I use a 6 Quart Instant Pot DUO)

3. Place chicken in the Instant Pot and cook on each side for 2-3 minutes, or until golden brown. This helps to seal in the juices and keep it tender. (You may have to work in batches depending on the size and amount of chicken you are using). Once browned, remove from Instant Pot and set aside.

4. Melt butter in Instant Pot and stir in the onions and garlic. Add lemon juice to deglaze pan and cook for 1 minute. Add Italian seasoning, lemon zest and chicken broth.

5. Place the chicken back into the Instant Pot, lock the lid, and turn the valve to SEALING.

6. Select the Manual (older models) or Pressure Cook (newer models) button and adjust the timer to 7 minutes.

7. It will take about 5-10 minutes to come to pressure and start counting down.

8. When done, release the pressure after 2 minutes, then remove your Instant Pot lid.

9. Remove chicken from Instant Pot using tongs and set aside on a large serving plate. Stir in heavy cream (if using) into the Instant Pot.

10. (If you like your sauce thicker - you can thicken with a cornstarch slurry (if not low carb) or 1/2 teaspoon of xanthum gum.)

11. Press off and turn Instant Pot to SAUTE function. Cook and allow sauce to bubble and thicken. Turn off and add chicken back to the Instant Pot to coat with sauce. Sprinkle chicken with chopped parsley and serve hot with your favorite sides. Spoon sauce over chicken and garnish with lemon slices, if desired.

12. Serve this Instant Pot lemon garlic chicken with a salad, cauliflower rice or spiralized zucchini noodles.

180. Seafood Gumbo

Ingredients

- 24 ounces sea bass filets patted dry and cut into 2" chunks
- 3 tablespoons ghee or avocado oil
- 3 tablespoons cajun seasoning or creole seasoning
- 2 yellow onions diced
- 2 bell peppers diced
- 4 celery ribs diced

- 28 ounces diced tomatoes
- 1/4 cup tomato paste
- 3 bay leaves
- 1 1/2 cups bone broth
- 2 pounds medium to large raw shrimp deveined
- sea salt to taste
- black pepper to taste

Instructions

1. Season the barramundi with some salt and pepper, and make sure they are as evenly coated as possible. Sprinkle half of the Cajun seasoning onto the fish and give it a stir- make sure it is coated well and set aside.

2. Put the ghee in the Instant Pot and push "Sauté". Wait until it reads "Hot" and add the barramundi chunks. Sauté for about 4 minutes, until it looks cooked on both sides. Use a slotted spoon to transfer the fish to a large plate.

3. Add the onions, pepper, celery and the rest of the Cajun seasoning to the pot and sauté for 2 minutes until fragrant. Push "Keep Warm/Cancel". Add the cooked fish, diced tomatoes, tomato paste, bay leaves and bone broth to the pot and give it a nice stir. Put the lid back on the pot and set it to "Sealing." Push "Manual" and set the time for just 5 minutes! The Instant Pot will slowly build up to a high pressure point and once it reaches that point, the gumbo will cook for 5 minutes.

4. Once the 5 minutes have ended, push the "Keep warm/Cancel" button. Cautiously change the "Sealing" valve over to "Venting," which will manually release all of the pressure. Once the pressure has been release (this will take a couple of minutes), remove the lid and change the setting to "Sauté" again. Add the shrimp and cook for about 3-4 minutes, or until the shrimp have become opaque. Add some more sea salt and black pepper, to taste. Serve hot and top off with some cauliflower rice and chives.

181. Chicken and Low Carb Gravy

Ingredients

- 6.5 pound whole chicken
- 2 tbsp olive oil s
- 1 tsp dried Italian seasonings
- 1/2 tsp onion powder
- 1/2 tsp garlic powder

- 1/2 tsp salt
- 1/2 tsp pepper
- 1.5 cups low sodium chicken broth
- 2 tsp guar gum

Instructions

1. Rub 1 tablespoon of oil all over the chicken and place the rest of the oil in the bottom of the Instant Pot.

2. Mix the dry seasonings together and sprinkle all over the chicken.

3. Press "Saute" and heat the oil, then add the whole chicken into the pot, breast side down. Hit "cancel".

4. Give it 5 minutes to brown then flip the chicken over and pour in the chicken broth.

5. Cover your pot and Press "Manual" and timer for 40 minutes. It will take about 10 minutes for pressure then the timer will begin.

6. Once time is done, hit "Cancel" and manually release pressure.

7. Be careful of the steam when removing the cover of the pot.

8. Remove chicken from the pot to make the gravy.

9. Sprinkle the guar gum over the hot broth in the pot and stir continually to thicken. If it's not thickening as quick as you'd like, simple hit "saute" to warm the broth and continue to stir until the gravy is thickened. You could also add 1 more teaspoon of guar gum if it's not as thick as you'd like.

10. Serve with gravy and a sprinkle of chopped parsley if desired.

182. Vegetable Beef Stew

Ingredients

- 4tablespoonsfat of choiceI used home-rendered tallow, but coconut oil, avocado oil, and ghee will work too.
- 1yellow oniondiced
- 3cupsceleriacpeeled and diced into 1/2" cubes
- 4carrotsdiced
- 4stalks celerydiced
- 1 15oz.can diced tomatoes
- 4cupsbone broth -- beefchicken, pork, venison, any broth will do

- 2poundsgrass-fed beef* -- ground beefstew meat, or a combination (See note.)
- 1tablespoonsalt
- 2teaspoonsherbes de Provence
- 2teaspoonsgarlic powder
- 1teaspoononion powder
- 1teaspoonwhite pepper
- 3/4cupfrozen green peasoptional

Instructions

1. Press the Saute button on the Instant Pot and melt your fat of choice.
2. Add the onion, celeriac root, carrots, and celery and saute 5 to 10 minutes, stirring occasionally. If using stew meat, you can add it in at this time also.
3. Next, pour in the bone broth, canned tomatoes, salt, and spices. If using browned ground beef, now is the time to add it.
4. Place the lid on the Instant Pot, check the seal, and make sure the vent is closed. Press Cancel to stop sauteing. Press the Manual and set the time to 20 minutes on high pressure.
5. Manually release pressure when the Instant Pot beeps.
6. Finally, stir in the frozen peas, if using.
7. Wait 5 minutes before serving.

183. Creamy Shrimp Scampi

Ingredients

- 2 tablespoons butter
- 1 pound shrimp, frozen
- 4 cloves garlic, minced
- 1/4-1/2 teaspoons red pepper flakes
- 1/2 teaspoons paprika
- 2 cups Carbanada low carb pasta (uncooked)

- 1 cup water or chicken broth
- 1/2 cup half and half
- 1/2 cup parmesan cheese
- salt, to taste
- pepper, to taste

Instructions

1. Melt the butter in the Instant Pot or saucepan.

2. Add in garlic and red pepper flakes and cook until the garlic is slightly browned 1-2 minutes.

3. Add the paprika and then the frozen shrimp, salt, pepper, and noodles.

4. Pour in the broth. If using broth, don't add salt above.

5. Cook under pressure for 2 minutes an use quick release.

6. Turn the pot to Saute, add in half and half and cheese, and stir until melted.

184. Chili Verde

Ingredients

- 2 pounds boneless skinless chicken thighs (about 8)

- 12 ounces tomatillos (about 7) husked and quartered

- 8 ounces poblano peppers (about 3) stemmed, seeded, and chopped

- 1/4 cup water

- 4 ounces jalapeño peppers (about 2) stemmed, seeded, and chopped

- 4 ounces onions (about 1/2) chopped

- 5 cloves garlic

- 2 teaspoons ground cumin

- 1 1/2 teaspoons salt

For finishing:

- 1/4 ounce chopped cilantro leaves (about 1/3 cup packed), plus more for garnish

- 1 tablespoon fresh lime juice (about 1 lime)

Instructions

1. Add tomatillos, poblanos, jalapeños, onions, and water to the pressure cooker. Distribute garlic, cumin, and salt on top. Lastly, add chicken thighs. Secure and seal the lid. Cook at high pressure for 15 minutes, followed by a manual pressure release.

2. Uncover and transfer only the chicken to a cutting board. Cut into bite-sized pieces. Set aside.

3. Add cilantro and lime juice to the pressure cooker. Use an immersion blender or countertop blender to puree the mixture.

4. Select the saute mode on the pressure cooker for medium heat. Return the chicken to the mixture. Boil for about 10 minute's to thicken the sauce, stirring occasionally. Serve and garnish with additional cilantro.

185. Chicken Tikka Masala

Ingredients

- 2 lbs boneless skinless chicken breast
- 1 small onion, chopped
- 1/2 yellow bell pepper, chopped
- 2 tablespoons butter or ghee for Whole30
- 1 teaspoon cumin
- 1 teaspoon coriander
- 2 teaspoons garam masala
- 1 teaspoon turmeric
- 1/4 teaspoon cayenne pepper (or more to taste)
- 1 1/2 teaspoon sea salt
- 15 oz can diced tomatoes
- 1/2 cup full fat coconut milk
- 3 cloves garlic, minced
- 1 teaspoon grated fresh ginger

Instructions

1. Set your Instant Pot to Saute. Add butter, onion, and yellow peppers and cook for 3-4 minutes until veggies start to soften.

2. Add garlic, ginger, spices and salt and cook for an additional 1-2 minutes.

3. Add tomatoes and coconut milk and stir well to combine. Place chicken on top of mixture. Close the lid and set to Poultry (or Manual setting for 15 minutes).

4. When cycle is complete, remove chicken and shred. Using an immersion hand blender, puree the sauce. Add the chicken back to the sauce and adjust seasoning to taste.

186. Kerala Ground Meat Coconut Curry

Ingredients

- 2 tablespoons coconut oil
- 1 teaspoon black mustard seeds
- 1 onion, diced
- 1 Serrano pepper or green chili, minced
- 20 curry leaves
- 3 teaspoons minced garlic
- 1 teaspoon minced ginger

Spices

- 2 teaspoons meat masala
- 1 ½ teaspoons salt
- 1 teaspoon coriander powder
- ½ teaspoon black pepper
- ½ teaspoon paprika
- ½ teaspoon turmeric
- 1 pound ground beef or ground meat of choice
- 3 carrots, chopped
- 1 potato, chopped
- ¼ cup water
- 1 (13.5 ounce) can full-fat coconut milk

1. Press the saute´ button, add the coconut oil. Once it melts, add the mustard seeds and when they begin to pop, add the onion, Serrano pepper and curry leaves. Stir-fry for 6-7 minutes, or until the onions begin to brown.

2. Add the garlic and ginger and stir-fry for 30 seconds. Add the spices, stir, then add the ground meat and cook until it is mostly browned.

3. Add the carrots, potatoes and ¼ cup water.

4. Secure the lid, close the pressure valve and cook for 4 minutes at high pressure.

5. Open the valve to quick release any remaining pressure.

6. Stir in the coconut milk.

187. Three-Pea Salad with Ginger-Lime Vinaigrette

Ingredients

- 1 cup snow peas
- 1 cup fresh or thawed frozen sweet peas
- 1 cup sugar snap peas

Vinaigrette:

- ¼ cup fresh lime juice
- 1/2 tbsp soy sauce, reduced sodium
- ½ tbsp fresh ginger, chopped
- ½ tbsp fresh lime zest
- 1 tbsp hot sesame oil
- 1 tbsp sesame seeds
- ½ cup grapeseed oil or canola oil

Optional: coarse black pepper (freshly cracked) to taste

Instructions

1. Roast some sesame seeds in a heated frying pan while twirling continuously for at most 3-5 minutes.

2. Setting the cooker to high heat, boil some water in a big pot and cook the peas for about 2 minutes, then drain. Immediately after, place the peas in cold water and drain again.

3. In another deep dish, make a fine mixture of cayenne pepper, lime juice, soy sauce, and some seasoning. Keep whisking for about 2 minutes.

4. Add some ginger into the mixture while still whisking. Drip some graveyard oil or canola and little sesame oil. Whisk the mixture properly till it is homogenous.

5. In a bigger deep dish, pour the pea mixture and the salad dip together and whisk until mixture is as smooth as possible, then remove the sesame seeds to be thrown away.

6. Add some cayenne pepper, then serve.

MARVELOUS

RECIPES

---

188. Crunchy Quinoa Salad

Ingredients

- 2 cups of water
- 1 cup rinsed quinoa
- ½ cup seeded and diced cucumbers
- 5 diced cherry tomatoes
- ¼ cup chopped fresh mint
- 3 chopped green onions
- 2 tbsp fresh lemon juice
- ½ cup chopped flat leaf parsley
- 4 tbsp olive oil
- 1 tbsp grated lemon rind (zest)
- ½ head Bibb or Boston lettuce parted into cups
- ¼ cup grated parmesan cheese

Instructions

1. Wash some quinoa well under running water and drain afterward. Set the flame to medium or high heat, then place the quinoa in a skillet and roast for 2 minutes. Ensure you keep stirring.

2. Add about 2 cups of clean drinking water and boil the contents.

3. After the mixture has started boiling, reduce the flame, cover the pan with its lid, and then let it cook for about 10 minutes. Use a fork to check when it is done.

4. Mix up the tomatoes, onions, cucumber, lemon juice, olive oil, and seasonings.

5. Then pour the quinoa into the mix.

6. Scoop the meal into little lettuce cups and sprinkle some cheese as toppings.

189. Dijon Chicken

Ingredients

- ½ tbsp curry powder
- 1/4 cup Dijon mustard
- 4 boneless chicken breasts
- ½ tbsp lemon Juice
- 3 tbsp honey

Instructions

1. Set the temperature of the oven to 350°F.

2. Put the chicken in a baking tray.

3. Make the sauce from mixing the curry powder, Dijon mustard, lemon juice, and honey.

4. Smear the whole chicken with the sauce.

5. Leave the chicken to bake for about 30 minutes until the chicken itself is hot as 165 degrees.

190. Fruity Chicken Salad

Ingredients

- 1 cup sliced almonds
- 12.5 ounces canned chicken or 2 cups cooked chicken breasts (cut into cubes)
- 1 chopped green onion
- 1 chopped stalk celery
- 1 cubed apple
- 2 cups seedless grapes
- 1/2 cup of sour cream
- 3/4 cup of raisins
- ½ tbsp unseasoned rice vinegar
- 1/4 cup mayo
- 1/2 tsp Chinese Five-Spice Blend
- 2 tsp sugar

Instructions

1. In one bowl, make a mixture of almonds, chicken, celery, green onions, grapes, raisins, and apples in a deep dish.

2. In another bowl, make another mixture of mayonnaise, rice, vinegar, sugar, sour cream and some Chinese special spice in another deep dish.

3. Mix both contents together.

191. Lemon Cure Chicken Salad

Ingredients

- 1/4 cup thawed frozen lemonade concentrate
- 1/4 cup vegetable oil
- 1/4 tsp powdered curry
- 1/8 tbsp ground ginger
- 1 1/2 cups cooked and diced chicken
- 1/8 tsp powdered garlic
- 1/2 cup sliced celery
- 1 1/2 cups halved grapes

Instructions

1. In a container, make a mixture of concentrated lemonade, oil, and spices.

2. Add the remaining required contents: vegetable oil, powdered curry, ground ginger, cooked diced chicken, garlic, celery, and grapes. Stir everything together gently.

3. Best served chilled.

192. Italian Eggplant Salad

Ingredients

- 1 chopped small onion
- 3 cups of cubed eggplant
- 1 clove of chopped garlic
- 2 tbsp white wine vinegar
- 1/4 tsp black pepper
- 1/2 tsp oregano
- 3 tbsp olive oil
- 1 chopped medium-sized tomato

Instructions

1. Boil some water in a skillet, then add some eggplants and keep boiling for a while.

2. Lower the flame, then cover the pot and keep cooking for about 10 minutes until the eggplants are soft. After, drain the water.

3. In a deep dish, pour the drained eggplant and some onions

4. In another deep dish, make a mixture of garlic, pepper, and vinegar.

5. Pour this vinegar mixture into the dish containing the eggplants.

6. Twirl and flip then stir some oil in the mixture as thoroughly as possible. Now, you can serve.

193. Hawaiian Chicken Salad

Ingredients

- 1-1/4 cups head of lettuce (shredded)
- 1/2 cup of celery (diced)
- 1 cup of drained pineapple chunks (unsweetened)
- 1-1/2 cups chicken (cooked and chopped)
- 1 tbsp lemon juice
- 1/4 tbsp sugar
- A dash of Tabasco sauce
- 1/2 cup mayonnaise
- A dash of paprika
- 1/4 tsp pepper

Instructions

1. Make a mixture of pineapple, celery, lettuce, and chicken in a deep dish.

2. Make another mixture in a separate deep-dish containing sugar, mayonnaise, lemon juice, and hot pepper.

3. Join both mixtures together and twirl for a homogenous mixture.

4. Spritz some slices of bell peppers and serve on a leaf of lettuce.

194. Curried Turkey and Rice

Ingredients

- 1-pound turkey breast cut into 8 cutlets
- ½ vegetable oil
- 1 tbsp margarine (unsalted)
- 1 chopped medium-sized onion,
- 2 tbsp flour
- 1 tbsp curry powder (Curry powder can be found in mild or spicy.)
- 1/2 cup creamer (non-dairy)
- 1 cup chicken broth (low sodium)
- 2 cups white rice (cooked)
- ½ tbsp sugar

Instructions

1. Pour a little oil in a big saucepan and put in the turkey. Keep sautéing for about 10 minutes and flip the turkey once until it changes color to a golden brown.
2. Dish the turkey into bowls and use foil to cover and act as warmer.
3. Using the same saucepan, pour onion and curry powder into melted margarine. Fry while stirring for about 5 minutes.
4. Add some flour while still stirring continuously.
5. Pour in the chicken broth, sugar, and creamer (non-milk product). Ensure you keep stirring even while adding those ingredients. Stir until the mixture in the pan becomes thick.
6. Pour the turkey back into the saucepan. Stir for another 2 minutes.
7. Serve rice with the turkey with its sauce.

195. Chicken Nuggets with Honey Mustard Sauce

Ingredients

- Nonstick cooking spray
- 1/2 cup mayonnaise
- 1-pound chicken breast (boneless) cut into 36 pieces, bite-sized
- 1 tbsp Dijon mustard
- 1 tbsp Worcestershire sauce
- 1/3 cup honey
- 2 tbsp liquid nondairy creamer
- 1 beaten, medium-sized egg
- 3 cups low sodium cornflakes (finely crushed)

Instructions

1. Pour honey, mustard, mayonnaise, and Worcestershire sauce in a deep dish and mix thoroughly.
2. Put the mix of honey, mustard, and Worcestershire sauce in the refrigerator. While refrigerating the mixture, cook some nuggets.
3. Serve cooked nuggets and use the mixture as the sauce.

4. Set oven to a temperature of 400°F.

5. Whisk together some eggs, and creamer (non-milk products).

6. Squash cornflakes and put the resulting bits in a Ziploc bag.

7. Pour pieces of chicken into the whisked egg mix and put in the cornflake's morsels.

8. Put some nuggets on an already butter-coated baking tray and bake for about 15 minutes or until it's well baked.

196. Low Salt Stir-fry

Ingredients

- 1/2 tsp sesame seeds
- 1 tbsp olive oil
- 4 cups (about 3/4 pound) mixed greens (lettuce, collard, beets)
- 1/4 tsp curry powder
- 1 cup thinly sliced onions
- 1/2 cup rice or white wine vinegar
- 1 tbsp soy sauce (low sodium)
- 1/2 tsp sesame oil
- 8 ounces cubed tofu

Instructions

1. Chop up the greens into long strips as long as 2 inches.

2. Pour oil in a frying pan and heat up.

3. Add onions and fry for about 2 minutes until onions are clear and almost transparent.

4. Spritz the onions with curry, sugar, and some greens.

5. Cover the pan with its lid and lower the flame.

6. Leave the veggies to simmer for about 8 minutes until they are soft while stirring from time to time.

7. If it gets sticky, add just the littlest volume of water.

8. Be wary of cooking for too long. Once your veggies start turning dark, this will let you know that you are on the brink of overcooking them.

9. Use a perforated spoon to scoop the veggies without the juice.

10. Add vinegar and soy sauce to the veggies juice and boil.

11. Wait till the juice is thick then drizzle the juice over the veggies.

12. Top with sesame oil and sesame seeds.

197. A pulled Pork BBQ style

Ingredients

- 4 pounds pork shoulder roast
- 1 cup tomato sauce (no-salt added)
- 1 cup ketchup (low sodium)
- 2/3 cup red wine vinegar
- 2/3 cup brown sugar
- 2 tsp liquid smoke
- 1/4 cup molasses
- 1/4 tsp onion powder
- 1/4 tsp garlic powder
- 1/2 tsp paprika
- 1/4 tsp chili powder
- 1/4 tsp cinnamon
- 1/4 tsp celery seed
- 1/2 tsp black pepper
- 1/4 tsp cayenne pepper

Instructions

1. Make the BBQ sauce by mixing the ingredients except for the pork in a deep dish.
2. Put the pork in a slow cooker and then pour the already made BBQ sauce in the pot too.
3. Set the cooker to low heat for overnight cooking or high heat for at least 6 hours.
4. When the temperature is set to 165°F, you will know when the meat is done and ready to be taken out.
5. Use two forks to split the pork into parts.
6. Serve with rice or in a hamburger roll.

198. Chicken Pot Pie Stew

Ingredients

- 2 quarts chicken stock (low sodium)
- 1½ pounds boneless and skinless, fresh chicken breast (natural)
- ½ cup flour
- ¼ cup canola oil
- ½ cup diced, fresh onions
- ½ cup diced, fresh carrots
- 1 tbsp black pepper
- ¼ cup diced, fresh celery
- 2 tsp chicken base (low sodium)
- 1 tbsp McCormick or any other sodium-free Italian seasoning
- ½ cup light cream
- ½ cup sweet peas (fresh or frozen), thawed
- 1 cup cheddar cheese (low-fat)
- 1 frozen, cooked and bite-size pieces pie crust

Instructions

1. Freeze the pulverized meat for about 30 minutes.

2. Dice some pulverized chicken when it is ready and thawed.

3. Pour the chicken with its broth into a big slow cooker and set to high heat for about 30 minutes.

4. While the chicken is cooking, put flour and oil in a bowl and mix it.

5. Pour the smooth mixture of oil and flour into the chicken stock slowly, stopping only when thick. Lower the heat to a low temperature and leave to cook for another 15 minutes.

6. Put in your onions, celery, carrots, cayenne pepper, bouillon, and spices.

7. Let everything cook for another 15 minutes.

8. Turn off the cooker and dribble cream and peas onto your meal. Stir well.

9. Serve in cups and garnish with cheese and cobbler.

199. Cabbage-Onion-Sweet Pepper Medley

Ingredients

- ½ cup fresh green bell pepper
- ½ cup fresh red bell pepper
- ½ cup chopped fresh onions
- ½ cup fresh yellow bell pepper
- 3 tbsp white vinegar
- 2 cups shredded cabbage (fresh)
- 1 ½ tsp brown sugar
- 1 tbsp canola oil
- 1 ½ tsp pepper
- 1 ½ tsp Dijon mustard

Instructions

1. Slice some bell pepper into strips of at least 2 inches long.

2. Using a slick, anti-adhesive saucepan, mix the peppers, some cabbage, and onions while stirring carefully.

3. Mix the other ingredients and some vinegar in a container and shake well.

4. Pour the well-shaken mixture into the vegetables in the saucepan and stir.

5. Set the pot to moderate heat and leave the contents to cook, stirring from time to time until the cabbage is soft.

200. Easy Cranberry Salad

Ingredients

- 1/3 cup sugar
- 1-1/3 cups raw cranberries
- 1-1/3 cups miniature marshmallows
- 2/3 cup whipped topping
- 2/3 cup canned pineapple chunks in juice

Instructions

1. Using a grinder or blender, blend some cranberries and add sugar.

2. Leave the cranberry juice to stand.

3. Chop up the pineapple into morsels and drain.

4. Stir the cranberry juice into the bowl of pineapple morsels and add some marshmallows.

5. Stir well and add some toppings.

6. Best served chilled.

201. Baked Pita Chips

Ingredients

- chili powder
- 3 (6″) pita rounds
- 3 tbsp olive oil

Instructions

1. Divide the pitas into two rounds using kitchen scissors.

2. Cut each of the pitas into eight wedges.

3. Next, brush the pita wedges using olive oil and sprinkle the pita with chili powder.

4. Transfer the pita into an oven and bake at 350°F for a maximum of 15 minutes (or until crisp).

202. Ice Cream Sandwiches

Ingredients

- 20 tbsp cool whip (non-dairy)
- 10 plain graham crackers

Instructions

1. Break the graham crackers into halves.

2. Sprinkle 2 teaspoons of cool whip on one half.

3. Place the other half of the cracker on the one that was sprinkled.

4. Place them on a tray and freeze it for a couple of hours.

5. Once it is frozen, wrap each of the sandwiches with Saran Wrap.

203. Sweet Cornbread Muffins with Citrus Honey Butter

Ingredients

- 1 cup flour
- 1 cup cornmeal
- 3 tbsp juiced lemon
- 1 ½ tsp baking soda
- 1 cup milk
- 1 egg, beaten
- 1 tbsp vanilla extract
- ½ stick melted, unsalted butter

Honey Butter:

- ½ tsp orange extract
- 2 tbsp honey
- 1 stick softened, unsalted butter
- ½ tsp orange zest
- ¼ tsp black pepper

Instructions

1. Preheat the oven at 400°F.

2. Get a large bowl, crack the eggs open and beat the eggs, add milk and butter together, then mix again.

3. Get a separate bowl and add baking soda and cornmeal. Mix well and add the liquid ingredients and mix until everything becomes smooth. Be careful not to overbeat.

4. With a muffin liner, line the muffin tin and fill each cup up to ¾ full. Bake for about 15–20 minutes on the center rack.

5. In another bowl, whisk the honey butter ingredients until it blends smoothly and spread it on top of the cornbread muffin, or you could just serve the honey butter on the side of the muffin.

204. Sunburst Lemon Bars

Ingredients

Crust

- ½ cup sugar (powdered)
- 2 cups flour (all-purpose)
- 1 cup room temperature butter (2 sticks), unsalted

Filling

- 1½ cups sugar
- 4 large eggs
- ½ tsp cream of tartar
- ¼ cup flour (all-purpose)
- ¼ cup juiced lemon
- ¼ tsp baking soda

Glaze

- 2 tsp juiced lemon
- 1 cup sifted, powdered sugar

Instructions

Crust

1. Preheat the oven to a temperature of 350°F.

2. Get a large bowl, mix the powdered sugar, flour, and 1 full cup of softened butter. Keep on mixing until it is crumbly. Transfer the mixture into a 9" x 13" baking pan.

3. Then place in the preheated oven and bake until it is lightly browned (about 15–20 minutes).

Filling

1. Get a medium-sized bowl and use it to whisk the eggs slightly.

2. In a separate bowl, add flour, sugar, baking soda, and cream of tartar. Add the whisked egg to the dry mixture. Now, add some lemon juice to the egg mixture then whisk again until the mixture becomes slightly thick.

3. Pour the mixture on the warm crust and bake until filling is set (or for another 20 mins).

4. Bring it out of the oven and allow it to cool.

Glaze

1. Get a small bowl and use it to stir the lemon juice into the already sifted powdered sugar until it becomes spreadable. Add little or more lemon juice as necessary.

2. Sputnik the mixture over the cooled filling. Once the glaze is set, cut into 24 bars. Store the extra lemon bars in a refrigerator.

205. Brown Bag Popcorn

Ingredients

- 1 brown paper lunch bag
- ½ tbsp canola oil
- 1/4 cup popcorn kernels

Instructions

1. Get a small bowl and mix the oil and popcorn.

2. Place the popcorn in a brown bag, then fold the bag to close the open and staple the folded top twice.

3. Next, put the popcorn in the microwave at a high temperature until 5 seconds between pops or for 3 minutes.

206. Dijon Chicken

Ingredients

- 1 tbsp juiced lemon
- 4 chicken breasts (boneless)
- 3 tbsp honey
- 1/4 cup Dijon mustard
- ½ tbsp curry powder

Instructions

1. Preheat the oven to about 350°F degrees.

2. Place the chicken on a baking dish.

3. Use a bowl to mix all the ingredients.

4. Brush both sides of the chicken with the mixed sauce.

5. Bake until the internal temperature of the chicken rises to about 165 degrees (or for about 30 minutes).

207. Chicken Parmesan Meatballs

Ingredients

- 1/4 tsp powdered garlic
- 1 pound of ground chicken
- 3 tbsp breadcrumbs
- 1 egg(large)
- 8 ounces pizza sauce
- 1 tbsp Parmesan cheese (grated)
- 1/4 tsp powdered onion
- 1/4tsp Italian seasoning
- 1/2 cup mozzarella cheese, shredded

Instructions

1. Preheat the oven to about 375°F. Use a cooking spray to spray a large baking sheet.
2. Mix the egg, ground chicken, 2 tablespoons of pizza sauce, spices, breadcrumbs, and Parmesan cheese in a large bowl.
3. Chop the chicken into about 30 small meatballs (about the size of a ping-pong ball). Place the meatballs on the prepared baking sheet.
4. Bake the meatballs for 15 minutes.
5. Before placing the baked meatballs in the glass baking dish, spread a thin layer of pizza sauce in the bottom of the baking dish. Pour the rest of the pizza sauce on top of the meatballs and add shredded mozzarella.
6. Place the meatballs back in the oven, then bake for another 10 minutes.

208. Dill Nibbles

Ingredients

- 28 ounces of rice cereal
- 13 ounces of corn cereal
- 1-1/2 tbsp dried dill weed
- 1-1/2 tsp garlic powder
- ½ Worcestershire sauce
- 1/2 cup butter (unsalted)
- 1/2 cup Parmesan cheese

Instructions

1. Preheat the oven to about 250°F.
2. Pour both cereals into a roasting pan or a large baking pan.
3. Dissolve the butter in a saucepan over low heat.
4. Add dill, garlic powder, Worcestershire sauce, and Parmesan cheese to the butter, then stir to blend.
5. Pour 1/4 of the melted butter mixture on the cereal in the baking pan then mix together to coat the cereal. After, bake the cereal for 15 minutes.
6. Bring out the cereal from the oven and pour another 1/4 of melted butter mixture over the cereal; then mix well. Again, bake for 15 minutes.
7. Step 6 should be repeated two more times or until all the butter mixture is added and the cereal becomes crisp (or for a total of 1 hour).

209. Black Bean Chili

Ingredients

- Large onion (1)
- Large carrots (2)
- Green bell pepper (1)
- Cooked black beans (6 cups)
- Organic crushed tomatoes (1 large can)
- Garlic cloves (2)
- Chili powder (2 tsp. or to your liking)
- Black pepper (2 tsp.)
- Vegetable broth or Olive oil (2 tbsp.)
- Salt (as desired)
- Smoked paprika (2 tsp.)
- Sweet potato chips
- Cilantro - chopped for garnish

Instructions

1. Prep the Veggies: Drain and rinse the beans. Chop the carrots, onions, seeded bell pepper, and cloves of garlic.
2. Warm up the broth/oil until hot in a large soup pot with a top.
3. Toss in the bell pepper, onion, carrots, and garlic. Simmer for three to five minutes.
4. Fold in the rest of the fixings. Leave the lid off and *gently* simmer for 30 minutes (low-med).
5. Taste test and cover the chili. Use the warmer in the oven 30 minutes or so.
6. Serve with a sprinkle of cilantro.

210. Broccoli Mushroom Rotini Casserole - Vegan

Ingredients - For the Casserole:

- Whole wheat rotini - spirals or elbows (16 oz.)
- Broccoli (1 cup)
- Sliced mushrooms (8 oz.)
- Onion (1 medium)
- Large cloves of garlic (3)
- Dried basil (.5 tsp.)
- Panko breadcrumbs (.25 cup)
- Dried oregano (.5 tsp.)

For the Cheesy Sauce:

- Almond milk (2 cups)
- Cashews (.25 tsp.)
- Cove of garlic (1 large)
- Nutritional yeast (.33 cup)
- Brown rice miso paste (5 tsp.)
- Smoked paprika (1 tsp.)
- Cornstarch (1 tbsp.)

For The Garnish

Paprika

- White pepper
- Herbamare or salt

Instructions

1. Warm the oven to reach 350° Fahrenheit.

2. Prepare a large pot of water with the salt.

3. Quarter and peel the onion.

4. Prepare the spirals or rotini for about 6 minutes just until al dente. (Don't overcook.)

5. Pulse the mushrooms, garlic, broccoli, and onions in a food processor. Toss into a sauté pan or wok.

6. Cook until softened (approx. 7 min.).

7. Pour in vegetable broth or water as needed.

8. Blend the sauce ingredients using a blender. Adjust the seasonings as desired.

9. Drain the rotini and toss into the pan. Add the sauce and toss to coat.

10. Prepare in a large casserole pan. Top with the panko breadcrumbs and smoked paprika.

11. Bake for 20 to 25 minutes. Enjoy when ready.

211. Brussel Sprouts With Lemon & Pistachios

Ingredients

- Olive oil (2 tbsp.)
- Pistachios (.75 cup)
- Lemon (1)
- Large brussels sprouts (16)
- Salt and pepper (as desired)

Instructions

1. Prepare the sprouts. Remove the leaves from the core, remove the end, and peel the leaves off.

2. Juice and zest the lemon. Shell the pistachios.

3. Warm up the oil in a skillet using the med-high temperature setting. Sauté the pistachios and lemon zest for 1 minute.

4. Fold in the Brussel leaves.

5. Toss until bright green but crispy (5 minutes).

6. Sprinkle the salt and pepper to your liking with a spritz of fresh lemon juice.

212. Butternut Squash With Spelt Pasta & Broccoli

Ingredients

- Olive oil (1 tbsp.)
- Spelt pasta (1 box)
- Butternut squash (1)
- Small onion (1)
- Vegetable broth (.5 to 1 cup)
- Basil, sage, or parsley (to your liking)
- Good-quality parmesan cheese (1 tbsp.)
- Salt and pepper (as desired)

Instructions

1. Warm up the oven to reach 375° Fahrenheit.

2. Prepare a baking tin with a layer of parchment paper or aluminum foil.

3. Cut the onion into quarters. Peel the squash and cut into 2-inch pieces.

4. Pour the oil into a skillet. Toss the onions and squash. Sprinkle with the pepper and salt. Roast for 30 to 40 minutes.

5. Cool slightly and pour into a food processor to puree. Slowly, add the stock until it's like you like it.

6. Prepare the pasta according to the manufacturer's directions.

7. Toss the florets of broccoli into the pot for about three minutes before the pasta is done.

8. Combine the pasta and squash sauce. Garnish as desired and serve.

213. Garbanzo Zucchini Cakes

Ingredients

- Garbanzo bean flour (.5 cup)
- Yellow onions (.25 cup)
- Green onions (.25 cup)
- Cayenne powder (.5 tsp.)
- Zucchini (2-3)
- Parsley (1 tsp.)
- Sea salt (1 tsp.)
- Oregano (1 tsp.)
- Onion powder (1 tsp.)
- Hemp milk (.25 cup)
- Grapeseed oil (as needed)
- *Also Needed*: Food Processor with Grater

Instructions

1. Chop the onions. Shred up the zucchini with a grater. Squeeze the moisture out of zucchini by hand using a strainer.

2. Mix the milk, zucchini, flour, onions, and seasonings.

3. Pour grapeseed oil to a skillet using the medium temperature setting to lightly fry the mixture.

4. Scoop the zucchini mixture and place in the skillet. Pat it down with the spatula.

5. Let the cake cool for about three to five minutes per side. Serve.

214. Plant-Based Dinner Burger

Ingredients

- Red onion (.75 cup)
- Olive oil (1 tbsp.)
- Raw walnuts (.5 cup)
- Red quinoa (.66 cup uncooked/1 cup dry)
- Garbanzo beans - canned (1.5 cups)

- Tapioca starch - dissolved in alkaline water (3 tbsp.)
- Salt (.5 tsp.)
- Pepper (.25 tsp.)
- Smoked paprika (.5 tsp.)
- Sriracha - use ketchup for a less spicy version (1 tbsp.)
- Low-sodium tamari (1 tbsp.)
- Spelt buns
- Sweet potato fries
- *For the Topping*: Lettuce, red onion slices, ketchup, and tomato slices

Instructions

1. Make the quinoa according to the package instructions.
2. Chop the walnuts into small bits. Gently toast them using the medium-low temperature setting.
3. Drain the can of beans.
4. Warm up the oil and dice the onions. Sauté until softened and lightly browned.
5. Add to the food processor bowl; the toasted walnuts, garbanzo beans, onions, cooked quinoa, salt, pepper, smoked paprika, sriracha, tamari, and the tapioca starch mixture.
6. Pulse the fixings several times until the components are well blended - not pureed.
7. Prepare a baking sheet with a sheet of parchment paper.
8. Shape each burger by scooping .33 cup of the mixture to form a ball. Flatten it gently into a burger shape. Place the burgers on the baking sheet and chill them for at least 15 minutes before cooking.
9. Warm up a few teaspoons of grapeseed oil in a frying pan for the crispiest burgers. Fry the burgers for about two minutes per side or until browned.
10. Serve on toasted spelt buns with lettuce, red onion slices, tomato, and ketchup. Sweet potato fries go great with these burgers.

215. Quinoa Stuffed Spaghetti Squash

Ingredients

- Spaghetti squash (1 large or 2 small)
- Coconut oil (2 tbsp.)
- Steamed green peas (1 cup)
- Shallot (1 medium)
- Orange or red bell pepper (1)
- Spring onions - white part (2 sliced)
- Chopped walnuts (.25 cup)
- Cooked quinoa (1.5 cups)
- Garlic powder (1 tsp.)
- Black pepper & Pink salt (as desired)
- Dried thyme (2 tsp.)

Instructions

1. Warm the oven to reach 400° Fahrenheit.
2. Wash and slice the squash in half. Remove the seeds and bake until tender (40 min.).

3. Heat half of the oil in a frying pan (1 tbsp.). Saute the finely chopped shallot and bell pepper until softened.

4. Toss in the spices, cooked quinoa, green peas, and walnuts. Simmer until warmed throughout. Dust with the pink salt and pepper.

5. Divide between the squash. Put the fixings back into the oven for another five to eight minutes.

6. Transfer from the oven. Serve with fresh greens on top.

7. You can scratch the flesh with a fork and it resembles spaghetti.

216. Raw Pad Thai & Zucchini Noodles

Ingredients

- Zucchini (3 medium)
- Carrots (3 large)
- Chopped spring onions (1)
- Shredded red cabbage (1 cup)
- Bean sprouts (.5 of 1 pkg. or to your liking)
- Cauliflower florets (1 cup)
- Coriander/cilantro - fresh roughly chopped (1 bunch)
- Coconut oil

The Sauce:

- Tahini (.25 cup)
- Almond butter (.25 cup)
- Tamari (.25 cup)
- Coconut sugar (1 tsp.)
- Lemon or lime juice (2 tbsp.)
- Clove garlic (1 minced)
- Ginger root (grated 1-inch)

Instructions

1. Use a sharp knife, a mandolin or spiralizer to prepare the carrot and courgette 'noodles'. Make the slices of the zucchini and carrot very thin strips.

2. Toss the strips to a large bowl with the shredded cabbage, spring onions, rinsed bean sprouts, cauliflower, and coriander.

3. Prepare the sauce by mixing the almond butter, tahini, coconut sugar, tamari, garlic, juice of choice, and grated ginger. If it needs to be thinned, just add a small amount of water.

4. Combine all of the fixings until everything is covered.

5. Serve with a sprig of coriander and a spritz of lemon or lime.

217. Spaghetti Squash Patties

Ingredients

- Spaghetti squash (1)
- Za'atar (.25 tsp.)
- Spring onion (1)
- Grated ginger (1 tbsp.)
- Coriander leaves (1 tbsp.)
- Ground flaxseed (1 tsp.)

- Oat flour - optional (2 tbsp.)
- Leeks (.25 cup)

The Dressing:

- Tahini (3 tbsp.)
- Water (5 tbsp.)

- Coriander (1 tsp.)
- Sunflower oil (2 tbsp.)

- Lemon juice (1 lemon)
- Himalayan salt (1 pinch)

Instructions

1. Warm up the oven to 350° Fahrenheit.
2. Finely chop the leeks and coriander leaves. Use a very sharp knife to cut the spaghetti squash in half (lengthways down the center). Discard the seeds and spritz with about half of the oil.
3. Bake for about 40 minutes.
4. Cool to the touch scoop out the insides with a fork, keeping the 'spaghetti' strands intact and toss into a bowl.
5. Add to the squash with the Za'atar, leeks, grated ginger, and ground flaxseed. Combine with the oat flour and chill in the fridge.
6. Prepare the dressing by adding all the fixings, whisking in a mason jar or a glass using a fork.
7. Warm up the remainder of the oil in a skillet. Once it's hot, make the patties and arrange them in the pan.
8. Sear until golden for about two minutes per side.
9. Serve with the tahini dressing and a green salad.

218. Stuffed Sweet Potato

Ingredients

- Medium-sized sweet potatoes (2)
- Red bell pepper (1 cubed)
- Broccoli florets (.66 cup)
- Parsley finely chopped (.33 cup)
- Clove of garlic (1)
- Caraway seeds (.25 tsp.)

- Melted coconut oil (2 tbsp.)
- Lemon juice and zest (1)
- Water (.25 cup)
- Fresh dill (.25 cup)
- Himalayan salt (1 pinch)
- Feta Cheese (.75 oz. - optional)

Instructions

1. Cut the pepper into cubes and the broccoli into florets. Finely chop the parsley. Juice and zest the lemon.
2. Heat up the oven to reach 350° Fahrenheit.
3. Drizzle the sweet potato with one tbsp. of the oil and a sprinkle of salt. Bake for 50 minutes.
4. Open the potato and scoop out the 'flesh' into a bowl. Try not to rip the outer layer.

5. Warm up the remainder of the oil with the grated garlic and caraway seeds. Sauté for 1 minute.

6. Add half of the water and add the broccoli florets, bell pepper, and parsley. Sauté for another two minutes.

7. Pour in the juice of the lemon and the flesh of the sweet potato. Mix together for two minutes.

8. Add the lemon zest, rest of the water, and chopped fresh dill. Sprinkle with the salt.

9. Stuff the loaded fixings back into the potato skins.

10. Top it off with a serving with a sprinkle of herbs, sprouts, herbs, or feta.

219. Sweet Potato Veggie Biryani - Vegan

Ingredients

- Oil (1 tbsp.)
- Cloves of garlic (2)
- Red pepper (1)
- Sweet potatoes (2)
- Onion (1)
- Cauliflower (.5 of 1)
- Paprika (1 tsp.)
- Cumin (2 tsp.)
- Coriander (2 tsp.)

- Turmeric (.5 tsp.)
- Ground ginger (1 tsp.)
- Cinnamon (.5 tsp.)
- Basmati rice (.75 cup)
- Vegetable stock (4 cups)
- Passata (1 container)
- Chickpeas (1 can - drained)
- Spinach leaves (2 large handfuls)
- Black pepper (to your liking)

Instructions

Warm the oven in advance to 400° Fahrenheit.

1. Chop the onions and garlic. Slice the red peppers.

2. Cut the cauliflower into small florets. Peel and dice the potatoes.

3. Empty the oil into a large ovenproof casserole dish. Put it into the oven for a few minutes to warm it up. Add the veggies and spices. Mix well to coat and roast for 10 minutes.

4. Combine the rice into the vegetables. Pour in the stock and add the seasoning.

5. Lower the oven temperature to 360° Fahrenheit.

6. Cover with a layer of foil.

7. Bake until the liquid has been absorbed (20 min.). The rice will be tender at that point.

8. Stir in the chickpeas, the passata, and spinach. Bake for an additional ten minutes.

9. Top it off with a portion of yogurt drizzled over the top if you wish before serving.

220. Tofu Chili Burger

Ingredients

- Firm tofu (2 cups)
- Green bell pepper (2 cups)
- Onions (.5 cup)
- Organic chili sauce (6 tsp.)
- Sea salt or organic salt (.5 tsp.)
- Olive oil (2 tsp.)
- Pepper (as desired)

Instructions

1. Chop the tofu, bell pepper, and the onions into small pieces.
2. Pour oil in a pan and stir-fry the onions and bell pepper for around five minutes. Fold in the tofu pieces. Stir-fry for another 15 minutes.
3. Pour in the chili sauce, salt, and the pepper. Mix well.
4. Add water as needed.
5. Serve when ready.

221. Wild Mushrooms & Spelt Pasta

Ingredients

- Cauliflower florets (12 oz. or 4-5 cups)
- Raw cashews (.5 cup)
- Chopped garlic (2 cloves)
- Wild mushrooms (2 oz.)
- Fresh mushrooms (4 oz.)
- Spelt pasta (.75 lb.)
- Finely minced chives (.25 cup)
- Nutritional yeast (2 tbsp.)
- Lemon wedges
- Smoked paprika (2 tsp.)
- Black pepper (.5 tsp.)
- Sea salt (1 tsp.)
- Olive oil (or vegetable broth if oil-free (2 tbsp.

Instructions

1. Soak the cashews and mushrooms (individually) in alkaline water to soften (30 min.). Drain and rinse well. Slice them into small pieces.
2. Warm up half of the oil in a large skillet.
3. Once it's *hot*, toss in the cauliflower. Stir-fry for three to five minutes.
4. Pour in the rest of the oil, pushing the cauliflower aside.
5. Toss in the mushrooms and sauté until they're reduced in size by half and combine with the cauliflower. Transfer from the burner and keep warm.
6. In a high-powered blender, add .5 cup of alkaline water, the drained cashews, smoked paprika, garlic, nutritional yeast, pepper, and salt. Whisk well until very creamy.
7. Empty the sauce over the cauliflower-mushroom mixture. Stir and cover until the pasta is ready.
8. Prepare the pasta in salted water. Combine and serve with a portion of chives and lemon wedges.

QUICK & EASY

RECIPES

222. Apple - Ginger & Carrot Soup - Vegan Style

Ingredients

- Carrots (1 lb.)
- Apple (large)
- Vegetable broth - low-sodium preferred (4 cups)
- Raw cashews (.5 cup)
- Ginger root (1 tbsp.)
- Unsweetened almond milk (1 tbsp.)
- Fine sea salt (as desired)

Instructions

1. Soak the cashews covered with alkaline water for at least eight hours.
2. Drain the cashews when ready to prepare.
3. Pour in the almond milk and freshly grated ginger root into a food processor, blending until smooth.
4. Peel, dice, and steam the carrots and apples until tender (5 min.).
5. Toss into a soup pot with the vegetable broth. Cool to room temperature.
6. Puree with an immersion blender until creamy.
7. Pour back into the soup pot. Stir in the cashew-ginger mixture with 2 tsp. of salt. Simmer, don't boil and serve while hot.

223. Asparagus & Ginger Broth

Ingredients

- Gluten-Free vegetable bouillon - ex. Marigold brand (3 cups)
- Filtered water (2 cups)
- Bragg Liquid Aminos or gluten-free tamari (1.5 tbsp.)
- Fresh ginger root (1-inch)
- Garlic cloves (2)
- Fresh red chilies (1)
- Asparagus (8 stalks)
- Kale (1 large handful)
- Spring onion(1)
- Fresh coriander (.5 cup)
- Olive oil (as needed)
- Coconut oil (2 tbsp.)
- Cracked black pepper (as desired)
- Himalayan salt (to your liking)

Instructions

1. Peel and grate the ginger. Chop the coriander, asparagus, kale, chili, and onion.
2. Use the medium heat setting to warm the filtered water, coconut oil, vegetable bouillon (stock), and Bragg Liquid Aminos or gluten-free tamari in a pan.
3. Stir in the chopped garlic, chili, and ginger.
4. Simmer for about 3 to 4 minutes.

151

5. Fold in the asparagus, kale, coriander, and spring onion.

6. Simmer for another 3 to 4 minutes and serve.

224. Beef Bone Broth - Crock Pot

Ingredients

- Cold water (18-20 cups)
- Beef bones & Marrow (4 lb.)
- Celery stalks (4)
- Carrots (4)
- Onions (2 medium)
- Garlic cloves (4)
- Whole peppercorns (1 tsp.)
- Kosher salt (1 tsp.)
- Bay leaves (2)
- Fresh thyme (3 sprigs)
- Fresh parsley (5-6 sprigs)
- Apple cider vinegar (.25 cup)
- *Also Needed:* 10-quart capacity crock pot

Instructions

1. Peel the onions and slice into quarters. Dice the garlic (peel on). Chop the celery and carrots. Pour in the water and toss each of the fixings into the cooker.

2. Wait for it to boil using the high-temperature setting. Lower the setting and gently simmer. Occasionally, scoop the fat that will rise to the surface. Simmer for 24 to 48 hours.

3. When it's ready, remove from the pot and cool slightly.

4. Strain the soup through a colander and trash the solids.

5. Cool until it's room temperature. Store in the fridge when cooled.

6. Use within seven days or freeze up to three months.

225. Black Bean & Tomato Soup

Ingredients

- Dry beans (2 lb.)
- Tomatoes (6-8)
- Medium onions (2)
- Olive oil (.5 cup)
- Cloves of garlic (2)
- Sea salt (to taste)
- Medium carrots (2)
- Bay leaves (2)
- Oregano (1 tsp.)
- Cayenne pepper (1 tsp.)
- Fresh cilantro (.5 cup)

Instructions

1. Dice the tomatoes, garlic, onions, and carrots.

2. Rinse and drain the beans. Cook until tender.

3. Warm up the oil and combine each of the fixings into the pan.

4. Add water to reach the desired consistency. Don't boil.

5. Serve while it's hot.

226. Broccoli - Mint & Ginger Soup

Ingredients

- Rough-crushed broccoli (1 large head or approx. 1.5 cups)
- Brown onion (1 small)
- Garlic (2 cloves)
- Fresh mint (.5 of 1 bunch)
- Cucumber (.5 of 1)
- Fresh root ginger (.5-inch grated)
- Organic vegetable stock (2 cups)
- Himalayan salt & Black pepper (as desired)
- Coconut or avocado oil (1 tbsp.)

Instructions

1. Mince the garlic and onion. Prepare a frying pan with oil and sauté for two to three minutes, and add the chopped broccoli.

2. Sauté for another one to two minutes.

3. Grate the ginger, and roughly chop the mint. Toss in and stir.

4. Pour in the stock to cover the broccoli, saving the remainder for blending to achieve the desired consistency.

5. Let this simmer for three to four minutes until the broccoli *just* starts to soften.

6. Roughly chop the cucumber. Transfer everything to a blender, adding the spinach and raw cucumber. Blend on the high-speed setting until everything is creamy smooth.

7. Pour in additional stock to get the consistency you like.

8. Serve with a sprig of mint atop each bowl with a drizzle of avocado or olive oil.

227. Cauliflower Soup

Ingredients

- Grapeseed or olive oil (2 tbsp.)
- Minced garlic (2 cloves)
- Sliced leeks - white parts only or Diced yellow onion (2 cups)
- Celtic sea salt (1 tsp. or more as desired)
- Cauliflower (1 large head)
- Vegetable broth (7 cups)
- Blanched slivered almonds or raw unsalted cashews (.25 cup)
- *For Serving*: Chopped chives (3 tbsp.)

Instructions

1. Warm up the oil using the medium heat temperature setting.

2. Saute the leeks, garlic, and .25 teaspoon of salt until the veggies are soft (3 min.).

3. Fold in the roughly chopped cauliflower. Continue to simmer for an additional minute.

4. Stir in the vegetable broth. Raise the temperature setting to high.

5. Once the water starts to bubble, lower the temperature setting to medium.

6. Simmer for 20 to 30 minutes or until the cauliflower is tender.

7. Take the pan from the burner and wait for the soup to cool slightly.

8. Stir in the nuts.

9. Pour the soup into a blender in batches if needed. Pulse using the high setting until creamy smooth (1 min.)

10. Return the soup back into the saucepan using the low heat setting. Stir in salt as desired. Simmer.

11. Ladle the soup into serving bowls. Top it off with either chopped chives or grated nutmeg.

228. Chicken Bone Broth

Ingredients

- Chicken necks/feet/wings (4 lb.)
- Carrots (3 chopped)
- Celery stalks (3 chopped)
- Onions (2 medium - peel on - sliced in half lengthwise & quartered)
- Garlic cloves (4 - peel on & smashed)
- Himalayan salt (1 tsp.)
- Whole peppercorns (1 tsp.)

- Apple cider vinegar (3 tbsp.)
- Parsley (5–6 sprigs)
- Bay leaves (2)
- Oregano (1 tsp.)
- Fresh thyme (3 sprigs)
- Cold water (18–20 cups)
- *Also Needed*: 10-quart slow cooker

Instructions

Toss all of the fixings into the slow cooker. Pour in the water.

1. Simmer for 24 - 48 hours. Skim away the fat occasionally.

2. Cool slightly.

3. Trash the solid parts and strain the rest through a colander into a container.

4. Cool the broth to reach room temperature, cover, and chill.

5. It will be good for up to a week. For longer shelf life of the broth, up to three months, just store in the freezer.

229. Curried Sweet Potato Soup

Ingredients

- Coconut oil (1 tbsp.)
- Ginger (.5-inch chunk)
- Cloves of garlic (4)
- Lime (1)
- Curry (2 tsp.)
- Sweet potatoes (3)
- Full-fat coconut milk (15 oz. can)
- Filtered water (2 cups)
- Chopped cilantro (.5 of 1 bunch)

Instructions

1. Warm up the coconut oil in a large saucepan using the medium temperature setting.
2. Zest and juice the lime. Slice the potatoes into 1-inch pieces with the peel on or off.
3. Slice and crush the ginger and mince the garlic and lime zest. Cook about three to four minutes.
4. Stir in the curry and simmer about one minute.
5. Fold in the sweet potatoes, water, and coconut milk. Let the mixture boil. Lower the temperature setting to low and simmer for 25 minutes.
6. Place a lid on the cooker. Extinguish the heat and leave on the stovetop for about 30 minutes for the flavors to meld.
7. Prepare the soup in a blender.
8. Top it off with the cilantro and lime juice.

230. Minestrone Specialty

Ingredients

- Eggplant - aubergine (.5 cup)
- Sweet potato (.5 cup)
- Zucchini - courgette (.5 cup)
- Carrot (.5 cup)
- Red onion(.25 cup)
- Cloves of garlic (2)
- Beans - kidney, navy, etc. (.5 cup)
- Coconut oil (1 tbsp.)
- Vegetable stock (1 cup)
- Basil (1 handful)
- Tomato juice - fresh or bought (1 cup)
- Himalayan salt & black pepper (to your liking)

Instructions

1. Wash and cube the eggplant, potato, and zucchini. Dice the carrot and onion.
2. Prepare a large pot. Gently saute the fixings in the coconut oil for about two minutes.
3. Stir in the beans, stock, and tomato juice. Once it's boiling, lower the temperature to simmer for 8 to 10 minutes.
4. Sprinkle with the basil and serve. Season how you like it.

231. Potato & Chickpea Curry

Ingredients

- Olive oil - for cooking
- Sweet potatoes (4 medium)
- Diced tomatoes (1 can)
- Cooked chickpeas (1 cup)
- Onion (1)
- Chili pepper (.5 of 1 or to taste)
- Cumin seeds (1 tsp.)
- Large garlic cloves (3)
- Turmeric powder (1 tsp.)
- Salt (.5 tsp.)
- Garam masala (1 tsp.)
- Bay leaves (3)
- Yellow mustard seeds (1 tsp.)
- Full-fat coconut milk (1 can)
- Fresh spring onions for garnishing

Instructions

1. Finely chop the pepper. Heat a large pan using the medium heat temperature setting. Pour in a portion of olive oil. Toss in the cumin and mustard seeds after the pan is hot. Fry the spices for 3 to 4 minutes or so.

2. Dice the onion and toss into the pan.

3. Finely chop the garlic and add to the pan. Saute for about five minutes.

4. Pour in the canned tomatoes. Stir in the remainder of the spices – whole bay leaves, chopped chili pepper, garam masala, turmeric, and salt. Saute for three minutes.

5. Peel the skin from the potatoes and dice into bite-size chunks. Toss into the pan. Stir well until they're evenly coated with the tomatoes.

6. Lastly, pour in the coconut milk. Cook for approximately 15 minutes.

7. Fold in the chickpeas. Stir well and simmer for an additional 18 to 20 minutes. The potatoes will be fork-tender when ready.

8. Extinguish the heat source. Let the curry to stay in the pan for about ten more minutes to thicken up.

9. Top it off with a serving of fresh spring onions.

232. Turmeric & Lentil Anti-Inflammatory Soup

Ingredients

- Pumpkin (200 grams - approximately .875 or 7/8 cup)
- Carrots (4)
- Sweet red potato (1)
- Tomatoes (4)
- Garlic (3 cloves)
- Mustard seeds (1 tsp.)
- Red onion (1)
- Vegetable stock (1.25 cups)

- Coconut cream (200 ml or .85 cup)
- Fresh coriander/cilantro (1 handful)
- Fresh turmeric root (1-inch)
- Red pepper (.5 of 1)
- Fresh ginger root (1-inch)
- Lentils (1 cup)
- Coconut oil (as needed)

Optional Toppings:

- Cashews (.5 cup)
- Pumpkin seeds (2 tbsp.)
- Clove of garlic (1 minced)
- Thinly sliced red chili

Instructions

1. Chop the tomatoes, red onion, coriander/cilantro, garlic, peeled ginger, and turmeric - roughly peeled).

2. Heat a portion of the coconut oil in a pan. Toss in the onion and saute one minute. Stir in the mustard seeds, ginger, turmeric, and garlic.

3. Stir in the root veggies (pumpkin, carrot, sweet potato), tomatoes and red pepper. Coat the veggies in the oil.

4. Pour in the lentils and stock. Lower the temperature setting to simmer until the veggies soften and the lentils cook.

5. Once everything has softened, fold in the coconut cream and chopped cilantro. Transfer to a blender and blend until smooth.

6. Prepare the optional topping. Mash the cashews on a chopping board. Cook with the pumpkin seeds and coconut oil with the minced garlic.

7. Serve the soup in bowls with, a drizzle of coconut cream, a sprig of cilantro, and the cashew topping with optional chili.

8. *Note*: If you're using dried lentils, you will need to add an additional .25 cup of the stock (allowing an additional 10 mins cooking time).

233. Vegetable Soup

Ingredients

- Brown onion (1)
- Garlic (2 cloves)
- Carrots (2)
- Cauliflower (.25 of 1 head)
- Broccoli (.25 of 1 head)
- Cabbage - any green variety (.25 of 1 head)
- Vegetable stock (1 cup)
- Organic chopped tomatoes (1 can or 8 fresh tomatoes or as desired)
- Himalayan pink salt & Black pepper
- Turmeric root (.5-inch root or 1 tsp. dried)
- Ginger root (.5-inch root or 1 tsp. dried)
- Coconut oil

Ingredients - Raw:

- Cucumber (.5 of 1)
- Tomatoes (3)
- Spinach (1 handful)
- Basil (.5 of 1 bunch)
- Coriander (.25 of 1 bunch)
- Chickpeas - garbanzos (.5 to 1 can as desired)

Instructions

1. Roughly chop the cabbage. Dice the carrots, garlic, and onions. Chop the tomatoes. Prepare the broccoli and cauliflower florets.
2. Saute the garlic and onions in a portion of coconut oil. After three minutes, toss in the cauliflower, carrots, cabbage, and broccoli. Simmer for another three minutes.
3. Pour in the stock and tomatoes/can of tomatoes. Simmer for 20 to 25 minutes until the veggies are softened.
4. Toss the raw foods into a blender and pulse until smooth.
5. After the soup has simmered for about 20 minutes, transfer it in batches and blend it all together until creamy smooth. It may take a couple of batches into the blender.
6. Serve with a sprig of coriander or basil and enjoy warm.

234. Asparagus & Celery Seed

Ingredients

- Asparagus (.5 to 1 bunch)
- Ground celery seed (.5 tsp)
- Ground clove (.5 tsp)
- Cinnamon (.25 tsp)
- Raw honey (.25 cup)
- Bragg's Liquid Amino (1 tbsp.)
- Cold-pressed oil ex. olive (.25 cup)
- Alkaline water (.25 cup)

Instructions

1. Wash the asparagus, and cut away the ends. Place in a shallow dish.
2. Combine the rest of the fixings in a blender.
3. Cover with this mixture and chill in the fridge for about 24 hours.
4. Serve and enjoy as a side dish.

235. Baked Beans

Ingredients

- Organic butter beans (1 cup)
- White onion (.25 of 1)
- Garlic cloves (1)
- 100% organic tomato paste (2 tbsp.)
- Dry mustard powder (1 tsp.)
- Coconut oil (1 tsp.)

- Cherry tomatoes (.5 cup)
- Cracked pepper & Sea salt (as desired)
- Smoked paprika (.5 tsp.)
- Liquid stevia (1 drop)
- Fresh baby spinach (1 cup)
- Avocado (.25 cup)

Instructions

1. Wash and drain the beans
2. Warm up a frying pan with the oil using the low-medium heat setting.
3. Dice and sauté the garlic and onion until softened. Slice the tomatoes into halves. Fold in the cherry tomatoes, butter beans, and tomato paste. Simmer for three minutes.
4. Add all the seasonings including the stevia and continue cooking for another three minutes.
5. Serve with spinach and sliced avocado.

236. Cauliflower Mashed Potatoes

Ingredients

- Coconut oil (2 tsp.)
- Cloves garlic (3)
- Onion (1)
- Cauliflower (1 head)
- Carrot (1)
- Vegetable broth - yeast free (.25 cup)
- Garlic powder (1 tsp.)
- Rosemary (2 tsp.)
- Parsley (2 tsp.)
- Black pepper & Sea salt - Redmond Real Salt or Himalayan (as desired)

Instructions

1. Chop the veggies.
2. Warm up the coconut oil in a large pot.
3. Toss in the garlic and onion. Sauté for about five minutes.
4. Fold in the carrots, cauliflower, and vegetable broth.
5. After it's boiling, reduce the temperature setting to low-medium.
6. Simmer for 10 minutes. Add more veggie broth if needed.
7. Combine and add the rosemary, garlic powder, salt, pepper, and parsley.
8. Use an immersion blender or a food processor to mash the cauliflower. Serve.

237. Roasted Root Veggies

Ingredients

- Pumpkin seeds (.25 cup)
- A mixture of the following root vegetables: Parsnips, radishes, turnips, carrots, beets, sweet potatoes (1-2 lbs. total)
- Coconut oil (2 tbsp.)

- Sea salt - Celtic Grey or Himalayan (as desired)

Instructions

1. Warm the oven to reach 425° Fahrenheit.
2. Dice the veggies into small pieces.
3. Toss with the salt and coconut oil.
4. Roast until lightly browned in spots and tender (30 to 40 minutes).
5. Toss the pumpkin seeds with coconut oil and sea salt.
6. Roast with the vegetables for the last few minutes before serving

238. Roasted Sweet Potato Salad with Chutney Vinaigrette

Ingredients

- Olive oil (3 tbsp.)
- Sweet potatoes (3)
- Salt (1 tsp.)
- Ground ginger (1 tsp.)
- Cumin (1 tsp.)
- Mango chutney (2 tbsp.)
- Dijon mustard (1 tbsp.)
- Garlic clove (1 tsp.)
- Balsamic vinegar (3 tbsp.)
- Olive oil (2 tbsp.)
- Scallions (1 cup)
- Toasted sliced almonds (.5 cup)
- Dried cranberries (.5 cup)

Instructions

1. Warm up the oven to reach 425° Fahrenheit.
2. Cover a large baking tin with a sheet of aluminum foil.
3. Use a sharp knife to peel and dice the potatoes into one-inch cubes. Mince the garlic and chop the scallions.
4. Scoop up the potatoes and mix with the olive oil, cumin, ginger, and salt onto the baking sheet.
5. Roast until the potatoes are tender (approx. 30 min.). Stir occasionally for even roasting.
6. Whisk the garlic, with the mustard, chutney, vinegar, and olive oil in a bowl.
7. Transfer the potatoes to the stovetop to cool slightly (approximately ten min.).
8. Toss the potatoes with the dressing mixture.
9. Serve with a garnish of the almond; either hot or at room temperature.

239. Sesame Ginger Shiitake Cauliflower Rice

Ingredients

- Cauliflower (1 large head)
- Toasted sesame oil (2 tbsp.)
- Grapeseed oil (2 tbsp.)
- Green chile - ribbed (1 small)

- Minced fresh ginger (2 tbsp.)
- Minced garlic cloves (4 tsp.)
- Green onions - white and green parts
- Shiitake mushrooms (4 cups)
- Wheat-free tamari (2 tbsp.)
- Cilantro (1 bunch or to your liking)
- Fresh lime juice (2 tsp.)
- Celtic sea salt (.5 tsp.)

Instructions

1. Remove the seeds and mince the chile, mince the garlic and ginger, and finely chop the rest of the veggies.
2. Squeeze the lime for juice.
3. Prepare the cauliflower rice. Roughly chop the cauliflower into florets. Discard the leaves and the tough middle core. Throw the cauliflower pieces into a food processor fitted with the 'S' blade.
4. Pulse a few seconds until the cauliflower is the consistency of rice (5 to 6 cups of cauliflower "rice").
5. Pour the oil into a deep skillet or wok. Heat the oil using the med-high temperature setting.
6. Saute the ginger, chile, green onions, garlic, and mushrooms with .25 teaspoon of salt for about 5 minutes or until softened.
7. Throw in the cauliflower rice and tamari. Sauté for another 5 minutes or until softened.
8. Stir in the lime juice, cilantro, and remaining salt. Tweak the flavors to taste.

240. Spinach & Chickpea Medley

Ingredients

- Olive oil (3 tbsp.)
- Garlic (4 cloves)
- Onion - thinly sliced (1 large)
- Grated ginger (1 tbsp.)
- Grape tomatoes (.5 of a 1-pint container)
- Lemon (1 large)
- Crushed red pepper flakes (1 tsp.)
- Chickpeas - ex. Eden Organic (1 large can or to your liking)
- Sea salt - to taste (Himalayan - Celtic Grey or Redmond Real Salt)

Instructions

1. Pour the oil to a large skillet.
2. Rinse and drain the beans.
3. Dice and toss in the onion. Sauté approximately five minutes or until they start browning.
4. Zest and juice the lemon. Toss in the grated ginger, minced garlic, tomatoes, lemon zest, and red pepper flakes. Sauté for about 3 to 4 minutes.
5. Fold in the chickpeas. Cook for another 3 to 4 minutes.

6. Toss in the spinach, and wait for it to wilt. Spritz with the lemon juice and sea salt.

7. Cook for an additional 2 minutes and serve.

241. Spinach & Tomatoes - Mac & Cheese

Ingredients

- Macaroni pasta (4 cups)
- Vegan spread (.33 cup)
- Plain flour (.33 cup)
- Plant milk (2 cups)
- Vegan cheese (1.5 cups)
- Cherry tomatoes (.5 cup)
- Spinach (Couple of handfuls)
- White onion (1 large)
- Optional: Nutritional yeast (2 tbsp.)
- Salt and pepper (as desired)
- Oil: Frying the onion

Instructions

1. Warm the oven in advance to 360° Fahrenheit.

2. Finely chop the onion.

3. Rinse the spinach. Wash and slice the tomatoes into halves.

4. Pour water into a pot and add to salt. Wait for it to boil.

5. Prepare the macaroni for 8 minutes on a low boil. Drain and rinse under the cold tap to prevent further cooking, set aside.

6. In a saucepan melt your vegan spread.

7. Once melted, add in the flour to form a smooth paste.

8. Simmer for two minutes, whisking as you go.

9. Pour in small portions of the milk.

10. Heat gently and continue to whisk, after approximately three to five minutes.

11. Season with salt and pepper as desired after the sauce has thickened.

12. Add in 3/4 of your grated cheese. Stir well until melted. Stir in the creme fraiche.

13. Sauté the onions until crispy. Add into the cheese sauce and save a few to sprinkle on top.

14. Combine the spinach and pasta into the cheese sauce. Pour into a large ovenproof dish.

15. Scatter the halved cherry tomatoes, nutritional yeast and remaining grated cheese over the top. Sprinkle with a dusting of pepper and a touch more salt.

16. Prepare in the heated oven for approximately 20 to 25 minutes.

17. Serve immediately while piping hot.

242. Summer Coleslaw

Ingredients

- Napa cabbage (1 cup)
- Red cabbage (1 cup)
- Red pepper thinly sliced (1)
- Carrots julienne sliced (1.5)

- Bok choy sliced (1 cup)
- Chives (1 small bunch)
- Raw sesame seeds and lightly toasted - if desired (1.5 tbsp.)

The Dressing:

- Bragg's liquid amino (1 tbsp.)
- Extra-virgin olive oil (1 tbsp.)
- Celtic sea salt (as desired)
- Fresh lemon juice (.25 cup)

- Toasted sesame oil (.5 tbsp.)
- Grated ginger (1 tsp.)
- Raw sesame tahini (1 tsp.)

Instructions

1. Finely slice the cabbage, peppers, bok choy (with some green parts and mostly white), and carrots. Chop the chives into 1-inch pieces.
2. Combine all of the veggies in a large bowl.
3. Whisk and pour the dressing fixings into a measuring cup.
4. Serve with the dressing over all these vegetables
5. Serve immediately.

243. Almond Flour Pineapple Upside down Cake - Vegan & Gluten-Free

Ingredients

- Unsweetened almond milk (.25 cup)
- Pineapple - canned preferred (9 slices)
- Optional: Maraschino cherries
- Flax eggs (2) - (2 tbsp. Golden Flaxseed Meal + 5 tbsp. filtered water)
- Almond flour (1.75 cups)
- Tapioca flour (.5 cup)

- Unrefined coconut sugar (.5 cup)
- Baking powder (1 tsp.)
- Pineapple juice (.25 cup)
- Unsweetened almond milk yogurt (.33 cup)
- *Also Needed*: 9-inch cake pan & parchment paper or coconut oil

Instructions

1. Set the oven temperature setting at 350° Fahrenheit.
2. Prepare the baking pan.
3. Arrange the pineapple slices along the bottom, using the cherries in the gaps. Place it to the side for now.

4. Prepare the cake batter. Mix the flax eggs in a mixing container and gel for five minutes.

5. Add in the pineapple juice, almond milk, coconut sugar, and yogurt.

6. Whisk until just combined.

7. Sift in the tapioca flour, almond flour, and baking powder.

8. Pour over the slices of pineapple. Smooth down with the back of a spatula.

9. Bake for 45-55 minutes. Cool in the pan for approximately ten minutes. Invert onto a cake stand or plate. Remove the cake pan.

10. Slice and serve.

244. Chocolate Chip Banana Bread

Ingredients

- Ground flaxseed (1 tbsp.)
- Warm water (2.5 tbsp.)
- Unsweetened almond milk (.75 cup)
- Mashed banana (1.5 cups)
- Melted coconut oil (3 tbsp.)
- Vanilla extract (1 tsp.)
- Liquid stevia (.5 tsp.)
- Baking powder (1 tbsp.)
- Ground cinnamon (.75 tsp.)
- Almond flour (1.5 cups)
- White rice flour (.75 cup)
- Tapioca starch (.25 cup)
- Old-fashioned oats (1 cup)
- Dairy-free chocolate chips (.5 cup)
- *Also Needed*: Regular-size loaf pan

Instructions

1. Warm up the oven to reach 350°Fahrenheit.

2. Grease a regular-sized loaf pan with cooking spray.

3. Whisk the flaxseed and water in a small bowl. Let it rest for 5 minutes.

4. Combine the bananas and milk in a large mixing container with the vanilla, oil, and stevia.

5. Stir until combined. Fold in the cinnamon, baking powder, and salt.

6. In another container, stir together the tapioca starch, almond flour, rice flour, and oats.

7. Combine everything and fold in the nuts, adding the chocolate chips last.

8. Pour the batter in the greased loaf pan.

9. Bake your bread for 1 hour to 1.25 hours until the center is set.

10. Cool before slicing.

245. German Chocolate Cake

Dry Recipe Ingredients

- Pre-sifted organic whole wheat flour (1.75 cups)
- Baking powder (1 tsp.)
- Fine grain salt (.5 tsp.)
- Baking Soda (2 tsp.)
- Cocoa powder (.25 cup)

Wet Recipe Ingredients

- Apple cider vinegar (1 tsp.)
- Coconut milk (1 cup)
- Freshly brewed coffee (1 cup)
- Coconut sugar (1.25 cups)
- Melted coconut oil (.5 cup)
- Eggs - room temperature (2 large)
- Molasses (1 tbsp.)

Recipe Ingredients - The Frosting:

- Pitted dates (1 cup)
- Coconut milk (1 cup)
- Molasses (1 tsp.)
- Coconut oil (.5 cup)
- Shredded coconut - unsweetened (2 cups)
- Pecans - optional (1 cup)

Instructions

1. Warm up the oven to 350° Fahrenheit.
2. Coat two 9-inch round baking pans liberally with coconut oil.
3. Dust with cocoa powder.
4. Sift whole wheat flour to make 1.75 cups of pre-sifted flour.
5. Sift or whisk each of the dry fixings.
6. In another container, mix together the wet ingredients until the sugar is completely dissolved.
7. Use a whisk to mix all of the fixings together well, or use a mixer on low speed to blend for 30 seconds.
8. Scoop the cake batter into the prepared pans.
9. Bake for 20 minutes.
10. *Note:* Depending upon your oven and where you live, the baking time may vary.
11. *Instructions for The Frosting:* Use a small cup blender to prepare the dates, molasses, coconut milk, and coconut oil until smooth.
12. Warm these in a small sauce pot to melt the oil and dates together.
13. Stir in shredded coconut and pecans (if using).

246. Gluten-Free Zucchini Muffins

Ingredients

- Shredded zucchini (2 cups)
- Buckwheat flour (2.5 cups)
- White rice flour (2 cups)
- Baking powder (1 tbsp.)
- Baking soda (1 tbsp.)
- Ground cinnamon (.5 tsp.)
- Unsweetened almond milk (1.5 cups)
- Coconut sugar or brown sugar or stevia or maple syrup (.25 cup)
- Coconut oil (6 tbsp.)
- Bananas - peeled and mashed (3 medium)

Instructions

1. Spread the zucchini out on a clean towel then roll it up.
2. Wring out as much moisture from the zucchini as you can and then set it aside.
3. Warm up the oven to 355° Fahrenheit.
4. Prepare the muffin tins with liners.
5. Whisk the buckwheat flour, baking powder, rice flour, baking soda, and cinnamon.
6. Combine and blend the rest of the fixings except for the zucchini in a food processor. Add the dry ingredients.
7. Once the mixture is smooth and well combined, fold in your grated zucchini.
8. Spoon the muffin batter into your prepared pan.
9. Fill each muffin cup about ¾ full.
10. Bake for 18 to 20 minutes until done.
11. Cool your muffins for approximately five minutes in the pan. Arrange on a wire rack to cool the rest of the way.

247. Marble Cake - Vegan

Ingredients

- Wheat flour or light spelled flour (2.33 cups)
- Sugar (1 cup)
- Water (1.25 cups)
- Baking powder (1 tbsp.)
- Tasteless vegetable oil - sunflower oil or grape seed oil (.5 cup)
- Cocoa powder (2.75 tbsp.)

Instructions

1. Warm up the oven to reach 355° Fahrenheit.
2. Grease the mold for the cake and dust with flour.
3. Sift the sugar, flour, and baking powder.

4. Stir in the oil and water with the whisk. Continue stirring until a lump-free dough is formed.

5. Pour 3/4 of the dough mixture into the baking pan.

6. Mix the remaining dough with the cocoa powder. Pour the resulting chocolate on the light layer. Pull with a fork through the dough to mix it - making it's marbled appearance.

7. Bake the cake for about 50 minutes.

8. Cool completely. Carefully topple out the beautiful cake out of the mold.

248. Orange & Almond Cake

Ingredients

- Eggs (6)
- Rice syrup or agave nectar (7 oz.)
- Zest of oranges (3 large)
- Ground almonds (1.75 oz.)
- *For The Syrup:*
- Orange juice (3 large)
- Rice syrup (3 tbsp.)

- *For The Cream:*
- Blanched almonds (8 oz.)
- Vanilla seeds (from .5 of 1 vanilla pod)
- Vanilla extract (.5 tsp.)
- Rice syrup (1 tsp.)

Instructions

Set the oven to 350° Fahrenheit.

1. Grease and line a 9-inch springform cake tin.

2. Separate the eggs and beat the yolks well with the rice syrup.

3. Combine and add in the orange zest and ground almonds.

4. Whisk the whites of the eggs to form stiff peaks. Gently fold into the mix.

5. Bake in the middle of the oven for 50 minutes.

6. While it's baking, warm up the syrup fixings. Boil to prepare a thick sauce.

7. Prick the cake and pour over the syrup while the cake is still warm. Let it cool thoroughly.

8. Make the blanched almonds. Toss the almonds in a blender with 8 ounces of water. Mix until smooth.

9. Toss in the vanilla seeds, extract, and rice syrup. Blend well.

10. Serve the cake with the almond cream on the side as an option.

249. Pumpkin Bread

Ingredients

- Water (3.5 to 5 tbsp.)
- Pumpkin (1 small)

- Baking powder (2 tsp.)
- GF flour (2.5 cups)

- Italian seasoning (1 tsp.)
- Oil -Hemp or flax (2 tbsp.)

Instructions

1. Warm up the oven in advance to 392° Fahrenheit.
2. Arrange the entire pumpkin in a baking pan.
3. Bake for a minimum of 40 to 50 minutes. The pumpkin will become softened.
4. Cool for 30 minutes. Discard the skin, seeds, and stalk.
5. Mash the pumpkin well and combine with the remaining fixings.
6. Place the pumpkin onto a floured surface.
7. Knead until the mixture becomes sponge-like. If it's too sticky, just add a little more water.
8. Shape the mixture into a circular loaf shape. Arrange on a lightly oiled baking tray. Make a pattern in the top of the loaf such as a cross.
9. Bake until done or for 30 to 40 minutes.

250. Alkaline Electric Banana Cream Pie

Ingredients - Pie Mixture:

- Baby bananas (6-8)
- Agave (3 - 4 tbsp.)
- Creamed coconut (7 oz.)
- Sea salt (.125 tsp.)
- Hemp milk (1 cup)

Crust

- Pitted dates (1.5 cups)
- Agave (.25 cup)
- TastyUnsweetened coconut flakes (1.5 cups)
- Sea salt (.25 tsp.)

Also Needed

- Food processor
- Hand or stand mixer
- Springform pan or pie dish

Instructions

1. Place each of the crust fixings into a food processor. Pulse for 20 to 30 seconds or until a ball is formed.
2. Line the springform pan with a sheet of parchment paper. Spread out the crust mixture evenly.
3. Thinly slice the bananas and arrange around the inside of the springform pan. Stick it in the freezer.
4. Add the pie mixture fixings. Blend until well combined.
5. Pour the pie mixture into the pan. Lightly shake the batter for an even texture.
6. Cover with a sheet of aluminum foil. Let it set in the freezer for three to four hours.
7. Flip the pie from the pan, top with coconut flakes and serve.

251. Live Apple Pie

Ingredients

- Ground raw walnuts (1 cup)
- Pitted dates (1 cup)
- Raw sunflower seeds (.5 cup)
- Shredded apples - any variety (4 cups)
- Cinnamon (2.5 tsp.)
- Fresh apple juice (.5 cup)
- Shredded coconut for garnishing (.5 cup)
- Raisins - dried figs or prunes - your choice (.66 cup)

Instructions

1. Soak the dates in alkaline water for 15 minutes.

2. Soak the sunflower seeds for 20 minutes; drain and rinse.

3. Prepare the food processor. Gather the fixings and add in the sunflower seeds, walnuts, dates and about two-thirds of the shredded coconut. Blend until fully incorporated.

4. Prepare the pie crust. Press the mixture into the pie plate and set aside for now.

5. Grate the apples using the processor or box grater. Add to a mixing container and pour in the apple juice with the cinnamon and figs, prunes, or raisins. Mix thoroughly to form your apple pie filling.

6. Load the pie crust with the apple filling. Sprinkle the completed pie with more shredded coconut.

7. Serve or refrigerate for later. It is best when eaten within two days.

252. Raw Pumpkin Pie

Ingredients - Pie Crust:

- Raw almonds (1 cup)
- Cinnamon (1 tsp.)
- Dates (1 cup)
- Coconut flakes - unsweetened (1 cup)

Pie Filling

- Organic pumpkin puree (12 oz.)
- Pecans (1 cup)
- Dates (6)
- Cinnamon (.5 tsp.)
- Nutmeg (.5 tsp.)
- Himalayan sea salt (.25 tsp.)
- Vanilla (1 tsp.)
- Optional: Gluten-free tamari (1 tsp.)
- *Also Needed:* Pie pan or 9-inch tart pan & Food processor

Instructions

The Crust

1. Use a food processor to prepare the pie crust. Blend the pie crust fixings until you see the oils

coming out of the mixture (food process 1-2 min.).

2. Pour the mixture into the chosen pan. Push it firmly against the sides, then the base of the mold to make it stick tightly.

Pie Filling

1. In a blender, mix the pie fixings.

2. Pour the mixture to fill in the pie crust.

3. Sprinkle cinnamon on top.

4. Store in the fridge to cool and set.

253. Almond Butter Fudge Squares

Ingredients

- Almond butter (1.5 cups)
- Raw cacao powder (.5 cup)
- Maple syrup (.5 cup)
- Almond milk - unsweetened (.25 cup)
- Almond extract (1 tsp.)
- Melted coconut oil (3 tbsp.)
- Roasted - unsalted almonds (.5 cup)
- *Also Needed*: 8x8 pan & lined with parchment paper

Instructions

1. Finely chop the almonds and set to the side.

2. Toss all of the fixings in a food processor (omit the almonds).

3. Process until the dough is formed. Shape into the paper-lined baking pan.

4. Evenly sprinkle the chopped almonds over the surface and securely cover with a layer of aluminum foil. Place it into the freezer for at least one hour.

5. Take it out and slice into individual portions.

6. Place the pieces close but not touching in rows on a large piece of baking paper.

7. Start at the shortest end of the paper. Roll the paper carefully into a "tube" shape. Freeze the roll in a freezer bag for at least an hour.

8. When you're ready; just unroll the paper and place the squares on a chilled plate.

9. Serve and enjoy frozen or just cold.

254. Chocolate Mousse - Vegan

Ingredients

- Soft tofu (14 oz.)
- Vegan 70% cacao - dark chocolate (6 oz.)
- Vanilla extract (1 tsp.)
- Maple syrup (3 tbsp.)
- Almond milk (4 tbsp.)
- *Also Needed:* Food Processor or blender

Instructions

1. Let the tofu become room temperature and drain well in towels.

2. Melt the chocolate in the microwave or double-boiler. Cool slightly.

3. Add all the fixings into a food processor. Blend until very smooth.

4. Chill for one hour (minimum).

5. Serve in individual glasses topped with a portion of fresh raspberries and cream.

255. Oven-Crisp Fish Tacos

Ingredients

- 5 (1 to 1-1/2 pounds) fish fillets (I prefer wild caught Flounder or Tilapia), cut into 2 inch wide strips (3 or 4 strips per fillet)
- ¼ cup white whole wheat flour
- 2 egg whites
- ¼ cup cornmeal
- ¼ cup whole wheat bread crumbs
- 2 tablespoons freshly squeezed lime juice (1 medium sized lime)
- 2 tablespoons Taco Seasoning, recipe for homemade Taco Seasoning
- 8 (6 inch) corn tortillas or 8 (6 inch) whole wheat flour tortillas
- 1 cup shredded lettuce or cabbage
- 1 cup salsa (no sugar added) or, 1 medium tomato, diced
- 1 cup non-fat Greek-style yogurt, optional non-fat sour cream

Instructions

1. Preheat the oven to 450 degrees F.

2. Line a baking sheet with foil. Place a cooling rack on top of the baking sheet and spray with olive oil or canola oil cooking spray.

3. Combine breadcrumbs, cornmeal and taco seasoning together in a shallow bowl.

4. In a separate shallow bowl, whisk the egg whites and lime juice until frothy.

5. Place flour in a shallow bowl.

6. Dip the fish strips gently into the flour to lightly coat on both sides. Dip into the egg whites and allow excess to drip off, then press the fish pieces on both sides into the seasoned cornmeal and breadcrumbs.

7. Place the breaded fish strips on the prepared rack and cook for 10 to 12 minutes, until the outside is golden crisp and the fish is opaque and flakes easily with a fork.

8. Coat a saute pan or griddle with cooking spray. Warm the tortillas over medium heat, for 30 seconds to 1 minute per side, until warmed through. Keep tortillas warm in a clean kitchen towel until ready to serve.

9. Place 2 strips of the fish into each tortilla, top with shredded romaine, salsa or tomato, and top with yogurt

256. Turkey Burrito Skillet

Ingredients

- 1 pound ground turkey
- 1 tablespoon chili powder
- 1 teaspoon ground cumin
- 1 tablespoon lime juice
- 1/2 teaspoon Kosher salt
- 1/4 teaspoon ground black pepper
- 1/4 cup water

- 1 cup no-sugar added chunky salsa
- 1 cup low-fat cheddar cheese
- 1/2 cup plain Greek yogurt
- 1 (15 ounce) can black beans, rinsed and drained
- 4 (6 inch) whole wheat flour tortillas, cut into 1 inch strips
- 1/4 cup fresh cilantro, chopped

Instructions

1. In a large skillet, cook the ground turkey until cooked through, breaking up the turkey into small pieces as it cooks. Stir in the chili powder, cumin, lime juice, salt, pepper, water, salsa, and beans. Bring to a boil and reduce to a simmer. Simmer for 3 to 5 minute, or until the sauce thickens.

2. Remove from the heat and stir in tortilla strips and top with shredded cheese. Cover until cheese has melted. Top each serving with Greek yogurt and fresh cilantro. Serve and enjoy!

257. Baked Lemon Salmon and Asparagus Foil Pack

Ingredients

- 4 (4 to 6 ounce) filets salmon
- 1 pound fresh asparagus, about 1 inch of bottom ends trimmed off
- 1 teaspoon Kosher salt
- 1/2 teaspoon ground black pepper

- 2 tablespoons olive oil
- 1/4 cup fresh lemon juice
- 1 tablespoon fresh thyme, chopped
- 2 tablespoons fresh parsley, chopped
- 2 tablespoons lemon zest

Instructions

1. Preheat the oven to 400 degrees.

2. Lay 4 large sheets of foil on a flat surface and spray with nonstick spray. Divide the asparagus between each of the packets and lay in a single layer side by side. Season with half the salt and pepper.

3. Place a salmon filet on top of each bed of asparagus. Drizzle with olive oil, lemon juice, thyme, and the remaining salt and pepper. Carefully fold up each side of the foil sheets to create a packet around the salmon and place in a single layer on a baking sheet. Bake for 15 minutes.

4. Remove from the oven and carefully open each packet, be cautious of the steam released once opened! Sprinkle lemon zest and parsley on top. Serve and enjoy!

5. Option: Try this recipe on the grill instead of in the oven for extra flavor!

258. Chicken and Broccoli Stir Fry

Ingredients

- 2 teaspoons sesame seeds
- 3 tablespoons light soy sauce, optional Tamari
- 1 tablespoon honey
- 2 teaspoons lemon
- 2 tablespoons sesame oil
- 1 tablespoon cornstarch or flour
- 1 tablespoon extra-virgin olive oil

- 1.25 pounds chicken breast filets, cubed
- 1 medium onion, coarsely chopped
- 1 (1-inch) ginger root, peeled and finely chopped
- 2 cups broccoli florets
- 1/4 teaspoon black pepper

Instructions

1. Whisk together soy sauce, honey, lemon juice, sesame oil, and cornstarch. Set mixture aside.

2. Over medium-low heat in a large skillet or wok, toast sesame seeds for 2 minutes, or until fragrant. Place toasted seeds in a bowl and set aside.

3. Add olive oil to the same skillet, turn to medium heat and cook chicken until lightly golden. Add onions, ginger, broccoli, and pepper. sauté for 4 minutes. Reduce heat to medium-low, add soy sauce mixture and toss to combine. Cook until sauce is desired thickness, but no more than 5 minutes. Sprinkle with toasted sesame seeds and serve. Enjoy!

259. 4-Ingredient Protein Pancakes

Ingredients

- 1/2 cup mashed banana
- 3 egg whites

- 1/4 teaspoon baking powder
- 1 scoop vanilla protein powder

Instructions

1. Combine all Ingredients in a mixing bowl until smooth

2. Lightly spray a skillet with non-stick spray and heat on medium heat. Pour about 1/4 cup of the batter into the pan. Cook about 3 to 4 minutes, or until pancakes begin to bubble in the center. Carefully flip and cook for another 2 to 3 minutes. Once cooked, remove pancake from the pan and repeat the process until all the batter has been used. Spray the skillet as needed with non-stick spray in-between cooking the pancakes.

3. Top with fresh fruit, honey, or your favorite nut butter! Enjoy!

260. Wild Cod with Moroccan Couscous

Ingredients

- 1/2 cup chicken broth, fat free, low sodium
- 1 (14.5 ounce) can diced tomatoes with green chilies
- 1 tablespoon plus 2 teaspoons extra-virgin olive oil
- 3/4 cup Moroccan couscous, (optional whole wheat couscous)
- Kosher or sea salt to taste
- Black pepper to taste
- 4 (4 ounce) wild caught cod fillets, thawed
- 1 tablespoon freshly squeezed lemon juice

Instructions

1. In medium pot add chicken broth, 2 teaspoons extra-virgin olive oil, and diced tomatoes with juice. Turn to medium-high heat and bring to a boil, add couscous, add salt and pepper. Stir, cover saucepan and remove from heat. Allow couscous to stand while preparing cod.

2. Season cod with sea salt and black pepper. Add 1 tablespoon oil to a large non-stick skillet, turn to medium-high and cook until filets flake with a fork, about 2-3 minutes on each side. Remove from heat and serve with couscous. Drizzle lemon juice over fillets.

261. Honey Garlic Shrimp Stir Fry

Ingredients

- 1 tablespoon coconut oil
- 1 pound raw shrimp, peeled and deveined
- 2 cloves garlic, minced
- 1 tablespoon fresh ginger, minced
- 1 small yellow onion, cut into thin strips
- 2 cups brown rice, cooked
- 1 small red bell pepper, cut into thin strips
- 1 cup peas
- 1/2 teaspoon kosher salt
- 2 tablespoons honey
- 1 tablespoon soy sauce
- 1 tablespoon orange zest

Instructions

1. In a large skillet on high heat, heat the coconut oil. Once hot, add the shrimp, half the garlic, and half the ginger. Cook, stirring constantly, just in the the shrimp are firm. Remove the shrimp and set aside.

2. In the same pan the shrimp was cooked in, add the onion, bell pepper, snap peas, and the remaining garlic and ginger. Cook, stirring constantly, on high heat just until the vegetables begin to soften.

3. Return the shrimp to the pan, season with the salt and stir in the honey, soy sauce, and orange zest. Cook until all ingredients are coated in the sauce and hot. Serve over the brown rice and enjoy!

262. Ham and Egg Breakfast Cups

Ingredients

- 12 thin slices all-natural and low-sodium ham
- 3 eggs
- 3 egg whites
- 1/2 cup skim milk
- 2 green onions, chopped

Instructions

1. Preheat oven to 350.

2. Lightly spray a muffin tin with non-stick spray. Press each ham slice into the muffin pan, creating a cup shape.

3. In a mixing bowl, whisk together the egg, egg whites, and milk. Stir in the green onion and pour into the ham cups until about 3/4 full. Bake until eggs are completely set, about 20 minutes. Remove and allow to cool slightly before serving.

4. Enjoy!

263. Sweet Potato and Turkey Skillet

Ingredients

- 1 tablespoon Extra-virgin olive oil
- 1 medium onion, minced
- 1 teaspoon cumin
- 1 pound lean ground turkey
- 2 medium sweet potatoes, diced in small cubes
- 2 fresh sage leaves, roughly chopped
- 1/2 teaspoon kosher or sea salt
- 1/4 teaspoon pepper
- 1/2 cup part-skim mozzarella cheese, grated

Instructions

1. Over medium-low heat, in a large saucepan with extra virgin olive oil sautè the onion until tender, about 4 minutes. Add the turkey, break up with a fork, and cook it is no longer pink. Drain off any fat. Add the sweet potatoes, cumin, sage, salt and pepper. Stir and cook until potatoes are tender but not falling apart, approximately 5 - 10 minutes.

2. When the sweet potatoes are tender, sprinkle the mozzarella on top, cover then turn off the heat.

3. Wait until the cheese melts before serving

264. Savory Lemon White Fish Fillets

Ingredients

- 4 (4 to 6 ounces) cod, halibut, or flounder
- 3 tablespoons olive oil, divided
- 1/4 teaspoon kosher or sea salt
- 1/4 teaspoon freshly ground black pepper
- 2 lemons, one cut in halves, one cut in wedges

Instructions

1. Allow the fish to sit in a bowl at room temperature for 10- 15 minutes.

2. Rub one tablespoon olive oil and sprinkle salt and pepper on both sides of each fillet. Place a skillet or sauté pan over medium-heat and add two tablespoons olive oil. When the oil is hot and shimmering, but not smoking, after about one minute, add the fish. Cook for two to three minutes on each side, so that each side is browned and the fish is cooked through.

3. Squeeze both lemon halves over the fish and remove from the heat. If there is any lemon juice left in the pan, pour it over the fish to serve. Serve with lemon wedges.

Tip: Make this into a meal by tossing arugula, baby kale, or other lettuce greens in lemon juice, olive oil, salt and pepper and having as a side salad.

RECIPES

YOU CAN TRUST

---

265. No-Bake Oatmeal Raisin Energy Bites

Ingredients

- 1 cup dry oats
- 1/4 cup peanut butter
- 2 tablespoons honey
- 1/4 cup semi-sweet mini chocolate chips
- 1/4 cup raisins
- 1/4 cup peanuts, chopped
- 1/2 teaspoon ground cinnamon
- 1 scoop vanilla protein powder

Instructions

1. Combine all ingredients and mix very well until the mixture is well blended and sticky.
2. Roll into 1 inch balls and place on a parchment lined baking sheet. Place in the refrigerator for about 30 minutes or until firm. Store covered and refrigerated in an air tight container.

266. Cucumber Quinoa Salad with Ground Turkey, Olives, Feta

Ingredients

- 1/2 pound ground turkey sausage
- 3 large cucumber, sliced into 1/4 inch half circles
- 1 small red onion, sliced thin
- 1 cup grape tomatoes, sliced in half
- 1/2 cup kalamata olives
- 1/2 cup fat free feta cheese crumbles
- 1 1/2 cup quinoa, cooked
- 2 tablespoons fresh mint, chopped
- 2 cloves garlic, minced
- 1 tablespoon fresh oregano, chopped
- 1 tablespoon lemon juice

Instructions

1. In a large skillet, cooked the turkey sausage. Break the sausage into small pieces as it cooks. Drain off any excess liquid and cool completely.
2. Once the turkey sausage is cool, combine the sausage with remaining ingredients. Mix well and chill before serving. Enjoy!

267. Skinny Salmon, Kale, and Cashew Bowl

Ingredients

- 12 ounces skinless salmon
- 2 tablespoons olive oil
- 1/2 teaspoon Kosher salt
- 1/4 teaspoon ground black pepper
- 2 cloves garlic, minced
- 4 cups kale, stems removed and chopped
- 1/2 cup shredded carrot
- 2 cups quinoa, cooked according to package
- 1/4 cup cashews, chopped

- Optional Lemon Yogurt Sauce:
- 3/4 cup Greek yogurt
- 1 teaspoon lemon juice
- 1 clove garlic, finely grated or minced
- 1/2 teaspoon lemon zest
- 1/4 teaspoon Kosher salt

Instructions

1. Preheat oven to 400 degrees, line a baking sheet with parchment paper. Place the salmon fillets on to the sheet. Brush the salmon with 1 tablespoon of the oil (reserve the second tablespoon for later) and season with salt and pepper. Bake for 15 minutes until firm and flaky.

2. Meanwhile, heat the remaining oil in a skillet. Once hot, add the garlic, kale, and carrot. Cook, stirring often, until the kale is wilted and soft. Add the quinoa and cashews. Cook, stirring, just until hot.

3. Spoon the kale and quinoa mixture into a serving bowl. Remove the salmon from the oven and place on top of the kale. Serve and enjoy.

4. Optional Yogurt Sauce:

268. Baked Chicken and Vegetable Spring Rolls

Ingredients

- 3 tablespoons extra virgin olive oil, divided
- 1 garlic clove, finely chopped
- 1 small onion, finely chopped
- 4 ounces chicken fillet, diced small
- 1 cup carrots, julienned
- 1 cup string beans or flat beans, ends taken away and sliced diagonally
- 1 cup cabbage, julienned
- 3 tablespoons low salt soy sauce
- 1/4 teaspoon salt
- 1/4 teaspoon ground pepper
- 8 spring rolls wrappers or 4 phyllo (filo) pastry sheets (layer 2 sheets at a time and cut into 4 squares with kitchen scissors)

Instructions

1. Preheat the oven to 400 degrees F.

2. Over medium heat, in a large saucepan with 2 tablespoons of extra virgin olive oil, sautè the garlic and onion for 1 minute.

3. Add the chicken and sautè for about 5 minutes.

4. Add all the vegetables then sautè them for about 15 minutes.

5. Add the soy sauce, salt and pepper then toss for 1 minute. Set aside.

6. Make the rolls by laying 2 squares of filo (1 square can easily break) or 1 spring roll wrapper on the working area. Spoon some sautèed chicken and vegetables at the part closer to you.

Roll, tuck in the sides then keep on rolling until the end. Wet your fingertips with water then dab the ends of the filo lightly to seal them. Work on the other spring rolls.

7. Line a baking tray with parchment paper and place the spring rolls on it.

8. Brush each spring roll with the remaining 1 tablespoon extra virgin olive oil.

9. Bake for 15 - 20 minutes or until they turn golden brown.

10. Serve with sweet and sour sauce or any desired dipping sauce

269. Skinny Turkey Meatloaf

Ingredients

- 1 pound lean ground turkey, recommend 93% lean
- 1 egg, lightly whipped with a fork
- 1/3 cup rolled oats (uncooked)
- 1/3 cup chunky salsa, no-sugar added
- 1/2 cup diced onion
- 1/2 teaspoon black pepper
- 1/4 teaspoon salt
- 1/3 cup ketchup

Instructions

1. Preheat oven to 375 degrees.

2. Combine all Ingredients, except ketchup, in a mixing bowl. Add mixture to a 5 x 7-inch loaf pan, press to foam a loaf. Bake 35 minutes uncovered.

3. Remove pan and evenly spread ketchup over the top. Bake an additional 10 minutes.

4. Allow to rest 5 minutes. Either remove the entire loaf and place on a serving platter, or slice first.

270. Sweet Potato Hash

Ingredients

- 2 large sweet potatoes, peeled and diced small
- 3 tablespoons olive oil
- 1/2 teaspoon kosher salt
- 1/4 teaspoon ground white pepper
- 1 tablespoon apple cider vinegar
- 2 cloves garlic, minced
- 1 teaspoon honey
- 1/4 cup yellow onion, diced small
- 1/4 cup green bell pepper, diced small
- 8 ounces low sodium sulfate free ham, diced small
- 1 tablespoon lemon juice
- 1 avocado, peeled, pit removed, and diced small

Instructions

1. Preheat oven to 450 degrees. Line a baking sheet with foil.

2. Toss the diced sweet potatoes, 1/2 tablespoon of the olive oil, salt, and pepper together and spread in an even layer on the baking sheet. Bake for about 15 minutes or until the potatoes are tender and just beginning to brown.

3. Meanwhile, combine the apple cider vinegar, garlic and honey in a small bowl. While whisking continuously, add 1 tablespoon of olive oil. Whisk until well combined. Set aside.

4. In a large skillet on medium heat, heat the remaining olive oil. Once hot, add the onion and green pepper. Cook just until the onions begin to soften and add the ham and cooked potatoes. Continue to cook until the ham begins to brown. Remove from heat and stir in the apple cider vinegar sauce.

5. Combine the lemon juice and avocado. Gently stir into the hash. Serve hot!

OPTIONAL TIP: Top with a poached egg for extra protein and a full meal!

271. Spicy Black Bean and Shrimp Salad

Ingredients

- 1/2 pound large raw shrimp, peeled and deveined
- 1/4 teaspoon crushed red pepper
- 1 teaspoon chili powder
- 1 teaspoon smoked paprika
- 1 teaspoon ground cumin
- 1/2 teaspoon Kosher salt
- 2 tablespoons olive oil
- 1 cup corn kernels
- 1/4 cup red onion, diced small

- 1 tablespoon lime juice
- 1 (15 ounce) can black beans, drained and rinsed
- 2 cups kale, shredded or finely chopped
- 2 cup romaine lettuce, shredded or finely chopped
- 1 cup grape tomatoes, cut in half
- 1 avocado, peeled and pit removed and sliced
- 2 tablespoons fresh cilantro, chopped

Instructions

1. In a small bowl, combine the shrimp, red pepper, chili powder, paprika, cumin, and salt. Toss well to coat the shrimp in the seasonings.

2. Heat 1 tablespoon of the olive oil in a large skillet. Once hot, add the seasoned shrimp. Cook, about 5 to 6 minutes, until pink and firm. Remove the shrimp from the skillet and keep hot.

3. Add the remaining tablespoon of olive oil to the pan the shrimp was just cooked in. Heat on high heat and once hot add the corn and onion. Cook, about 5 minutes, until the corn begins to char and the onions are soft. Stir in the lime juice, black beans, and cooked shrimp. Cook just until the beans are hot.

4. In a large salad bowl, toss together the kale and romaine. Top with the shrimp mixture, tomato, and avocado. Sprinkle the cilantro on top and serve

272. Turkey Sausage with Pepper and Onions

Ingredients

- 1 pound turkey rope sausage, cut into thick half moons
- 1/2 tablespoon olive oil
- 1 cup sliced green pepper
- 1 cup sliced yellow pepper
- 1 cup sliced red onion

Instructions

1. In a large skillet on medium high heat, add all the ingredients. Cook until peppers and onions just begin to soften and stir often.

2. Serve with a side such as quinoa or brown rice. Enjoy!

273. Chia pudding

Ingredients

- 1/2 cup Quaker Oats rolled oats
- 1/4 cup chia seeds
- 1 cup milk or water
- pinch of salt and cinnamon
- maple syrup or other sweetener to taste
- 1 cup frozen berries of choice (or yesterday's smoothie leftovers)
- yogurt for topping
- berries for topping

Instructions

1. Place the oats, seeds, milk, salt, and cinnamon in a jar with a lid. Refrigerate overnight.

2. Puree the berries. (I usually incorporate this into my smoothie routine, so I either use leftover smoothie or just blend up a huge smoothie batch so I have a little extra for the oats. You don't HAVE to do this, but it's a nice way to add some fruit and color.)

3. Stir oats with your frozen berry puree and top with yogurt and more berries, nuts, honey and whatevs you like.

274. Chinese chicken salad

Ingredients

For the dressing

- 1 teaspoon minced garlic
- 1/4 cup reduced-sodium soy sauce
- 2 tablespoons rice vinegar
- 1 1/2 tablespoons honey
- Pinch of ground ginger

For the salad

- 1 cup cooked chicken breast, chopped or shredded
- 1 cup shelled edamame beans, cooked according to package Directions and cooled
- 2 medium bell peppers, diced
- 1 cup shredded carrots
- 4 cups tricolor coleslaw mix
- 1/2 cup chopped cilantro
- 3 green onions, chopped, optional
- 1/4 cup toasted almonds, optional
- 1 tablespoon sesame seeds, optional

Instructions

1. Mix the garlic, soy sauce, rice vinegar, honey, and ginger in a small bowl to make the dressing.
2. Place the chicken, edamame, bell peppers, carrots, and coleslaw mix in a large bowl. Toss to combine.
3. Add the dressing to the salad, and combine until the salad is fully coated. Add the cilantro, and mix again.
4. Sprinkle the green onions, toasted almonds, and sesame seeds on top, if desired.
5. Serve immediately, or let it chill for the best taste possible

275. Spicy chicken chili

Ingredients

- 1 tablespoon canola oil
- 1 cup chopped red onion
- 1 cup chopped green pepper
- 2 cloves garlic, finely chopped
- 2 jalapeños, thinly sliced
- 1-1/2 pounds ground chicken
- 1/4 cup chili powder
- 2 cups canned crushed tomatoes
- 1 tablespoon chicken stock
- 1 tablespoon brown sugar
- 1 tablespoon apple cider vinegar
- 1 tablespoon hot sauce
- 1 tablespoon salt
- 2 cans dark red kidney beans, drained
- To garnish: (optional)
- Cilantro

Instructions

1. In a large Dutch oven, heat canola oil over high heat. Add onion, pepper, jalapeños and garlic. Cook over medium heat until the onion is tender (about five minutes.)
2. Add chicken — cook, stirring to break up lumps until the chicken loses its pink color (about five minutes). Stir in chili powder, and cook one minute.

3. Stir in tomatoes, broth, sugar, vinegar, hot sauce, and salt. Reduce heat to low; cover and simmer, stirring often until the chili is thickened (about 45 minutes.)

4. Stir in beans, cook until heated through, about 15 minutes. Uncover for the last 15 minutes of cooking.

5. Top with garnish of your choice, and enjoy!

276. Chip protein shake

Ingredients

- 3/4 cup nonfat Greek yogurt
- 1/4 cup fresh mint, tightly packed
- 1 cup almond milk
- 1/4 cup dark chocolate chips
- 1 cup baby spinach
- 1 tablespoon maple syrup
- 2 cups ice

Instructions

Blend all the ingredients together until smooth, and enjoy.

277. Vegan chickpea salad

Ingredients

For the dressing:

- 3 tablespoons tahini
- 1 1/2 tablespoons extra-virgin olive oil
- 2 tablespoons pure maple syrup
- 2 tablespoons water
- Juice of half a lemon
- 2 teaspoons apple cider vinegar
- 1 tablespoon curry powder
- 1 teaspoon turmeric
- Freshly ground black pepper
- For the salad:
- 2 15-ounce cans chickpeas, drained and rinsed
- 1/2 cup green onions, chopped
- 1/2 cup cilantro, chopped
- 1 bell pepper, chopped
- 1/2 cup raisins
- 1/2 cup
- cashews, chopped
- 1/2 teaspoon salt

Instructions

1. Whisk together all dressing Ingredients in a small bowl. I blended mine in my Nutribullet.

2. Place salad ingredients in a large bowl. Add dressing and toss to combine

184

278. Mexican tempeh quinoa salad

Ingredients

- 1 cup quinoa
- 2 cups water
- 1 tablespoon olive oil
- 1/2 onion, chopped
- 1 red pepper, diced
- 1 (8-oz.) package tempeh, diced into bite-size pieces
- 1 cup salsa
- Juice from one lime
- 1 teaspoon cumin
- 1/4 teaspoon salt
- 1/4 teaspoon pepper
- 1 (15-oz.) can black beans, drained and rinsed
- 1 cup fresh corn (or frozen)
- 1/2 cup cherry tomatoes, halved
- 2 tablespoons fresh cilantro
- Salt and pepper, to taste
- 1 avocado, diced
- 1/4 teaspoon cayenne pepper

Instructions

1. Place the quinoa and water in a covered pot on high heat. Once it starts to boil, reduce to simmer and cook for 20 minutes or until the water is absorbed and the quinoa is fluffy.

2. While the quinoa is cooking, prepare the tempeh. Heat the oil in a pan on medium heat, and add the chopped onion. Cook for 5 minutes.

3. Add the diced red pepper, tempeh, salsa, lime juice, cumin, cayenne pepper, and salt and pepper.

4. Cook the tempeh mixture, stirring occasionally, for about 15 minutes.

5. Once the quinoa and tempeh are cooked, pour both into a glass bowl and mix together. Add the beans, corn, tomatoes, cilantro, and a little salt and pepper, and mix well. Serve and top with a few pieces of diced avocado.

6. Enjoy as is, or use as a delicious filling for burritos.

279. Vegan vanilla protein shake

Ingredients

- 1/2 cup soft tofu
- 1 cup vanilla soy milk
- 1 frozen banana
- 1/2 Tablespoon Peanut Butter

Instructions

Place everything in a blender and mix until smooth, about one minute. Enjoy!

280. Tuna salad pita sandwiches

Ingredients

- 2 whole-wheat pitas
- 1 can tuna canned in water without salt
- Lemon juice from 2 wedges
- 2 tsps olive oil
- 1/2 small onion diced (purple or red onion adds color)
- 1/2 cup diced red bell pepper
- 1 tbsp chopped parsley
- Salt and pepper

Instructions

1. Open can of tuna, drain it, and place in a bowl.
2. Stir in lemon juice and olive oil.
3. Add bell pepper, onion, and parsley.
4. Salt and pepper to taste.
5. Pop into the pita and eat!

281. Asian fried "rice"

Ingredients

- 3 slices bacon, crosscut into 1/4-inch pieces
- 1 medium cauliflower head, cut into uniform pieces
- Kosher salt & 2 large eggs
- Freshly ground black pepper
- 2 tablespoons ghee (or fat of choice)
- 1 small yellow onion, minced
- 4 ounces cremini mushrooms, thinly sliced
- 1 (1-inch) piece fresh ginger, peeled and finely grated (about 1 tablespoon)
- 2 tablespoons coconut aminos
- 1 teaspoon coconut vinegar
- 1 teaspoon Paleo-friendly fish sauce (I used Red Boat Fish Sauce)
- 2 scallions, thinly sliced
- 2 tablespoons chopped cilantro

Instructions

1. Cook the bacon in a large skillet over medium heat, stirring occasionally. Once it crisps up, about 15 minutes, transfer the crunchy bacon to a paper-towel-lined plate with a slotted spoon.
2. While you're crisping the bacon, toss the cauliflower into a food processor, and pulse until it's the size of rice grains. Pro tip: don't overdo it. We don't want liquid cauliflower.
3. In a small bowl, whisk the eggs together with salt and pepper to taste. Pour the eggs in the hot bacon drippings, and fry up a thin egg omelet. Remove the omelet from the pan, slice it into ribbons, and set aside.

4. Melt the ghee in the same skillet of medium-high heat, and add the onions along with a sprinkle of kosher salt and pepper. Once the onions are soft and translucent, about 5 minutes, throw in the sliced mushrooms. When the mushrooms are browned, add the grated ginger and stir for 30 seconds to incorporate.

5. Add the cauliflower "rice," season with a bit more salt and pepper, and mix the ingredients together. Place a lid on the skillet, turn the heat down to low, and cook for about 5 minutes with the skillet covered. The "rice" is ready when it's tender but not mushy.

6. Season with the coconut aminos, coconut vinegar, and fish sauce. Before serving, mix in the scallions, cilantro, omelet sliced, and reserved crispy bacon.

282. Egg muffins

Ingredients

- 3 cups kale, de-stemmed and chopped into thin ribbons

- 1/4 small onion, diced, or 4 green onions, finely sliced

- 2 tablespoons fresh cilantro, minced

- 1 jalapeño, very finely diced (de-seed and remove the white parts to decrease spice)

- 1 tablespoon dried oregano

- 11 egg whites (I use a small carton of organic, free-range liquid egg whites. You can also just use 12 whole eggs if you don't like egg whites)

- 7 whole eggs

- Salt and pepper

Instructions

1. Preheat oven to 375°F. Spray a muffin tin with cooking spray and line it with muffin liners (optional).

2. In a medium microwave-safe bowl, steam prepped kale in the microwave for 2–3 minutes until soft and wilted. Place in a large bowl and set aside.

3. In that same microwave-safe bowl, add diced onions and microwave for about 1 minute. This helps take away some of the strong, raw oniony taste. Add onions to the bowl with the kale.

4. Add cilantro, oregano, jalapeño, salt, and pepper to the same onion/kale mix. Stir to combine. Set aside for now.

5. In a separate large bowl, whisk together whole eggs, egg whites, salt, and pepper. You want the mixture to ribbon off the whisk and be fully scrambled.

6. Distribute the veggie mixture evenly between your 12 muffin cups.

7. Distribute egg mixture evenly between the cups, pouring over the veggie mix. I usually use a 1/3-cup measuring cup to do the job.

8. Bake for about 30 minutes until the muffins are golden brown and puffed up.

9. Let cool in pan for a few minutes and then remove to a cooling rack. Try to remove them to a rack as soon as you can safely do so, while keeping the muffins intact. If they sit in the pan too long, they continue to steam, and the texture can get rubbery.

10. Store in your fridge and reheat in a counter-top oven or microwave.

283. Broccoli slaw salad

Ingredients

- 1/2 cup plain yogurt
- 1 teaspoon lemon juice
- 1 tablespoon apple cider vinegar
- 2 tablespoons blue cheese crumbles
- 2 cups broccoli slaw (I used Trader Joe's)
- 2 ounces chicken breast, grilled or baked
- 1 teaspoon sliced green onions

Instructions

1. Combine yogurt, lemon juice, apple cider vinegar, and blue cheese crumbles in a small bowl. Mix well.

2. In another bowl, add the broccoli slaw, then pour in your dressing, and mix well until all the slaw is coated evenly.

3. Top off your slaw with the chicken breast, and sprinkle green onions on top. Enjoy!

284. Lemon garlic chicken drumsticks

Ingredients

- Kosher salt
- Pepper, freshly cracked
- 10-16 skin-on chicken drumsticks
- 1 tablespoon olive oil
- 4 tablespoons butter
- 3 garlic cloves, finely chopped
- Zest of 1 lemon, plus 1 tablespoon lemon juice
- 2 tablespoons parsley, chopped

Instructions

1. Generously season the drumsticks with salt and pepper, and let sit at room temperature for 30 minutes, time permitting. Pat the drumsticks dry with paper towels just before cooking.

2. Heat a 12-inch, heavy-bottomed skillet (preferably not nonstick) over medium-high heat. If you don't have a large enough skillet, use two smaller skillets. Add the oil and half the butter. When the butter is foaming, brown the drumsticks on all sides in batches; transfer the browned drumsticks to a plate.

3. Reduce the heat to medium-low, add all the drumsticks back to the skillet(s), cover with the lid, and cook for 20-25 minutes, rearranging the drumsticks every 5-10 minutes for even cooking. Remove the lid and add the remaining butter, garlic, lemon zest, and lemon juice. Gently toss

to coat the drumsticks. Take the skillet off the heat and leave the flavors to infuse for a few minutes (this also allows the chicken to rest). Sprinkle with parsley, and serve hot.

285. 50-calorie chocolate coconut protein balls

Ingredients

- 1 cup raw almonds
- 1 cup golden raisins
- 1 1/2 scoops chocolate plant-based protein powder (1 scoop is about 35 grams; I used Vega)
- 1/8 teaspoon sea salt
- 2 tablespoons unsweetened shredded coconut

Instructions

1. Add almonds to a food processor or high-speed blender. Process nuts a few minutes until a creamy almond butter forms.
2. Add raisins and mix until smooth.
3. Add in the protein powder and salt; blend until thoroughly combined.
4. Roll dough into 24 balls, coat each ball with shredded coconut, and place on a plate or pan.
5. Enjoy immediately, or if you like a firmer consistency, refrigerate for at least 20 minutes. Store uneaten balls in an airtight container.

286. Taco salad

Ingredients

- 1 tablespoon olive oil
- 1/2 jalapeño, seeded and thinly sliced
- 1 clove of garlic, minced
- 1/2 pound of ground beef
- 3/4 teaspoon plus 1/2 teaspoon cumin
- 1/2 teaspoon chili powder
- 3/4 teaspoon plus 1/2 teaspoon salt
- 1/2 teaspoon plus 1/4 teaspoon black pepper
- 1/2 cup canned black beans, rinsed
- 3/4 cup cotija cheese, crumbled
- 3 radishes, thinly sliced
- 2 green onions, thinly sliced
- 1 cup tortilla chips, crumbled
- 1 cup cherry tomatoes, halved
- 5 tablespoons extra-virgin olive oil
- 3 tablespoons minced cilantro
- 1 head of red leaf lettuce and 1 large lime, juiced

Instructions

1. Heat the olive oil in a large sauté pan. Add the jalapeños and garlic and cook for about a minute.
2. Add the ground beef, 3/4 teaspoon cumin, chili powder, 3/4 teaspoon salt, and 1/2 teaspoon pepper. Stir to break up the ground beef and cook through, about 10 minutes. Set aside.

3. Wash and dry the lettuce. Tear apart. Distribute to two large bowls. Evenly arrange the beans, cheese, radishes, green onions, tomatoes, and tortilla chips. Split the ground beef mixture between the two bowls.

4. In another small bowl, combine 1/2 teaspoon cumin, 1/2 teaspoon salt, 1/4 teaspoon black pepper, and minced cilantro. Add the lime juice and olive oil. Whisk together.

5. Pour dressing evenly over salads and toss together.

287. Thai citrus chicken salad

Ingredients

For the salad:

- 1 chicken breast, about 7 to 8 ounces, cubed
- 1 clove garlic, minced
- 1 1/2 cup Napa cabbage, shredded
- 1 cup red cabbage, shredded
- Salt
- Pepper

- 1 cup papaya, cut into matchsticks
- 1 cup carrots, shredded
- 1/2 cup daikon, shredded
- 1/4 cup green onion, minced
- 1/4 cup cilantro, chopped
- 1 tablespoon olive oil
- 1/2 lime, cut into wedges

For the dressing:

- 1 tablespoon fresh lime juice
- 1 tablespoon soy sauce
- 1 tablespoon fish sauce
- 1 teaspoon rice vinegar

- 1 teaspoon sugar
- 1/2 teaspoon olive oil
- 2 cloves garlic, minced
- 1/2 to 1 jalepeno, or to taste

Instructions

1. Sprinkle cubed chicken breast with salt and pepper, and add minced garlic. Set aside for a few minutes.

2. Over medium-high heat, heat a skillet or pan and add olive oil.

3. When oil is hot, add chicken breast and cook, turning occasionally to brown on both sides. Remove when done, about seven minutes. Squeeze juice from a wedge of lime on the chicken, and set aside to cool.

4. In a large bowl, mix together the rest of the salad ingredients (red and Napa cabbage, carrots, papaya, daikon, green onion, and cilantro). Set aside.

5. In a small bowl, combine all salad dressing Ingredients and mix together.

6. Pour dressing into a blender, and blend until emulsified.

7. Add chicken and dressing to salad, and mix to combine. Serve with a lime wedge.

288. Protein smoothie

Ingredients

- 1 cup unsweetened almond milk
- 1 scoop chocolate protein powder of your choice (I used a chocolate whey)
- 1 banana
- 1 cup blackberries

Instructions

1. Combine all Ingredients in blender, and mix until smooth.
2. Enjoy!

289. Avocado chicken salad

Ingredients

For the chicken salad:

- 1/4 avocado
- 2 tablespoons plain yogurt
- 1 teaspoon lemon juice
- 3/4 cup shredded chicken, precooked

For the sandwich:

- 1 whole wheat English muffin
- Handful of lettuce or sunflower sprouts
- 2 slices tomato

Instructions

1. In a small bowl, mash the avocado together with yogurt and lemon juice until completely combined.
2. Add the chicken to the bowl, and mix with a spoon until all the chicken is coated.

Serve your chicken salad on top of a bed of lettuce, or split on top of two English muffins with a tomato slice and sunflower sprouts

290. Mediterranean quinoa salad

Ingredients

For the dressing:

- 3 tablespoons lemon juice
- 2 tablespoons red wine vinegar
- 1/2 tablespoon olive oil
- Pinch of oregano

For the salad:

- 1 cup quinoa, cooked
- 2 cups spinach

- 1 red pepper, diced
- 10 grape tomatoes, halved
- 10 kalamata olives, sliced
- 1/4 cup feta cheese

Instructions

1. Whisk together all the dressing ingredients in a small bowl. Set aside.

2. In a large bowl, combine the quinoa, spinach, and about half of the prepared dressing. Mix well with a wooden spoon.

3. Add the red pepper, tomatoes, olives, and remainder of the dressing to bowl. Mix well.

4. Fold in the feta, and either refrigerate or enjoy immediately!

291. Paleo breakfast bar

Ingredients

- 1 cup desiccated coconut
- 1/2 cup shelled hemp seeds
- 1/2 cup sesame seeds
- 1/2 cup pumpkin seeds
- 1 1/2 cups mixed nuts, chopped into small chunks (I added cashews, walnuts, almonds & pistachios to a high-powered blender and pulsed for a few seconds)
- 1/2 cup raisins
- 1 tsp ground cinnamon
- 1/2 cup cashew butter, or nut butter of your choice
- 4 tbsp maple syrup or date paste
- 1 tsp vanilla extract

Instructions

1. Preheat the oven to 180C/ 350F and line a brownie tin with parchment paper.

2. In a large bowl, combine the coconut, seeds, nuts, raisins and cinnamon.

3. In a large saucepan, melt the cashew butter with the maple syrup on a medium heat. Once it's well combined and smooth, remove from the heat and stir in the vanilla extract.

4. Add the contents of the bowl to the saucepan and mix until everything is well combined. If you need to, you can add a small drop of water to help it stick together.

5. Transfer to the brownie tin and press down as firmly as possible to create a flat, even layer.

6. Bake for approximately 15 minutes until golden brown.

7. Leave to cool completely before cutting into 12 bars. Keep in an air-tight tin for up to a week. Enjoy!

292. Smashed avocado chickpea salad

Ingredients

- 1 ripe avocado
- 1/4 cup tahini or Goddess Salad Dressing
- Juice from 1/2 a lemon (or 1 lemon if you prefer)
- 15-ounce can of chickpeas, rinsed and drained
- 1/2 cucumber, diced
- 2 stalks celery, chopped
- 1 large carrot, chopped
- 2 tablespoons fresh dill
- 3 tablespoons salted sunflower seeds
- Sea salt and pepper, to taste
- 2 English muffins

Instructions

1. Add the avocado, tahini, juice from half a lemon, and chickpeas to a bowl. Using a fork or potato masher, smash these ingredients until coarsely mashed.

2. Add the cucumber, celery, carrot, dill, and sunflower seeds, and mix to combine. Season with salt and pepper.

3. Serve 1/4 of the chickpea mixture on top of half a toasted English muffin, top with four slices of cherry tomatoes, and enjoy

293. Peanut chicken and veggies

Ingredients

For the peanut sauce:

- 1/3 cup creamy peanut butter
- 1 tablespoon sesame oil
- 1 tablespoon freshly squeezed lime juice
- 2 cloves garlic — minced
- 1 tablespoon minced fresh ginger
- 1 tablespoon low-sodium soy sauce
- 2 teaspoons honey
- 5-6 tablespoons water
- 1/2 teaspoon red pepper flakes — plus additional to taste

For the chicken and stir fry veggies:

- 2 cups cooked shredded chicken — about 8 ounces; if your chicken is not yet cooked, try this easy Method for how to cook shredded chicken
- 1 tablespoon extra-virgin olive oil
- 3 cups chopped broccoli florets — about 1 small head or 8 ounces
- 2 large red bell peppers — cut into thin slices
- 2 medium carrots — peeled and cut into thin, 1/8-inch coins

- 1 small bunch green onions — chopped, with white and green parts divided
- 1 cup shelled edamame — I use frozen and thawed
- 2 cloves garlic — minced
- 1 tablespoon minced fresh ginger
- 1 tablespoon low-sodium soy sauce
- Cooked brown rice — quinoa, soba noodles, or brown rice noodles
- For topping: chopped fresh cilantro — chopped peanuts, toasted sesame seeds, additional green onions, additional red pepper flakes

Instructions

1. In a small saucepan over medium heat, whisk together the sauce ingredients: peanut butter, sesame oil, lime juice, garlic, ginger, soy sauce, honey, 5 tablespoons water, and red pepper flakes. Heat and stir until the sauce is smooth and thickens a little. If the sauce is a thicker than you'd like, add a bit more water. Add the chicken, and toss to coat it with the sauce and warm it through. Turn off the heat and cover the saucepan to keep the chicken warm.

2. Meanwhile, heat the olive oil in a large nonstick skillet or wok over medium high. Add the broccoli, bell pepper, carrots, and white and light green parts of the green onions. Cook the vegetables until crisp tender, about 6 to 8 minutes. Add the edamame, garlic, ginger, soy sauce, and the green parts of the green onions. Stir to coat and cook 1 additional minute.

3. To serve, spoon the rice into individual serving bowls. Top with the veggies, peanut chicken, and any other desired toppings. Enjoy hot.

294. Spicy squash and feta frittata with mint yoghurt

Ingredients

- 2 onions, thinly sliced
- 680g/1lb 8oz butternut squash, peeled, very thinly sliced
- 2 garlic cloves, grated
- 5cm/2in fresh root ginger, peeled and finely grated
- 1 tsp ground cumin
- 2 tsp smoked paprika
- ½ tsp ground chilli
- 8 free-range eggs, beaten
- 160g/5¾oz feta, crumbled
- freshly ground black pepper
- For the mint yoghurt
- 25g/1oz fresh mint leaves
- ½ green chilli, roughly chopped
- 1 lime, juice and finely grated zest
- 4 tbsp low-fat plain yoghurt
- ½ tsp sea salt flakes
- 1 tbsp olive oil
- ½ tsp sea salt flakes

Instructions

1. Preheat the oven to 200C/180C Fan/Gas 6.

2. Tip the onions and squash into a roasting tin. Add the garlic, ginger, spices, oil, salt and a pinch of pepper. Mix well and cover tightly with kitchen foil. Bake for 35 minutes.

3. Meanwhile, to make the mint yoghurt, put the mint, chilli, lime juice and zest, yoghurt and salt in a blender and blend well. Set aside.

4. Stir the squash, then pour over the eggs. Scatter over the feta and bake for 20 minutes, or until the eggs are just set in the middle.

5. Cut the frittata into squares and serve hot or at room temperature with the mint yoghurt.

295. Greek yogurt chicken salad sandwich

Ingredients

- 2 cups leftover rotisserie chicken
- 1/2 cup diced red onion
- 1/2 cup diced apple & 8 slices bread
- 1/2 cup grapes, halved
- 1/4 cup dried cranberries
- 1/4 cup slivered almonds
- 1/2 cup plain Greek yogurt
- 1 tablespoon freshly squeezed lemon juice, or more, to taste & 4 leaves Boston bibb lettuce
- 1/2 teaspoon garlic powder
- Kosher salt and freshly ground black pepper

Instructions

1. In a large bowl, combine chicken, red onion, apple, grapes, dried cranberries, sliced almonds, Greek yogurt, lemon juice, garlic powder, salt and pepper, to taste.

2. Serve sandwiches on bread with chicken mixture and lettuce.

296. Spicy chilli con carne with guacamole

Ingredients

For the chilli con carne:

- drizzle olive oil
- 1 large onion, very finely chopped
- 2 garlic cloves, very finely chopped
- 2 bay leaves
- 2 sprigs fresh rosemary, leaves only, very finely chopped
- 2 tsp ground cumin
- 1 red chilli, chopped (optional)
- 1-3 tsp chilli powder, to taste
- 500g/1lb 2oz lean beef mince
- 1 x 400g tin chopped tomatoes
- 1 tbsp clear honey
- 250ml/9fl oz red wine or beef stock
- boiled long-grain rice, to serve
- salt and freshly ground black pepper

For the avocado salsa:

- 1 ripe avocado, skin and stone removed, finely diced
- ½ red onion, finely diced
- ¼ cucumber, finely diced
- ½ lemon, juice only
- handful roughly chopped fresh coriander leaves (optional), plus extra to serve

Instructions

1. For the chilli con carne, heat the oil in a medium frying pan over a low heat.

2. Add the onion and fry for 4-5 minutes, or until it is beginning to soften. Add the garlic and fry for a further 1-2 minutes, stirring regularly. Stir in the bay leaves, rosemary, cumin, chilli (if using) and chilli powder (to taste) until well combined.

3. Increase the heat to high and add the beef mince, breaking it up with a wooden spoon and frying for 4-5 minutes, or until golden-brown throughout.

4. Pour in the tinned tomatoes, honey and red wine (or stock), stir well and bring the mixture to the boil. Reduce the heat until the mixture is simmering and simmer for 25-30 minutes, seasoning, to taste, with salt and freshly ground black pepper, halfway through cooking.

5. Meanwhile, for the avocado salsa, mix the diced avocado, onion and cucumber together in a bowl until well combined. Season, to taste, with salt and freshly ground black pepper and a squeeze of lemon juice. Garnish with the coriander leaves, if using.

6. Serve the chilli con carne with the salsa and steamed rice. Finish with more chopped coriander, if using.

297. Salmon and bulgur wheat pilaf

Ingredients

- 475g/1lb 1oz salmon, boned and skinned
- 250g/8oz bulgur wheat
- 85g/3oz frozen peas
- 200g/7oz runner beans, chopped
- 2 tbsp chopped chives
- 2 tbsp chopped flat leaf parsley
- salt and freshly ground black pepper

To serve

- 2 lemons, halved
- 4 tbsp low-fat yoghurt

Instructions

1. Preheat the oven to 180C/160C Fan/Gas 4.

2. Wrap the salmon in foil and cook for 15 minutes, or until the salmon is cooked through.

3. Meanwhile, place the bulgur wheat in a medium sized lidded pan. Add boiling water to reach 1cm/½in above the bulgur wheat. Cover with the lid and simmer over a medium heat for 12-15 minutes, or until the bulgur wheat is tender and has absorbed the water.

196

4. Cook the peas and beans in a pan of boiling water until done to your liking, then drain.

5. Flake the salmon and mix it into the bulgur wheat with the peas and beans. Add in the chives and parsley. Season with salt and freshly ground black pepper.

6. Serve with lemon halves and yogurt.

298. Pear & gorgonzola flatbread

Ingredients

- 4Naan flatbreads (Stonefire Original)
- 1/2 cup butter
- 1 pear, peeled and diced & 8 sage leaves
- 1/2 cup gorgonzola cheese, crumbled
- 1/4 cup chopped walnuts
- 1/4 lb prosciutto

Instructions

1. Place butter in a small light colored saucepan. (You need to be able to see the butter turn brown.) Melt butter over medium heat, stirring constantly. The butter will start to foam. Continue cooking until brown specks start to appear in the bottom of the pan. Drop 2 sage leaves into the butter and remove from heat. Pour butter into small dish to stop the cooking process.

2. Preheat oven to 400°F.

3. Brush naan flatbreads with half of the browned butter. Top each flatbread with prosciutto, pear, walnuts and gorgonzola. Chop remaining sage and sprinkle over top of flatbreads.

4. Place flatbreads on baking sheet and bake for 12-15 minutes. Drizzle remaining browned butter over flatbreads.

299. Chorizo beans on toast

Ingredients

- 100g/3½oz cooking chorizo, diced
- 200g/7oz tinned chickpeas, drained and rinsed
- 200g/7oz tinned chopped tomatoes
- 1 tbsp chopped fresh thyme leaves
- salt and freshly ground black pepper

To serve

- 2 slices toast
- 1 tbsp chopped fresh parsley leaves

Instructions

1. Place a saucepan over a medium heat. When the pan is hot, add the chorizo and fry for 1-2 minutes, or until starting to crisp.

2. Add the drained chickpeas and tinned tomatoes, then stir in the thyme. Season, to taste, with salt and freshly ground black pepper. Simmer for 4-5 minutes, or until the sauce has warmed through and thickened to your liking.

3. To serve, spoon the chickpea mixture on top of the toast and garnish with parsley.

300. Blackened salmon with salsa

Ingredients

- 3 tbsp Cajun seasoning
- 1 tsp dried oregano
- 4 salmon fillets, about 75g/3oz each
- sunflower oil, to brush
- lime wedges, to garnish
- For the salsa
- 400g tin black-eyed beans, rinsed and drained
- 2 tbsp olive oil
- 1 avocado, peeled, stoned and chopped
- 2 plum tomatoes, finely chopped
- 1 yellow pepper, deseeded and finely chopped
- 2 tbsp lime juice
- salt and freshly ground black pepper

Instructions

1. Mix together the Cajun seasoning and oregano in a shallow bowl.
2. Brush the salmon on both sides with a little oil and coat with the spice mix, making sure the fish is completely covered. Set aside.
3. Meanwhile, for the salsa mix together all the ingredients in a bowl. Season to taste and set aside.
4. Heat a frying pan over medium heat, dry fry the salmon for 4 minutes on each side.
5. Slice the salmon and spoon the salsa over, garnish with lime wedges and serve

301. Heirloom Tomato & Coconut Bacon BLT with Basil Aioli

Ingredients

- 2 cups coconut chips
- 1 tablespoon olive oil
- 2 tablespoons soy sauce
- 1 teaspoon smoked paprika
- 1 tablespoon maple syrup
- 1 tablespoon chopped garlic
- 1/2 teaspoon liquid smoke & 3 eggs yolks
- 1 1/2 cups canola oil
- 1 tablespoon lemon juice
- Salt and pepper to taste
- 3 different varieties of heirloom tomatoes, sliced
- 1 loaf thick sliced bread, toasted (we used brioche)
- 2 ripe avocados
- 1 bunch of leaf lettuce
- 1 tablespoon chopped basil

Instructions

1. Preheat oven to 325°F.
2. To make coconut bacon: Mix coconut, olive oil, soy sauce, paprika, maple syrup, liquid smoke, salt, and pepper. Spread on a sheet pan and bake for 6 minutes. Stir and bake for another 5 minutes. Stir and bake for another 3 minutes. Let cool.

3. To make aioli: Place egg yolks in a small bowl. Gently whisk the oil into the yolks. Add garlic, lemon, and salt and pepper.

4. Assemble the BLT by spreading half of an avocado on one piece of bread and aioli on the other. Layer with tomatoes, lettuce, coconut bacon, and a drizzle of aioli.

302. Steak fajitas

Ingredients

- 300g/10½oz lean beef steak, such as sirloin or rump, visible fat trimmed and cut into thin strips
- 1½ tbsp extra virgin or sunflower oil
- 2 yellow peppers, deseeded and thinly sliced
- 2 red peppers, deseeded and thinly sliced
- 2 red onions, cut into thin wedges
- 1 tsp ground cumin
- 1 tsp ground coriander
- 1 tsp smoked paprika
- 400g tin red kidney beans, drained and rinsed
- 200g/7oz cherry tomatoes, halved
- 1 long red chilli, finely chopped, or ½ tsp dried chilli flakes
- 25g/1oz fresh coriander, chopped, plus extra to garnish
- lime wedges, for squeezing
- 4 x 40g/1½oz white or wholemeal flour tortillas, warmed, to serve
- 2 Little Gem lettuces, trimmed and shredded, to serve
- 6 tbsp natural yoghurt, to serve
- sea salt and freshly ground black pepper

Instructions

1. Season the beef with pepper. Heat half a tablespoon of the oil in large, non-stick frying pan and stir-fry the beef for 1½ minutes, or until lightly browned but not quite cooked through. Tip onto a plate, set aside and return the pan to the heat.

2. Add the remaining oil, peppers and red onions to the pan and stir-fry for 5–6 minutes, or until only just softened. Add the cumin, coriander and paprika. Season with salt and pepper and cook for 30 seconds, then stir in the beans, cherry tomatoes and cooked beef. Cook for 2–3 minutes, or until the beans and beef are hot.

3. Stir in the chilli and season with salt and pepper. Cook for a few seconds more. Remove from the heat, scatter over the coriander and add a squeeze of lime. Toss lightly.

4. Divide the tortillas between four warmed plates. Top with shredded lettuce then pile the beef mixture on top. Spoon the yoghurt over each tortilla and garnish with the coriander. Serve immediately, with extra lime wedges for squeezing.

303. Lentil stew with sweet onions

Ingredients

- a good handful, chopped unsmoked bacon or pancetta
- 4 medium sized onions
- 3 small carrots
- ½ tsp mild paprika
- ½ tsp ground cinnamon
- 300g/10oz Puy lentils
- 500ml/1pint stock
- a handful parsley
- knob of butter
- 100g/4oz crème fraiche
- ½ nutmeg, for grating

Instructions

1. Cook the bacon or pancetta in a deep pan over a moderate heat to let the fat slowly ooze out . Roughly chop two of the onions and add them to the pan. Cut the carrots into chunks and add to the pan. Cover and let it steam for a few minutes. Add the paprika, cinnamon, then grate in ½ of the nutmeg. Add the lentils, stock and 500ml water, cover and leave for 30 minutes until the lentils have softened.

2. While that is slowly cooking, slice the remaining two onions and, in another pan, cook them very slowly in butter until golden brown. Finish with a grate of nutmeg.

3. The last thing to add to the lentils is a handful of chopped parsley. Serve with a dollop of crème fraiche and pile the caramelised onions on top.

304. Chicken Cobb salad

Ingredients

For the Dressing

- 1 teaspoon finely minced shallots
- 3 tablespoons apple cider vinegar
- kosher salt and freshly ground pepper
- 1 tablespoon dijon mustard
- 3 tablespoons extra virgin olive oil

For the salad

- 4 hardboiled eggs halved
- 12 ounces center cut bacon
- 1 pound chicken breasts thinly sliced
- 1 large head romaine lettuce chopped
- 6 ounces grape tomatoes cut in half
- 2 avocados sliced
- 3 ounces blue cheese crumbles
- 2 tablespoon minced chives

Instructions

1. In a small bowl, combine shallots and apple cider vinegar. Let set 2-3 minutes to let flavors combine. Then whisk in mustard, olive oil and a pinch of kosher salt and pepper.

2. In a large skillet, cook chopped bacon over medium heat until crispy. Remove bacon from skillet and set on a paper towel lined plate to drain.

3. Remove all but 2 tablespoons of bacon drippings from pan, pat thinly sliced chicken breasts dry and season with salt and pepper. Cook chicken breast in skillet over medium heat until golden brown on both sides and cooked through. Set chicken aside to cool.

4. Whisk remaining pan drippings into dressing, taste and season with additional salt and pepper as needed. Once chicken has cooled, slice.

5. Assemble salad. In a large bowl, toss romaine lettuce with half of dressing. Then arrange remaining ingredients on top of lettuce. Top with remaining dressing, salt and pepper and a sprinkle of fresh chives.

FEARLESS

FLAVOR

RECIPES

---

305. Chicken traybake with chorizo, tomato and red peppers

Ingredients

- 2 onions, quartered
- 2 red peppers, seeds removed, quartered
- 1 yellow pepper, seeds removed, quartered
- 8 large tomatoes, preferably on the vine
- 80g/3oz chorizo, sliced
- 4 garlic cloves, bashed
- 400g tin cannellini beans, drained and rinsed
- 2 sprigs fresh rosemary
- 8 chicken thighs, skin-on, bone-in
- 2 tbsp olive oil
- 1 tsp sea salt flakes
- freshly ground black pepper

Instructions

1. Preheat the oven to 200C/180C Fan/Gas 6.

2. Put the onions, peppers, tomatoes, chorizo, beans, garlic and rosemary in a very large roasting tin (you may choose to use two tins). Top with the chicken, then drizzle with the oil.

3. Scatter with the salt and a big pinch of pepper. Roast for 1 hour, or until the chicken is cooked through and the skin is golden brown. To check if the chicken is cooked, pierce the thickest part with a skewer; the juices should run clear. If there is any sign of pink, return the bake to the oven until the chicken is cooked.

4. Leave the chicken to rest for 10 minutes, then serve with the vegetables.

306. Italian broccoli and egg salad

Ingredients

- 4 free-range eggs
- 300g/10½oz broccoli, cut in to florets
- 2 small leeks, about 300g/10½oz in total, trimmed, slit and thickly sliced
- 4 tbsp lemon juice
- 2 tbsp olive oil
- 2 tbsp clear honey
- 1 tbsp capers, well drained
- 2 tbsp chopped tarragon
- salt and freshly ground pepper

Instructions

1. Place the eggs in a large pot, cover with cold water and bring to the boil. Once the water is boiling cook for a further 7-10 minutes. When cooked plunge the eggs in ice-cold water for 1 minute, remove and set aside.

2. Meanwhile, place the broccoli in the top of a steamer, cook for 3 minutes. Add the leeks and cook for a further 2 minutes.

3. For the dressing, mix together the lemon juice, oil, honey, capers and tarragon in a salad bowl. Season with salt and freshly ground black pepper.

4. Shell and roughly chop the eggs.

5. Add the broccoli and leeks to the dressing and toss together. Sprinkle with the chopped eggs and serve.

307. Mason Jar Ramen

Ingredients

- 1 teaspoon bouillion paste (I used Better than Bouillion vegetable paste, but you could also use chicken, beef, pork, miso or Thai curry paste.)
- 3 Tablespoons kimchi (or more if you like spice!) If kimchi isn't your thing, try sesame seed oil, chili sauce or Sriracha.
- veggies! I used corn, carrots and sautéed mushrooms. You could add spinach, peppers or bok choy. There are endless possibilities here.
- 1 cup cooked brown rice noodles. You can also try udon, soba noodles, vermicelli or spaghetti. Get creative!
- green onions on top (optional)
- mason jar (the wide mouth containers work best)

Instructions

- Add bouillion paste to the bottom of a mason jar.
- Next add in your kimchi.
- Pack in your veggies.
- Put noodles on top.
- Top with green onions.
- When ready to eat, remove lid and pour hot water into the mason jar. Let sit for a few minutes, then enjoy!

308. Jerk pork with sweet potato mash

Ingredients

- 2 tsp jerk seasoning
- 1½ tsp runny honey
- 100ml/3½fl oz pineapple juice (from 227g tin pineapple rings)

- 300g/10½oz pork tenderloin
- 1 tsp olive oil
- 1 x 350g/12oz sweet potato, peeled and cut into 3cm/1¼in pieces

For the salsa

- 2 tinned pineapple rings (about 100g/3½oz), drained and finely chopped
- 3 spring onions, thinly sliced
- 2 tbsp roughly chopped fresh coriander leaf

- ½ lime, juice only
- 1 tsp olive oil
- ½ red chilli, deseeded and finely diced
- pinch salt

Instructions

1. Mix the jerk seasoning, honey and pineapple juice in a shallow bowl large enough to hold the pork. Add the pork loin and place in the fridge, covered, for at least 30 minutes or overnight, turning the pork over a couple of times.

2. Preheat the oven to 200C/180C Fan/Gas 6 and line a baking tray with kitchen foil.

3. Remove the meat from the marinade, reserving the liquid, and pat it dry with kitchen paper. Heat the oil in a frying pan over a high heat. Brown the meat on one side, turn over and brown on the other side.

4. Place the meat in the baking tray, pour over the marinade and roast for 20–25 minutes, turning the pork over after 15 minutes. Cut into the thickest part of the steak to check that it is juicy but cooked through.

5. Meanwhile, bring a saucepan of lightly salted water to the boil and simmer the sweet potato for 15 minutes until tender. Drain, mash and season with salt and pepper.

6. To make the salsa, mix the pineapple, spring onion, coriander, a squeeze of lime juice, olive oil, chilli and salt together in a bowl and set aside for at least 10 minutes.

7. Turn the meat over in its reduced marinade and leave to rest for 5 minutes. Cut the pork into 2cm/¾in-thick slices and serve with the mash and salsa.

309. Healthy chicken pasta

Ingredients

- 1-2 skinless chicken breasts, bones removed
- 1 tbsp olive oil, plus extra for rubbing
- 2 garlic cloves, finely chopped
- pinch chilli flakes
- 1 tbsp tomato purée
- 300g/10½oz tomato passata
- sea salt and freshly ground black pepper

- 200g/7oz wholewheat penne pasta
- 200g/7oz broccoli, sliced into bite-sized chunks
- 125g/4½oz baby spinach, washed (optional)
- ½ bunch basil, leaves picked (optional)
- 1-2 tbsp finely grated parmesan (optional)

Instructions

1. Carefully slice the breast almost in half horizontally, not quite cutting through to the other edge. Keep that edge intact and open up the breast like you are opening up a book. This will make the meat a uniform thickness to ensure a quick and even cooking.

2. Heat a large saucepan over a medium-low heat. Add the olive oil to the pan. Once warm, add the garlic and chilli flakes and cook for two minutes, then stir in the tomato purée and cook for two more minutes. Add the passata to the pan, season with pepper, stir to mix well and reduce the heat to a gentle simmer. Leave to simmer gently while you prepare the rest of the dish.

3. Bring a large pan of salted water to the boil, add the pasta and cook according to the packet instructions. Add the broccoli three minutes before the end of cooking. Drain thoroughly.

4. Meanwhile heat a griddle pan over a high heat until smoking. Rub the chicken with a little oil and season with a tiny bit of salt and pepper then griddle for 3-5 minute's on each side. Set aside to rest for five minutes before slicing into bite-sized pieces.

5. Add the cooked pasta and broccoli to the pan with the tomato sauce (if the sauce has thickened too much while simmering then add a little hot water from the pasta). Stir to mix well and then add the cooked and sliced griddled chicken, spinach and the picked basil leaves (if using). Season again with plenty of black pepper and allow the spinach and basil to wilt. Sprinkle with parmesan, if using, and serve.

310. Chickpea Lettuce Wraps

Ingredients

- 1 (15 oz) can chickpeas drained and rinsed
- 2 tablespoons low fat mayonnaise
- 2 tablespoons non fat plain greek yogurt
- 3 tablespoon lemon juice
- 1 teaspoon hot madras curry powder
- 1/4 teaspoon salt & Cilantro finely minced
- 3 tablespoons raisins & Green onions thinly sliced
- 1/2 stalk celery chopped
- 1/4 cup chopped walnuts
- bibb lettuce washed, left whole

Instructions

1. In a medium sized bowl, mash half a can of chickpeas using a potato masher.
2. Once they're mashed, stir in the other half can of whole chickpeas and set aside.
3. In a small bowl, mix together the sauce ingredients: mayo, greek yogurt, lemon juice, curry powder, and salt.
4. Pour the sauce over the chickpeas and stir in the raisins, chopped celery and chopped walnuts.
5. Cover the bowl with saran wrap and let chill in the fridge until cold, about 30 minutes.
6. Once chilled, spoon the mixture into each lettuce leaf and top with thinly sliced green onion, finely minced cilantro, and more chopped walnuts! I also like to drizzle these with a little extra greek yogurt.
7. Serve immediately and enjoy!

311. Fiery prawn and tomato pasta

Ingredients

- 125g/4½oz dried spaghetti or linguine
- 150g/5½oz broccoli, cut into small florets
- 100g/3½oz cherry tomatoes, halved
- 150g/5½oz large cold water prawns, such as North Atlantic or Canadian, completely thawed and drained
- 1 tbsp extra virgin olive oil
- ½ tsp dried chilli flakes, to taste
- sea salt and freshly ground black pepper
- lemon wedges, for squeezing (optional)

Instructions

1. Half-fill a large, non-stick saucepan with water and bring to the boil. Add the pasta to the boiling water, return to the boil and cook for 8 minutes, stirring occasionally. Add the broccoli to the pan and cook for 2 minutes more.

2. Drain the pasta and broccoli. Return to the pan and add the tomatoes, prawns, oil, chilli flakes and season well. Cook for 2–3 minutes, tossing with two wooden spoons until the spaghetti is evenly coated with the spices from the pan and the prawns and tomatoes are hot.

3. Squeeze over a little lemon juice, if using, and serve immediately.

312. Haddock parcels and coconut rice

Ingredients

- 4 haddock fillets, about 150g/5½ oz each
- 4 tbsp chopped fresh coriander
- 1 red chilli, chopped
- 1 shallot, thinly sliced
- 1 lime, sliced, plus extra lime halves to serve
- 2 lemongrass stalks, 1 roughly chopped and 1 bashed
- 300g/10½oz basmati rice
- 2 fresh or dried kaffir lime leaves
- 50ml/2fl oz reduced-fat coconut milk

Instructions

1. Preheat the oven to 180C/160C Fan/Gas 4.

2. Cut 4 pieces of nonstick baking paper, each 30cm/12in square. Put a haddock fillet in the centre of each piece and arrange some of the coriander, chilli, shallot, lime and chopped lemongrass stalk evenly over each. Wrap them up into neat parcels. Transfer the parcels to a baking sheet and bake for 20 minutes.

3. Put the rice in a lidded pan, cover with water and bring to the boil. Simmer with the lid on for 10 minutes, or until the rice is soft. When the rice is cooked and the water absorbed, stir in the coconut milk.

4. Serve with the rice alongside the haddock parcels, with some extra lime halves.

313. Egg and Vegetable Sandwich

Ingredients

- 1 Thomas' Everything Bagel Thin
- ¾ cup egg whites
- 2 slices tomato
- 2-4 slices avocado
- kosher salt
- 10-15 fresh spinach leaves
- 1 wedge Laughing Cow Herb & Garlic Cheese
- Cholula hot sauce

Instructions

1. Toast bagel thin in the toaster or toaster oven. In a small bowl (I used disposable bowls at the office) add egg whites and spinach leaves, season with kosher salt. Place in microwave for 1 minute 30 seconds, keeping an eye on the eggs so they don't overflow.

2. Smear wedge of cheese on toasted bagel thin and add slices of tomato. Spoon egg out of bowl in a single patty and place on top of cheese and tomato, top with avocado. Season with more salt and hot sauce if desired.

314. Hoisin salmon with broccoli and noodles

Ingredients

- 4 x 125g/4oz salmon fillets, with skin left on
- 2 heaped tbsp hoisin sauce (from a jar or bottle)
- 150g/5½oz cherry tomatoes, halved
- 140g/5oz medium egg noodles
- 200g/7oz long-stemmed broccoli, trimmed
- freshly ground black pepper
- dark soy sauce, to serve (optional)

Instructions

1. Preheat the oven to 220C/200C Fan/Gas 7 and line a small, shallow ovenproof dish with kitchen foil.

2. Place the salmon fillets into the dish, skin-side down, and brush generously with the hoisin sauce. Make sure the fillets are placed at least 5cm/2in apart from each other. Scatter the cherry tomatoes around them. Cook for 15 minutes, or until the salmon is cooked through.

3. Meanwhile, prepare the noodles. Half-fill a saucepan with water and bring to the boil. Add the noodles, return to the boil and cook for 1 minute, stirring to separate the strands. Add the broccoli and cook for 3 more minutes, stirring occasionally.

4. Divide the noodles and broccoli between four warmed plates. Top with the salmon fillets and scatter with the cherry tomatoes. Season with pepper and serve sprinkled with a little soy sauce, if using.

315. Chicken with red kidney beans

Ingredients

- low-calorie cooking spray
- 1 onion, roughly chopped
- 1 red pepper, cored, deseeded and roughly chopped
- 1 garlic clove, halved
- 250g/9oz boneless, skinless chicken thighs, cut into 3cm/1¼in chunks & salt and freshly ground black pepper
- 2 tsp mild chilli powder
- 200g/7oz easy-cook long-grain rice
- 400g can red kidney beans, rinsed and drained
- 400g can cherry tomatoes, in natural juice
- 200ml/7fl oz chicken stock

To garnish

- Fresh coriander leaves, roughly chopped
- Lime wedges

Instructions

1. Heat a large frying pan with a flameproof handle over a medium heat and lightly spray with oil. Add the onion, red pepper, garlic and chicken. Cook for 3 minutes, stirring continuously.

2. Preheat the grill to a hot setting.

3. Add the chilli powder, rice, beans, tomatoes and stock to the pan. Season to taste with salt and freshly ground black pepper. Bring to the boil, then reduce the heat and simmer for 15 minutes.

4. Place the pan under the grill and cook until golden.

5. Divide between four plates, garnish with coriander and serve with lime wedges

316. Open-Face Chicken Caprese Sandwiches

Ingredients

- 2 small chicken breasts (or 1 large breast)
- salt & pepper
- 4 slices French or country-style bread
- softened butter
- 2 vine-ripened tomatoes, cut into 1/4" slices
- 4-5 fresh basil leaves, torn into small pieces
- 2oz fontina or mozzarella cheese, cut into slices

Instructions

1. Season chicken with salt & pepper on both sides, then saute in a non-stick sprayed skillet over medium-heat until chicken is no longer pink in the center, about 3-4 minutes a side. Remove to a plate, and set aside.

2. Position oven rack in the second slot under the broiler, about 6-7 inches away from the heat. Lightly butter one side of each bread slice, then place on a foil-lined baking sheet. Broil until golden brown around the edges.

3. Place cooked chicken on top of toasted bread slices, then top with tomatoes, basil, and cheese. Place back under the broiler until cheese is melted. Crack black pepper over the top, then serve.

317. Spicy mozzarella aubergines with green beans and chickpeas

Ingredients

- 2 aubergines, halved
- 400g tin chickpeas, drained and rinsed
- 2 tbsp olive oil, plus extra if needed
- ½ tsp sea salt, plus extra for sprinkling
- 2 garlic cloves, crushed
- 175g/6oz green beans

- 125g/4½oz reduced-fat mozzarella, roughly torn
- 25g/1oz panko breadcrumbs
- 1 red chilli, deseeded and finely chopped
- 25g/1oz fresh flat-leaf parsley, finely chopped, to garnish

Instructions

1. Preheat the oven to 220C/200C Fan/Gas 7.

2. Without cutting all the way through, cut cross-hatches into the aubergine flesh. Put into a roasting tin with the chickpeas, olive oil, salt and garlic. Mix thoroughly to combine. Roast for 20 minutes.

3. Reduce the oven to 200C/180C Fan/Gas 6.

4. Add the green beans to the tin and mix to coat in the oil, adding a little more if needed. Cover the aubergine flesh with the torn mozzarella, a pinch of sea salt, the panko breadcrumbs and half the chilli. Cook for a further 30 minutes, or until the topping is crisp and golden and the aubergine flesh is soft.

5. Garnish with the remaining chilli and parsley and serve immediately.

318. Tamarind and lemongrass beef

Ingredients

- 1 tbsp oil
- 500g/1lb 2oz lean beef, cut into strips
- 2 lemongrass stalks, chopped
- 6 shallots, chopped
- 2 tsp brown sugar
- 2 green chillies, chopped
- 3 tbsp tamarind paste
- 2 tbsp lime juice
- 2 tsp Thai fish sauce
- 200g/7oz shredded green papaya

Instructions

1. Heat the oil in a wok or frying pan, toss in the beef and cook over a high heat for 2-3 minutes.

2. Add the lemongrass, shallots and chillies and stir-fry for a 5 minutes, or until the meat is well browned.

3. Add the tamarind paste, lime juice, fish sauce, sugar and papaya and stir-fry for 4 minutes.

4. Divide between four bowls and serve.

319. Shrimp stuffed avocado

Ingredients

- 1 lime
- 16 cooked and peeled shrimp
- small bunch cilantro, finely chopped
- 2 scallions, chopped
- ¼ red onion, peeled and finely chopped
- ¼ red bell pepper, de-seeded and finely chopped
- 2 ripe avocados

- 10 cherry tomatoes, halved

- 1 packed cup pea shoots (or other salad leaves)

For the dressing:

- 6 Tablespoons mayonnaise

- 1 teaspoon lime juice

- 1 Tablespoon hot chili sauce (we used sriracha)

- ¼ teaspoon salt

- ¼ teaspoon ground black pepper

- 1 Tablespoon tomato ketchup

Instructions

1. Slice the avocados in half and remove the stone. Zest the lime, and squeeze one teaspoon of juice out for the dressing.

2. Make the dressing first by mixing all of the dressing Ingredients together in a small bowl.

3. Place the shrimp in a bowl and add half of the dressing. Add the cilantro, all but one teaspoon of the scallions, the chopped red onion and all but one teaspoon of the chopped bell pepper. Mix together until the shrimp is coated in the mixture.

320. Chicken and cashew noodle stir-fry

Ingredients

- 1 tbsp vegetable oil

- 1 head of pak choi, chopped

- 250g/9oz chicken breast, cut into thin strips

- 300g/10½oz straight-to-wok fine egg noodles

- 1 tbsp runny honey

- small bunch fresh coriander, roughly chopped

- 1 garlic clove, crushed

- 1 tbsp chopped fresh ginger

- 1 tbsp dark soy sauce

- ½ red chilli, finely chopped

- 1 tbsp toasted sesame oil

- 3 spring onions, chopped

- 1 lime, finely grated zest and juice

- 1 small carrot, sliced

- 25g/1oz unsalted, toasted cashew nuts

Instructions

1. Heat a large wok over a high heat. Add half the oil and the chicken. Stir fry for 1 minute, then add the honey and fry until the chicken is fully cooked and a rich golden-brown. Remove from the wok and set aside.

2. Add the remaining oil to the wok and fry the garlic, ginger and chilli for 20 seconds over a medium heat. Add the vegetables and stir-fry until they are just tender but retain some bite. Add the pre-cooked noodles and sauté for a minute or so before returning the chicken to the pan.

3. Add the coriander, soy sauce, sesame oil and lime zest and juice and toss well.

4. Serve with a scattering of cashews over the top.

321. Mediterranean-style lamb chops

Ingredients

- 2 tbsp chopped fresh mint
- 1 tsp finely chopped fresh rosemary
- 3 garlic cloves
- 2 tbsp olive oil
- 4 lean lamb chops or cutlets
- 1 aubergine, sliced

- 4 courgettes, sliced
- 2 red peppers, cut into large chunks
- 2 yellow peppers, cut into large chunks
- 85g/3oz feta cheese, crumbled
- 250g/9oz cherry tomatoes

To serve

Mixed leaf salad

Instructions

1. Preheat the oven to 180C/355F/Gas 4.

2. Using a pestle and mortar or food processor, blend together the mint, rosemary and the garlic, then add one tablespoon of the olive oil. Smear the herb mixture over the lamb chops.

3. Place the aubergine, courgette and peppers on a baking sheet. Drizzle with the remaining olive oil and place the lamb chops on top. Place into the oven to roast for 20-25 minutes.

4. Remove from the oven and top the chops with the feta and add the cherry tomatoes to the tray. Return to the oven for a further 10 minutes until the cheese just starts to brown and the lamb chops are just cooked through.

5. Serve the chops with the roasted vegetables and mixed leaf salad.

322. Grilled Thai Chicken Sandwich

Ingredients

- ½ cup "lite" coconut milk
- ¼ cup smooth natural peanut butter
- 2 tablespoons lime juice
- 2 tablespoons chile-garlic sauce, divided
- 1 tablespoon reduced-sodium soy sauce
- 1 pound prepared pizza dough, preferably whole-wheat

- 1 tablespoon canola oil, divided
- 2 6-ounce boneless, skinless chicken breasts
- 1 large red bell pepper, quartered
- 1 large onion, sliced into ½-inch-thick rounds
- 2 tablespoons chopped fresh cilantro

Instructions

1. Preheat grill to medium-high. Whisk coconut milk, peanut butter, lime juice, 1 tablespoon chile-garlic sauce and soy sauce in a bowl until well combined. Working on a lightly floured surface,

divide dough into 5 equal pieces. Roll each piece into a 6-inch disk with a rolling pin or press into a disk with your hands. Using 1½ teaspoons oil, brush one side of each disk. Oil the grill rack; place the dough, oiled-side down, on the grill and cook until light brown and puffed, 1 to 2 minutes. Brush the dough with the remaining 1½ teaspoons oil, flip and grill until cooked through, but still a little soft, 1 to 2 minutes more.

2. Wrap in foil to keep warm. Brush chicken with the remaining 1 tablespoon chile-garlic sauce. Place the chicken, bell pepper and onion on the grill. Grill the chicken, turning once, until an instant-read thermometer inserted into the thickest part registers 165°F, 10 to 14 minutes. Grill the pepper and onion, turning once, until lightly charred and cooked through, 8 to 10 minutes. Slice the pepper and onion. Toss with ½ cup of the reserved dressing in a medium bowl. When the chicken is cool enough to handle, slice or shred into bite-size pieces. Top flatbreads with equal portions of the vegetables and chicken; drizzle with the remaining dressing and sprinkle with cilantro. Fold to eat.

3. Oiling a grill rack before you grill foods helps ensure that the food won't stick. Oil a folded paper towel, hold it with tongs and rub it over the rack. (Do not use cooking spray on a hot grill.) When grilling delicate foods like tofu and fish, it is helpful to coat the food with cooking spray.

323. Quick chicken stew with vegetables

Ingredients

- 1 tbsp light olive oil
- 1 onion, roughly chopped
- 2 garlic cloves, finely chopped
- 8 chicken thighs, boneless, skin removed, cut into bite-sized pieces
- 700ml/1¼ pint chicken stock
- 2 tbsp finely chopped fresh tarragon
- salt and freshly ground black pepper
- 2 level tbsp plain flour

- 1 level tbsp wholegrain mustard
- 2 celery sticks, sliced
- 2 large carrots, peeled and cut into 1.5cm/½in cubes
- 1 cinnamon stick & 1 star anise
- 300g/10½oz small new potatoes, scrubbed and halved
- 200g/7oz frozen soya beans, defrosted

Instructions

1. Heat the oil in a wide frying pan over a medium heat. Add the onion, garlic and chicken and stir-fry for 2–3 minutes.

2. Meanwhile, pour the stock into a saucepan and bring to the boil.

3. Stir the flour into the chicken and gradually add the hot stock. Stir in the mustard, star anise, cinnamon, celery, carrots and potatoes. Bring to the boil, cover and reduce the heat to medium. Cook for 15–20 minutes.

4. Uncover, increase the heat, and cook for 5 minutes, or until the chicken is cooked through and the vegetables are tender.

5. Stir in the soya beans and cook for 2–3 minutes. Season well and stir in the tarragon. Serve immediately in four warm bowls.

324. Lemon and pomegranate couscous

Ingredients

- 1 large or 2 small pomegranates
- 200g/7oz couscous
- 250ml/9fl oz pints boiling chicken stock or water
- sea salt and freshly ground black pepper
- 2 lemons, juice only
- 6 tbsp olive oil
- 4 tbsp chopped, fresh mint or coriander

Instructions

1. Cut the pomegranates in half and scoop out the seeds using a teaspoon and remove the white membrane around the seeds.

2. Place the couscous in a bowl. Pour the boiling stock or water onto the couscous and and mix in the olive oil and lemon juice. Season with sea salt and freshly ground black pepper.

3. Cover tightly with clingfilm and allow the couscous to sit in a warm place for 5-10 minutes, or until the liquid has been absorbed. Remove the clingfilm and fluff the grains with a fork. Allow the couscous to cool completely.

4. Stir the chopped herbs and pomegranate seeds into the couscous. Add more olive oil, salt, pepper and herbs to taste.

325. Grilled Eggplant & Portobello Sandwich

Ingredients

- 1 small clove garlic, chopped
- ¼ cup low-fat mayonnaise
- 1 teaspoon lemon juice
- 1 medium eggplant (about 1 pound), sliced into ½-inch rounds
- 2 large or 3 medium portobello mushroom caps, gills removed
- Canola or olive oil cooking spray
- ½ teaspoon salt
- ½ teaspoon freshly ground pepper
- 8 slices whole-wheat sandwich bread, lightly grilled or toasted
- 2 cups arugula, or spinach, stemmed and chopped if large
- 1 large tomato, sliced

Instructions

1. Preheat grill to medium-high. Mash garlic into a paste on a cutting board with the back of a spoon. Combine with mayonnaise and lemon juice in a small bowl. Set aside.

215

2. Coat both sides of eggplant rounds and mushroom caps with cooking spray and season with salt and pepper.

3. Grill the vegetables, turning once, until tender and browned on both sides: 2 to 3 minutes per side for eggplant, 3 to 4 minutes for mushrooms.

4. When cool enough to handle, slice the mushrooms. Spread 1½ teaspoons of the garlic mayonnaise on each piece of bread.

5. Layer the eggplant, mushrooms, arugula (or spinach) and tomato slices onto 4 slices of bread and top with the remaining bread.

326. Healthy beef and mushroom stroganoff

Ingredients

- 150g/5½oz brown basmati rice
- 1 tbsp light olive oil
- 4 shallots, finely chopped
- 1 tsp sweet smoked paprika & cider vinegar
- 1 red pepper, seeds removed, roughly chopped
- 200g/7oz chestnut mushrooms, thinly sliced

- 2 garlic cloves, finely chopped
- 150ml/5fl oz beef stock
- 200g/7oz lean sirloin steak, visible fat removed, thinly sliced
- 100ml/3½fl oz fat-free plain fromage frais
- 2 level tbsp roughly chopped gherkins
- 2 tbsp finely snipped fresh chives
- salt and freshly ground black pepper

Instructions

1. Cook the rice according to the packet Directions and keep warm.

2. Meanwhile, heat the oil in a wide frying pan and fry the shallots for 5 minutes, or until softened.

3. Add the paprika, pepper, mushrooms and garlic and fry for 6–8 minutes, or until softened.

4. Add the vinegar and mustard and bring to the boil. Cook until the liquid has almost evaporated. Pour over the stock and cook for 3–4 minutes, or until slightly thickened.

5. Add the steak and cook over a high heat for 2–3 minutes, or until sealed and cooked to your liking.

6. Turn the heat down to low and stir in the fromage frais, gherkins and half the chives. Season.

7. Serve the stroganoff with the rice, garnished with the remaining chives.

327. Ham and Swiss Crustless Quiche

Ingredients

- cooking spray
- 1 3/4 cups diced ham steak or leftover ham (9 oz)
- 1 cup chopped steamed broccoli (fresh or frozen)
- 1 cup fresh grated Swiss cheese
- 2/3 cup 2% milk
- 1/4 cup half & half cream
- 5 large eggs
- 1/2 teaspoon kosher salt
- 1/8 teaspoon ground black pepper
- pinch of nutmeg

Instructions

1. Preheat the to 350F degrees. Spray a pie dish with oil.
2. Evenly spread the broccoli in the dish and top it evenly with the ham.
3. Make the custard mixture by whisking together the milk, half and half, eggs, salt, black pepper, and the nutmeg.
4. Pour the custard into the dish and top with Swiss Cheese.
5. Bake 35 to 40 minutes, until the center is set.
6. Cut the quiche into 6 pieces and serve.

328. Tortillas

Ingredients

- 1 cup blanched almond flour
- 3 tablespoons coconut flour
- 2 teaspoons xanthan gum
- 1 teaspoon baking powder
- 1 pinch salt
- 2 teaspoons apple cider vinegar
- 1 egg
- 3 tablespoons water
- cooking spray

Instructions

1. Combine almond flour, coconut flour, xanthan gum, baking powder, and salt in the bowl of a food processor; pulse until well combined. Pour apple cider vinegar into the mixture and blend until smooth. Add egg and water, 1 tablespoon at a time, and blend until a sticky dough ball is formed. Place the dough on a surface sprinkled with almond flour and knead until soft, about 2 minutes. Wrap dough in plastic wrap and let it stand for 10 minutes. Divide dough into 8 equal balls; roll out each ball into a 5-inch disc between two sheets of parchment paper.
2. Heat an iron skillet over medium-high heat and grease with cooking spray. Place dough disc in the hot skillet for just 5 seconds; flip it immediately with a spatula, and cook until lightly golden, about 40 seconds. Flip and cook for another 40 seconds.

329. Chicken and Asparagus Lemon Stir Fry

Ingredients

- 1 1/2 pounds skinless chicken breast, cut into 1-inch cubes
- Kosher salt, to taste
- 1/2 cup reduced-sodium chicken broth
- 2 tablespoons reduced-sodium shoyu or soy sauce (Coconut aminos for GF, W30)
- 2 teaspoons cornstarch (arrowroot powder or tapioca starch for whole30)
- 2 tablespoons water
- 1 tbsp canola or grapeseed oil, divided
- 1 bunch asparagus, ends trimmed, cut into 2-inch pieces
- 6 cloves garlic, chopped
- 1 tbsp fresh ginger
- 3 tablespoons fresh lemon juice
- fresh black pepper, to taste

Instructions

1. Lightly season the chicken with salt.
2. In a small bowl, combine chicken broth and soy sauce.
3. In a second small bowl combine the cornstarch and water and mix well to combine.
4. Heat a large non-stick wok over medium-high heat, when hot add 1 teaspoon of the oil, then add the asparagus and cook until tender-crisp, about 3 to 4 minutes.
5. Add the garlic and ginger and cook until golden, about 1 minute. Set aside.
6. Increase the heat to high, then add 1 teaspoon of oil and half of the chicken and cook until browned and cooked through, about 4 minutes on each side.
7. Remove and set aside and repeat with the remaining oil and chicken. Set aside.
8. Add the soy sauce mixture; bring to a boil and cook about 1-1/2 minutes.
9. Add lemon juice and cornstarch mixture and stir well, when it simmers return the chicken and asparagus to the wok and mix well, remove from heat and serve.

330. Tomato Salad

Ingredients

- 5 large (8 cups) medium ripe red heirloom or beefsteak tomatoes, cut into 1-inch cubes
- 1/2 cup red onion, chopped
- 8 to 10 fresh basil leaves, chopped
- 1 tablespoon extra virgin olive oil
- 1 clove garlic, minced
- Kosher salt and fresh ground pepper to taste
- good crusty bread, for serving (optional)

Instructions

- In a large bowl combine the tomatoes, red onion, basil, olive oil, garlic and season liberally with salt and pepper.
- Let the tomato mixture sit room temperature for about 20 minutes to let the flavors blend (the juices from the tomatoes will release and create a kind of dressing). Toss well.
- When ready to serve, toss the tomato mixture and divide in 4 bowls. Eat with crusty bread if desired.

331. Basil Chicken and Tomato Salad

Ingredients

- 3 large ripe tomatoes, cut into wedges
- chicken breast from 1 rotisserie chicken (12 ounces)
- 5 ounces avocado, sliced
- 2 tablespoons extra virgin olive oil
- 1 lemon
- 1/2 cup small fresh basil leaves
- kosher salt
- fresh black pepper

Instructions

1. Divide the tomatoes between 4 plates or bowls.
2. Shred the chicken breast into large pieces and arrange over tomatoes with the avocado.
3. Drizzle with olive oil, squeeze with lemon juice and season with salt and fresh pepper, to taste.
4. Top with fresh basil.

332. Chicken and Avocado Soup

Ingredients

- 2 tsp olive oil
- 1-1/2 cups scallions, chopped fine
- 2 cloves garlic, minced
- 1 medium tomato, diced
- 5 cups reduced sodium chicken broth
- 2 cups shredded chicken breast (12 oz)
- 8 ounces (from 2 small) ripe hass avocados, diced
- 1/3 cup chopped cilantro
- 4 lime wedges
- kosher salt and fresh pepper, to taste
- 1/8 teaspoon cumin
- pinch chipotle chile powder (optional)

Instructions

1. Heat a large pot over medium heat.
2. Add the oil, 1 cup of scallions and garlic. Sauté about 2 to 3 minutes until soft then add the tomatoes and sauté another minute, until soft.
3. Add chicken stock, cumin and chile powder and bring to a boil. Simmer, covered on low for about 15 minutes.
4. In four bowls, fill each with 1/2 cup chicken, 1/2 avocado, remainder of the scallions, and cilantro. Ladle 1 cup chicken broth over the chicken and serve with a lime wedge.

333. Cauliflower Rice Chicken Biryani

Ingredients

- 1 pound NeverAny! Fresh ABF Chicken Breasts, cut into 1 inch chunks
- 2 teaspoon kosher salt
- 1 teaspoons grated ginger
- 1 teaspoons minced garlic
- 1 teaspoon garam masala
- 3/4 teaspoon ground turmeric
- 1/4 teaspoons chili powder
- 1 tablespoon fresh lemon juice
- 3 teaspoons Carlini Ghee Clarified Butter
- 1 large yellow onion, diced
- 1 to 2 hot green chili pepper, sliced
- 2 packages (6 cups) frozen Season's Choice Plain or Garlic Riced Cauliflower
- 1/4 cup chopped cilantro
- lemon wedges, for serving

Instructions

1. Season the chicken with 1 teaspoon salt, ginger, garlic, 1/2 teaspoon garam masala, chili powder, 1/4 teaspoon turmeric and lemon juice.

2. In a large skillet over high heat, add 1 teaspoon ghee. Add half of the chicken and cook until browned, and cooked through, about 5 minutes stirring halfway.

3. Set aside and repeat with the remaining ghee and chicken. Set aside.

4. Add 2 teaspoons ghee to the skillet, reduce heat to medium-high and add the onion, cook until they become golden about 3 to 4 minutes.

5. Add the green chili, cauliflower rice, remaining 1 teaspoon of salt, 1/2 teaspoon garam masala and 1/2 teaspoon turmeric.

6. Cook, stirring until tender, about 6 minutes.

7. Stir in chicken and garnish with cilantro.

8. Serve with lemon wedges.

334. Meal Prep Taco Salad

Ingredients

Dressing

- 1/2 cup jarred mild salsa
- 4 teaspoons extra virgin olive oil
- juice of 1/2 lime

Meat

- 1 lb 93% ground turkey
- 1 teaspoon garlic powder
- 1 teaspoon cumin
- 1 teaspoon kosher salt
- 1/2 teaspoon chili powder
- 1/2 teaspoon paprika
- 1/2 teaspoon oregano
- 1/2 small onion, minced
- 2 tablespoons bell pepper, minced
- 1/2 cup water
- 4 ounces canned tomato sauce (1/2 can)

For the Salad

- 6 cups chopped romaine lettuce
- 1 cup pico de gallo
- 1/2 cup shredded cheddar
- 4 lime wedges, for serving
- (optional) greek yogurt or sour cream

Instructions

1. Brown the turkey in a large skillet breaking it into smaller pieces as it cooks.

2. When no longer pink add dry seasoning and mix well.

3. Add the onion, pepper, water and tomato sauce and cover.

4. Simmer on low for about 20 minutes.

5. Divide the meat equally between the 4 meal prep containers.

6. Meanwhile, while the meat is cooking, make the dressing: combine the salsa, olive oil and lime juice; transfer to 4 small containers.

7. Divide the lettuce in 4 ziplock bags.

8. Divide pico de gallo, sour cream or yogurt, if using and cheese in small containers. Cover and refrigerate.

9. To serve, remove the lettuce and containers, heat the meat then make a salad by placing the lettuce in a bowl or plate.

10. Top with the meat, pico de gallo, cheese and finish with dressing.

335. Air Fryer Turkey Breast

Ingredients

- 4 pound turkey breast, on the bone with skin (ribs removed)
- 1 tablespoon olive oil
- 2 teaspoons kosher
- 1/2 tablespoon dry turkey or poultry seasoning (I used Bell's which has not salt)

Instructions

- Rub 1/2 tablespoon of oil all over the turkey breast. Season both sides with salt and turkey seasoning then rub in the remaining half tablespoon of oil over the skin side.
- Preheat the air fryer 350F and cook skin side down 20 minutes, turn over and cook until the internal temperature is 160F using an instant-read thermometer about 30 to 40 minutes more depending on the size of your breast. Let is rest 10 minutes before carving.

336. Air Fryer Bacon Wrapped Chicken Bites

Ingredients

- 1.25 lbs (3) boneless skinless chicken breast, cut in 1-inch chunks (about 30 pieces)
- 10 slices center cut bacon, cut into thirds
- optional, duck sauce or Thai sweet chili sauce for dipping

Instructions

1. Preheat the air fryer.

2. Wrap a piece of bacon around each piece of chicken and secure with a toothpick.

3. Air fry, in batches in an even layer 400F for 8 minutes, turning halfway until the chicken is cooked and the bacon is browned.

4. Blot on a paper towel and serve right away.

337. Roasted Salmon with Fresh Herbs

Ingredients

- 2 lemons
- 8 to 10 parsley sprigs
- extra virgin olive oil
- 1 whole skin-on side of wild salmon, such as sockeye or coho, about 2 pounds
- 1/2 teaspoon kosher salt
- fresh black pepper, to taste
- 2 tablespoons chopped fresh dill
- 1 tablespoons chopped fresh chives
- 1 tablespoons chopped fresh parsley

Instructions

1. Slice 1 of the lemons thin, the second into wedges.
2. Place the lemon slices on a large sheet pan arranged in the center just under the fish.
3. Top with parsley sprigs and drizzle with 1 teaspoon of olive oil.
4. Drizzle the remaining 1 teaspoon of olive oil over the flesh side of the fish and rub all over, season with salt and pepper.
5. Transfer to the pan over the lemon slices, skin side down.
6. Preheat the oven to 450F.
7. Roast 15 to 20 minutes, depending on the thickness of the fish, until the thickest part of the fish is cooked though in the center.
8. Top with fresh herbs and serve with lemon wedges.

338. Huevos Pericos (Colombian Scrambled Eggs)

Ingredients

- 2 teaspoons olive oil
- 3 to 4 medium scallions, white and green parts, sliced thin
- 1 medium roma or vine tomato, seeded and diced
- 6 large eggs, beaten with fork
- kosher salt or adobo seasoning salt

Instructions

1. Heat olive oil in a medium nonstick skillet over medium heat.
2. Add the scallions and cook until they soften, about 3 to 4 minutes.
3. Add the tomato and season with adobo or salt, cook until the liquid from the tomato evaporates, about 3 to 4 minutes.
4. Add the beaten eggs to pan with more adobo or salt to taste and cook over medium heat, stirring a few times until just cooked.

339. Instant Pot Deviled Eggs

Ingredients

- 6 large eggs
- 1 cup water
- rack that comes with the Instant Pot
- 2 tablespoons mayonaisse
- 1 tablespoon 2% milk
- 1 teaspoon dill pickle juice
- 1/8 teaspoon salt
- fresh black pepper, to taste
- paprika for sprinkling
- fresh dill, for garnish

Instructions

1. Place the rack in the bottom of the pot. Pour the water in the pot. Place the eggs on the rack.
2. High pressure on manual 5 minutes.
3. Natural release 5 minutes then use quick release, then quickly run the eggs under cold running water until cool enough to hold.
4. Peel the eggs and slice in half lengthwise. Remove yolks and transfer to a medium-sized bowl.
5. Add the mayo, milk, pickle juice, salt, pepper then use a fork to mash well.
6. Spoon filling into each egg white. Sprinkle with paprika, dill and serve.

340. Cream of Asparagus Soup

Ingredients

- 2 lbs asparagus (2 bunches), tough ends snapped off
- 1 tbsp unsalted butter
- 1 medium onion, chopped
- 6 cups reduced sodium chicken broth
- 2 tbsp low fat sour cream
- kosher salt and fresh pepper, to taste

Instructions

1. Melt butter over low heat in a large pot. Add onion and sauté until soft, about 2-minutes.
2. Cut the asparagus in half and add to the pot along with chicken broth and black pepper, to taste. Bring to a boil, cover and cook low about 20 minutes or until asparagus is very tender.
3. Remove from heat, add sour cream and using your hand held blender, puree until smooth (or in two batches in a large blender).

341. Instant Pot Corned Beef and Cabbage

Ingredients

- 2 pounds trimmed, lean corned beef brisket
- 3 medium carrots, peeled and cut into 1-inch chunks

- 1 cup frozen pearl onions
- 1/4 cup chopped fresh parsley
- 2 bay leaves
- 1/8 tsp whole peppercorns
- 1 medium head cabbage, cut into 6 wedges

Instructions

1. Place the corned beef brisket, carrots, pearl onions, parsley, bay leaves and peppercorns in the Instant pot and add 3 cups of water.
2. Cover and cook on high pressure 1 1/2 hours. Natural release then open.
3. Add the cabbage to the top, cover and cook on high pressure 3 minutes, quick release.
4. Remove meat and slice into 6 pieces.

342. Perfect Hard Boiled Eggs Every Time

Ingredients

- 4 large eggs with no cracks
- enough water to cover eggs

Instructions

1. Place the eggs in a medium pan, and cover with about an inch of cold water.
2. Turn heat on to medium and bring the water to a boil. When the water boils, shut the flame off and cover for 20 minutes, the steam will cook them. Run under cold water to let the eggs cool, then peel.

343. Green Bean Salad

Ingredients

- 24 oz (6 cups) string beans beans, ends trimmed
- 2.25 ounce can sliced black olives, drained (check labels for Whole30)
- 3 tablespoons balsamic vinegar
- 3 tablespoons extra virgin olive oil
- 3 medium scallions, chopped
- 3/4 teaspoon kosher salt
- fresh black pepper, to taste
- 5 hard boiled eggs, peeled and sliced

Instructions

1. Place green beans in a large pot and cover with water, about 6 cups. Bring to a boil, then cover and cook until tender crisp, about 6 minutes (don't overcook or they will get mushy).
2. Drain and rinse under cold water when done to prevent them from overcooking, drain.
3. In a large bowl, combine balsamic, oil, salt and pepper. Toss in the green beans, scallions and olives.
4. Mix well and top with sliced eggs. Refrigerate and serve chilled or room temperature.

344. Chicken and Asparagus Lemon Stir Fry

Ingredients

- 1 1/2 pounds skinless chicken breast, cut into 1-inch cubes
- Kosher salt, to taste
- 1/2 cup reduced-sodium chicken broth
- 2 tablespoons reduced-sodium shoyu or soy sauce (Coconut aminos for GF, W30)
- 2 teaspoons cornstarch (arrowroot powder or tapioca starch for whole30)
- 2 tablespoons water
- 1 tbsp canola or grapeseed oil, divided
- 1 bunch asparagus, ends trimmed, cut into 2-inch pieces
- 6 cloves garlic, chopped
- 1 tbsp fresh ginger
- 3 tablespoons fresh lemon juice
- fresh black pepper, to taste

Instructions

1. Lightly season the chicken with salt.
2. In a small bowl, combine chicken broth and soy sauce.
3. In a second small bowl combine the cornstarch and water and mix well to combine.
4. Heat a large non-stick wok over medium-high heat, when hot add 1 teaspoon of the oil, then add the asparagus and cook until tender-crisp, about 3 to 4 minutes.
5. Add the garlic and ginger and cook until golden, about 1 minute. Set aside.
6. Increase the heat to high, then add 1 teaspoon of oil and half of the chicken and cook until browned and cooked through, about 4 minutes on each side.
7. Remove and set aside and repeat with the remaining oil and chicken. Set aside.
8. Add the soy sauce mixture; bring to a boil and cook about 1-1/2 minutes.
9. Add lemon juice and cornstarch mixture and stir well, when it simmers return the chicken and asparagus to the wok and mix well, remove from heat and serve.

345. Instant Pot Bolognese

Ingredients

- 4 ounces pancetta (or center cut bacon), chopped
- 1 tablespoon unsalted butter
- 1 large white onion, minced
- 2 celery stalks (about 3/4 cup), minced
- 2 carrots (about 3/4 cup), minced
- 2 lb lean ground beef
- 1/4 cup dry white wine, such as Pinot Grigio
- 2 (28 oz) cans crushed tomatoes (I love Tuttorosso)
- 3 bay leaves
- 1/2 teaspoon kosher salt and fresh black pepper, to taste

- 1/2 cup half & half cream
- 1/4 cup chopped fresh parsley

Instructions

1. Press saute on the Instant Pot, sauté the pancetta over low heat until the fat melts, about 4-5 minutes.
2. Add the butter, onion, celery and carrots and cook until soft, about 6 to 8 minutes.
3. Add the meat and season it with 3/4 teaspoons salt and black pepper to taste and sauté until browned, about 4 to 5 minutes, breaking the meat up into smaller pieces with a wooden spoon as it cooks.
4. Add the wine and cook until it reduces down, about 3-4 minutes.
5. Add crushed tomatoes, bay leaves, 3/4 teaspoon salt and fresh cracked black pepper; cover and cook high pressure 15 minutes.
6. Natural release, stir in the half & half and garnish with parsley; serve over your favorite pasta, zucchini noodles or spaghetti squash.

346. Sautéed Brussels Sprouts with Pancetta

Ingredients

- 2 oz pancetta, minced
- 2 lb brussels sprouts (weight after outer leaves and stems removed)
- 1.5 tbsp extra virgin olive oil
- 4 cloves garlic, minced or sliced thin
- kosher salt and fresh ground pepper

Instructions

1. With a large sharp knife, finely shred the brussels sprouts after thoroughly washing.
2. In a deep heavy saute pan, sauté pancetta on medium-low heat until fat melts and pancetta becomes golden, about 5 minutes. Add olive oil and garlic and sauté until golden. Add shredded brussels sprouts, salt and pepper to taste and sauté on high heat for about 6 to 10 minutes, until tender crisp.
3. Makes about 7 cups.

347. Tuna Salad Deviled Eggs

Ingredients

- 8 large hard boiled eggs, halved (Instant Pot hard boiled egg recipe here)
- 2 (6 oz) cans albacore tuna, packed in water, drained
- 1 tbsp red onion, minced
- 1/3 cup light mayo (use compliant mayo for whole30)
- 1 teaspoon red wine vinegar
- chopped fresh chives
- salt and pepper, to taste

Instructions

1. In a medium bowl combine the egg yolks with mayo and mash.

2. Add tuna, red onion and red wine vinegar.

3. Scoop heaping spoonfuls of the tuna salad into the 16 halved eggs. Garnish with chives.

348. Smoked Salmon Pinwheels

Ingredients

- 8 ounces thinly sliced cold smoked salmon (I like Nova Lox)

- 4 ounces 1/3 less fat cream cheese

- 1/4 medium cucumber, cut into matchsticks

- 2 tablespoons finely chopped red onion

- 2 tablespoons capers, drained

- 1/2 lemon, sliced thin

Instructions

1. Lay a large piece of plastic wrap on a work surface.

2. Arrange the slices of salmon in an overlapping fashion to create a rectangle about 6 inches wide by 12 inches long, with one of the longest sides facing you.

3. Gently spread the cream cheese over the salmon trying not to dislodge any of the pieces. Lay the cucumber along one side of the rectangle about 1/2 inch from the edge.

4. Using the plastic wrap to guide you, roll the salmon up tightly around the cucumber sticks. Refrigerate until firm at least 30 minutes.

5. Using a sharp knife, cut the roll into 16 1/2-inch thick slices.

6. Sprinkle with red onion and capers and serve with lemon slices.

349. Easy No-Cook Salsa Recipe

Ingredients

- 1/4 small onion
- 2 small cloves peeled garlic
- 1/2 jalapeño, seeded and membranes removed or leave in for spicy
- 14.5 ounce can diced tomatoes (not with basil) I use Tuttorosso
- handful cilantro
- juice of 1 lime
- 1/4 teaspoon kosher salt

Instructions

Place everything in the chopper of food processor and pulse a few times until combined and chunky. Don't over process.

350. Instant Pot Garlicky Cuban Pork

Ingredients

- 3 lb boneless pork shoulder blade roast, lean, all fat removed
- 6 cloves garlic
- juice of 1 grapefruit (about 2/3 cup)
- juice of 1 lime
- 1/2 tablespoon fresh oregano
- 1/2 tablespoon cumin
- 1 tablespoon kosher salt
- 1 bay leaf
- lime wedges, for serving
- chopped cilantro, for serving
- hot sauce, for serving
- tortillas, optional for serving
- salsa, optional for serving

Instructions

Pressure Cooker

1. Cut the pork in 4 pieces and place in a bowl.
2. In a small blender or mini food processor, combine garlic, grapefruit juice, lime juice, oregano, cumin and salt and blend until smooth.
3. Pour the marinade over the pork and let it sit room temperature 1 hour or refrigerated as long as overnight.
4. Transfer to the pressure cooker, add the bay leaf, cover and cook high pressure 80 minutes. Let the pressure release naturally.
5. Remove pork and shred using two forks.
6. Remove liquid from pressure cooker, reserving then place the pork back into pressure cooker. Add about 1 cup of the liquid (jus) back, adjust the salt as needed and keep warm until you're ready to eat.

Slow Cooker

1. Cut the pork in 4 pieces and place in a bowl.
2. In a small blender or mini food processor, combine garlic, grapefruit juice, lime juice, oregano, cumin and salt and blend until smooth.
3. Pour the marinade over the pork and let it sit room temperature 1 hour or refrigerated as long as overnight.
4. Transfer to the slow cooker, add the bay leaf, cover and cook low 8 hours.
5. Remove pork and shred using two forks.
6. Remove liquid from slow cooker, reserving then place the pork back into slow cooker. Add about 1 cup of the liquid (jus) back, adjust the salt as needed and keep warm until you're ready to eat.

351. Blackened Scallops with Horseradish Sauce

Ingredients

- 1 tablespoon paprika
- 1/2 teaspoon cayenne (or more to taste)
- 1/4 teaspoon garlic powder
- 1 teaspoon dried thyme
- 1 teaspoon dried oregano
- 3/4 teaspoon kosher salt
- 1/8 teaspoon black pepper
- 1 tablespoons butter
- 16 large sea scallops (20 ounces) room temperature

Horseradish Cream

- 1/4 cup reduced fat sour cream
- 1 tablespoon prepared grated horseradish
- 1 tablespoon water
- 1/4 teaspoon Dijon mustard
- 1/8 teaspoon kosher salt
- black pepper, to taste

Instructions

1. Preheat the oven to 350F.
2. In a small bowl combine the horseradish cream ingredients and set aside.
3. In another small bowl, add the paprika, cayenne, garlic powder, thyme, oregano, salt, black pepper and mix to blend. Coat the scallops on all sides with the spices.
4. Heat a large heavy-bottomed pan or cast iron skillet over medium heat, and melt the butter.
5. When very hot add the scallops and saute 1 minutes on each side.
6. Transfer to the oven to finish cooking 4 to 5 minutes, or until the scallops are just cooked through and just opaque in the middle. (Warning, you may want to open your windows, you kitchen will get smokey.) Serve with sauce.

352. Roasted Asparagus

Ingredients

- 1 bunch fresh asparagus, about 18 ounces
- olive oil spray
- kosher salt, to taste
- fresh black pepper

Instructions

1. Preheat oven to 400°F.
2. Wash and trim hard ends off asparagus. Place in a single layer in roasting pan.
3. Spray all over with olive oil and season with salt and pepper.
4. Roast in oven approximately 10 minutes, or until render crisp.

353. Pork Chops with Dijon Herb Sauce

Ingredients

- 1 tsp butter
- 4 pork chops (22 oz with bone, fat removed), 1 inch thick, trim all visible fat
- 1/2 tsp salt
- fresh ground pepper
- 3 tbsp chopped onion
- 3/4 cup chicken stock or broth
- 1 tbsp dijon mustard
- 2 tbsp chopped, fresh herbs like parsley, chives

Instructions

1. In a large skillet melt the butter over moderately low heat.
2. Season the pork with salt and pepper.
3. Raise heat to medium and add the chops to the pan and sauté for 7 minutes. Turn and cook until chops are browned and done to medium, about 7-8 minutes longer. Remove the chops and put in a warm spot.
4. Add the onion to the pan and cook, stirring, until soft, about 3 minutes. Add the stock and boil until it reduces to 1/2 cup, about 2 to 3 minutes.
5. Stir in the mustard, herbs, and 1/8 tsp pepper.
6. Put the chops on a platter and pour the sauce over the meat.

354. Classic Deviled Eggs

Ingredients

- 4 large hard boiled eggs, cooled and peeled
- 2 tablespoon light mayonnaise (regular for Keto)
- 1 teaspoon Dijon mustard
- paprika, for garnish
- Kosher salt and fresh black pepper, to taste
- 2 tablespoons chopped fresh chives

Instructions

1. Use the Stove Top Hard Boiled Egg cooking method or the Instant Pot Hard Boiled Egg method to cook your eggs.
2. Cut eggs in half lengthwise. Remove yolks and put them in a bowl.
3. Add mayonnaise, mustard, salt and pepper to the yolks and mash.
4. Transfer them to a plastic bag, snip the corner and pipe them into the egg whites.
5. Top with chopped chives and paprika.

355. Zucchini Pork Dumplings

Ingredients

- 12 ounces napa cabbage leaves, roughly chopped
- 1 teaspoon salt
- 2/3 pound ground pork
- 1 tablespoon grated fresh ginger (using a zester)
- 1/4 cup minced green onions (white and green parts), plus ¼ cup finely minced, green parts only, for serving
- 1/4 teaspoon ground white pepper
- 1½ tablespoons reduced sodium soy sauce, plus more for serving (or coconut aminos for gf, whole30, paleo)
- 1 tablespoon rice wine
- 2 teaspoons sesame oil
- 5 to 6 medium zucchini (about 1½ inches in diameter)
- Crushed red pepper flakes, for serving

Instructions

1. Preheat the oven to 400 degrees.
2. In a food processor, add the cabbage and pulse until finely minced. Set aside on a large, thin kitchen towel in the sink.
3. Sprinkle with salt and let stand for 10 to 15 minutes.
4. Wrap the cabbage up in the towel and wring out excess moisture over the sink (should eliminate about ⅓ cup of moisture). Set the cabbage aside.
5. Meanwhile, wipe out the food processor and add in the pork, ginger, green onions, pepper, soy sauce, rice wine, and sesame oil and pulse to mix the ingredients well, being careful not to over-pulse. (You don't want the mixture to become paste-like.)
6. Transfer to a large bowl and add the cabbage. Mix together with your hands to combine thoroughly. Set aside.
7. Using a mandoline, slice the zucchini into 1/16-inch-thick strips. Set 1 strip down and then set another one down on top of it to create a cross shape. Repeat with 2 more zucchini strips on an angle to create an 8-cornered star shape.
8. Spoon about 2 tablespoons of filling onto the center of the zucchini star. Bring the ends of the zucchini together, laying them over the filling.
9. Flip the dumpling over so the seam side is down.
10. Arrange on a baking sheet and repeat with remaining zucchini strips and dumpling filling, lining them up on the baking sheets as you go.
11. You should create 18 to 20 total dumplings.
12. Bake for 15 minutes, or until dumplings are firm and edges start to brown and crisp up.

13. Transfer the zucchini dumplings to serving platters, and sprinkle with green onions and red pepper flakes.

14. Serve with soy sauce.

356. Peruvian Green Sauce

Ingredients

- 2 tablespoons olive oil
- 1/4 cup chopped red onion
- 1/2 cup light Hellman's mayonnaise (use compliant mayo for whole30)
- 2 tablespoons white vinegar
- 4 teaspoons yellow mustard (Guldens)
- 1/2 teaspoon kosher salt

- 1/4 teaspoon freshly ground black pepper
- 3 jalapeños, roughly chopped seeded but keeping the ribs (about 1 cup/3 oz)
- 2 cups chopped fresh cilantro leaves and stems (2 oz) rinsed well
- 3 medium cloves garlic, crushed through a press

Instructions

1. Saute the onion in a small skillet with 1 teaspoon of the oil until soft, 3 to 4 minutes.

2. Transfer to the blender then add the remaining oil, mayo, vinegar, mustard, salt and pepper.

3. Then add the chopped jalapeno, cilantro and garlic and blend on high speed until the sauce is smooth and creamy, about 30 seconds.

357. Chicken Shawarma Kebab Salad

Ingredients

- 1 pound (2) boneless, skinless chicken thighs
- 1 tablespoons extra virgin olive oil
- Juice from 1 medium lemon
- 3 garlic cloves, minced
- 1 teaspoon cumin
- 1 teaspoon smoked paprika

- 1/4 teaspoon turmeric
- 1/4 teaspoon curry powder
- 1/8 teaspoon cinnamon
- Pinch red pepper flakes
- 1 teaspoon kosher salt
- Freshly ground black pepper, to taste

For the salad

- 1 tablespoon olive oil
- 1 tablespoon red wine vinegar
- Kosher salt and freshly cracked black pepper

- 3 Persian cucumbers, chopped
- 1 cup (145 g) cherry tomatoes, halved
- 1/4 red onion, thinly sliced

- 1/4 cup feta (the kind that comes in brine), crumbled
- 4 cups butter lettuce, torn
- 1 cup Skinny Tzatziki (from my blog)

Instructions

1. Cut the chicken thighs into 1-inch pieces.
2. In a medium bowl, combine olive oil and lemon juice. Whisk until combined.
3. Add the garlic, cumin, paprika, turmeric, curry powder, cinnamon, red pepper, salt and black pepper and whisk again. Pour the marinade over the chicken making sure it evenly coat (careful it will stain your fingers). Refrigerate and marinate for at least 30 minutes, up to overnight.
4. Preheat an outdoor grill or indoor grill pan to medium-low heat.
5. Thread the chicken pieces among 4 wooden or metal skewers, discarding the marinade in the bowl.
6. Grill the chicken, turning the skewers occasionally, until golden brown and cooked through in the center, about 15 to 18 minutes.To make the salad:
7. For the salad: In a medium bowl, whisk together the oil and vinegar and season with salt and pepper. Add the cucumbers, cherry tomatoes, and red onion and toss to combine.
8. Divide the lettuce between 4 bowls, top with tomato salad, feta and grilled chicken. Serve with Tzaziki for dipping.

358. Skillet Taco Cauliflower Rice

Ingredients

- 1 lb 93% lean ground turkey
- 1 1/4 tsp kosher salt
- 1 tsp garlic powder
- 1 tsp cumin
- 1 tsp chili powder
- 1 tsp paprika
- 1/2 tsp dried oregano
- 1/2 small onion, minced
- 2 tbsp bell pepper, minced
- 3/4 cup water
- 4 oz canned tomato sauce (1/2 can)
- 4 cups uncooked riced cauliflower

For the toppings

- 4 ounces avocado (1 small)
- chopped cilantro
- 1 cup chopped lettuce
- 1/4 cup jarred salsa
- lime wedges

Instructions

1. Over high heat, brown the turkey in a large skillet breaking it into smaller pieces as it cooks, about 5 minutes.
2. When no longer pink add 1 teaspoon salt and the dry seasoning and mix well.
3. Add the onion, pepper, water and tomato sauce and cover.
4. Simmer on low for about 15 minutes.

5. Remove the cover and add the cauliflower, add 1/4 teaspoon salt and cook until tender, about 8 minutes.

6. Transfer to a plate and serve with avocado, lettuce, salsa and lime.

359. Chicken Salad with Lemon and Dill

Ingredients

- 10 1/2 ounces cooked skinless boneless chicken breasts (from 1 whole rotisserie chicken)
- 2 tablespoons fresh dill
- zest and juice of 1 lemon
- 1 tablespoon extra virgin olive oil
- 1/4 teaspoon kosher salt

Instructions

1. Remove the chicken legs, wings and thighs from the rotisserie chicken and set aside for another meal.

2. Remove the skin from the 2 breasts and remove the meat from the bones. Break the chicken into chunks with your hands or a knife and place into a large bowl. Add the fresh dill, lemon juice, lemon zest, olive oil and salt.

3. Refrigerate until ready to eat.

360. Nut Butter

Ingredients

- 16 ounces (3 cups) raw almonds, walnuts or pecans*
- 1/4 teaspoon salt
- Optional: ½ teaspoon vanilla extract
- Optional to taste: ground cinnamon
- Optional to taste: maple syrup or honey

Instructions

1. Preheat the oven to 350F. Spread the almonds, walnuts or pecans on a large, rimmed baking sheet and toast the almonds about 10 minutes, mixing halfway. (Don't let them get dark).

2. Let them cool about 10 minutes when they are warm, not hot.

3. Transfer the nuts to a high-speed blender or food processor. Blend until creamy, scraping down the sides as necessary. Be patient, it may seem like it will never turn to butter, but it will! It will go from clumps, to a ball against the side of the food processor (keep scraping the sides), then finally it will turn very creamy. If the mixture gets too hot, stop and let it cool down for a few minutes.

4. Once the nut butter is very creamy, blend in the salt. If you wish to add additional flavors such as vanilla, cinnamon or honey, let the mixture cool, add the optional add ins and blend until

creamy once again. Keep in mind, the texture will harden slightly if you add honey or maple syrup.

5. Let the nut butter cool to room temperature, then transfer the mixture to a glass jar and tighten the lid. Store in the refrigerator for up to 3 to 4 weeks, or until you see any signs of spoilage.

361. Braised Chicken with Tomatoes and Rosemary

Ingredients

- 10 skinless chicken thighs on the bone, 5 oz each
- kosher salt and fresh black pepper
- 3 – 4 small sprigs fresh rosemary
- 1 tbsp + 1 tsp olive oil
- 1 large yellow onion, finely chopped
- 4 garlic cloves, chopped
- 1 celery stalk, chopped
- 1 carrot, chopped

- pinch red pepper flakes, optional
- 2 cups Imported crushed tomatoes (Tuttoroso)
- 1/4 tsp dried marjoram
- 1/4 cup dry white wine (Omit for Whole30)
- 2 cups low sodium, fat free chicken broth
- kosher salt and fresh black pepper

Instructions

Dutch Oven

- Lightly season the chicken with salt and fresh pepper. Place a Dutch Oven or large heavy pot on medium-high heat. Add 1 tbsp oil, when hot add the chicken and sear until browned on all sides, about 6-7 minutes on each side. Transfer chicken to a dish and set aside.

- Sauté garlic and onions (and red pepper flakes if using) in remaining oil; sauté until golden, about 3 minutes, stirring occasionally. Add celery and carrots and saute on medium-low for about 2-3 minutes, until soft. Add the wine and chicken broth, scraping any caramelized bits from the bottom with a wooden spoon.

- Add tomatoes, marjoram, and reduce heat to low, adjust salt and pepper to taste and simmer for 30 minutes.

- Add the chicken and rosemary to the sauce, partially cover and cook slowly on low heat for another 25 – 30 minutes, stirring occasionally, adding water if needed.

Slow Cooker

- Start with the same directions step 1 and 2 on the stove, reducing the chicken broth to 1 cup. Transfer to the slow cooker with the remaining ingredients and cook on low for 8 hours.

Instant Pot

- Lightly season the chicken with salt and fresh pepper. Press saute on the Instant Pot and add 1/2 tbsp oil, brown half of the chicken and sear until browned on all sides, about 6-7 minutes on each side. Transfer chicken to a dish and set aside, repeat with the remaining 1/2 tbsp oil and chicken. Set aside.

- Add remaining teaspoon oil, add garlic, onions (red pepper flakes if using) celery and carrots and saute on medium-low for about 3 to 4 minutes, until soft. Add the wine and 1 cup chicken broth, scraping any caramelized bits from the bottom with a wooden spoon.

- Add tomatoes, marjoram, adjust salt and pepper to taste and mix, return the chicken to the pot, add the rosemary to the sauce, cover and cook high pressure 30 minutes, natural release.

362. Easy Shredded Harrisa Chicken

Ingredients

- 1 pound boneless, skinless chicken breasts
- 1/2 teaspoon ground cumin
- 1/4 teaspoon garlic powder
- 1/2 teaspoon Kosher salt
- 1 cup mild Harissa sauce (I like Mina)
- optional, serve with Tzatziki

Instructions

Slow Cooker Instructions

1. Season the chicken with the cumin, garlic powder, pinch of salt, and pepper.
2. Place chicken in a slow cooker, pour the harissa over the chicken, and cover. Cook on HIGH for 2 hours or LOW 4 hours.
3. Remove chicken from the slow cooker and shred with two forks.

Pressure Cooker Instructions

4. Season the chicken with the cumin, garlic powder, pinch of salt, and pepper.
5. Place chicken in the pressure cooker, pour the harissa over the chicken and cook high pressure 20 minutes. Quick or natural release then shred with two forks. If using frozen chicken breasts, cook 25 minutes.

363. Bacon Parmesan Spaghetti Squash

Ingredients

- 4 slices center cut bacon, sliced
- 1 medium spaghetti squash (yields 3 cups cooked)
- pinch Kosher salt
- 1 1/2 tablespoons extra virgin olive oil
- 1/2 cup course grated Parmigiano Reggiano
- fresh black pepper, to taste

Instructions

1. Heat a medium skillet over medium heat.

2. Add the bacon and cook until crisp, about 5 to 6 minutes. Transfer bacon to a paper towel with a slotted spoon.

3. Preheat oven to 400F degrees.

4. Line a baking sheet with foil. Cut the squash in half lengthwise, and use a spoon to scrape out the seeds and soft yellow strands. Lightly season with salt and pepper, place the squash face down on the baking sheet and bake for 60 to 65 minutes or until the flesh easily pierces with a fork.

5. When soft, transfer to a bowl and combine with olive oil, parmesan, and bacon.

364. Ham and Swiss Crustless Quiche

Ingredients

- cooking spray
- 1 3/4 cups diced ham steak or leftover ham (9 oz)
- 1 cup chopped steamed broccoli (fresh or frozen)
- 1 cup fresh grated Swiss cheese

- 2/3 cup 2% milk
- 1/4 cup half & half cream
- 5 large eggs
- 1/2 teaspoon kosher salt
- 1/8 teaspoon ground black pepper
- pinch of nutmeg

Instructions

1. Preheat the to 350F degrees. Spray a pie dish with oil.

2. Evenly spread the broccoli in the dish and top it evenly with the ham.

3. Make the custard mixture by whisking together the milk, half and half, eggs, salt, black pepper, and the nutmeg.

4. Pour the custard into the dish and top with Swiss Cheese.

5. Bake 35 to 40 minutes, until the center is set.

6. Cut the quiche into 6 pieces and serve.

365. Ranch Chicken Salad

Ingredients

- 1/2 cup 1% buttermilk
- 3 tablespoons mayonnaise
- 2 tablespoon fresh finely chopped chives
- 1/2 teaspoon kosher salt
- 1/4 teaspoon garlic powder
- 1/4 teaspoon onion powder

- 1/4 teaspoon dried parsley
- 1/4 teaspoon dried basil
- fresh black pepper, to taste
- 2 cups shredded boneless chicken breast, from rotisserie chicken or leftover

- In a medium bowl combine the buttermilk, mayo, chives, salt, garlic powder, onion powder, parsley, basil and black pepper and mix.
- Add the shredded chicken and mix well. Refrigerate until ready to eat.

366. Veggie Ham and Cheese Egg Bake

Ingredients

- olive oil spray
- 2 cups shredded reduced fat sharp cheddar (for gf, check labels)
- 1 tbsp olive oil
- 1/3 cup sliced scallions
- 5 oz sliced shiitake mushrooms
- 1/2 cup chopped red bell pepper
- 7 oz finely diced lean ham steak
- 3/4 cup diced tomatoes, seeded
- 1 cup finely chopped broccoli florets
- 7 large whole eggs
- 5 large egg whites
- 1/4 cup fat free milk
- 1/2 tsp kosher salt
- 1/4 tsp ground black pepper

Instructions

1. Preheat the oven to 375°F. Spray a 9 x 13 baking dish with oil.
2. Place 1 cup of cheese into the baking dish.
3. Heat the oil in a large nonstick skillet over medium heat; add scallions, mushrooms and red pepper and sauté until vegetables are tender, about 5 to 6 minutes. Add the tomatoes and cook 2 – 3 minutes. Add the ham and broccoli and remove from heat. Spread evenly over the cheese mixture.
4. In a large bowl combine the eggs, egg whites, milk, salt and pepper and whisk well. Slowly pour over the vegetables in the baking dish and top with remaining cheese.
5. Bake until a knife inserted near the center comes out clean, 32 to 35 minutes. Let stand 8 to 10 minutes before cutting into 12 pieces.

367. Crustless Broccoli & Cheddar Quiche

Ingredients

- cooking spray
- 3 cups chopped broccoli florets
- 1 cup grated cheddar cheese
- 2/3 cup 2% milk
- 1/4 cup half & half cream
- 5 large eggs
- 3/4 teaspoon kosher salt
- 1/8 teaspoon ground black pepper
- pinch freshly grated nutmeg

Instructions

1. Preheat your oven to 350 degrees. Spray a pie dish with oil.
2. Steam the chopped broccoli florets in the microwave with 1 tablespoon water until tender crisp and green but not mushy, about 2 1/2 to 3 minutes.
3. Evenly spread the broccoli in the dish and top it evenly with the grated cheddar cheese.

4. Make the custard mixture by whisking together the milk, half and half, eggs, salt, black pepper, and the nutmeg. Pour the custard into the dish and bake 35 to 40 minutes, until the center is set.

5. Cut the quiche into 6 pieces and serve.

368. Jalapeno Popper "Nachos"

Ingredients

- Reynolds Wrap Non-Stick Foil
- olive oil spray
- 1/2 pound 99% lean ground turkey
- 1 clove garlic, minced
- 2 tablespoons chopped onion, minced
- 1 tbsp chopped fresh cilantro
- 1/2 teaspoon garlic powder
- 1/2 teaspoon cumin powder

- 1/2 teaspoon kosher salt
- 1/2 tablespoon tomato paste
- 2 tablespoons water
- 8 jalapeno peppers, halved and seeded and membranes removed (use gloves)
- 3 ounces 1/3 less fat cream cheese
- 1 large scallions, green part only, sliced
- 1/2 ounce shredded sharp cheddar cheese

Toppings

- 1/2 cup shredded sharp cheddar cheese
- chopped scallions and cilantro, for garnish

- 2 tablespoons sour cream plus 2 teaspoons water, for drizzling
- 1/2 cup pico de gallo
- 2 tablespoons sliced black olives

Instructions

1. Preheat oven to 400F and line a large baking sheet with nonstick aluminum foil.

2. Heat a medium nonstick skillet over medium heat and spray with oil. Add onion, cilantro and garlic and saute about 2 minutes, until soft. Add ground turkey, salt, garlic powder, cumin and cook meat for 4 to 5 minutes until meat is completely cooked through breaking it up with a spoon. Add the tomato paste and water, mix well and simmer on medium for about 2 to 3 minutes, remove from heat.

3. Meanwhile, combine cream cheese, cheddar and scallions in a medium bowl. Using a small spoon or a spatula, spoon about 1 teaspoon of the cream cheese filling into the peppers.

4. Arrange in a single layer, cut-side up close together. Bake until soft, about 12 to 15 minutes.

5. Top with meat and cheese and bake until melted, about 3 minutes more.

6. Remove from oven and top with pico de gallo, olives and drizzle with sour cream. Garnish with cilantro and scallions and serve immediately.

369. Buffalo Chicken Dip

Ingredients

- 2 boneless skinless chicken breasts (16 ounces)
- 4 oz 1/3 less fat cream cheese, softened (Philadelphia)

- 1 cup fat-free sour cream or Greek yogurt (I prefer sour cream)
- 1/2 cup Franks red hot sauce (or whatever hot sauce you like)

240

- 1/2 cup crumbled blue cheese
- 1 teaspoon white vinegar
- scallions, optional for garnish
- cut up celery sticks and carrot sticks, for dipping

Instructions

1. To make the shredded chicken, place chicken in the slow cooker and add enough water or chicken broth to cover. Cook high 4 hours. Remove and shred with two forks, discard the liquid.

2. Meanwhile, combine the cream cheese, sour cream, vinegar and hot sauce together until smooth. Add half of the blue cheese.

3. Transfer to the slow cooker with the chicken, mixing well and return to the slow cooker, cook low 2 to 3 hours.

4. Transfer to a serving dish and top with the remaining blue cheese, garnish with scallions. Serve hot.

Oven Method

1. To bake this in the oven, you can use cooked shredded chicken breast from a rotisserie chicken, then mix all the ingredients and place them in a baking dish. Bake 350F until hot, about 20 to 25 minutes.

2. Instant Pot Method:

3. Cook chicken covered in water or broth 15 min high pressure. Once you shred and drain set the instant pot to the slow cooker mode, combine Ingredients and proceed.

370. Chicken Thighs with Shallots in Red Wine Vinegar

Ingredients

- 32 oz (8 lean and trimmed) boneless, skinless chicken thighs
- kosher salt and fresh pepper
- 1/2 cup red wine vinegar
- 1 cup chicken broth
- 1 tbsp honey
- 1 tbsp tomato paste
- 1 tsp butter
- 1 large shallot, thinly sliced (3/4 cup)
- 2 cloves garlic, thinly sliced
- 1/2 cup dry white wine
- 2 tbsp light sour cream
- 2 tbsp fresh chopped parsley

Instructions

1. Season the chicken with salt and pepper.

2. In a medium saucepan, combine vinegar, honey, 3/4 cup chicken broth and tomato paste. Boil about 5 minutes, until it reduces down to about 3/4 cup. Remove from heat.

3. In a large skillet, melt butter over medium-low heat and add chicken. Cook on both sides, until brown, about 6-8 minutes. Remove chicken and set aside. Add the shallots and garlic to the

skillet and cook on low until soft, about 5 minutes. Pour the sauce over the chicken, add the wine, remaining broth salt and pepper. Cover and simmer about 20 minutes until tender.

4. Remove the chicken, add sour cream and stir into the sauce (if sauce dries up, add more broth). Boil a few minutes then return chicken to skillet. Top with fresh parsley.

371. Fish Florentine

Ingredients

- 4 (5 oz) thick pieces of skinless white firm fish fillet (such as grouper, bass or halibut)
- 1 tablespoons extra virgin olive oil
- 1 tablespoon salted butter
- 1 cup red bell pepper chopped
- 2 cloves garlic minced

- 9 ounces fresh baby spinach (from two bags)
- 2 ounces 1/3 less fat cream cheese (I like Philadelphia)
- ¼ cup half & half cream
- 3 tablespoons grated Parmesan cheese
- kosher salt
- fresh black pepper

Instructions

1. In a large skillet over medium heat add 1/2 tablespoon of olive oil and 1/2 tablespoon of butter, red bell pepper and garlic and cook for about 4 minutes.

2. Add spinach season with a pinch of salt and pepper mix until the spinach wilts down.

3. Add cream cheese, half & half and parmesan cheese mix well until cream cheese is melted and resembles creamed spinach.

4. Heat a separate skillet on medium high heat, add remaining oil and butter.

5. Season fish on both sides with salt and pepper and place on the hot pan.

6. Cook 6 minutes on first side and flip fish over and cook other side an additional 5 minutes, until cooked through and browned.

7. Divide the spinach mixture on the bottom of each plate and top with piece of fish.

CLASSIC

RECIPES

---

372. Classic Egg Salad

Ingredients

- 6 hard boiled eggs, peeled and chopped
- 3 tablespoons mayonnaise
- 1 teaspoon finely chopped red onion
- 1/4 teaspoon kosher salt
- fresh black pepper, to taste
- 1/8 teaspoon sweet paprika, for garnish
- chopped chives, for garnish

Instructions

Combine all the Ingredients and refrigerate until ready to eat.

373. Instant Pot Chicken Parmesan

Ingredients

- 1 teaspoon extra virgin olive oil
- 2 garlic cloves, thinly sliced
- 1-1/2 cups prepared marinara sauce
- 3 tablespoons grated Parmesan cheese
- Freshly ground black pepper
- 4 thin chicken cutlets (12 ounces total)
- ½ teaspoon kosher salt, or more to taste
- ½ teaspoon dried oregano
- 4 ounces fresh mozzarella cheese, grated
- Chopped basil, for garnish (optional)

Instructions

1. Using the sauté function (on low, if possible), heat the oil in the pressure cooker pot. Stir in the garlic and cook until just turning golden, about 2 minutes. Stir in the marinara sauce, 2 tablespoons of the Parmesan, and 1/4 teaspoon pepper.

2. Increase the sauté heat to medium.

3. Season the chicken with the salt, oregano, and pepper to taste. Nestle the cutlets into the sauce, overlapping as little as possible, then spoon the sauce over to cover the chicken.

4. Lock the lid into place and cook on low pressure for 3 minutes. Manually release the pressure.

5. Sprinkle the mozzarella and the remaining 1 tablespoon Parmesan evenly over the chicken. Cover the pot with the lid (but don't lock it on) and let it sit for 4 to 5 minutes to melt the cheese.

6. Serve as is or, for deeper flavors and a little bit of crispiness, broil the cheese until golden and bubbling: Heat the broiler with a rack 4 inches from the heat source. Scoop the chicken and sauce into a greased small rimmed baking sheet, trying to keep the cheese on top. Broil until the cheese has browned, 2 to 3 minutes. Sprinkle with basil, if desired.

374. Roast Chicken with Rosemary and Lemon

Ingredients

- 1 (3 lb) chicken, washed and dried, fat removed
- 1/2 onion, chopped in large chunks
- 2 cloves garlic, smashed
- 1 lemon, halved
- 3 sprigs fresh rosemary
- 1 tbsp dried herbes de Provence (or dried rosemary)
- kosher salt and fresh pepper

Instructions

Heat oven to 425F

1. Season chicken inside and out with salt, pepper, and herbs de Provence.
2. Squeeze half of the lemon on the outside of the chicken and stuff the remains of the lemon along with onion, garlic, rosemary sprigs inside the chicken. Transfer to a sheet pan, and tie the chicken by taking kitchen twine and plumping up the breast, then coming around with the string to lasso the legs and tie them together. Don't forget to tuck the wing tips under themselves so they don't burn.
3. Roast the chicken with the feet towards the back of the oven, until the juices run clear, and internal temperature is 160°F, about 50-60 minutes (Insert thermometer between the thickest part of the leg and the thigh).
4. Let the bird rest for 10 minutes, tenting with foil before carving.
5. Serve chicken, either one breast, or one thigh/drumstick, skin is optional.

375. Chopped Feta Salad

Ingredients

- 8 cups chopped romaine lettuce
- 1/2 English cucumber, peeled and diced in large chunks
- 1/3 cup Feta cheese, crumbled
- 1/8 small red onion, sliced lengthwise
- 1/4 cup olive oil
- 2 tablespoon red wine vinegar
- 1 1/2 tablespoons fresh chopped dill
- 1/2 teaspoon kosher salt
- fresh black pepper, to taste

Instructions

Toss all the Ingredients together and serve right away.

376. Ranch Chicken Salad

Ingredients

- 1/2 cup 1% buttermilk
- 3 tablespoons mayonnaise
- 2 tablespoon fresh finely chopped chives
- 1/2 teaspoon kosher salt
- 1/4 teaspoon garlic powder
- 1/4 teaspoon onion powder
- 1/4 teaspoon dried parsley
- 1/4 teaspoon dried basil
- fresh black pepper, to taste
- 2 cups shredded boneless chicken breast, from rotisserie chicken or leftover

Instructions

- In a medium bowl combine the buttermilk, mayo, chives, salt, garlic powder, onion powder, parsley, basil and black pepper and mix.
- Add the shredded chicken and mix well. Refrigerate until ready to eat.

377. Low Carb Potato Salad

Ingredients

- 1 pound cauliflower florets, chopped into 1/2 inch pieces
- Kosher salt
- 1/2 cup olive oil mayonnaise (I love Sir Kensington)
- 1 teaspoon yellow mustard
- 1 ½ teaspoon fresh dill
- Freshly ground black pepper, to taste
- 1/4 cup finely chopped dill pickle
- 1 medium celery stalk, finely chopped
- 1/4 cup chopped red onions
- 1 tablespoon pickle juice
- 6 hard boiled eggs, sliced
- paprika, for garnish

Instructions

1. Place 1 inch of water in a large pot with 1 teaspoon salt and bring to a boil. Add the cauliflower and cook until tender, 8 to 10 minutes. Drain and set aside in a large bowl.
2. Meanwhile, in a small bowl, combine the mayonnaise, mustard, dill, pinch of salt and pepper. Set aside.
3. Chop 4 of the eggs and add to the bowl with the cauliflower. Slice the remaining two eggs for topping.
4. Add pickle, celery, 1/4 teaspoon salt, pepper, and red onion. Add the mayo mixture and pickle juice to the cauliflower and toss gently to evenly coat. Garnish with remaining sliced eggs and sprinkle with paprika.

378. Shrimp Scampi Foil Packets

Ingredients

- Reynolds Wrap Heavy-Duty Aluminum Foil
- 4 garlic cloves, 2 grated, 2 thinly sliced
- 1/2 teaspoon kosher salt
- 1 tablespoons extra virgin olive oil
- 40 jumbo peeled and deveined shrimp (slightly over 1 pound)
- 1/4 cup dry white wine
- 1 tablespoon fresh lemon juice
- 4 pinches red pepper flakes
- 2 tablespoons unsalted butter, melted
- 3 tablespoons chopped parsley
- whole wheat crusty bread, optional for serving
- 1 lemon, cut into wedges

Instructions

1. Whisk the grated garlic, salt, oil in a medium bowl. Add shrimp, toss to coat, and chill, uncovered, at least 30 minutes and up to 1 hour.

2. Make foil packets. Tear off 4 16" sheets of Reynolds Wrap Heavy-Duty Aluminum Foil.

3. Place 10 shrimp on the center of each foil sheet. Top each with remaining garlic slices, 1 tablespoon wine, lemon juice, pinch red pepper flakes and 1/2 tablespoon melted butter over each.

4. Bring up the long sides of the foil, so the ends meet over the food. Double fold the ends, leaving room for heat to circulate inside. Double fold the two short ends to seal the packet

5. Grill over high heat, 8 minutes. Use gloves or tongs to remove and carefully open. Top with chopped parsley. Serve with lemon wedges.

6. (To bake in the oven, preheat oven to 425F and cook about 10 minutes.)

379. Chicken and Mushrooms in a Garlic White Wine Sauce

Ingredients

- 8 chicken tenderloins, 16 oz total
- 2 tsp butter
- 2 tsp olive oil
- 1/4 cup all-purpose flour* (use rice flour for gluten free, omit for paleo, w30)
- 3 cloves garlic, minced
- 12 oz sliced mushrooms
- 1/4 cup white wine (omit for w30, paleo and add more broth)
- 1/3 cup fat free chicken broth
- salt and fresh pepper to taste
- 1/4 cup chopped fresh parsley

Instructions

1. Preheat oven to 200°F.

2. Season chicken with salt and pepper. Lightly dredge in flour.

3. Heat a large skillet on medium heat; when hot add 1 tsp butter and 1 tsp olive oil.

4. Add chicken to the skillet and cook on medium heat for about 5 minutes on each side, or until chicken is no longer pink.

5. Set aside in a warm oven.

6. Add additional oil and butter to the skillet, then garlic and cook a few seconds; add mushrooms, salt and pepper stirring occasionally until golden, about 5 minutes.

7. Add wine, chicken broth, parsley; stir the pan with a wooden spoon breaking up any brown bits from the bottom of the pan. Cook a few more minutes or until the liquid reduces by half.

8. Top the chicken with the mushroom sauce and serve.

380. BLT Lettuce Wraps

Ingredients

- 4 slices center cut bacon, cooked and chopped
- 1 medium tomato, diced
- 1 tbsp light mayonnaise (or whole30 approved mayo)
- 3 large iceberg lettuce leaves
- fresh cracked pepper
- 1 ounce avocado optional (add 1 point)

Instructions

1. Carefully remove 2 large outer leaves of a head of lettuce. If you rip or tear one, just save it for the 3rd leaf you need to shred. Shred the 3rd leaf and set aside.

2. Dice tomato and set aside in a bowl.

3. Combine diced tomato with mayonnaise and fresh black pepper.

4. Place lettuce cups on a plate, top with shredded lettuce. Add tomato then bacon and roll it like a wrap and dig in!

381. Chicken Pesto Bake

Ingredients

- 2 (16 oz total) boneless, skinless chicken breasts
- kosher salt and fresh pepper to taste
- 4 teaspoons Skinny Basil Pesto
- 1 medium tomatoes, sliced thin
- 6 tbsp (1.5 oz) shredded mozzarella cheese
- 2 teaspoons grated parmesan cheese

Instructions

- Wash chicken and dry with a paper towel. Slice chicken breast horizontally to create 4 thinner cutlets. Season lightly with salt and fresh pepper.

- Preheat the oven to 400° F. Line baking sheet with foil or parchment if desired for easy clean-up.

- Place the chicken on prepared baking sheet. Spread about 1 teaspoon of pesto over each piece of chicken.
- Bake for 15 minutes or until chicken is no longer pink in center. Remove from oven; top with tomatoes, mozzarella and parmesan cheese. Bake for an additional 3 to 5 minutes or until cheese is melted.
- To Grill: Grill chicken over medium flame on both sides until cooked through in the center. Lower flame, top chicken with pesto, tomatoes and cheese, and close grill until cheese melts.

382. Grilled Steak with Tomatoes, Red Onion and Balsamic

Ingredients

- 2 lb flank or london broil steak
- kosher salt and fresh pepper
- garlic powder
- 1 tbsp extra virgin olive oil
- 2 tbsp balsamic
- 1/3 cup red onion, chopped
- 3-4 tomatoes, chopped (about 3 1/2 cups)
- 1 tbsp fresh herbs such as oregano, basil or parsley

Instructions

1. Pierce steak all over with a fork. Season generously with salt, pepper and garlic powder and set aside about 10 minutes at room temperature.
2. In a large bowl, combine onions, olive oil, balsamic, salt and pepper. Let onions sit a few minutes with the salt and balsamic to mellow a bit. Combine with tomatoes and fresh herbs and adjust seasoning if needed.
3. Heat grill or broiler on high heat. Cook steak about 7 minutes on each side for medium rare or longer to taste. Remove from grill and let it rest on a plate for about 5 minutes before slicing.
4. Slice steak thin on the diagonal; top with tomatoes and serve.

383. Grilled Garlic and Herb Chicken and Veggies

Ingredients

- 1 1/2 lbs boneless, skinless thin sliced chicken cutlets
- 3 ounce package Delallo garlic and herb veggie marinade
- kosher salt
- 1 lb asparagus (1 bunch), tough ends removed
- 1 medium 8 ounce zucchini, sliced 1/4-inch thick

- 1 medium yellow squash, sliced 1/4-inch thick
- 1 red bell pepper, seeded and sliced into strips
- olive oil cooking spray

Instructions

1. Shake marinade well. Season chicken with 1/2 teaspoon salt and 2 tablespoons of the veggie herb marinade at least 1 hour, or as long as overnight.
2. Marinate the veggies with the remaining marinade.
3. Heat a grill over medium-high, be sure grates are clean and well oiled to prevent sticking.
4. Put veggies on 1 large grill tray or 2 smaller trays (or cook in batches), season with 3/4 teaspoon salt and black pepper and cook, turning constantly until the edges are browned, about 8 minutes. Set aside on a platter.
5. Cook the chicken about 4 to 5 minutes on each side, until grill marks appear and the chicken is cooked though, transfer to a platter with the veggies and serve.

384. Buffalo Brussels Sprouts with Crumbled Blue Cheese

Ingredients

- 2 tbsp olive oil
- 1 lb brussels sprouts, trimmed and halved
- 1/4 cup Franks Hot Sauce
- 2 tbsp crumbled blue cheese, for topping

Instructions

1. Preheat oven to 425°F. Heat an oven-safe nonstick 12-inch sauté pan over medium-high heat and add olive oil and brussels sprouts in one layer and let cook undisturbed for about 3 minutes until beginning to caramelize. Turn occasionally for an additional 2-3 minutes until golden all over.
2. Transfer to the oven and roast for 8-10 minutes, until softened a bit but still slightly al dente. Drizzle with hot sauce, toss and top with crumbled blue cheese.

385. California Spicy Crab Stuffed Avocado

Ingredients

- 2 tablespoons light mayo (I used Hellmans) *for whole30 use compliant mayo
- 2 teaspoons sriracha, plus more for drizzling
- 1 teaspoon chopped fresh chives
- 4 oz lump crab meat
- 1/4 cup peeled and diced cucumber
- 1 small Hass avocado (about 4 oz avocado when pitted and peeled)

- 1/2 teaspoon furikake (I like Eden Shake or use sesame seeds)
- 2 teaspoons gluten-free soy sauce (coconut aminos for whole30/paleo)

Instructions

1. In a medium bowl, combine mayo, sriracha and chives.
2. Add crab meat and cucumber and chive and gently toss.
3. Cut the avocado open, remove pit and peel the skin or spoon the avocado out.
4. Fill the avocado halves equally with crab salad.
5. Top with furikake and drizzle with soy sauce.

386. Instant Pot Chicken Cacciatore

Ingredients

- 4 chicken thighs, with the bone, skin removed
- kosher salt and fresh pepper to taste
- olive oil spray
- 1/2 can (14 oz) crushed tomatoes (Tuttorosso my favorite!)
- 1/2 cup diced onion
- 1/4 cup diced red bell pepper
- 1/2 cup diced green bell pepper
- 1/2 teaspoon dried oregano
- 1 bay leaf
- 2 tablespoons chopped basil or parsley for topping

Instructions

1. Season chicken with salt and pepper on both side.
2. Press saute on the Instant Pot, lightly spray with oil and brown chicken on both sides a few minutes. Set aside.
3. Spray with a little more oil and add onions and peppers. Sauté until soften and golden, 5 minutes.
4. Pour tomatoes over the chicken and vegetables, add oregano, bay leaf, salt and pepper, give it a quick stir and cover.
5. Cook high pressure 25 minutes; natural release.
6. Remove bay leaf, garnish with parsley and serve over pasta, squasta or whatever you wish!

387. Philly Cheesesteak Stuffed Portobello Mushrooms

Ingredients

- 6 ounces thin sliced sirloin steaks
- 1/8 teaspoon kosher salt
- black pepper to taste
- cooking spray
- 3/4 cup diced onion
- 3/4 cup diced green pepper

- 1/4 cup light sour cream
- 2 tablespoons light mayonnaise
- 2 oz light cream cheese, softened
- 3 oz shredded mild provolone cheese (or cheese of your choice)
- 4 medium portobello mushrooms, with no cracks

Instructions

1. Preheat the oven to 400F. Spray a baking sheet with oil.
2. Gently remove the stems, scoop out the gills and spray the tops of the mushrooms with oil, season with 1/8 tsp salt and fresh pepper.
3. Season steak with salt and pepper on both sides.
4. Spray a large skillet with cooking spray and heat on high, let the pan get very hot then add the steak and cook on high heat about 1 to 1 1/2 minutes on each side, until cooked through.
5. Transfer to a cutting board and slice thin, set aside.
6. Reduce the heat to medium-low, spray with more oil and saute onions and peppers 5 to 6 minutes, until soft.
7. Combine all the ingredients in a medium bowl. Transfer to the mushroom caps, about 1/2 cup each.
8. Bake in the oven until the cheese is melted and the mushrooms are tender, about 20 minutes.

388. Chicken and Shrimp Laap

Ingredients

- 1 teaspoon coconut flour
- 1 teaspoon oil
- 1 small shallot, thinly sliced
- 1 pound ground chicken thighs
- ½ pound large shrimp, peeled and chopped coarsely
- 2 tablespoons Asian fish sauce
- 2 tablespoons fresh lime juice
- ½ teaspoon cayenne pepper
- 2 scallions, thinly sliced
- ¼ cup chopped cilantro
- ¼ cup minced fresh mint leaves
- 1 head butter lettuce, washed and spun dry, and separated into leaves

Instructions

1. On a parchment-lined baking tray, toast the coconut flour in a 300°F oven for 5 to 7 minutes or until the flour turns golden brown. (You can also toast the coconut flour in a dry pan over low heat instead.) Set aside.
2. In the meantime, heat the oil in a large skillet over medium-high heat. Add the sliced shallot and sauté for 2 to 3 minutes or until softened.
3. Add the ground chicken, and break it up with a spatula. Cook, stirring, for 3 to 5 minutes until no longer pink.

4. Add the shrimp and stir-fry for another 2 to 3 minutes or until the shrimp is cooked through.

5. Remove the pan from the heat and add the fish sauce, lime juice, toasted coconut flour, and cayenne pepper. Adjust the seasoning to taste.

6. Sprinkle the chopped herbs on top. To eat, wrap a 1/3 cup of laap in a lettuce leaf and devour.

389. Buffalo Brussels Sprouts with Crumbled Blue Cheese

Ingredients

- 2 tbsp olive oil
- 1 lb brussels sprouts, trimmed and halved
- 1/4 cup Franks Hot Sauce
- 2 tbsp crumbled blue cheese, for topping

Instructions

1. Preheat oven to 425°F. Heat an oven-safe nonstick 12-inch sauté pan over medium-high heat and add olive oil and brussels sprouts in one layer and let cook undisturbed for about 3 minutes until beginning to caramelize. Turn occasionally for an additional 2-3 minutes until golden all over.

2. Transfer to the oven and roast for 8-10 minutes, until softened a bit but still slightly al dente. Drizzle with hot sauce, toss and top with crumbled blue cheese.

390. One Skillet Chicken with Bacon and Green Beans

Ingredients

- 4 strips center-cut bacon, chopped
- 1 pound boneless, skinless chicken breasts, cut lengthwise into thin cutlets
- kosher salt
- freshly ground black pepper
- 2 tablespoons minced shallot
- 2 cloves garlic, minced
- ¾ cup low-sodium chicken broth
- ½ cup crisp white wine, such as Sauvignon Blanc (use broth for Whole30 or Paleo)
- 1 teaspoon chopped fresh thyme
- 8 ounces French green beans

1. Heat a large non-stick skillet over medium heat. Add the bacon and sauté until brown and crisp. Remove bacon pieces with a slotted spoon, transfer to a paper towel lined plate and set aside. Discard the majority of the bacon grease, leaving a very thin coating in the pan.

2. Season both sides of the chicken pieces with 1/4 tsp salt and black pepper and add to the skillet. Cook 4 minutes per side, or until cooked through. Transfer to a plate and tent with foil.

3. Add the shallots to the now empty skillet and sauté 1 minute, scraping up brown bits. Add the garlic and sauté 30 seconds more. Add the broth, wine and thyme and stir. Add the green beans, increase the heat to medium-high and cook for about 8 minutes, or until the sauce has reduced and the green beans are crisp tender, stirring occasionally.

4. Transfer the chicken breasts and green beans to a serving platter. Season beans with 1/8 teaspoon salt and fresh pepper. Pour chicken juices into sauce with 1/8 teaspoon salt, stir and cook for an additional 30 seconds. Pour sauce over the chicken and green beans and top with chopped bacon.

391. Arugula Salad with Crispy Proscuitto, Parmesan and Fried Eggs

Ingredients

- 2 ounces sliced proscuitto (4 slices)
- 5 cups baby arugula
- 1/4 cup shaved parmesan cheese

- olive oil spray
- 2 large eggs
- fresh black pepper, to taste

Dressing:

- 2 tbsp minced shallots
- 2 tbsp extra virgin olive oil
- 1 tbsp sherry vinegar

- 2 tsp Dijon mustard
- 1/4 tsp honey

Instructions

1. Preheat oven to 375°F. Line a large baking sheet with parchment paper.

2. Arrange the proscuitto on the prepared baking sheet and bake 15 minutes or until lightly browned and crisp. Crumble into large pieces.

3. Meanwhile, whisk the dressing Ingredients in a large bowl. Add the arugula and toss well. Divide on two plates and top with crumbled proscuitto and parmesan.

4. To cook the eggs heat a large nonstick skillet over medium-low heat, spray with oil and gently break the eggs. Season with salt and cook, covered until the whites are set and the yolks are still runny, or longer if desired. Place the egg on top of each salad and serve with fresh pepper, if desired.

392. Chicken with Roasted Red Pepper Cream Sauce

Ingredients

- 1 tablespoon clarified butter or avocado oil
- 4 chicken thighs or 2 thighs and 2 drumsticks
- 1/4 small yellow onion thinly sliced
- 2 large cloves garlic crushed
- 1/2 cup water
- 1/4 teaspoon salt
- 1/4 teaspoon black pepper
- 4 oz cream cheese
- 2 tablespoons roasted red bell pepper minced
- 1/2 teaspoon dried Italian herb seasoning

Instructions

1. Turn pressure cooker on, press "Sauté", and wait 2 minutes for the pot to heat up. Add the ghee or oil and the chicken thighs (skin down), and cook until browned, about 2 minutes per side. Press "Cancel" to stop sautéing.

2. Add the onion, garlic, water, salt, and black pepper to the pot. Turn the pot on Manual, High Pressure for 15 minutes and then do a quick release.

3. Use thongs to transfer the pieces of chicken to a plate; let them cool slightly, and then remove the skin (unless you don't mind soggy skin).

4. Press "Sauté", and whisk in the cream cheese, roasted red bell pepper, and dried Italian herb mix. Continue whisking until the sauce is smooth and thickened slightly, about 4 to 5 minutes. Return the chicken back to the sauce.

5. Serve along with cauliflower mash, cauliflower rice, or something else to soak up the sauce.

393. Pressure Cooker Pot Roast

Ingredients

- 2 to 3 pound roast
- 1 tsp salt
- 1 tsp pepper
- 2 cloves garlic
- 2 tbsp. worstershire
- 16 ounces radishes
- 1 medium onion
- 8 ounces mushrooms
- 1 cup beef stock
- 2 tbsp. avocado oil

Instructions

1. Slice mushrooms and cut radishes in half.

2. Quarter onions. Set aside

3. Place a tbsp of avocado oil into instant pot and set to saute.

4. Add vegetables to the Instant Pot. Cook until onions have caramelized. Radishes will not be fully cooked though.

5. Remove veggies and set aside

6. Add remaining tbsp of oil.

7. Salt and Pepper roast on both sides

8. Place roast on saute and brown roast on both sides

9. Pour in beef broth and Worcestershire sauce. Hit Manual high pressure for 45 minutes.

10. Allow Instant Pot to depressurize naturally then add back your veggies.

11. Hit manual. Change time to 1 minute high pressure. Once timer goes off, use quick pressure release.

12. Let roast and veggies sit in Instant Pot for ~5 minutes before eating.

394. Steamed Crab Legs

Ingredients

- 3 clusters fresh crab legs
- 1 cup water

Instructions

1. Insert steaming rack into your Instant Pot.

2. Pour 1 cup of water.

3. Add fresh or thawed crab legs (if using frozen) to the pot.

4. Place the lid on the Instant Pot and seal the vent.

5. Press the manual button and set the time to 2 minutes.

6. Once the Instant Pot beeps, quick release the pressure.

7. Use tongs to remove the crab legs.

395. Low Carb Grilled Swordfish Skewers with Pesto Mayo

Ingredients

- 1 lb swordfish, cut into 1 inch cubes
- 16 cherry tomatoes
- salt and pepper
- 1 tsp olive oil to coat
- 1/4 cup pesto
- 1/4 cup mayonnaise

Instructions

1. Divide the swordfish cubes into four equal portions.

2. Alternate the swordfish with the cherry tomatoes on your skewers.

3. Brush with olive oil and season with salt and pepper.

4. Preheat the grill for at least 5 minutes, then carefully place your skewers on the hot grill.

5. Cook for about 1 minute per (four) sides of your cubes – a little longer if your swordfish pieces are really thick.

6. Serve warm or chilled with a salad.

7. Combine the pesto and mayonnaise in a small bowl and stir well. Serve with the skewers.

396. Thai Shrimp Soup

Ingredients

- 2 tbsp unsalted butter or ghee, divided in half
- ½lb (225g) medium uncooked shrimp, peeled and deveined
- ½ yellow onion, diced
- 2 cloves garlic, minced
- 4 cups chicken broth
- 2 tbsp fresh lime juice
- 2 tbsp fish sauce, this brand is whole30 compliant
- 2½ tsp red curry paste, like this one

- 1 tbsp coconut aminos (paleo whole30) or can use 1 tbsp tamari sauce for low carb
- 1 stalk lemongrass, bruised (smashed) and finely chopped
- 1 cup sliced fresh white mushrooms
- 1 tbsp grated fresh ginger root
- 1 tsp sea salt
- ½ tsp freshly ground black pepper
- 1 (13.66-ounce) can unsweetened, full-fat coconut milk (this brand is whole30 compliant)
- 3 tbsp chopped fresh cilantro

Instructions

1. Press the Sauté button once. Once the inner pot becomes hot, add 1 tbsp butter. Once butter is melted, add the shrimp and stir until shrimp turns pink and begins to curl. Immediately transfer shrimp to a medium bowl. Set aside.

2. Add remaining 1 tbsp butter to the inner pot. Once butter is melted, add onions and garlic and sauté until garlic is fragrant and onions become translucent. Press Cancel to turn off the heat.

3. Add chicken broth, lime juice, fish sauce, red curry paste, coconut aminos or tamari sauce, lemongrass, mushrooms, grated ginger root, sea salt, and black pepper. Stir to combine.

4. Cover, lock the lid and flip the steam release handle to the Sealing position. Select Pressure Cook on high and set the cooking time for 5 minutes. When the cook time is complete, allow the pressure to release Naturally for 5 minutes (Don't touch the pot for 5 minutes), and then carefully quick release the remaining pressure by flipping the steam release handle to "Venting". Press Cancel to turn off the heat.

5. Remove the lid. Add shrimp and coconut milk to the pot, and stir.

6. Press the Sauté button twice ("more or high" setting will light up), and let the soup come to a boil. Once boiling Press Cancel to turn off the heat. Let soup rest for 2 minutes in the pot.

7. Ladle the soup into bowls, sprinkle cilantro over the top to garnish and serve.

397. Bacon Cheddar Egg Bites

Ingredients

- 9-10 eggs
- 1/2 cup heavy cream (Sub coconut milk if preferred)
- 1 cup bacon, cooked and chopped or crumbled (about 6-8 slices)
- 1/2 cup cheddar cheese, shredded
- 1 tsp dried basil
- 1 tsp salt
- 1/4 tsp black pepper

Instructions

1. Spray silicone molds or 4 oz. jelly jars liberally with non-stick cooking spray. Set aside.
2. Crack eggs into medium-sized bowl and gently whisk to scramble.

Mix in remaining Ingredients.

3. Pour egg mixture into silicone molds or jelly jars, distributing evenly.
4. Cover molds or jars loosely with aluminum foil.
5. Place trivet in bottom of Instant Pot cooking pot. Add recommended minimum amount of water.
6. Gently lower first silicone mold into pot to rest on top of trivet. (If using jelly jars, place first layer of jars on trivet, leaving about an inch between jars.)
7. Carefully lower second silicone mold and lay it to rest on top of the first mold. Be sure to rotate the mold so the cups are offset (make sure the bottom of the cups on the top mold rest on the spaces between the cups of the bottom mold). If using jelly jars, place second layer of jars, making sure to offset them from the first layer.
8. Close lid, seal vent, and set Instant Pot to cook on HIGH for 14 minutes.
9. Once cook time has ended, allow the Instant Pot to release pressure naturally for 5 minutes, then quick release the remaining pressure.
10. Remove lid and carefully take out molds or jars. You may need to use tongs or chopsticks if space is tight.
11. Place a plate on top of a mold, and holding the plate and mold together, invert, so that the plate is on bottom and the mold is upside-down on top. This should pop egg bites out of the mold. If not, gently press on the top of the mold cups to release.

To freeze:

1. Place egg bites, not touching, on parchment-lined baking sheet and place in freezer for minimum of 1 hour, up to 4 hours.
2. Once frozen, remove egg bites from tray and place into freezer storage bag.
3. Label and date, then place bag back into freezer.
4. To reheat:
5. From thawed, microwave for 30 seconds.
6. From frozen, microwave for 1 1/2 to 2 minutes.

398. Instant Pot Soft-Boiled Eggs

Ingredients

1. 2 cups water
2. 4 eggs

Instructions

1. Pour the 2 cups of water into the insert of the Instant Pot. (Note: Do measure 2 cups as opposed to using the markings on the inside of the insert.) Lay the steamer insert inside. Place 4 eggs on top.

2. Cover the pot. Using the manual button, set the pot to 3 minutes and low pressure. Make sure the valve on top is set to sealing. Fill a bowl with ice water or cold tap water.

3. When the 3 minutes are up, which will take more like 9 minutes, switch the valve to venting, let the steam escape for no more than 1 minute, carefully remove the lid to avoid steaming your face, transfer eggs to water bath, let cool for 30 seconds or so, then peel, season and eat.

399. Ropa Vieja

Ingredients

- 1 (3 – 3 ½) pound chuck roast
- 1 onion, sliced
- 4 teaspoons minced garlic
- 2 ½ teaspoons dried oregano
- 2 teaspoons cumin
- 2 teaspoons paprika
- 2 teaspoons salt
- 1 teaspoon smoked paprika
- ½ teaspoon black pepper
- ½ teaspoon ground cloves
- 1 (14.5 ounce) can diced tomatoes
- 2 bay leaves

Add Later:

- 3 bell peppers (I use a combo of green, red and yellow), sliced
- Green olives with pimentos, garnish

Instructions

1. Add all of the Ingredients (except the ones listed under add later) to an Instant Pot.
2. Secure the lid, close the valve and cook for 90 minutes.
3. Naturally release pressure.
4. Shred the beef using two forks.
5. Press the sauté button, add the bell peppers and cook for 4-5 minutes, or until tender.
6. Stir in the green olives..

400. Pan-Seared and Roasted Mahi Mahi with Mediterranean Salsa and Feta

Ingredients

- 2 Mahi Mahi pieces, about 6 oz. each
- 2 tsp. + 2 tsp. olive oil
- 1/2 C diced onion (or more if you're fond of onion)
- 1 large green bell pepper, stem cut out and seeds remove and then chopped in to 1/2 inch pieces
- 1 tsp. finely minced or crushed garlic
- 1 tsp. Greek seasoning
- 1/2 cup mild tomato salsa from a jar (I used Pace Picante Sauce)
- 1/4 cup homemade chicken stock or chicken broth
- 2 T sliced Kalamata olives (or use regular black olives if you're not a Kalamata olive fan)
- salt and fresh ground black pepper to taste
- 2 T crumbled Feta cheese

Instructions

1. Thaw frozen fish overnight in the refrigerator (or in a pinch you can thaw in cold water, but thawing overnight is preferable.)
2. Preheat oven to 425F/220C.
3. Let fish come to room temperature.
4. Heat 2 teaspoons olive oil in a large frying pan, add onion and green pepper and saute over medium-high heat until they're starting to brown.
5. Add the minced garlic and Greek seasoning and cook a minute or so more.
6. Add the salsa, homemade chicken stock , and olives, and simmer over medium low heat until the mixture has slightly reduced and thickened, about 5-6 minutes.
7. Remove salsa to a bowl.
8. Wipe out the pan, then add the other 2 teaspoons of olive oil and heat about a minute over medium-high heat.
9. Add the fish and sear 2 minutes.
10. Turn fish over and sear for 2 minutes more on the second side.
11. Spray a glass or crockery baking dish with olive oil or non-stick spray.
12. Arrange the seared fish in the baking dish, spoon salsa over, and roast 6 minutes.
13. Remove from oven and sprinkle with crumbled Feta.
14. Serve hot.

401. Herbed Cauliflower "Rice" with Pine Nuts

Ingredients

- 1 large (2 lbs/900 g) head of cauliflower, cut into large florets
- 3 tablespoons grass-fed ghee (clarified butter) or olive oil (or a mixture of both; see Note below)
- ½ teaspoon salt
- ? teaspoon black pepper
- 2 tablespoons minced fresh flat parsley
- 2 tablespoons minced fresh chives
- 1 teaspoon minced fresh rosemary
- 3 tablespoons toasted pine nuts

Instructions

1. Add the cauliflower florets to a medium to large-sized saucepan. Cover the cauliflower completely with water, then put a lid on the saucepan and bring to a boil over high heat. Once boiling, turn the heat down a bit and cock the lid so it doesn't boil over; cook until the cauliflower is fork-tender but not mushy, about 3 to 4 minutes. Drain well and cool slightly.

2. Add half the cooked cauliflower florets to a food processor and pulse until the cauliflower is chopped into very small pieces (about the size of rice), but not pureed (scrape down the sides as necessary). Transfer the chopped cauliflower to a bowl and process the rest of the florets the same way.

3. Add the ghee or olive oil to a large nonstick skillet over medium-high heat. Add the cauliflower, salt, and pepper, and cook until the cauliflower's moisture is cooked off, about 3 to 5 minutes.

4. Turn off the heat and stir in the herbs.

5. Transfer to a serving dish, sprinkle the pine nuts on top, and serve.

402. Chinese Beef Short Ribs

Ingredients

- 4-4.5 pounds beef short ribs cut in 4"-6" lengths (usually this is already done by the butcher)
- 1 cup bone broth
- 2/3 cup coconut amino acids, or 1/3 cup real fermented soy sauce
- 1/3 cup honey
- 1/3 cup toasted sesame oil
- 1/4 cup fresh ginger, freshly grated or minced
- 10 cloves garlic minced or crushed
- 2 teaspoons Chinese five spice powder

Instructions

1. Add all Ingredients to liner pot. Put on and lock lid.
2. Set Instant Pot on "Stew/Meat."
3. The IP will automatically set itself for 35 minutes on high pressure.
4. Make sure steam valve is closed.

5. The Instant Pot will automatically switch over to warm when the cooking time has elapsed. Let it rest and allow it to release the pressure on its own slowly.

6. After 20 minutes the IP will switch to the "Warm" setting. Open the top.

7. Serve. Or puree sauce with cooked winter squash, to make an easy and delicious side dish.

403. Steak Cobb Salad With Cilantro-Lime Vinaigrette

Ingredients

- 3 ounces grass-fed hanger steak
- 1 teaspoon avocado oil
- 1 pasture-raised egg
- 1 slice pasture raised bacon
- 1 cup riced cauliflower
- 1/2 avocado
- 1 cup arugula

- 1 cup mixed greens
- 2 tablespoons olive oil
- 1 teaspoon Brain Octane Oil or MCT oil
- ½ teaspoon lime juice
- 1 teaspoon apple cider vinegar
- ¼ teaspoon sea salt
- ¼ cup diced cilantro

Instructions

Bacon Cauliflower Rice

1. Add minced bacon to a pan over medium heat, cook until no longer translucent

2. Add cauliflower rice to the pan and cook for 4 minutes

3. Grass-Fed Hanger Steak

4. Pat the steak dry and salt both sides generously

5. Add avocado oil to pan over medium heat

6. Add steak to the pan and cook for 4 minutes a side

7. Let the steak rest for 5 minutes and then slice against the grain

Soft-Boiled Egg

1. Bring 6 cups of water to rolling boil

2. Set eggs into the water, cover and cook for 7 minutes

3. Cilantro-Lime Dressing

4. Add lime juice, apple cider vinegar, sea salt, cilantro, brain octane and olive oil in a food processor and blend until there are no more large chunks of cilantro.

Salad

Add mixed greens, arugula and all toppings in a bowl and toss

404. Creamy Chicken Bacon Chowder

Ingredients

Prep

- 6 boneless chicken thighs
- 8 ounce cream cheese full fat
- 4 t minced garlic
- 1 C frozen chopped onion celery mix

- 6 ounce sliced mushrooms
- 4 T butter
- 1 t thyme
- salt and pepper to taste

On Cooking Day

- 3 C chicken broth
- 1 C heavy cream

- 1 pound cooked bacon chopped
- 2 C fresh spinach

Instructions

To Assemble

Cube chicken thighs and add to large zipper bag.

Add remaining Ingredients to chicken in zipper bag. Zip to seal. (Store in fridge until ready to cook)

To Cook

- Pour chicken mixture into Instant Pot, add chicken broth and cook for 30 minutes (soup setting).
- Mix well then add spinach and cream. Cover and let sit for 10 minutes to wilt spinach. Top with chopped bacon.

405. Paleo Beef Brisket Pho

Ingredients

- 1.75 - 2 lbs. Beef brisket
- 1-1.25 lbs beef shank soup bones, , beef knuckle bones, or a combination
- 1 ¼ cups dry shiitake mushrooms*, (rehydrate overnight in room temperature water)
- 3 loose carrots, , roughly chopped*
- 1 medium size yellow onion, , peeled but not sliced (leave it as a whole)

- 1 large size leek, , roughly diced into segments
- Water
- 2 ½ tsp fine sea salt*
- 1 tbsp Red Boat fish sauce
- 1 tsp five spice powder, (optional)
- Tea bags or cheese cloth

Pho Aroma Combo:

- 2 fat thumb size ginger, (scrub clean, no need to peel)

- 4 star anise
- 2 cinnamon sticks

- 8 green cardamom
- 3 medium size shallots

- 4-5 cilantro roots, (alt. 1 ½ tsp coriander seeds)

Garnish

- Lime wedges
- Baby bok choy
- Bean sprouts
- Red or green fresno chili peppers

- Mint leaves
- Asian/Thai basil, (optional)
- Cilantro, (optional)
- Hot chili pepper sauce, (optional)

Instructions

Pre-Cooking:

1. Soak the dry shiitake mushrooms overnight in room temperature water. If rush on time, soak in warm temperature water until the mushrooms are soft and tender.

2. Pre-boil the bones and brisket: add the bones and brisket to a large stockpot and cover with water. Bring the water to boil over high heat, then reduce to medium and simmer for 10 more minutes. Rinse the bones and meat over room temperature tap water. Set aside. Discard the broth.

3. Grill the Ingredients under "Pho Aroma Combo" in a cast iron over medium heat. No oil added. Rotate and flip the Ingredients frequently until you can smell a nice and lovely fragrant. Be careful not to burn the aroma combo. Slightly charred outer surface is okay but not burnt.

4. Slice the mushrooms. Save the mushroom water. Roughly dice leek. Add aroma combo and leeks to large tea bags or cheesecloth tied with a string.

Instant Pot Cooking:

1. In a 6-quart size instant pot, add beef bones, brisket (fatty side up), diced carrots, aroma combo and leeks (in tea bags). Strain the mushroom water as you add the liquid to the pot. Fill the pot with more tap water until it reaches the 4 liter mark. Close the lid in Sealing position - Press Soup - Adjust to 40 minutes/High pressure/More.

2. Allow the instant pot come to natural pressure release (valve dropped), discard the whole onion and aroma combo in tea bags.

3. Remove the brisket and soak it in cold water for at least 10 minutes. This will prevent the meat from turning dark color. Discard aroma & leek tea bags, yellow onion, and beef bones. Season the broth with 2 ½ tsp fine sea salt, 1 tbsp fish sauce, and 1 tsp five spice powder (optional).

4. Thin slice the brisket in 45 degree angle and against the grain. Ladle the broth over bean sprouts, carrots, mushrooms, mint leaves, Asian basil, chili peppers, and sliced brisket. Serve hot with lime wedges.

SUPER

DELICIOUS

RECIPES

406.   Chicken Breast Recipe (Shredded Chicken)

Ingredients

- 4 lb Chicken breast
- 1 tbsp Italian seasoning (or any spices you like)
- 1/2 tsp Sea salt
- 1/2 tsp Black pepper
- 1 cup Chicken broth (or use homemade)

Instructions

1. Place the chicken into the pressure cooker. Season with Italian seasoning, sea salt, and black pepper (or any other spices you like). Pour the chicken broth around the sides of the chicken.

2. Close the lid and select the either the "Poultry" or "Manual" setting. Set the time to 8 minutes for fresh chicken breast, or 13 minutes for frozen chicken breast. (These times are for typical 6-8 ounce chicken breasts. If yours are larger, add a couple of minutes.)

3. When done, let the pressure naturally release for at least 5 minutes. After that, you can turn the valve to "vent" for quick release if you're in a hurry, or continue natural release for the most tender texture.

4. Unplug the pressure cooker and use two forks to shred the chicken. (I prefer to do this right in the pressure cooker, mixing with the juices.) Drain if serving right away, or store with the broth to retain moisture.

407. Instant Pot Chorizo Chili

Ingredients

- 1 1/2 tablespoons olive oil or coconut oil
- 1 large brown onion, roughely chopped
- 1 medium carrot (or 2 small ones), peeled and diced into small cubes
- 1 celery stick, diced into small cubes
- 7 oz / 200 g chorizo sausage, peeled and diced
- 1 long red chilli, finely diced
- 2.2 lb / 1 kg ground beef (grass-fed, if possible)
- 3 cloves garlic, finely diced
- 2 teaspoons ground cumin
- 2 teaspoons ground coriander seed
- 2 cups / about 400 g tinned chopped tomatoes
- 4 tablespoons tomato paste
- 1 tablespoon Tamari or soy sauce (coconut aminos for those on Whole30/paleo)
- 2 teaspoons salt
- 2 bay leaves
- 3 tablespoons of port or fortified red wine (optional but adds lots of depth)

To serve: flash pan-fried zucchini or cooked white rice, chopped avocado and cilantro.

Instructions

1. Turn the Instant Pot on and press the Sauté function key (it should say High, 30 mins). Add the oil, onion, carrot, celery, chorizo and chili and cook together for 3-4 minutes.

2. Add the beef, garlic, spices and stir. Add the tinned tomatoes and paste and stir. Add the rest of the Ingredients and stir together. Press Keep Warm/Cancel.

3. Place and lock the lid, make sure the steam releasing handle is pointing to Sealing. Press MANUAL (High Pressure) and set to 15 minutes. After 3 beeps the pressure cooker will start going.

4. Once the time is up, let the pressure release naturally for 5 minutes, then use the quick release to let off the rest of the steam.

5. If storing in the freezer, make sure to cool down the chili first.

408. Instant Pot Keto Crustless Quiche

Ingredients

- 6 large eggs
- 3/4 cup heavy cream
- 1/2 cup chopped fresh spinach
- 1/4 cup chopped sun dried tomatoes, drained
- 1/4 teaspoon crushed red pepper

- 3/4 cup shredded fontina cheese, or gouda
- 1/2 cup crumbled feta cheese
- 1 teaspoon fresh chopped rosemary
- Salt and pepper

Instructions

1. Butter a 7-8 cup soufflé dish. Place the rack inside the Instant Pot. Then add 1 1/2 cups water to the pot and place the soufflé dish down on the rack.

2. Crack the eggs into a mixing bowl. Whisk well. Then whisk in the cream, 1/2 teaspoon salt, and 1/4 teaspoon ground black pepper.

3. Stir in all remaining Ingredients. Pour the mixture into the soufflé dish.

4. Lock the Instant Pot lid into place. Set on manual Pressure Cook High for 30 minutes. Once the timer goes off, turn the Instant Pot off and perform a Quick Release.

5. Allow the quiche to sit in the Instant pot for 5-10 minutes. Make sure the steam valve has dropped, then unlock the lid.

409. Perfectly Steamed Wild-Caught Crab Legs In The Instant Pot

Ingredients

- 2poundswild-caught Snow Crab legs
- 1cupwater
- 1/3cupsaltedgrass-fed butter, melted (or ghee)
- lemon slices

Instructions

1. Place the metal trivet in the bottom of your Instant Pot.
2. Add 1 cup water.
3. Add the crab legs to the pot. If it helps to thaw them slightly so you can fit them all in the Instant Pot, that's fine.
4. Place the lid on the Instant Pot and seal the vent.
5. Press the "Manual" button and adjust the time to 3 minutes.
6. Quick release the pressure as soon as the Instant Pot beeps.
7. Use tongs to carefully transfer the cooked crab legs to a platter for serving.
8. Serve with melted grass-fed butter and lemon slices!

410. Beef Tongue into Delicious CRISPY BEEF

Ingredients

- 1 beef tongue
- 3 cups water
- 2-3 Tablespoons lard or other traditional fat
- 2-3 teaspoons sea salt
- freshly ground black pepper to taste (omit for AIP)
- 1 teaspoon garlic powder optional
- 1 teaspoon cumin optional (omit for AIP)

Instructions

1. Place whole tongue and water into Instant Pot. (See Recipe Notes below if you don't have an IP.) Seal lid and close valve. Select Stew setting. IP will cook for 35 minutes. Allow pressure to release naturally for 30 minutes, then put dish towel over valve and release pressure.
2. Using tongs, remove tongue to cutting board to cool slightly. When cool enough to handle, peel tongue, making a cut through the skin to begin. (See photo.)
3. Slice tongue starting at the tip, in 1/2" slices, at a slight angle to get larger pieces at the tip.
4. beef tongue into crispy beef- slicing before frying
5. Heat large cast iron skillet or other pan over medium-high heat. Add 1 Tablespoon fat to pan, spreading it around. Place meat slices closely together. Sprinkle with 1 tsp. sea salt, freshly ground pepper, to taste, and optional spices. Cook for 5 minutes, then reduce heat to medium

for an additional 3 minutes. Check the surface that's frying. When it's crispy flip each piece. beef tongue into crispy beef- frying

6. Lightly salt second side of meat. Fry on second side until crispy. Remove first batch and start second batch of meat frying: repeat frying steps with any meat that remains, using lard, sea salt and spices as you did with the first batch.

7. Remove meat to a cutting board and cut into thin strips, as desired. Serve in Mexican food settings, such as tacos, big salads, over eggs with green chilies, inside soft tortillas etc. with accompaniments: fresh cilantro, sweet onions, salsa, avocado, sour cream, cheese, fresh radishes etc.

411. Instant Pot Low-Carb Green Chile Chicken Burrito Bowl

Ingredients

Green Chile Chicken Ingredients

- 4 boneless, skinless chicken breasts, trimmed and cut into strips
- 1 cup green chile salsa (Look for a green chile salsa without much sugar, see notes for what we used.)
- 1 can (4 oz.) diced green chiles (Anaheim chiles, not jalapenos!)

Tomato-Avocado Salsa Ingredients:

- 2 avocados, diced and tossed with 1 T lime juice
- 1 1/2 cups diced tomato or cherry tomatoes cut in half
- 2 green onions, thinly sliced
- 1 T olive oil

- 3 T fresh lime juice (1 T is for tossing with avocado and the rest is for the salsa. See note about the lime juice I used.)
- salt to taste

Cauliflower Rice Ingredients:

- About 6 cups frozen cauliflower rice (We used two 12 oz. packages, but if you have the big package from Costco, just measure out 6 cups.)
- 2 T olive oil
- 1 onion, chopped small
- 1 large Poblano chile pepper, seeds and stem removed and finely diced (These are often called Pasilla Peppers in U.S. grocery stores.)
- 1 tsp ground cumin
- salt and fresh-ground black pepper to taste
- 2 T fresh lime juice to toss with the cooked rice (optional)

269

Instructions

1. Measure out about 6 cups frozen cauliflower rice, break apart lumps, and let it thaw on the counter.

2. Trim chicken breasts and cut each one lengthwise into 2 or 3 strips (so you'll have shorter pieces of chicken when you shred the cooked chicken apart.)

3. Put chicken into the Instant Pot with the Salsa Verde and diced green chiles.

4. Lock the lid and set Instant Pot to MANUAL, HIGH PRESSURE, 8 minutes.

5. When the cooking time is up, use NATURAL RELEASE for 10 minutes, then release the rest of the pressure manually.

6. Remove chicken to a cutting board to cool while you turn the Instant Pot to SAUTE, MEDIUM HEAT and cook the sauce to reduce it, about 8-10 minutes.

7. When it's cool, shred shred chicken apart and put it back into the Instant Pot to mix with the flavorful green chile sauce. You can use the pressure cooker to keep it warm if needed.

8. While chicken cooks, dice avocados and toss with 1 T lime juice, dice tomatoes, and slice green onions. Toss the diced avocado, diced tomato, and sliced green onion with the olive oil, other 2 T fresh lime juice, and a little salt to make the salsa. (If you're doing Weekend Food Prep, I would only make half the salsa and make the rest when you eat the leftovers.)

9. Chop the onion and cut out seeds and stem from the Poblano chile and finely chop the chile.

10. Heat 2 T olive oil in a large non-stick frying pan over medium high heat; add the chopped onion and cook 2-3 minutes. Add the finely diced poblano and cooker 2-3 minutes more. The add the ground cumin and cook about a minute more.

11. Add the cauliflower rice and cook, stirring frequently, until all the liquid has evaporated, the rice is hot, and it's cooked through. This will take about 6-8 minutes, depending on how thawed the cauliflower is, but start to check after about 5 minutes. Season the cooked cauliflower rice with salt and fresh-ground black pepper to taste, and stir in the lime juice if you like the idea of an extra touch of lime.

12. To assemble the finished bowl meal, put a generous amount of cauliflower rice into a bowl, top with a generous scoop of the green chile chicken with sauce, and top with Tomato-Avocado salsa.

13. If you're making this for Weekend Food Prep, I would only make half the amount of salsa when you eat this the first time. Refrigerate the leftover shredded chicken and cooked cauliflower rice separately. When you're ready to eat leftovers, make the rest of the salsa and heat the chicken and cauliflower rice in the microwave or in a pan on the stove.

412. Paleo Beef Barbacoa

Ingredients

- 3 pounds grass-fed chuck roast fat cut off and cut into large chunks
- 1 large onion, peeled and sliced
- 6 garlic cloves
- 2 4oz can of green chilis
- 1 tablespoon oregano
- 1 teaspoon salt
- 1 teaspoons pepper
- 3 dried chipotle peppers stems removed and broken into pieces
- juice of 3 limes
- 3 tablespoons coconut vinegar
- 1 tablespoon cumin
- 1/4 cup water

Instructions

Add all Ingredients to the Instant Pot and stir.

1. Place lid on, make sure vent is closed, and hit the "manual" button. Increase time to 60 minutes.
2. Once done, let naturally release or press "cancel" and release the pressure.
3. Remove lid, shred with a fork, and hit the "sauté" button. Stir regularly as the juices reduce. This may take up to 20-30 minutes to fully reduce.

413. Instant Pot Taco Meat

Ingredients

- 2 pounds ground beef
- 4 tablespoons oil
- 2 red onions, diced
- 3 green bell peppers, diced
- 5 garlic cloves, minced
- 2 teaspoons chili powder
- 2 teaspoons oregano
- 1 teaspoon salt
- 1 teaspoon dried basil
- ½ teaspoon turmeric
- ½ teaspoon black pepper
- 1 teaspoon paprika
- 1 teaspoon cumin
- ½ teaspoon cayenne
- ½ teaspoon chipotle powder
- Cilantro, garnish

Instructions

Add all of the Ingredients to the Instant Pot except for the ground beef.

- Press the "sauté" button and stir-fry for 5-6 minutes.
- Then add the ground beef to the pot and cook until mostly brown.
- Secure the lid, close the pressure valve and cook for 10 minutes at high pressure.
- Naturally release pressure (or you can quick release too if you're in a hurry).
- Open the lid, and if the meat released any liquid then press the sauté button to boil it off.
- Garnish with cilantro and serve.

414. Balsamic Beef Pot Roast

Ingredients

- One boneless chuck roast, approximately 3 lbs.
- 1 Tbsp kosher salt
- 1 tsp black ground pepper
- 1 tsp garlic powder
- 1/4 cup of balsamic vinegar
- 2 cups water
- 1/2 cup onion, chopped
- 1/4 tsp xanthan gum
- Fresh parsley, chopped to garnish

Instructions

1. Cut your chuck roast in half so you have two pieces. Season the roast with the salt, pepper, and garlic powder on all sides. Using the saute feature on the instant pot, brown the roast pieces on both sides.

2. Add 1/4 cup of balsamic vinegar, 1 cup water, and 1/2 cup onion to the meat. Cover and seal, then using the manual button set the timer for 40 minutes. When the timer runs out, release the pressure by moving the lever to the "venting" setting. Once all the pressure is released, uncover the pot.

3. Carefully remove the meat from the pan to a large bowl. Break carefully into chunks and remove any large pieces of fat or other refuse.

4. Use the saute function to bring the remaining liquid to a boil in the pot, and simmer for 10 minutes to reduce.

5. Whisk in the xanthan gum, then add the meat back to the pan and stir gently.

6. Turn off the heat and serve hot over cauliflower puree, garnished with lots of fresh chopped parsley.

415. Lemon Garlic Chicken

Ingredients

- 6-8 boneless chicken thighs skinless or with skin*
- sea salt and pepper to taste
- 1/2 teaspoon garlic powder
- 2 tablespoons olive oil
- 3 tablespoons butter
- 1/4 cup chopped onion
- 4 garlic cloves , sliced or minced
- 2 - 4 teaspoons Italian seasoning (I actually usually use 1 - 1 1/2 tablespoon but feel free to adjust to your liking)
- zest of half a lemon
- Juice of one lemon
- 1/3 cup 1/3 cup homemade or low sodium chicken broth Chopped fresh parsley and lemon slices for garnish if desired
- 2 tablespoons heavy cream

272

- Instant Pot (I have the 6 Quart DUO)
- OR Cast Iron Skillet

Instructions

1. Season the chicken with salt, pepper, garlic powder and chili flakes.

2. Press the Sauté function (Normal setting) on the Instant Pot and add the olive oil to the pot. (I use a 6 Quart Instant Pot DUO)

3. Place chicken in the Instant Pot and cook on each side for 2-3 minutes, or until golden brown. This helps to seal in the juices and keep it tender. (You may have to work in batches depending on the size and amount of chicken you are using). Once browned, remove from Instant Pot and set aside.

4. Melt butter in Instant Pot and stir in the onions and garlic. Add lemon juice to deglaze pan and cook for 1 minute. Add Italian seasoning, lemon zest and chicken broth.

5. Place the chicken back into the Instant Pot, lock the lid, and turn the valve to Sealing.

6. Select the Manual (older models) or Pressure Cook (newer models) button and adjust the timer to 7 minutes.

7. It will take about 5-10 minutes to come to pressure and start counting down.

8. When done, release the pressure after 2 minutes, then remove your Instant Pot lid.

9. Remove chicken from Instant Pot using tongs and set aside on a large serving plate. Stir in heavy cream (if using) into the Instant Pot.

10. (If you like your sauce thicker - you can thicken with a cornstarch slurry (if not low carb) or 1/2 teaspoon of xanthum gum.)

11. Press off and turn Instant Pot to SAUTE function. Cook and allow sauce to bubble and thicken. Turn off and add chicken back to the Instant Pot to coat with sauce. Sprinkle chicken with chopped parsley and serve hot with your favorite sides. Spoon sauce over chicken and garnish with lemon slices, if desired.

12. Serve this Instant Pot lemon garlic chicken with a salad, cauliflower rice or spiralized zucchini noodles.

416. Instant Pot Seafood Gumbo

Ingredients

- 24 ounces sea bass filets patted dry and cut into 2" chunks
- 3 tablespoons ghee or avocado oil
- 3 tablespoons cajun seasoning or creole seasoning
- 2 yellow onions diced
- 2 bell peppers diced
- 4 celery ribs diced

- 28 ounces diced tomatoes
- 1/4 cup tomato paste
- 3 bay leaves
- 1 1/2 cups bone broth
- 2 pounds medium to large raw shrimp deveined
- sea salt to taste
- black pepper to taste

Instructions

1. Season the barramundi with some salt and pepper, and make sure they are as evenly coated as possible. Sprinkle half of the Cajun seasoning onto the fish and give it a stir- make sure it is coated well and set aside.

2. Put the ghee in the Instant Pot and push "Sauté". Wait until it reads "Hot" and add the barramundi chunks. Sauté for about 4 minutes, until it looks cooked on both sides. Use a slotted spoon to transfer the fish to a large plate.

3. Add the onions, pepper, celery and the rest of the Cajun seasoning to the pot and sauté for 2 minutes until fragrant. Push "Keep Warm/Cancel". Add the cooked fish, diced tomatoes, tomato paste, bay leaves and bone broth to the pot and give it a nice stir. Put the lid back on the pot and set it to "Sealing." Push "Manual" and set the time for just 5 minutes! The Instant Pot will slowly build up to a high pressure point and once it reaches that point, the gumbo will cook for 5 minutes.

4. Once the 5 minutes have ended, push the "Keep warm/Cancel" button. Cautiously change the "Sealing" valve over to "Venting," which will manually release all of the pressure. Once the pressure has been release (this will take a couple of minutes), remove the lid and change the setting to "Sauté" again. Add the shrimp and cook for about 3-4 minutes, or until the shrimp have become opaque. Add some more sea salt and black pepper, to taste. Serve hot and top off with some cauliflower rice and chives.

417. Whole Chicken and Low Carb Gravy

Ingredients

- 6.5 pound whole chicken
- 2 tbsp olive oil s
- 1 tsp dried Italian seasonings
- 1/2 tsp onion powder
- 1/2 tsp garlic powder

- 1/2 tsp salt
- 1/2 tsp pepper
- 1.5 cups low sodium chicken broth
- 2 tsp guar gum

Instructions

1. Rub 1 tablespoon of oil all over the chicken and place the rest of the oil in the bottom of the Instant Pot.

2. Mix the dry seasonings together and sprinkle all over the chicken.

3. Press "Saute" and heat the oil, then add the whole chicken into the pot, breast side down. Hit "cancel".

4. Give it 5 minutes to brown then flip the chicken over and pour in the chicken broth.

5. Cover your pot and Press "Manual" and timer for 40 minutes. It will take about 10 minutes for pressure then the timer will begin.

6. Once time is done, hit "Cancel" and manually release pressure.

7. Be careful of the steam when removing the cover of the pot.

8. Remove chicken from the pot to make the gravy.

9. Sprinkle the guar gum over the hot broth in the pot and stir continually to thicken. If it's not thickening as quick as you'd like, simple hit "saute" to warm the broth and continue to stir until the gravy is thickened. You could also add 1 more teaspoon of guar gum if it's not as thick as you'd like.

10. Serve with gravy and a sprinkle of chopped parsley if desired.

418. Low Carb Taco Salad

Ingredients

Taco Seasoning

- 2 Tablespoons Chili powder
- 2 Teaspoons Ground cumin
- 2 Teaspoons Garlic powder
- 1/2 Teaspoon Onion powder

- 1/2 Teaspoon Dried oregano
- 1/4 Teaspoon Paprika
- 1 Teaspoon Sea salt
- 1/2 Teaspoon Cayenne pepper

Taco Salad

- 16 Ounces Ground Beef (80-20 Blend)
- 1 Head Green leaf lettuce (chopped)
- 2 Tablespoons Taco seasoning (recipe above)
- 8 Ounces Grape tomatoes (halved)
- 8 Ounces Cheddar cheese (shredded)
- 1 Medium Avocado (cubed)
- 8 Ounces Red onion (chopped)
- 1/3 Cup Mexican cream
- 2 Tablespoons Cilantro (chopped)

Instructions

Taco Seasoning

Mix all of the Ingredients together in a canning jar, make sure the lid is tight and shake until well combined.

Taco Salad

1. Add the ground beef to a skillet on medium-high. Stir fry and separate the beef using a wooden spatula for about 10 minutes, until browned.

2. Drain the beef of any excess grease and then stir in 2 Tablespoons of taco seasoning and combine well. About 5 minutes.

3. Combine the rest of the Ingredients in a bowl. Add the ground beef mixture and top with Mexican cream and cilantro.

419. Chicken Fajita Soup in the Instant Pot

Ingredients

- 2 lbs boneless skinless chicken breasts mine were frozen
- 2 cans of diced tomatoes 10 oz
- 2 cups of chicken broth
- 2 tablespoons of taco seasoning I used homemade taco seasoning
- 2 teaspoons of minced garlic
- 1/2 cup of onion chopped
- 1 green bell pepper chopped
- 1 red bell pepper chopped

Instructions

1. Combine all the ingredients in the Instant Pot.
2. Lock the lid on top and set the valve to sealing.
3. Set the timer for 30 minutes.
4. Do a quick release.
5. Remove the chicken and shred.
6. Return the chicken to the pot and Stir to combine the flavors.

420. Eggs Benedict

Ingredients

- 1 tbsp melted butter
- 1/4 tsp baking powder
- 1 tbsp almond meal/flour
- 2 egg whites

Poached Eggs

- 1 egg (per person)
- 1 cup water no matter how many eggs you are poaching
- Hollandaise Sauce (per person)
- 2 egg yolks (leftover from muffin)
- 1/2 tbsp lemon juice
- 1/4 tsp salt omit if using salted butter
- 4 tbsp unsalted butter melted and bubbling

Additional Ingredients (per person)

- 1-2 sliced bacon or ham also known as Canadian bacon
- 2-4 leaves spinach (optional)

Instructions

Low-Carb Muffins

1. Place the butter in a ramekin or flat bottom coffee mug. Microwave the butter for 10-15 seconds to melt the butter.

2. Using a fork, mix in the baking powder and almond flour. Once the almond flour is mixed, crack the eggs and separate the white from the yolk. The eggs white should be placed your batter, and the egg yolks should be saved for the hollandaise sauce.

3. Mix the muffin batter well with the fork. Then place the muffin in the microwave for 90 seconds. The muffin will rise up quite a bit but will lower as it cools.

4. When the muffin is done, run a knife around the edge to loosen then remove from the ramekin. Let the muffin cool then cut it in half and toast it.

Poached Eggs

1. Add 1 cup of water to the Instant Pot then place a trivet at the bottom.

2. Grease ramekins, a silicone trays, or silicone muffin liners. Then crack an egg into each cup/container. You do not need to cover the container. Lower the container to rest of the trivet in the Instant Pot.

3. Close the lid and turn the pressure valve to seal. Cook the eggs for 1-2 minutes using the "manual" or "pressure cook" setting. When the timer beep quickly release the pressure and remove the eggs.

4. To remove the poached eggs carefully run a spoon around the edge and then scoop the poached eggs out of the container.

Hollandaise Sauce

- Add the egg yolks, salt, and lemon juice to a blender. Turn it on.
- While the blender is going slowly pour the melted butter into the blender from the top. Make sure the butter is very hot and bubbling. Let the blender run for about 30 seconds and then turn it off. You hollandaise sauce is done.

Assembling

Place half the toasted muffin on a plate. Layer the spinach, back bacon or ham, and a poached egg on top. Drizzle a spoonful of hollandaise sauce over top and enjoy!

421. Super Easy Buffalo Chicken Dip

Ingredients

- 4 oz 115 g cream cheese, softened slightly
- 1 cup 240 g sour cream
- 1/2 to 3/4 cup 120 to 180 ml Frank's RedHot sauce (more or less to taste)
- 1 teaspoon Worcestershire sauce
- 1 teaspoon garlic powder
- 1 teaspoon onion powder
- 4 cups shredded cheddar divided
- 2 cups cooked shredded chicken great use for a rotisserie!
- 2 scallions green and white parts, thinly sliced

Instructions

- Add all Ingredients to the instant pot (using cooked chicken) except for the 1 cup of shredded cheese.
- Close the lid and set to manual high pressure for 1 minute.
- Allow the Instant Pot to natural pressure release for 5 minutes and then manually release the rest of the pressure.
- Transfer contents to an oven safe dish. Top with shredded cheese.
- Cook under the broiler until cheese is melted and browned.
- Enjoy!

422. Mongolian Beef

Ingredients

- 2 lb flank steak thinly sliced against the grain
- 2 tbsp avocado oil (any oil suitable for high heat will work fine)
- 3 cloves garlic minced
- 2 tsp grated fresh ginger or 1 tsp of dried ground ginger
- 2/3 cup soy sauce or coconut aminos
- 1 pinch red pepper flakes optional
- 1/2 cup brown sugar substitute (such as sukrin gold)
- 10-20 drops liquid stevia or to taste
- 1 tsp Xanthan Gum
- 2 green onions thinly sliced optional
- 2 tsp Sesame Seeds optional

Instructions

- Heat the oil in the instant pot on the saute setting on high. (press saute, then adjust then the plus button until the red indicator light moves to 'more)

- Add 1/2 of the thinly sliced beef and sear a couple of minutes. Remove from the instant pot and repeat with the remaining beef.

- Return all the beef to the instant pot and add the garlic, ginger, soy sauce, red pepper flakes, brown sugar substitute, and about 10 drops of liquid stevia.

- Place the lid on the instant pot, set the steam valve to 'sealing' and set the instant pot to cook for 12 minutes on high pressure using the manual setting. (press 'manual' > 'pressure' to select high pressure > '+ or -' to change the time to 12 minutes)

- Allow the pressure to naturally release, then open the pot and remove the beef, leaving the liquid in the pot. Taste the liquid and add more liquid stevia if desired.

- Stir in the xanthan gum 1/4 tsp at a time, whisking after each addition to thicken the liquid. Stop when it reaches the desired consistency. You can skip this step but you will have a more liquid sauce. If you opt to thicken it, you will likely not need the entire tsp of xanthan gum. I only usually only need 1/2 of a tsp.

- Return the beef to the pot and stir with the sauce. Serve topped with green onions and sesame seeds.

423. Instant Pot Whole Chicken

Ingredients

- 1 whole chicken innards removed
- 1 lemon cut in half
- 1 onion cut in half
- 1 recipe Rotisserie blend

Rotisserie Seasoning

- 1 tablespoon kosher salt
- 2 teaspoons pepper
- 1 tablespoon garlic powder
- 1 tablespoon onion powder
- 1 tablespoon paprika
- 1 teaspoon dried thyme
- dash of cayenne pepper

Instructions

Homemade Rotisserie Seasoning

Mix together all Ingredients well.

1. For Pressure Cooker Whole Roasted Chicken
2. Place trivet in instant pot pan and pour in 1 cup COLD water into instant pot. Use 2 cups water if you have an 8 quart instant pot.
3. Place cut lemon and onion inside cavity of chicken and place chicken on trivet in instant pot.
4. Sprinkle seasoning evenly over chicken.
5. Place lid on pressure cooker and be sure valve is turned to sealed.
6. Set on high pressure for 6 minutes per pound of chicken. If your chicken seems like it is really thick (the chicken breasts are large) you may want to increase time to 7 minutes per pound. A smaller organic chicken only needs 6 minutes per pound.
7. Once cooking time is finished, allow pressure to release naturally for at least 10 minutes, preferably closer to 20 minutes.

424. Rosemary Bagels

Ingredients

- 1 1/2 cups almond flour
- 3/4 teaspoon baking soda
- 3/4 teaspoon xanthan gum
- 1/4 teaspoon salt
- 3 tablespoons psyllium husk powder
- 1 whole egg
- 3 egg whites
- 1/2 cup warm water
- 1 tablespoon rosemary, chopped
- Avocado oil

Instructions

1. Preheat oven to 250F.
2. Mix almond flour, xanthan gum, baking soda and salt together in a bowl.
3. In a separate bowl, whisk eggs and warm water together. Stir in psyllium husk until there are no clumps.

Add liquid Ingredients to dry Ingredients.

1. Coat bagel mold with avocado oil.
2. Press dough into mold.
3. Sprinkle rosemary on top.
4. Place in oven and bake for 45 minutes.
5. Remove and cool for 15 minutes before slicing.

425. Instant Pot Hard Boiled Eggs

Ingredients

- 6 Large Eggs
- 1 cup Water

Instructions

- Add the trivet and the water to the Instant Pot. Place the eggs on top of the trivet.
- Seat the lid and set the cook time to 6 minutes high pressure. After the cooking time is up, release the pressure with a quick release.
- Carefully remove the inner pot from the Instant Pot and set in the sink. Pour cold water into the pot until the water in the pot is cold. When the eggs are cool enough to handle, peel by cracking all around the egg and the peel should slide right off.

426. Low-Carb (Pressure Cooker) Buffalo Chicken Soup

Ingredients

- 2 Boneless Skinless Chicken Breasts Frozen is ok, no need to thaw.
- 3 cups Chicken Bone Broth
- 1/2 cup diced Celery
- 1/4 cup Onion
- 1 clove Garlic
- 1 tablespoon ranch dressing mix
- 2 tablespoons Ghee or butter
- 1/3 cup hot sauce
- 2 cups cheddar cheese, shredded
- 1 cup Heavy Cream

Instructions

- In your pressure cooker combine all Ingredients EXCEPT cream & cheese.
- Cook under pressure for 10 minutes then quick depressurize.

- Carefully remove chicken, shred and return to soup. Add heavy cream and cheese, stir to combine.

427. Low Carb Grilled Swordfish Skewers with Pesto Mayo

Ingredients

- 1 lb swordfish, cut into 1 inch cubes
- 16 cherry tomatoes
- salt and pepper
- 1 tsp olive oil to coat
- 1/4 cup pesto
- 1/4 cup mayonnaise

Instructions

- Divide the swordfish cubes into four equal portions.
- Alternate the swordfish with the cherry tomatoes on your skewers.
- Brush with olive oil and season with salt and pepper.
- Preheat the grill for at least 5 minutes, then carefully place your skewers on the hot grill.
- Cook for about 1 minute per (four) sides of your cubes – a little longer if your swordfish pieces are really thick.
- Serve warm or chilled with a salad.
- Combine the pesto and mayonnaise in a small bowl and stir well. Serve with the skewers.

428. Low Carb Keto Indian Butter Chicken

Ingredients

Spice Mix (you'll use the entire mix for this recipe)

- 1 tablespoon garam masala spice mix
- 1 teaspoon cumin
- ½ teaspoon coriander
- ½ teaspoon turmeric
- ¼ teaspoon black pepper
- ¼ teaspoon cinnamon
- ¼ teaspoon fenugreek

Chicken

- 1 lb (450 g) boneless, skinless chicken breast
- 2 teaspoons Spice Mix (from recipe above)
- ½ teaspoon sea salt
- 2 large cloves garlic, crushed
- 2 tablespoons fresh lemon juice
- 3 tablespoons sour cream

Sauce

- 4 tablespoons grass-fed clarified butter (ghee)
- 1 medium yellow onion, diced
- 3 large cloves garlic, crushed
- 1-inch piece fresh ginger, grated
- Remaining Spice Mix (from recipe above)
- ½ teaspoon sea salt

- ¼ teaspoon crushed red pepper flakes (more or less to taste)
- 1½ cups (355 ml) low-sodium chicken bone broth or water
- 4 tablespoons tomato paste
- ½ cup (120 ml) grass-fed heavy whipping cream

For serving (optional)

- A small handful of fresh cilantro leaves
- Sliced red onion

Instructions

- Mix together all of the spices for the mix and set aside.

- Mix together all Ingredients for the chicken in a medium bowl. Cover and refrigerate at least 2 hours, but up to 2 days. Cook the chicken until fully done (it's no longer pink in the center) skewered on a grill or in a 400F oven for about 10 to 12 minutes.

- For the sauce, heat the ghee in a medium-large deep-sided skillet over medium heat. Once hot, add the onion and cook until softened and starting to caramelize, about 20 minutes, stirring occasionally. Stir in the garlic, ginger, and remaining spice mix and cook 1 minute, stirring constantly. Stir in the salt, crushed red pepper flakes, chicken broth, and tomato paste. Bring up to a boil, and then reduce the heat to simmer and cook 10 minutes. Cool slightly and then carefully puree using an immersion or regular blender. Return the sauce to the skillet.

- Stir the cooked chicken and heavy whipping cream into the sauce.

- Serve garnished with fresh cilantro and sliced red onion, if desired.

429. Low Carb Instant Pot Beef Stew

Ingredients

- 4 tablespoons ghee divided
- 2 lbs grass-fed beef chuck steak cut into 2-inch cubes
- 1 medium onion chopped
- 1 medium carrot cut into 2-inch pieces
- 1 medium parsnip cut into 2-inch pieces
- 8 oz button mushrooms quartered
- 6 cloves garlic minced
- 1/2 cup dry red wine
- 2 cups water or low-sodium beef stock
- 2 tablespoons tomato paste
- 1 tablespoon grass-fed beef gelatin
- 1/2 tablespoon dried Italian herb mix
- 1/2 teaspoon salt
- 1/2 teaspoon black pepper
- Fresh thyme for garnish (optional)
- Cauliflower mash for serving (optional)

Instructions

- Turn pressure cooker on, press "Sauté", and wait 2 minutes for the pot to heat up. Add the ghee and once melted, add the beef and cook until seared, about 3 to 5 minutes, flipping once halfway through. Transfer the beef to a bowl. (You may need to sear the beef in 2 batches so you don't crowd the pot.)

- Add the remaining 2 tablespoons ghee, onion, carrot, parsnip, and mushrooms. Cook briefly until the vegetables take on a little color, about 2 minutes, stirring frequently. Add the garlic and cook 30 seconds more, stirring constantly. Stir in the red wine and cook 1 minute, scraping up any brown bits from the bottom of the pot. Press "Cancel" to stop sautéing.

- Add the beef back to the pot along with the water, tomato paste, beef gelatin, Italian herb seasoning, salt, and black pepper. Turn the pot on Manual, High Pressure for 35 minutes and then let the pressure naturally release for 10 minutes before doing a quick release.

- Serve garnished with fresh thyme on top of cauliflower mash.

430. Easy Chicken Cordon Blue Casserole

Ingredients

- 1 tablespoon unsalted butter
- ½ small onion, diced
- 2 large cloves garlic, crushed
- 1 cup (240 ml) chicken bone broth
- 4 oz (115 g) cream cheese, at room temperature
- 2 oz (60 g) Emmental cheese, shredded (or Swiss cheese)
- 2 tablespoons chopped fresh parsley
- ½ teaspoon Worcestershire sauce
- ½ teaspoon black pepper
- 1 lb (450 g/about 2 medium) zucchini, sliced
- 2 cups cooked, shredded chicken (see Note)
- 2 tablespoons cured pork belly, crisped (see Note)
- 2 tablespoons grated Parmesan

Instructions

- Preheat the oven to 375F; get out a 1.5-quart casserole dish.

- Add the butter to a medium skillet over medium heat. Once hot, add the onion and cook until softened, but not browned, about 3 minutes, stirring occasionally. Add the garlic and cook 1 minute more, stirring constantly. Add the broth and bring up to a simmer. Whisk in the cream cheese until smooth; let it simmer a couple minutes until thickened slightly, whisking frequently. Whisk in the Emmental cheese a handful at a time until fully incorporated. Stir in the parsley, Worcestershire, and black pepper. Remove from the heat.

- Add the zucchini and chicken to the casserole dish and pour in the sauce. Sprinkle on the crisped pork belly and then the Parmesan. Cover with foil and bake until the zucchini is tender, about 45 minutes. Remove the foil and broil a couple minutes to brown the top.
- Serve.

431. Instant Pot Beef and Broccoli

Ingredients

- 1.5 pound flank steak, thinly sliced against the grain
- 2–3 crowns broccoli broken into florets
- 3/4 cup beef broth
- 1/2 cup coconut aminos
- 2 tablespoons avocado oil (I use Primal Kitchen) or olive oil
- 2 tablespoons sesame oil
- 1 tablespoon minced garlic
- 1 tablespoon arrowroot flour
- 1/2 tablespoon grated ginger
- 1/2 teaspoon onion powder
- 1/4 teaspoon salt
- 1/4 teaspoon red pepper flakes
- 1/8 teaspoon pepper
- Sesame seeds to garnish
- Chopped green onions to garnish

Instructions

- Turn instant pot onto "sauté" mode and add avocado or olive oil.
- Once oil is sizzling, sear sliced beef (about 30 seconds-1 minute on each side) in batches, ensuring not to overcrowd or over cook. Transfer to a plate once browned
- Once all beef is browned and on the plate, add minced garlic to the instant pot and sauté until fragrant, about 1 minute
- Add in the beef broth, ginger, coconut aminos, sesame oil, onion powder, red pepper flakes, salt, and pepper. Add beef and juices from plate to the instant pot, close the lid, and set to "sealing"
- Select manual and set the time for 10 minutes
- While beef and sauce is cooking, place broccoli florets in a microwave safe dish filled 3/4th's with water. Microwave for 3 minutes until lightly steamed for al dente broccoli. Drain water and set aside. Mix in with the beef after cooking. *See notes for additional way to cook the broccoli
- Once beef is done, do a quick release, and put the instant pot back into "sauté" mode
- Slowly add in arrowroot flour, using a fork to whisk into the liquid as you add it. Add in broccoli and continue stirring as the sauce thickens
- Remove beef and broccoli with a slotted spoon and arrange in a large serving dish or meal prep containers. Allow the remaining liquid to continue simmering and thickening
- Once it's thick and bubbling, pour sauce over beef and broccoli
- Garnish with sesame seeds, green onions or additional red pepper flakes

432. Chicken Bone Broth Soup Recipe!

Ingredients

- 3 tablespoons organic grass-fed clarified butter ghee
- 1 cup chopped onion
- 4 cloves garlic minced or crushed
- 1 cup chopped carrot
- 1 cup chopped celery
- 1 cup peeled chopped turnip
- 4 cups low-sodium chicken stock
- 2 tablespoons Vital Proteins Chicken Bone Broth Collagen
- 1 tablespoon dried Italian herb seasoning
- 1 rotisserie chicken meat pulled off and chopped (about 3 cups chopped chicken, white and dark meat)
- 2 tablespoons chopped fresh parsley for garnish (optional)

Instructions

- Heat the ghee in a 5-quart soup pot over medium-high heat. Add the onion and cook 1 minute, stirring constantly, and then add the garlic and cook 10 seconds, continuing to stir constantly.
- Stir in the carrot, celery, turnip, chicken stock, Vital Proteins Chicken Bone Broth Collagen, and dried Italian herb seasoning. Bring up to a boil, and then cover the pot, turn the heat down to simmer, and cook until the vegetables are softened, about 20 minutes.
- Stir in the chicken, cover the pot, and cook 5 minutes more.

433. Instant Pot Barbacoa Beef

Ingredients

- 2 Tbsp avocado oil
- 2 lb beef chuck roast
- 2/3 cup beef broth
- 1/4 cup lime juice
- 3 Tbsp cider vinegar
- 3 chipotle chilis in adobo sauce
- 1 Tbsp ground cumin
- 1 Tbsp dried oregano
- 1.5 tsp sea salt to taste

Instructions

- Blend the beef broth, lime juice, cider vinegar, chilis, cumin, oregano, and sea salt in a small blender and set aside.
- Cut the beef roast into 4-6 large chunks.
- Press the Saute button on the Instant Pot and add the oil. Once hot, carefully place the chunks of meat on the surface. Brown 2 minutes per side.
- Pour the adobo sauce over the browned meat and secure the lid on the Instant Pot. Pressure cook on high for 60 minutes.

- When the pot has finished its cycle and beeps, allow the pressure to naturally release.

- Remove lid and transfer the chunks of beef to a cutting board. Use 2 forks to shred the beef and place the meat back in the pot. Stir well and allow beef to sit 15 minutes or longer to absorb the juices.

- Serve barbacoa beef in tacos, burritos, or bowls.

434. Paleo and Egg Shakshuka with Kale

Ingredients

- 1 tablespoon olive oil
- 1/2 onion, diced
- 1/2 red bell pepper, diced
- 2 cloves garlic, minced
- 1 teaspoon chili powder
- 1/2 teaspoon smoked paprika
- 1/2 teaspoon ground cumin

- 2 cups baby kale
- 1 1/2 cups marinara sauce
- 1/2 teaspoon sea salt
- 1/2 teaspoon ground black pepper
- 4 eggs
- 1 tablespoon chopped fresh parsley

Instructions

Turn on a multi-functional pressure cooker (such as Instant Pot(R)) and select Saute function. Heat olive oil and cook onion, red bell pepper, garlic, chili powder, paprika, and cumin until soft, about 3 minutes. Add kale and cook until soft, about 2 minutes. Stir in marinara sauce and season with salt and pepper; turn off the pot and let cool for 5 minutes.

Crack eggs carefully in the pot, evenly spaced. Close and lock the lid. Select low pressure according to manufacturer's instructions; set timer for 1 minute. Once it beeps, release pressure carefully using the quick-release method according to manufacturer's Instructions, about 2 minutes. Unlock and remove the lid. Sprinkle with parsley.

435. Pan-Seared and Roasted Mahi Mahi with Mediterranean Salsa and Feta

Ingredients

- 2 Mahi Mahi pieces, about 6 oz. each
- 2 tsp. + 2 tsp. olive oil
- 1/2 C diced onion (or more if you're fond of onion)

- 1 large green bell pepper, stem cut out and seeds remove and then chopped in to 1/2 inch pieces
- 1 tsp. finely minced or crushed garlic
- 1 tsp. Greek seasoning

- 1/2 cup mild tomato salsa from a jar (I used Pace Picante Sauce)
- 1/4 cup homemade chicken stock or chicken broth
- 2 T sliced Kalamata olives (or use regular black olives if you're not a Kalamata olive fan)
- salt and fresh ground black pepper to taste
- 2 T crumbled Feta cheese

Instructions

- Thaw frozen fish overnight in the refrigerator (or in a pinch you can thaw in cold water, but thawing overnight is preferable.)
- Preheat oven to 425F/220C.
- Let fish come to room temperature.
- Heat 2 teaspoons olive oil in an large frying pan, add onion and green pepper and saute over medium-high heat until they're starting to brown.
- Add the minced garlic and Greek seasoning and cook a minute or so more.
- Add the salsa, homemade chicken stock, and olives, and simmer over medium low heat until the mixture has slightly reduced and thickened, about 5-6 minutes.
- Remove salsa to a bowl.
- Wipe out the pan, then add the other 2 teaspoons of olive oil and heat about a minute over medium-high heat.
- Add the fish and sear 2 minutes.
- Turn fish over and sear for 2 minutes more on the second side.
- Spray a glass or crockery baking dish with olive oil or non-stick spray.
- Arrange the seared fish in the baking dish, spoon salsa over, and roast 6 minutes.
- Remove from oven and sprinkle with crumbled Feta.
- Serve hot.

436. Pressure Cooker Garlic "Butter" Chicken Recipe

Ingredients

- 4 chicken breasts, whole or chopped
- ¼ cup turmeric ghee (or use regular ghee with 1 teaspoon turmeric powder)
- 1 teaspoon salt (add more to taste)
- 10 cloves garlic, peeled and diced

Instructions

1. Add the chicken breasts to the pressure cooker pot.
2. Add the ghee, (turmeric), salt, and diced garlic to the pressure cooker pot.
3. Set pressure cooker on high pressure for 35 minutes. Follow your pressure cooker's instructions for releasing the pressure.
4. Shred the chicken breast in the pot.
5. Serve with additional ghee if needed.

437. Low-Carb Fish Taco Cabbage Bowls

Ingredients

- 3 large or 4 small fillets of any mild white fish
- 2 tsp. + 2 tsp. olive oil
- 2 tsp. fish rub of your choice, see notes
- 1 tsp. ground cumin
- 1/2 tsp. chile powder
- 1 medium head green cabbage, thinly sliced
- 1/2 medium head red cabbage, thinly sliced (You could also make this with pre-sliced coleslaw mix if you don't want to slice the cabbage.)
- 1/2 cup thinly sliced green onion (or more if you're a big green onion fan like I am)
- guacamole, for serving (completely optional, but good, see notes)

Dressing Ingredients:

- 1/2 cup mayo (Or use a mix of mayo and Greek Yogurt if you'd like a lighter option.)
- 2 T fresh-squeezed lime juice; see notes
- 2 tsp. Green Tabasco Sauce (more or less to taste).
- salt or Vege-Sal to taste (I used about 1/2 tsp. Vege-Sal.)

Instructions

- Thaw fish overnight in the refrigerator if frozen.
- Mix the fish rub, ground cumin, and chile powder in a small dish.

- When you're ready to cook, pat fish dry with paper towels, then rub both sides with 2 tsp. of the olive oil followed by the fish rub mixture.

- Let the fish come to room temperature while you prep the other ingredients.

- Cut away the core of the cabbage and discard, then use a knife or a Mandoline Slicer to cut the cabbage into thin slices; we used the 3 cm blade for the mandoline. (You can also use pre-sliced coleslaw mix if you don't want to bother cutting the cabbage.)

- Thinly slice the green onion.

- Whisk together the mayo, lime juice, Green Tabasco Sauce, and Vege-Sal (or salt) to make the dressing.

- Brush a stove-top grill pan or heavy frying pan with the other 2 tsp. olive oil and heat the pan about a minute at medium-high heat. Then add the fish and cook about 4 minutes on the first side.

- Turn gently and cook about 4 minutes more on the other side. (Actual cooking time will depend on how thick your pieces of fish are. Fish should feel barely firm to the touch when it's done.)

- While the fish cooks, mix about half the green onions into the cabbage mixture and stir in enough dressing to barely moisten the cabbage.

- When the fish is done, let it cool slightly on a cutting board, then use two forks to shred the fish apart.

- Fill bowl with 1/4 of the cabbage mixture and top with desired amount of fish. Drizzle a little more dressing over the top.

- Serve right away, with green onions for garnish and guacamole if desired.

438. Bruschetta Chicken

Ingredients

- 2 lbs chicken breast boneless, skinless cut into 6-8 tenders
- 1 tbsp olive oil
- 1/2 cup chicken broth
- salt and pepper to taste

Tomato Sauce

- 1 can diced tomatoes 15 oz
- 1 tsp oregano, dried
- 4 cloves garlic
- 1/4 cup balsamic vinegar
- 1 tsp basil, dried

Instructions

- Combine all Ingredients for the tomato sauce in a bowl. Set aside.

- Set your Instant Pot to saute. Let it sit for two minutes and add olive oil. Place 4-5 chicken tenders in the pot and allow to sear for 30 seconds. Flip and sear for another 30 seconds. Transfer to plate and repeat with the remaining chicken. Lightly season with salt and pepper. Turn the pot to off/keep warm. Tip: I find as soon as I lay the last one in the pot it is time to flip the first one.

- Add chicken broth and use a wooden spoon to deglaze anything left on the pot.

- Add one-half of the tomato mixture and the chicken to the pot. Secure lid and flip the vent to "sealing". Press manual>high>7 minutes.

- When the pot has finished cooking allow a natural release for five minutes and then do a quick release to remove any remaining pressure.

- Remove the chicken and serve over your favorite noodles. Top with the remaining tomato sauce and garnish with fresh basil. You can also use any cooking liquid sauce left in the Instant Pot but it will likely be quite thin.

439. Instant Pot (Pressure Cooker) Mexican Beef

Ingredients

- 2½ pounds boneless beef short ribs beef brisket, or beef chuck roast cut into 1½- to 2-inch cubes
- 1 tablespoon chili powder
- 1½ teaspoons Diamond Crystal kosher salt
- 1 tablespoon ghee or fat of choice
- 1 medium onion thinly sliced
- 1 tablespoon tomato paste

- 6 garlic cloves peeled and smashed
- ½ cup roasted tomato salsa like the Salsa Roja Asada from my cookbook or iPad app—or just buy some
- ½ cup Instant Pot bone broth
- ½ teaspoon Red Boat fish sauce
- freshly ground black pepper
- ½ cup minced cilantro optional
- 2 radishes thinly sliced (optional)

Instructions

- The process is pretty much the same regardless of whether you use a stove-top pressure cooker or an electric one. The only difference is that your cooking time under high pressure will be slightly shorter with the stove top cooker than with an electric cooker (e.g. 30 minutes vs. 35 minutes).

- In a large bowl, combine cubed beef, chili powder, and salt.

- Press the "Sauté" button on your Instant Pot and add the ghee to the cooking insert. Once the fat's melted, add the onions and sauté until translucent. (If you're using a stove top pressure cooker, melt the fat over medium heat and sauté the onions.)

- Stir in the tomato paste and garlic, and cook for 30 seconds or until fragrant.

- Toss in the seasoned beef, and pour in the salsa, stock, and fish sauce.

- Cover and lock the lid, and press the "Keep Warm/Cancel" button on the Instant Pot. Press the "Manual" or "Pressure Cook" button to switch to the pressure cooking mode. Program your IP to cook for 35 minutes under high pressure. If your cubes are smaller than mine, you can press the "minus" button to decrease the cooking time. Once the pot is programmed, walk away. (If you're using a stove-top pressure cooker, you won't have all those buttons to press. Just cook on high heat until high pressure is reached. Then, reduce the heat to low to maintain high pressure for about 30 minutes.)

- When the stew is finished cooking, the Instant Pot will switch automatically to a "Keep Warm" mode. If you're using a stove-top pressure cooker instead, remove the pot from the heat. In either case, let the pressure release naturally (~15 minutes).

- Unlock the lid and season to taste with salt and pepper. At this point, you can plate and serve—or store the beef in the fridge for up to 4 days and reheat right before serving.

- When you're ready to eat, top the hot stew with cilantro and radishes.

440. Instant Pot Buffalo Chicken Meatballs

Ingredients

- 1.5 lb ground chicken
- 3/4 cup almond meal
- 1 tsp sea salt
- 2 garlic cloves minced
- 2 green onions thinly sliced

- 2 tbsp ghee
- 6 tbsp hot sauce
- 4 tbsp ghee or butter
- Chopped green onions, for garnish

Instructions

- In a large bowl, combine chicken, almond meal, salt, minced garlic cloves, and green onions.

- Use your hands to combine everything together, but be careful not to overwork the meat.

- Grease your hands with ghee or coconut oil, then shape the meat into balls 1-2 inches wide.

- Set your Instant Pot to sauté setting and add 2 tbsp of ghee.

- Working in batches, gently place the chicken meatballs in the Instant Pot to brown them. Turn them every minute until all sides are brown.

- While the meatballs are browning, combine hot sauce and 4 tbsp of butter or ghee and heat them in the microwave or the stove top until the butter is completely melted. Use a spoon to stir. This is your buffalo sauce.

- Place all the browned meatballs in the Instant Pot, then pour the buffalo sauce evenly over the meatballs.

- Screw on the lid to the Instant Pot, make sure that the pressure valve is set to "sealing," then set it to "Poultry."

- Once the meatballs are finished cooking (about 15-20 minutes), the Instant Pot will beep. If you are eating right away, hit "Cancel" then release the pressure valve, making sure your hand is away from the opening where the steam escapes. If not, the Instant Pot will automatically switch to the "Warm" setting for the next 10 hours and the pressure will slowly lower on its own.

- Serve over rice, cauliflower rice, zoodles. Or just eat on its own!

441. Low-Carb Cauliflower Sushi

Ingredients

- 500 g raw cauliflower including the stalk cut into chunks
- 100 g cream cheese full fat
- 1 spring onion thinly sliced
- 1 tbsp white vinegar
- salt and pepper to taste
- vegetables of choice (see recipe notes)
- fish of choice (see recipe notes)
- 4 nori sheets

Instructions

- Place the raw cauliflower chunks into your food processor with the blade attachment.

- Blitz with the blade until small pieces of cauliflower rice appear.

- Add the cream cheese, spring onion, and vinegar, salt and pepper to the food processor. Blitz until thoroughly mixed. You don't want any visible chunks of cream cheese or cauliflower, but you don't want a puree either.

- Taste the cauliflower rice and adjust the seasonings to your preference. Some like it with more salt or more vinegar than others.

- Spread the cream cheese cauliflower rice mixture along the nori sheet, leaving 2 inches of the nori sheet bare.

- Place your selection of vegetables, avocado and fish along the centre. Dampen the bare edge of the nori sheet then roll up tightly.

- Repeat with the remaining nori sheets and fillings. Slice with a sharp wet knife.

- Serve with wasabi, soy sauce or coconut aminos.

PLATINUM

RECIPES

---

442. Easy Pressure Cooker Green Chili With Chicken Recipe

Ingredients

- 3 pounds bone-in skin-on chicken thighs and drumsticks
- 3/4 pound tomatillos, quartered, husks discarded (about 4 tomatillos)
- 1 pound poblano peppers, roughly chopped, seeds and stems discarded (about 3 peppers)
- 6 ounces Anaheim or Cubanelle peppers, roughly chopped, seeds and stems discarded (about 2 peppers)
- 2 Serrano or jalapeño chilies, roughly chopped, stems discarded
- 10 ounces white onion, roughly chopped (about 1 medium)
- 6 medium cloves garlic, peeled
- 1 tablespoon whole cumin seed, toasted and ground
- Kosher salt
- 1/2 cup loosely packed fresh cilantro leaves and fine stems, plus more for garnish
- 1 tablespoon Asian fish sauce, such as Red Boat
- Fresh corn tortillas and lime wedges, for serving

Instructions

- Combine chicken, tomatillos, poblano peppers, Anaheim peppers, Serrano peppers, onion, garlic, cumin, and a big pinch of salt in a pressure cooker. Heat over high heat until gently sizzling, then seal pressure cooker, bring to high pressure, and cook for 15 minutes. Release pressure.

- Using tongs, transfer chicken pieces to a bowl and set aside. Add cilantro and fish sauce to remaining contents of pressure cooker. Blend with a hand blender or in a standing blender and season to taste with salt. Return chicken to sauce, discarding skin and bones and shredding if desired. Transfer to a serving platter, garnish with chopped cilantro, and serve immediately with tortillas and lime wedges.

443. Pressure Cooker Italian Beef

Ingredients

- 5 lbs. boneless beef roast
- 3 tbsp garlic-infused olive oil
- 2 tsp crushed red pepper
- 2 tsp oregano
- 1 tbsp basil
- 2 tbsp pink Himalayan salt
- 1 tbsp freshly cracked black pepper
- 1 32 oz jar Mezzetta Peperoncini
- 1 cup beef broth, homemade or store-bought (if store-bought, ensure that neither garlic nor onions are listed as Ingredients)

Instructions

- Using a sharp serrated knife, chop beef into 1-inch cubes and place in storage bag.
- Add garlic-infused olive oil and spices to bag and gently rotate the bag to distribute the oil and spices.
- Place storage bag in the refrigerator and allow to marinate for at least 2 hours, preferably overnight.
- After marination of beef, pour jar of Mezzetta Peperoncini (including juice), beef, and beef broth into pressure cooker insert.
- Set Instant Pot to "Beef/Stew" and set timer to 120 minutes.
- After the pressure cooker has completed the cooking process, allow it to naturally depressurize for 20 minutes. After 20 minutes, rotate the lid nozzle to fully depressurize.
- Serve Italian Beef in bowls topped high with Mezzetta Peperoncini and enjoy!

444. Instant Pot Cashew Chicken

Ingredients

- 1.5–2 lbs boneless, skinless chicken breasts, cut into 1"-1.5" pieces
- 2 tbsp sesame oil, divided
- 1/2 cup coconut aminos
- 3 tablespoons sugar-free ketchup
- 3 tbsp rice vinegar
- 1 tbsp coconut sugar*
- 1 tbsp honey*
- 1 tbsp minced garlic
- 1 tbsp minced ginger
- 2 tbsp arrowroot flour, divided
- 1/2 tsp Chinese Five Spice powder
- 1/2 tsp red pepper flakes, or to taste
- 1/4 tsp salt, or to taste
- 1/4 tsp pepper, or to taste
- 2 tbsp water
- 1 cup cashews

Instructions

- In a medium bowl, combine 1 tbsp sesame oil, coconut aminos, ketchup, vinegar, coconut sugar, honey, garlic, ginger, Five Spice, and red pepper flakes. Whisk well to combine and set aside.

- In a bowl or baggie, coat chicken pieces with 1 tbsp of the arrowroot flour, salt and pepper. Add 1 tbsp sesame oil to the bottom of the instant pot and turn it to "sauté".

- Allow oil to heat up and then sear chicken for 1-2 minutes. Press "cancel" and pour the sauce into the instant pot. Stir the sauce in with the chicken to evenly distribute. Cover, set the valve to "sealing" and press "manual" and adjust the time to 10 minutes.

- Right before the instant pot is done, combine 1 tbsp arrowroot flour with 2 tbsp water and stir well to dissolve. Once the instant pot is done, do a quick release and open the lid. Press the "sauté" button and pour the water and flour mixture into the instant pot and whisk into the sauce.

- Add the cashews and then continue stirring until the sauce has thickened. If you'd like it thicker after 1-2 minutes, add an additional 1/2 tbsp arrowroot dissolved in 1 tbsp water. Once the sauce has thickened, add any additional salt and pepper and serve.

- Serve over broccoli, cauliflower rice, on it's own with a side, over spaghetti squash "lo mien" noodles, etc. Garnish with any additional cashews, green onion, or sesame seeds

445. Beef Stroganoff In The Instant Pot

Ingredients

- 1 brown onion sliced and quartered
- 2 cloves garlic crushed
- 2 slices streaky bacon diced
- 500 g beef, stewing steak cubed
- 1 tsp smoked paprika
- 3 tbsp tomato paste
- 250 g mushrooms quartered
- 250 ml beef stock
- sour cream to garnish

Instructions

- Pour some oil in the Instant Pot dish, and using the saute function gently fry the onion, garlic and bacon until cooked but not browned.
- Add the diced beef and saute until the beef is browned on all sides.
- Add the paprika, tomato paste, mushrooms and beef broth. Stir together then pop the lid on and turn until it clicks indicating it is fully sealed.
- Cook on High Pressure for 30 minutes.
- Use the quick release valve to release the pressure.
- Serve with zoodles or mashed cauliflower, and garnish with sour cream

446. Balsamic Beef Pot Roast

Ingredients

- One boneless chuck roast, approximately 3 lbs.
- 1 Tbsp kosher salt
- 1 tsp black ground pepper
- 1 tsp garlic powder
- 1/4 cup of balsamic vinegar
- 2 cups water
- 1/2 cup onion, chopped
- 1/4 tsp xanthan gum
- Fresh parsley, chopped to garnish

Instructions

- Cut your chuck roast in half so you have two pieces. Season the roast with the salt, pepper, and garlic powder on all sides. Using the saute feature on the instant pot, brown the roast pieces on both sides.
- Add 1/4 cup of balsamic vinegar, 1 cup water, and 1/2 cup onion to the meat. Cover and seal, then using the manual button set the timer for 40 minutes. When the timer runs out, release the pressure by moving the lever to the "venting" setting. Once all the pressure is released, uncover the pot.

- Carefully remove the meat from the pan to a large bowl. Break carefully into chunks and remove any large pieces of fat or other refuse.
- Use the saute function to bring the remaining liquid to a boil in the pot, and simmer for 10 minutes to reduce.
- Whisk in the xanthan gum, then add the meat back to the pan and stir gently.
- Turn off the heat and serve hot over cauliflower puree, garnished with lots of fresh chopped parsley.

447. Schlemmerfilet Bordelaise – Herbed Almond and Parmesan Crusted Fish

Ingredients

- 1 lb = 450 g Alaska pollock OR other white fish fillets, frozen
- 3 oz = 75 g salted butter, softened
- 2/3 cup = 160 ml almond flour OR crushed pork rinds
- 2/3 cup = 160 ml freshly grated Parmesan
- 2 teaspoons Italian herb seasoning OR Herbes de Provence
- (Optional: to taste unrefined sea salt OR Himalayan salt)

Instructions

- Preheat the oven to 350 °F (175 °C).
- Place the fish fillets into a glass or ceramic baking dish.
- Prepare the topping: combine the butter, almond flour (or crushed pork rinds), Parmesan, herb seasoning and the salt (if using) in a medium bowl. Mix with an electric mixer until well-combined.
- Press the topping evenly on top of the fish fillets.
- Bake in the preheated oven for 35-40 minutes, or until the juices run clear and the topping is golden brown.

448. Almond Coconut Curry on Veges

Ingredients

For the curry mixture

For the veges

- 1 tsp coconut oil
- 400 ml coconut milk
- 2 cups mushrooms
- 125 g almond butter (100% ground almonds)

- 4 cups spinach
- 1 tbsp tomato paste
- 2 cups brocolli (chopped into florets)
- 1 tbsp curry powder

Instructions

For the curry mixture

- Put the coconut drain, almond spread, tomato glue and curry powder in a blender. Mix for around 20 seconds or until smooth.
- Add the curry blend to a pan on low-medium warmth and warmth for 10-15 minutes or until warmed through. Blend habitually to abstain from staying.

For the veges

- Heat the coconut oil in a container on medium-high warmth and include the broccoli and mushrooms. Sear for around 3 minutes. Include the spinach and warmth for one more moment.
- Serve the veges in a bowl with the curry blend poured over the best.

449. Sheet Pan Hibachi Beef and Vegetables

Ingredients

For the marinade:

- 1 tablespoon minced fresh ginger
- 1 tablespoon minced fresh garlic
- 1/4 cup gluten free soy sauce (aka. tamari)

- 1 tablespoon sesame oil
- 1 tablespoon granulated erythritol sweetener (I used Swerve)

For the beef and vegetables:

- 1 pound beef tenderloin or boneless ribeye, cut into 1 inch pieces.
- 2 slices of peeled onion, 1/2 inch thick
- 2 cups chopped zucchini

- 1 cup white mushrooms, cut into quarters
- 1/2 cup chopped red bell pepper

- 2 tablespoons avocado or other light tasting oil
- 1/2 teaspoon kosher salt
- 1/4 teaspoon ground black pepper

Instructions

- Preheat the oven to 425 degrees F.
- Combine all of the marinade Ingredients in a medium sized bowl.
- Add the pieces of beef (or other protein) to the marinade, and stir to coat.
- Separate the onion rings and form into two cones on a large baking sheet. (OR just toss the rings with the other vegetables before roasting.)
- Combine the remaining vegetables on the same baking sheet.
- Add the oil, salt, and pepper and stir to coat the vegetables.
- Spread the vegetables out on the sheet and place in the oven. Bake for 20 minutes.
- Remove the pan from the oven and move the vegetables to one side to make room for the beef.
- Add the beef to the pan, making sure the pieces are separated. Pour the marinade over the beef.
- Return the pan to the oven and roast for another 8 minutes, or until the meat is cooked to your liking. Don't overcook or it will become dry and chewy.
- Remove from the oven and stir the beef and vegetables together with the sauce.
- Serve immediately over cooked cauliflower rice if desired.

450. Pancakes

Ingredients

- 1/2 c. almond flour
- 4 oz. cream cheese, softened
- 4 large eggs
- 1 tsp. lemon zest
- Butter, for frying and serving

Instructions

- In a medium bowl, whisk together almond flour, cream cheese, eggs, and lemon zest until smooth.
- In a nonstick skillet over medium heat, melt 1 tablespoon butter. Pour in about 3 tablespoons batter and cook until golden, 2 minutes. Flip and cook 2 minutes more. Transfer to a plate and continue with the rest of the batter.
- Serve topped with butter.

451. Easy Tomato Feta Soup Recipe

Ingredients

- 2 tbsp olive oil or butter
- 1/4 cup chopped onion
- 2 cloves garlic
- 1/2 tsp salt
- 1/8 tsp black pepper
- 1 tsp pesto sauce — optional
- 1/2 tsp dried oregano
- 1 tsp dried basil
- 1 tbsp tomato paste — optional

- 10 tomatoes, skinned, seeded and chopped — or two 14.5 oz cans of peeled tomatoes
- 1 tsp honey, sugar or erythritol — optional
- 3 cups water
- 1/3 cup heavy cream
- 2/3 cup feta cheese — crumbled

Instructions

- Heat olive oil (butter) over medium heat in a large pot (Dutch Oven). Add the onion and cook for 2 minutes, stirring frequently. Add the garlic and cook for 1 minute. Add tomatoes, salt, pepper, pesto (optional), oregano, basil, tomato paste and water. Bring to a boil, then reduce to a simmer. Add sweetener.

- Cook on medium heat for 20 minutes, until the tomatoes are tender and cooker. Using an immersion blender, blend until smooth. Add the cream and feta cheese. Cook for 1 more minute.

- Add more salt if needed. Serve warm.

452. Fat Bombs

Ingredients

- 8 oz. cream cheese, softened to room temperature
- 1/2 c. keto-friendly peanut butter
- 1/4 c. coconut oil, plus 2 tbsp.
- 1/2 tsp. kosher salt
- 1 c. keto-friendly dark chocolate chips (such as Lily's)

Instructions

- Line a small baking sheet with parchment paper. In a medium bowl, combine cream cheese, peanut butter, ¼ c coconut oil, and salt. Using a hand mixer, beat mixture until fully combined, about 2 minutes. Place bowl in freezer to firm up slightly, 10 to 15 minutes.

- When peanut butter mixture has hardened, use a small cookie scoop or spoon to create golf ball sized balls. Place in the refrigerator to harden, 5 minutes.

- Meanwhile, make chocolate drizzle: combine chocolate chips and remaining coconut oil in a microwave safe bowl and microwave in 30 second intervals until fully melted. Drizzle over peanut butter balls and place back in the refrigerator to harden, 5 minutes. Serve.

To store, keep covered in refrigerator.

453. Brunch Spread

Ingredients

- 4 large eggs
- 24 asparagus spears
- 12 slices of pastured, sugar free bacon

Instructions

- Pre-heat your oven to 400F.

- Trim your asparagus about an inch from the bottoms. Then in pairs, wrap them with one slice of bacon. Hold your spears firmly and close together with one hand as you wind the slice of bacon starting from the bottom, to the top of the spear. Gently pull the bacon as you wind it, so it wraps tightly. Place it on a sheet pan.

- Repeat with the remaining asparagus, so you have 12 pairs wrapped in bacon.

- Place in the oven, set the timer for 20 minutes.

- In this time, bring a small pot of water to a rapid boil. Gently place 4 large eggs in the boiling water. Set another time for 6 minutes.

- Prepare a bowl with ice water. When the 6 minutes are up, use a slotted spoon or tongs to quickly transfer your eggs to the ice bath. Let them sit for 2 minutes before peeling the tops off.

- Gently crack the top of the egg on a hard surface and peel away shell to reveal the tip of the egg.

- When the asparagus are ready, serve on a tray or cutting board. If you don't have an egg holder use espresso cups to hold your eggs up.

- With a small spoon scoop out the tops of the soft boiled eggs to reveal a perfectly runny yolk.

- Dip your asparagus spears into your eggs. Feast, enjoy!

454. Cheesy Pizza Chicken in a Skillet Recipe

Ingredients

- 1 tablespoon olive oil
- 6 bone-in chicken thighs
- 1 cup low carb tomato sauce
- 3 ounces sliced pepperoni
- 1 1/2 cups shredded mozzarella cheese
- salt and pepper

Instructions

- Preheat the oven to 350°F.
- Heat the oil in a 12-inch cast-iron skillet over medium heat.
- Season the chicken with salt and pepper then add to the skillet.
- Cook for 3 to 4 minutes on each side until browned.
- Pour the low-carb tomato sauce over the chicken and spread it evenly.
- Top the chicken with pepperoni slices and sprinkle with mozzarella.
- Bake for 25 minutes until the cheese is melted then place under a broiler to brown the cheese.
- Remove from heat and let rest for 5 minutes before serving.

455. Mushroom omelet

Ingredients

- 3 eggs
- 1 oz. butter, for frying
- 1 oz. shredded cheese
- 1/5 yellow onion
- 3 mushrooms
- salt and pepper

Instructions

- Crack the eggs into a mixing bowl with a pinch of salt and pepper. Whisk the eggs with a fork until smooth and frothy.
- Add salt and spices to taste.
- Melt butter in a frying pan. Once the butter has melted, pour in the egg mixture.
- When the omelet begins to cook and get firm, but still has a little raw egg on top, sprinkle cheese, mushrooms and onion on top (optional).
- Using a spatula, carefully ease around the edges of the omelet, and then fold it over in half. When it starts to turn golden brown underneath, remove the pan from the heat and slide the omelet on to a plate.

456. Salmon & Avocado Nori Rolls (Paleo Sushi)

Ingredients

- 3 square nori sheets (seaweed wrappers)
- 150-180 g / 5-6 oz cooked salmon or tinned salmon
- ½ red pepper, sliced into thin strips
- ½ avocado, sliced into strips
- ½ small cucumber, sliced into strips
- 1 spring onion/scallion, cut into 2-3" pieces
- 2 tablespoons mayonnaise
- 1 tablespoon hot sauce or Sriracha sauce
- 1 teaspoon black or white sesame seeds
- Coconut aminos for dipping, optional

Instructions

- Place the nori sheet on a flat surface, such as a cutting board, shiny side down. Look at the fibres of the wrapper to see which way it needs to be rolled.
- Add a third of the salmon to the right or left third of the nori sheet and top with two strips of pepper, cucumber and avocado. Add some green onion and a drizzle of mayonnaise and hot sauce. You can sprinkle with sesame seeds now or at a later stage, once the rolls are cut.
- Lightly wet the top part of the nori sheet (the side you are rolling towards), just 1-2 cm of the wrapper. Pick up the opposite outer edge of the roll and start wrapping it over the Ingredients, using your fingers to keep it nice and tight. This can take a bit of practice, but don't worry if your roll doesn't look perfect. Roll it until the top edge of the wrapper overlaps the roll and press it tightly to stick. Place the roll on the cutting board with the seam facing down and then cut into bite-size pieces.
- Serve right away with some coconut aminos or extra mayo for dipping, or pack in a container to take for lunch or keep as a snack in the fridge.

457. Instant Pot Beef Bourguignon

Instant Pot Beef Bourguignon is a pressure cooker recipe with beef, mushrooms, onions, and carrots cooked in red wine. Low carb, keto, and gluten free.

Ingredients

- 1.5 - 2 pounds beef chuck roast cut into 3/4-inch cubes
- 5 strips bacon diced
- 1 small onion chopped
- 10 ounces cremini mushrooms quartered
- 2 carrots chopped
- 5 cloves garlic minced
- 3 bay leaves
- 3/4 cup dry red wine
- 3/4 teaspoon xanthan gum (or corn starch, read post for Instructions)

- 1 tablespoon tomato paste
- 1 teaspoon dried thyme
- salt & pepper

Instructions

- Generously season beef chunks with salt and pepper, and set aside. Select the saute mode on the pressure cooker for medium heat. When the display reads HOT, add diced bacon and cook for about 5 minutes until crispy, stirring frequently. Transfer the bacon to a paper towel lined plate.

- Add the beef to the pot in a single layer and cook for a few minutes to brown, then flip and repeat for the other side. Transfer to a plate when done.

- Add onions and garlic. Cook for a few minutes to soften, stirring frequently. Add red wine and tomato paste, using a wooden spoon to briefly scrape up flavorful brown bits stuck to the bottom of the pot. Stir to check that the tomato paste is dissolved. Turn off the saute mode.

- Transfer the beef back to the pot. Add mushrooms, carrots, and thyme, stirring together. Top with bay leaves. Secure and seal the lid. Cook at high pressure for 40 minutes, followed by a manual pressure release.

- Uncover and select the saute mode. Remove bay leaves. Evenly sprinkle xanthan gum over the pot and stir together. Let the stew boil for a minute to thicken while stirring. Turn off the saute mode. Serve into bowls and top with crispy bacon.

458. Curry Tofu Scramble with Avocado

Ingredients

- 1 tbsp coconut oil
- 2 tbsp olive oil
- 300 g tofu (extra firm)
- 1 tsp turmeric
- 1 tbsp nutritional yeast
- 1 tbsp curry powder
- 1/2 cup zucchini (chopped)
- 1 cup mushrooms (chopped)
- 1 tomato (chopped)
- cilantro (optional)(to garnish)
- 300-gram avocado

Instructions

- The initial step is to dry the tofu so it ingests the flavor.
- Cut the tofu into 1 inch long strips, spread out the strips on a paper towel,
- put another paper towel to finish everything and after that a slashing board.
- Place something substantial over this, for example, a few books.
- Abandon it to sit for around 15 minutes.
- Add the coconut oil to the dish and disintegrate the tofu into the skillet with your hands.
- Cook for around 5 minutes, mixing every now and again.

- Include the turmeric, nourishing yeast and curry powder and 1 tbsp of the olive oil,

- blend and cook for a further 4 minutes.

- Add whatever remains of the olive oil, zucchini, mushroom and tomato and sear for a further 4 minutes blending much of the time.

- Serve with 1 little medium size avocado (roughly 100g) cut.

459. Chicken Enchilada Bowl

Ingredients

- 2 tablespoons coconut oil (for searing chicken)

- 1 pound of boneless, skinless chicken thighs

- 3/4 cup red enchilada sauce (recipe from Low Carb Maven)

- 1/4 cup water

- 1/4 cup chopped onion

- 4 oz can diced green chiles

Toppings (feel free to customize)

- 1 whole avocado, diced

- 1 cup shredded cheese (I used mild cheddar)

- 1/4 cup chopped pickled jalapenos

- 1/2 cup sour cream

- 1 roma tomato, chopped

Optional: serve over plain cauliflower rice (or mexican cauliflower rice) for a more complete meal!

Instructions

- In a pot or dutch oven over medium heat melt the coconut oil. Once hot, sear chicken thighs until lightly brown.

- Pour in enchilada sauce and water then add onion and green chiles. Reduce heat to a simmer and cover. Cook chicken for 17-25 minutes or until chicken is tender and fully cooked through to at least 165 degrees internal temperature.

- Careully remove the chicken and place onto a work surface. Chop or shred chicken (your preference) then add it back into the pot. Let the chicken simmer uncovered for an additional 10 minutes to absorb flavor and allow the sauce to reduce a little.

- To Serve, top with avocado, cheese, jalapeno, sour cream, tomato, and any other desired toppings. Feel free to customize these to your preference. Serve alone or over cauliflower rice if desired just be sure to update your personal nutrition info as needed.

460. Crab Stuffed Mushrooms with Cream Cheese

Ingredients

- 20 ounces cremini (baby bella) mushrooms (20-25 individual mushrooms)
- 2 tablespoons finely grated parmesan cheese
- 1 tablespoon chopped fresh parsley
- salt

Filling

- 4 ounces cream cheese softened to room temperature
- 4 ounces crab meat finely chopped
- 5 cloves garlic minced

- 1 teaspoon dried oregano
- 1/2 teaspoon paprika
- 1/2 teaspoon black pepper
- 1/4 teaspoon salt

Instructions

- Preheat the oven to 400 F. Prepare a baking sheet lined with parchment paper.
- Snap stems from mushrooms, discarding the stems and placing the mushroom caps on the baking sheet 1 inch apart from each other. Season the mushroom caps with salt.
- In a large mixing bowl, combine all filling Ingredients and stir until well-mixed without any lumps of cream cheese. Stuff the mushroom caps with the mixture. Evenly sprinkle parmesan cheese on top of the stuffed mushrooms.
- Bake at 400 F until the mushrooms are very tender and the stuffing is nicely browned on top, about 30 minutes. Top with parsley and serve while hot.

461. Low Carb Donuts Recipe - Almond Flour Keto Donuts (Paleo, Gluten Free)

Ingredients

Donuts

- 1 cup Blanched almond flour
- 1/3 cup Erythritol
- 2 tsp Gluten-free baking powder
- 1 tsp Cinnamon
- 1/8 tsp Sea salt

- 1/4 cup Butter (unsalted; measured solid, then melted)
- 1/4 cup Unsweetened almond milk
- 2 large Egg
- 1/2 tsp Vanilla extract

Cinnamon Coating

- 1/2 cup Erythritol
- 1 tsp Cinnamon

- 3 tbsp Butter (unsalted; measured solid, then melted)

Instructions

- Preheat the oven to 350 degrees F (177 degrees C). Grease a donut pan well.

- In a large bowl, stir together the almond flour, erythritol, baking powder, cinnamon, and sea salt.

- In a small bowl, whisk together the melted butter, almond milk, egg, and vanilla extract. Whisk the wet mixture into the dry mixture.

- Transfer the batter evenly into the donut cavities, filling them 3/4 of the way. Bake for about 22-28 minutes (or longer for a silicone pan!), until dark golden brown. Cool until donuts are easy to remove from the pan.

- Meanwhile, in a small bowl, stir together the erythritol and cinnamon for the coating.

- When the donuts have cooled enough to easily remove from the molds, transfer them to a cutting board. Brush both sides of one donut with butter, then press/roll in the sweetener/cinnamon mixture to coat. Repeat with the remaining donuts.

462. Bacon and Spinach Frittata

Ingredients

- 6 duck eggs or 8 hen eggs
- 1 tablespoon grass-fed ghee
- 4 ounces pasture-raised bacon, cut in 1/2-inch pieces
- 1 1/2 cups green beans, cooked and cut in half
- 2 cups of spinach or collard greens, steamed and roughly chopped
- 4 ounces cherry tomatoes, sliced in half (optional)
- 1 rosemary sprig, finely chopped

Instructions

- Preheat convection oven to 350 F

- In an oven-proof wide saucepan (I used a 12-inch pan) over medium heat, add the ghee, bacon and rosemary. Cook for 3 minutes until the bacon is slightly crisp.

- To the same pan, add the green vegetables and tomatoes to heat up and soften.

- Whisk the eggs in a bowl and then add to the pan, making sure they cover and reach all corners of the pan. Leave to cook for 5 minutes to set on the base and sides.

- Transfer the pan to the oven and allow to cook for another 5 minutes until the top of the frittata has set. Remove and allow to cool.

- Slice into 3 portions and serve with salad.

463. Lemon Butter Sauce for Fish

Ingredients

Lemon Butter Sauce:

- 60 g / 4 tbsp unsalted butter , cut into pieces
- 1 tbsp fresh lemon juice
- Salt and finely ground pepper

Crispy Pan Fried Fish:

- 2 x thin white fish fillets (120-150g / 4-5oz each), skinless boneless (I used Bream, Note 1)
- Salt and pepper
- 2 tbsp white flour
- 2 tbsp oil (I use canola)

Serving:

- Lemon wedges
- Finely chopped parsley, optional

Instructions

- Place the butter in a light coloured saucepan or small skillet over medium heat.
- Melt butter then leave on the stove, whisking / stirring very now and then. When the butter turns golden brown and it smells nutty - about 3 minutes, remove from stove immediately and pour into small bowl.
- Add lemon juice and a pinch of salt and pepper. Stir then taste when it has cooled slightly. Adjust lemon/salt to taste.
- Set aside - it will stay pourable for 20 - 30 minutes. See Note 3 for storing.

Crispy Pan Fried Fish:

- Pat fish dry using paper towels. Sprinkle with salt & pepper, then flour. Use fingers to spread flour. Turn and repeat. Shake excess flour off well, slapping between hands if necessary.
- Heat oil in a non stick skillet over high heat. When the oil is shimmering and there are faint wisps of smoke, add fish. Cook for 1 1/2 minutes until golden and crispy on the edges, then turn and cook the other side for 1 1/2 minutes (cook longer if you have thicker fillets).
- Remove immediately onto serving plates. Drizzle each with about 1 tbsp of Sauce (avoid dark specks settled at the bottom of the bowl), garnish with parsley and serve with lemon on the side. Pictured in post with Kale and Quinoa Salad.

310

464. Jalapeño Popper Egg Cups

Ingredients

- 12 slices bacon
- 10 large eggs
- 1/4 c. sour cream
- 1/2 c. shredded Cheddar
- 1/2 c. shredded mozzarella
- 2 jalapeños, 1 minced and 1 thinly sliced
- 1 tsp. garlic powder
- kosher salt
- Freshly ground black pepper
- nonstick cooking spray

Instructions

- Preheat oven to 375°.

- In a large skillet over medium heat, cook bacon until slightly browned but still pliable. Set aside on a paper towel-lined plate to drain.

- In a large bowl, whisk together eggs, sour cream, cheeses, minced jalapeño and garlic powder. Season with salt and pepper.

- Using nonstick cooking spray, grease a muffin tin. Line each well with one slice of bacon, then pour egg mixture into each muffin cup until about two-thirds of the way to the top. Top each muffin with a jalapeño slice.

- Bake for 20 minutes, or until the eggs no longer look wet. Cool slightly before removing from the muffin tin. Serve.

465. Lamb Kofta Kebabs

Ingredients

- 1/2 pound ground grass-fed lamb
- 1/2 cup parsley
- 1/2 inch fresh turmeric, grated
- 1/4 teaspoon sea salt

Instructions

- Gather 4 wooden kebab skewers. Soak skewers in water for 1 hour.
- Preheat oven to 300 degrees.
- In a food processor, add parsley and process for 30 seconds, or until finely chopped.
- Add lamb and grated turmeric to the processor and run until evenly mixed.
- Form lamb tightly around the kebab skewers. Salt the exterior of the meat.
- Line a baking sheet with foil and place an oven-safe rack on top of it so there is at least one inch of space between the rack and the pan. You may use a cast iron grill pan to get grill marks instead.

- Place kebabs on the grill and place in the upper third of your oven. Bake for 18-20 minutes, or until the internal temperature has reached 160 degrees.
- Remove lamb kofta from oven and garnish with grated turmeric and parsley sprigs.

466. Chicken Pot Pie

Ingredients

For the Chicken Pot Pie Filling:

- 2 tablespoons of butter
- 1/2 cup mixed veggies could also substitute green beans or broccoli
- 1/4 small onion diced
- 1/4 tsp pink salt
- 1/4 tsp pepper
- 2 garlic cloves minced
- 3/4 cup heavy whipping cream
- 1 cup chicken broth
- 1 tsp poultry seasoning
- 1/4 tsp rosemary
- pinch thyme
- 2 1/2 cups cooked chicken diced
- 1/4 tsp Xanthan Gum

For the crust

- 4 1/2 tablespoons of butter melted and cooled
- 1/3 cup coconut flour
- 2 tablespoons full fat sour cream
- 4 eggs
- 1/4 teaspoon salt
- 1/4 teaspoon baking powder
- 1 1/3 cup sharp shredded cheddar cheese or mozzarella shredded

Instructions

- Cook 1 to 1 1/2 lbs chicken in the slow cooker for 3 hours on high or 6 hours on low.
- Preheat oven to 400 degrees.
- Sautee onion, mixed veggies, garlic cloves, salt, and pepper in 2 tablespoons butter in an oven safe skillet for approx 5 min or until onions are translucent.
- Add heavy whipping cream, chicken broth, poultry seasoning, thyme, and rosemary.
- Sprinkle Xanthan Gum on top and simmer for 5 minutes so that the sauce thickens. Make sure to simmer covered as the liquid will evaporate otherwise. You need a lot of liquid for this recipe, otherwise, it will be dry.
- Add diced chicken.
- Make the breading by combining melted butter (I cool mine by popping the bowl in the fridge for 5 min), eggs, salt, and sour cream in a bowl then whisk together.
- Add coconut flour and baking powder to the mixture and stir until combined.
- Stir in cheese.

- Drop batter by dollops on top of the chicken pot pie. Do not spread it out, as the coconut flour will absorb too much of the liquid.
- Bake in a 400-degree oven for 15-20 min.
- Set oven to broil and move chicken pot pie to top shelf. Broil for 1-2 minutes until bread topping is nicely browned.

467. Cauliflower Bread With Crispy Bacon, Poached Eggs & Avocado

Ingredients

- 2 cups grated cauliflower
- 1-2 tablespoons of coconut flour
- ½ tsp salt
- 4 eggs
- ½ tsp garlic powder
- ½ – 1 Tbsp psyllium husk
- 3-4 slices of organic, chemical-free bacon diced
- ¼ spring onion, finely sliced
- 1 avocado

Instructions

- Preheat the oven to 350F. Line two baking trays with baking paper.
- Mix the 2 cups of grated cauliflower, salt, 2 eggs, 1 tablespoon of coconut flour, psyllium and garlic powder together. Add up to 1 tablespoon more of flour, if needed, to thicken.
- Split the cauliflower mix in 2. Place each cauliflower blob onto one of the lined baking trays and use your hands or a spatula to shape the mixture into even rectangles. Try not to make them too thick as you want it to cook through, and try not to make it too thin otherwise they will fall apart.
- Place them in the oven for 15 minutes.
- Check the cauliflower toasts and rotate them in the oven. Bake for another 10 minutes, or until they're golden brown and cooked through.
- Add the bacon to the second baking tray and spread it out. Place it in the oven and cook until it's golden brown.
- Meanwhile bring a small saucepan of water to the boil and add a dash of apple cider vinegar and a pinch of salt.
- When the water is boiling, crack 2 eggs into the water to poach. Cook them until the whites are fully cooked and the yolk is still slightly running.
- Remove them with a slotted spoon and place them onto some paper towel to remove the excess water.
- When the bacon and cauliflower toasts are ready, begin plating. Place the cauliflower toasts onto two plates. Top them with the poached eggs, crispy bacon, spring onion and avocado.
- Serve and enjoy.

468. Low Carb Lasagna

Ingredients

- 1 tablespoon butter, ghee, coconut oil, or lard
- 1/2lb spicy Italian sausage or sweet Italian sausage
- 15oz ricotta cheese
- 2 tablespoons coconut flour
- medium-high large whole egg
- 1 1/2 teaspoon salt
- 1/2 teaspoon pepper
- 1 teaspoon garlic powder
- a large clove garlic (finely chopped)

- 1 1/2 cup mozzarella cheese
- 1/3 cup parmesan cheese
- 4 large zucchini's
- 16oz Rao's marinara sauce
- 1 tablespoon mixed Italian herb seasoning
- 1/4 to 1/2 tsp red pepper flake (depending on how spicy you want this dish)
- 1/4 cup basil

Instructions

- Slice the zucchini then sprinkle generously with sea salt. Place your salted zucchini on a paper towel for 30 minutes. Once 30 minutes is up, wring the zucchini noodles with a paper towel one last time to extract any moisture.

- Heat 1 tablespoon of butter or fat of choice in a large skillet over medium-high heat. Crumble and brown Italian sausage. Remove from heat and let cool.

- Preheat oven to 375 degrees and coat a 9×9 baking dish with cooking spray or butter.

- Add ricotta cheese, 1 cup of mozzarella cheese, 2 tablespoons of parmesan cheese, 1 egg, coconut flour, salt, garlic, garlic powder, and pepper to a small bowl and mix until smooth. Set aside. Add Italian seasoning and red pepper flakes to a jar of marinara, stir well. Set aside.

- Add a layer of sliced zucchini to the bottom of greased dish. Spread 1/4 cup of cheese mixture over zucchini, sprinkle with 1/4 of the Italian sausage and then add a layer of sauce. Repeat process 3-4 times until ingredients are all gone, ending with a layer of sauce. Add remaining mozzarella cheese and sprinkle with remaining parmesan cheese.

- Cover with foil and bake for 30 minutes. Remove foil and bake for an additional 15 minutes until golden brown. Remove from oven and let sit for 5-10 minutes before serving. Sprinkle with fresh basil if desired.

469. Pigs in a Blanket Recipe

Ingredients

- 2 cups shredded mozzarella
- 2 ounces cream cheese (softened)
- 1/2 cup coconut flour
- 1 teaspoon dried oregano
- 3/4 teaspoon onion powder
- 1/2 teaspoon garlic powder
- 1/2 teaspoon baking powder
- 2 large eggs (whisked)
- 12 all-beef hotdogs
- 1 teaspoon sesame seeds

Instructions

- Preheat the oven to 400°F and line a baking sheet with parchment.
- Combine the mozzarella and cream cheese in a microwave-safe bowl and heat until melted then stir smooth and set aside.
- Combine the coconut flour, oregano, onion powder, garlic powder, baking powder, and eggs in a mixing bowl then stir in the melted cheese until a dough forms – wet your hands because it will be sticky.
- Divide the dough into 12 pieces and roll into balls.
- Roll out each dough ball between two pieces of parchment into 8-inch circles.
- Wrap each dough circle around a hotdog and place on the baking sheet.
- Sprinkle with sesame seeds then bake for 15 to 20 minutes until browned.

470. Cannoli Stuffed Crepes – Low Carb

Ingredients

For the crepes:

- 8 ounces cream cheese, softened
- 8 eggs
- 1/2 teaspoon ground cinnamon
- 1 tablespoon granulated erythritol sweetener
- 2 tablespoons butter, for the pan

For the cannoli filling:

- 6 ounces mascarpone cheese, softened
- 1 cup whole milk ricotta cheese
- 1/2 teaspoon lemon zest
- 1/2 teaspoon ground cinnamon
- 1/4 teaspoon unsweetened vanilla extract
- 1/4 cup powdered erythritol sweetener

For the optional chocolate drizzle (not included in nutrition info)

3 squares of a Lindt 90% chocolate bar

Instructions

For the crepes:

- Combine all of the crepes Ingredients in a blender and blend until smooth.
- Let the batter rest for 5 minutes and then give it a stir to break up any additional air bubbles.
- Heat 1 teaspoon of butter in a 10 inch or larger nonstick saute pan over medium heat.
- When the butter is melted and bubbling, pour in about 1/4 cup of batter (you can eyeball it) and if necessary, gently tilt the pan in a circular motion to create a 6-inch (-ish) round crepe.
- Cook for two minutes, or until the top is no longer glossy and bubbles have formed almost to the middle of the crepe.
- Carefully flip and cook for another 30 seconds. Remove and place on a plate.
- Repeat until you have 8 usable crepes.

471. Quiche Recipe

Ingredients

- 3 tablespoons coconut oil 45 ml, to cook with
- 6 slices bacon 168 g, diced
- 2 medium bell peppers 240 g, diced
- 1 medium onion 110 g, diced
- 4 cups spinach 120 g, chopped
- 2 small tomatoes 180 g, diced
- 12 medium eggs whisked
- 15 olives 45 g, diced
- 1/4 cup fresh basil leaves 8 g, chopped
- 3 cloves garlic 9 g, minced or finely diced
- 3/4 cup coconut cream (from the top of 1 refrigerated can of coconut milk) 180 ml
- Salt and pepper to taste

Instructions

- Preheat oven to 350 F (175 C).
- In a large skillet, melt the coconut oil over medium-high heat. Add the bacon and sauté until crispy, about 3 to 4 minutes. Remove the bacon with a slotted spoon and set aside.
- In the same skillet, add the bell pepper and onion to the bacon fat and sauté for 5 minutes.
- Add the spinach to the skillet and saute until wilted, about 1 to 2 minutes. Remove from the heat and let cool.
- In a large bowl, combine the tomato, eggs, olives, basil, garlic, coconut cream, bacon, and spinach mixture. Season with salt and pepper. Pour the egg mixture into a 9-inch by 9-inch (23-cm by 23-cm) square baking dish.
- Place in the oven and bake for 30 minutes until the eggs are soft but set.

472. One-Pan Chicken Stir-Fry Recipe

Ingredients

- 1/3 cup soy sauce
- 2 tablespoon rice vinegar
- 2 tablespoons So Nourished granulated erythritol
- 1 tablespoon sesame oil
- 1 teaspoon garlic powder
- 1 pound boneless chicken thighs

- 2 medium red peppers (cored and chopped)
- 2 cups green beans (sliced)
- 1 cup cauliflower florets
- 1 1/2 tablespoons olive oil
- 2 tablespoons sesame seeds

Instructions

- Whisk together the soy sauce, rice vinegar, granulated erythritol, sesame oil, and garlic powder in a small bowl.
- Chop the chicken into 1-inch pieces and place them in a zippered freezer bag.
- Pour in the sauce and shake to coat then chill for at least 4 hours.
- Preheat the oven to 425°F and line a large baking sheet with foil.
- Drain the chicken and spread it on the baking sheet and bake for 8 minutes.
- Toss the veggies with the olive oil and sprinkle onto the baking sheet with the chicken.
- Bake for another 12 to 15 minutes until the chicken is done then sprinkle with sesame seeds to serve.

SUPER SIMPLE

RECIPES

---

473. Classic Chocolate Cake Donuts

Ingredients

Donuts

- 1/3 cup coconut flour
- 1/3 cup Swerve Sweetener
- 3 tbsp cocoa powder
- 1 tsp baking powder
- 1/4 tsp salt

- 4 large eggs
- 1/4 cup butter melted
- 1/2 tsp vanilla extract
- 6 tbsp brewed coffee or water coffee intensifies the chocolate flavour

Glaze:

- 1/4 cup powdered Swerve Sweetener
- 1 tbsp cocoa powder
- 1 tbsp heavy cream

- 1/4 tsp vanilla extract
- 1 1/2 to 2 tbsp water

Instructions

Donuts:

- Preheat the oven to 325F and grease a donut pan very well.
- In a medium bowl, whisk together the coconut flour, sweetener, cocoa powder, baking powder, and salt. Stir in the eggs, melted butter, and vanilla extract, then stir in the cold coffee or water until well combined.
- Divide the batter among the wells of the donut pan. If you have a six-well donut pan, you may need to work in batches.
- Bake 16 to 20 minutes, until the donuts are set and firm to the touch. Remove and let cool in the pan for 10 minutes, then flip out onto a wire rack to cool completely.

Glaze:

- In a medium shallow bowl, whisk together the powdered sweetener and cocoa powder. Add the heavy cream and vanilla and whisk to combine.
- Add enough water until the glaze thins out and is of a "dippable" consistency, without being too watery.
- Dip the top of each donut into the glaze and let set, about 30 minutes.

474. BBQ Pulled Beef Sando

Ingredients

- 3lbs Boneless Chuck Roast
- 2 tsp Pink Himalayan Salt
- 2 tsp garlic powder
- 1 tsp onion powder
- 1 tsp black pepper
- 1 tbsp. smoked paprika
- 2 tbsp. tomato paste
- 1/4 cup apple cider vinegar
- 2 tbsp. coconut aminos
- 1/2 cup bone broth
- 1/4 cup melted Kerrygold Butter

Instructions

- Trim the fat off of the beef and cut in to two large pieces.
- In a small bowl mix together the salt, garlic, onion, paprika and black pepper. Then rub it all over the beef. Place the beef in your slow cooker.
- In another bowl melt the butter, whisk in the tomato paste, vinegar and coconut aminos. Pour it all over the beef. Then add the bone broth to the slow cooker, pouring it around the beef.
- Set on low and cook for 10-12 hours. When done, remove the beef, set the slow cooker to high and let the sauce thicken. Shred the beef then add it back in to the slow cooker and toss with sauce. Serve!

475. 2 Ingredient Pasta

Ingredients

- 1 cup shredded part skim low moisture mozzarella cheese
- 1 large egg

Instructions

- Add the mozzarella to a large microwave-safe bowl and microwave for about 1 minute. Stir until cheese is completely melted. If needed, heat for an additional 30 seconds or until cheese is completely melted.
- Allow the mozzarella to cool for 1 minute, so that it will not cook the egg. You don't want to cool the cheese too long though because it needs to stay melted.
- Add in egg and stir and mix into the cheese, until you have a uniform yellow dough.
- Place your dough on a flat surface lined with parchment paper. Place another parchment paper on top of the dough.
- Use a rolling pin over the top piece of parchment paper, and roll dough until it is 1/8 inch thick.
- Remove the top piece of parchment and cut the dough into ½ inch wide strips. Refrigerate the pasta for at least 6 hours or overnight.

- When ready to cook, bring a pot of water to boil. Do not add salt to the water. Add in pasta. Cook for about 40 seconds to 1 minute. Be careful not to cook too long, otherwise the pasta will lose its form, break down and become a melted cheese mess.

- Remove pasta from pot and run under cold water to cool it down. Gently separate strands sticking together. Allow pasta to cool until it is only slightly warm to the touch. When the pasta cools, it will firm back up, so that it is no longer just melty cheese and it will taste more like pasta rather than just cheese sticks. Serve with your favorite pasta sauce.

476. Lamb Kofta Kebabs

Ingredients

- 1/2 pound ground grass-fed lamb
- 1/2 cup parsley
- 1/2 inch fresh turmeric, grated
- 1/4 teaspoon sea salt

Instructions

- Gather 4 wooden kebab skewers. Soak skewers in water for 1 hour.

- Preheat oven to 300 degrees.

- In a food processor, add parsley and process for 30 seconds, or until finely chopped.

- Add lamb and grated turmeric to the processor and run until evenly mixed.

- Form lamb tightly around the kebab skewers. Salt the exterior of the meat.

- Line a baking sheet with foil and place an oven-safe rack on top of it so there is at least one inch of space between the rack and the pan. You may use a cast iron grill pan to get grill marks instead.

- Place kebabs on the grill and place in the upper third of your oven. Bake for 18-20 minutes, or until the internal temperature has reached 160 degrees.

- Remove lamb kofta from oven and garnish with grated turmeric and parsley sprigs.

477. Korean Paleo Bibimbap

Ingredients

- 12 ounces cauliflower rice
- 1 teaspoon toasted sesame oil
- 1 teaspoon coconut aminos

Vegetables

- 1 cup matchstick carrots
- 1 cup bean sprouts (omit for strict paleo)
- 1 cup cucumber (julienned)
- 2 cups spinach
- 4 scallions
- 1 teaspoon toasted sesame oil divided
- sea salt to taste

Other Toppings

- 2-4 eggs
- Kimchi I like this
- Sriracha

Instructions

- Heat a skillet over medium high heat with 1 teaspoon sesame oil. Add in the cauliflower rice and cook until soft and toasted, about 5 minutes. Remove and divide between two bowls.

- Wipe out the pan and add 1/4 teaspoon sesame oil and carrots. Saute for about 30 seconds just until soft. Add a small pinch of salt. Remove from pan and set aside. Repeat with bean sprouts.

- To the same pan once you've removed the sprouts add in 1/2 teaspoon of sesame oil and spinach. Cook for about 1 minute or until wilted.

- Grill the scallions over high heat just until charred. I simply lay them over my gas burner but you can also use a regular grill or grill pan. See notes for another option.

- Fry the eggs in a small ceramic or well seasoned cast iron skillet with a bit of sesame oil just until the whites are crispy and set but the yolk is still runny.

- Divide the vegetables between the two plates, top with eggs, kimchi, cucumbers, and the grilled or sliced scallions. Serve with Sriracha.

478. Easy, vegan and keto approved thai curry.

Ingredients

- 1 tofu pack 454g, cut into 16 cubes.
- 2 Bell peppers (Red & Green) Cut into strips
- 2 tbsp coconut oil
- 1 tbsp tomato paste
- 1 15 oz can coconut milk full fat
- 2 tsp chili flakes
- 1 tsp thai curry paste
- 1 tbsp almond butter
- Thumb sized piece of ginger peeled

- 1 stalk of lemon grass cut into 3 pieces
- 1 clove or garlic
- 1/4 cup soy sauce

Instructions

- Heat a pan at medium heat and melt your coconut oil. Mince your ginger and garlic and add to the pan. Add your bell pepper strips and lemon grass pieces. Stir for 30 seconds and add your coconut milk and chill flakes. Stir again.

- Add your soy sauce, thai curry paste, tomato paste, and almond butter. Stir for 1 minute and add your Tofu cubes. Let your curry cook for 5-10 minutes, or until the sauce thickens and take off the heat.

- Serve with chopped coriander and green onions to add a bit of freshness to the dish.

479. Feta Frittata

Ingredients

- 1 green onion, thinly sliced
- 1 small garlic clove, minced
- 2 large eggs
- 1/2 cup egg substitute
- 1/3 cup chopped plum tomato
- 4 tablespoons crumbled feta cheese, divided
- 4 thin slices peeled avocado
- 2 tablespoons reduced-fat sour cream

Instructions

- Heat a lightly oiled 6-in. nonstick skillet over medium heat. Saute onion and garlic until tender. Whisk the eggs, egg substitute and 3 tablespoons feta cheese. Add egg mixture to skillet (mixture should set immediately at edges). Cover and cook until nearly set, 4-6 minutes.

- Sprinkle with tomato and remaining feta cheese. Cover and cook until eggs are completely set, 2-3 minutes longer. Let stand for 5 minutes. Cut in half; serve with avocado and sour cream.

480. Slow Cooker Mexican Shredded Beef

Ingredients

- 3 1/2 pounds pastured beef short ribs or beef shank
- 2 teaspoons ground turmeric
- 1 teaspoon salt
- 1/2 teaspoon pepper
- 2 teaspoons ground cumin
- 2 teaspoons ground coriander
- 1/2 cup water
- 1 cup cilantro stems, coarsley chopped
- Optional: 4 cloves of garlic (crushed), 1 teaspoon chipotle powder and 2 teaspoons paprika

Instructions

In a small bowl, combine dry ingredients.

- Add short ribs to slow cooker and lightly coat each piece in the spice mix.
- Sprinkle cilantro stems and optional garlic over the ribs. Carefully add water without rinsing spices off the meat.
- Cook on low for 6-7 hours, or until it is falling apart. Check the meat at 6 hours and cook longer if it is not tender enough.
- If desired, drain cooking liquid into a small saucepan and reduce for 10-15 minutes over medium heat.
- Return liquid to the crock pot. Using two forks, pull the meat apart and shred the beef.
- Serve hot with Bulletproof guacamole, silverbeet leaves as a taco, roasted pumpkin, cucumbers, green beans and fresh cilantro.

481. Herb Butter Salmon and Asparagus Foil Packs

Ingredients

- 4 boneless skineless salmon fillets
- salt and pepper to taste
- 1 pound asparagus, ends trimmed
- 1 lemon, thinly sliced, (plus additional wedges for garnish)
- 1/2 cup butter, at room temperature
- 3 teaspoons Italian seasoning
- 3 teaspoons minced garlic
- fresh thyme or parsley, for garnish

Instructions

- Season salmon generously with salt and pepper on both sides. Arrange one salmon fillet and 1/4 of the asparagus in the center of one 12x12 inch piece of foil. Repeat with remaining salmon and asparagus on 3 other pieces of foil. Slide lemon slices under the salmon and asparagus.

- In a small bowl mix butter, Italian seasoning, and garlic. Drop large dollops of the herb butter on top of the salmon and asparagus.

- Fold the foil tightly around the salmon and asparagus, being sure to seal the ends together tightly so the juices and butter doesn't run out while cooking. Grill over medium high heat for 6-8 minutes on each side, OR bake at 400 degrees for 20 minutes, until asparagus is tender and salmon is flaky.

- Drizzle fresh lemon juice over the top and serve immediately.

482. Bacon and Asparagus Frittata

Ingredients

- 12 ounces bacon
- 2 cups sliced fresh asparagus (cut in 1/2-inch pieces)
- 1 cup chopped onion
- 2 garlic cloves, minced
- 10 large eggs, beaten

- 1/4 cup minced parsley
- 1/2 teaspoon seasoned salt
- 1/4 teaspoon pepper
- 1 large tomato, thinly sliced
- 1 cup shredded cheddar cheese

Instructions

- In a 9- or 10-in. ovenproof skillet, cook bacon until crisp. Drain, reserving 1 Tbsp. drippings. Heat reserved drippings on medium-high. Add asparagus, onion and garlic; saute until onion is tender. Crumble bacon; set aside a third. In a large bowl, combine remaining bacon, eggs, parsley, salt and pepper.

- Pour egg mixture into skillet; stir. Top with tomato, cheese and reserved bacon. Cover and cook over medium-low until eggs are nearly set, 10-15 minutes. Preheat broiler; place skillet 6 in. from heat. Broil until lightly browned, about 2 minutes. Serve immediately.

483. Fish Cakes with Avocado Lemon Dipping Sauce

Fish Cakes Ingredients

- 1 pound raw white boneless fish (preferably local and wild caught)
- 1/4 cup cilantro (leaves and stems)
- Pinch of salt
- Pinch of chilli flakes

- 1-2 garlic cloves (optional)
- 1-2 tablespoons coconut oil or grass-fed ghee for frying
- Neutral oil for greasing your hands, such as avocado oil

More Recipes From Bulletproof

- Keto Salted CBD Brownies

- 20 Low-Carb Fish Recipes You Can Make in a Flash

- Fluffy Keto Almond Flour Biscuits
- The Perfect Zucchini Chocolate Cake

Dipping Sauce Ingredients

- 2 ripe avocados
- 1 lemon, juiced
- Pinch of salt
- 2 tablespoons water

Instructions

- In a food processor, add fish, herbs, garlic (if using), salt, chili, and fish. Blitz until everything is combined evenly.
- In a large frying pan on medium-high heat, add coconut oil or ghee and swirl the pan to coat.
- Oil your hands and roll the fish mixture into 6 patties.
- Add cakes to the heated frying pan. Cook on both sides until golden brown and cooked through.
- While fish cakes are cooking, add all dipping sauce Ingredients (starting lemon juice) to a small food processor or blender and blitz until smooth and creamy. Taste the mixture and add more lemon juice or salt if desired.
- When fish cakes are cooked, serve warm with dipping sauce.

484. Harissa Portobello Mushroom "Tacos"

Ingredients

Portobello Mushrooms

- 1 pound (450g) portobello mushrooms
- 1/4 cup (60g) spicy harissa, or use a mild harissa
- 3 tablespoons olive oil, divided
- 1 teaspoon ground cumin
- 1 teaspoon onion powder
- 6 collard green leaves

Guacamole

- 2 medium ripe avocados
- 2 tablespoons chopped tomatoes
- 2 tablespoons chopped red onion
- 1 1/2 to 2 tablespoons lemon or lime juice
- pinch of salt
- 1 tablespoon chopped cilantro

Optional Toppings

- cashew cream
- chopped tomatoes
- chopped cilantro

Instructions

- Remove the stem of the portobellos. Rinse mushrooms and pat dry.
- Mix harissa, 1 1/2 tablespoons olive oil, cumin, and onion powder in a bowl. Brush each mushroom with the harissa mixture, making sure to cover the edges of the mushroom as well. Let mushroom marinade for 15 minutes.

- While the mushrooms are marinating, prepare guacamole. Halve and pit the avocados and scoop out the flesh. Mash avocados and mix in chopped tomatoes, red onion, lemon (or lime) juice, salt, and cilantro. Set aside.

- Rinse collard greens. Chop off the tough stems and set aside.

- When the mushrooms are done marinating, heat 1 1/2 tablespoons of olive oil in a skillet or sauté pan over medium-high heat. Place the portobello mushrooms in the pan and cook for 3 minutes. Flip over and cook for another 2 to 3 minutes. Each side should be browned.

- Turn off the heat and let the mushrooms rest for 2 to 3 minutes before slicing.

- Take a collard green leaf and fill it with a few slices of portobello. Add guacamole, chopped tomatoes, cashew cream and cilantro to your liking.

485. Southwestern Omelet

Ingredients

- 1/2 cup chopped onion
- 1 jalapeno pepper, minced
- 1 tablespoon canola oil
- 6 large eggs, lightly beaten
- 6 bacon strips, cooked and crumbled
- 1 small tomato, chopped

- 1 ripe avocado, cut into 1-inch slices
- 1 cup shredded Monterey Jack cheese, divided
- Salt and pepper to taste
- Salsa, optional

Instructions

- In a large skillet, saute onion and jalapeno in oil until tender; remove with a slotted spoon and set aside. Pour eggs into the same skillet; cover and cook over low heat for 3-4 minutes.

- Sprinkle with the onion mixture, bacon, tomato, avocado and 1/2 cup cheese. Season with salt and pepper.

- Fold omelet in half over filling. Cover and cook for 3-4 minutes or until eggs are set. Sprinkle with remaining cheese. Serve with salsa if desired.

486. Shrimp Zucchini Noodles Meal Prep

Ingredients

- 2 tablespoons unsalted butter
- 2 tablespoons olive oil
- 1 pound medium shrimp, peeled and deveined
- 1 shallot, minced
- 4 cloves garlic, minced

- 1/4 teaspoon red pepper flakes, or more, to taste
- Kosher salt and freshly ground black pepper, to taste
- 1/4 cup vegetable stock

- 2 tablespoons freshly squeezed lemon juice
- 1 teaspoon lemon zest
- 1 1/2 pounds (4 medium-sized) zucchini, spiralized
- 2 tablespoons freshly grated Parmesan

Instructions

- Combine butter and olive oil in a large skillet over medium high heat. Add shrimp, shallot, garlic and red pepper flakes; season with salt and pepper, to taste. Cook, stirring occasionally, until pink, about 2-3 minutes.
- Stir in vegetable stock, lemon juice and lemon zest; season with salt and pepper, to taste. Bring to a simmer; stir in zucchini noodles until heated through, about 1-2 minutes.
- Place zucchini into meal prep containers, garnished with Parmesan, if desired.

487. Low Carb Crack Slaw Egg Roll in a Bowl Recipe

Ingredients

- 1 tbsp Avocado oil
- 4 cloves Garlic (minced)
- 3 tbsp Fresh ginger (minced or grated; or use 3/4 tsp ground ginger)
- 1 lb Ground beef
- 1 tsp Sea salt
- 1/4 tsp Black pepper (or more if you want it spicy)
- 1 lb Shredded coleslaw mix (~4 cups)
- 1/4 cup Coconut aminos
- 2 tsp Toasted sesame oil
- 1/4 cup Green onions

Instructions

- Heat avocado oil in a large saute pan over medium-high heat. Add garlic and ginger. Saute for about a minute, until fragrant.
- Add ground beef. Season with sea salt and black pepper. Cook until browned, about 7-10 minutes.
- Reduce heat to medium. Add the coleslaw mix and coconut aminos. Stir to coat. Cover and cook for about 5 minutes, until the cabbage is tender.
- Remove from heat. Stir in the toasted sesame oil and green onions.

488. Ham Steaks with Gruyere, Bacon & Mushrooms

Ingredients

- 2 tablespoons butter
- 1/2 pound sliced fresh mushrooms
- 1 shallot, finely chopped
- 2 garlic cloves, minced
- 1/8 teaspoon coarsely ground pepper
- 1 fully cooked boneless ham steak (about 1 pound), cut into four pieces
- 1 cup shredded Gruyere cheese
- 4 bacon strips, cooked and crumbled

- 1 tablespoon minced fresh parsley, optional

Instructions

- In a large nonstick skillet, heat butter over medium-high heat. Add mushrooms and shallot; cook and stir 4-6 minutes or until tender. Add garlic and pepper; cook 1 minute longer. Remove from pan; keep warm. Wipe skillet clean.

- In same skillet, cook ham over medium heat 3 minutes. Turn; sprinkle with cheese and bacon. Cook, covered, 2-4 minutes longer or until cheese is melted and ham is heated through. Serve with mushroom mixture. If desired, sprinkle with parsley.

489. Slow Cooker Mexican Shredded Beef

Ingredients

- 3 1/2 pounds pastured beef short ribs or beef shank
- 2 teaspoons ground turmeric
- 1 teaspoon salt
- 1/2 teaspoon pepper
- 2 teaspoons ground cumin
- 2 teaspoons ground coriander
- 1/2 cup water
- 1 cup cilantro stems, coarsley chopped
- Optional: 4 cloves of garlic (crushed), 1 teaspoon chipotle powder and 2 teaspoons paprika

Instructions

In a small bowl, combine dry Ingredients.

- Add short ribs to slow cooker and lightly coat each piece in the spice mix.

- Sprinkle cilantro stems and optional garlic over the ribs. Carefully add water without rinsing spices off the meat.

- Cook on low for 6-7 hours, or until it is falling apart. Check the meat at 6 hours and cook longer if it is not tender enough.

- If desired, drain cooking liquid into a small saucepan and reduce for 10-15 minutes over medium heat.

- Return liquid to the crock pot. Using two forks, pull the meat apart and shred the beef.

- Serve hot with Bulletproof guacamole, silverbeet leaves as a taco, roasted pumpkin, cucumbers, green beans and fresh cilantro.

490. Poached Butter Shrimp

Ingredients

- 1 pound large wild-caught raw shrimp, peeled and deveined (about 32 shrimp)
- 1 cup grass-fed ghee, or butter cut into cubes
- 3 tablespoons water
- 1 bay leaf
- 6 sprigs fresh oregano, or 1/2 teaspoon dried oregano
- Zest of 1 lemon
- Fresh basil to garnish
- Salt to taste

Instructions

- In a pan, bring water to a boil over high heat. Reduce heat to medium and whisk in butter or ghee. Continue constantly whisking until the sauce becomes smooth, evenly textured, and emulsified.
- Add bay leaf, oregano, lemon zest, and shrimp to the pan. Season generously with salt. Stir to coat the shrimp in the butter mixture, and spread them so that they lay evenly across the pan.
- Bring liquid up to a light simmer over medium low heat and cook shrimp until pink and cooked through, about 5 minutes.
- Serve butter shrimp with a thin pool of sauce and fresh torn basil to garnish.

491. Mediterranean Omelet

Ingredients

- 4 large eggs
- 1/4 cup water
- 1/8 teaspoon salt
- Dash pepper
- 1 tablespoon butter
- 1/4 cup crumbled feta or goat cheese
- 1/4 cup chopped tomato
- 1 green onion, chopped

Instructions

- In a small bowl, whisk eggs, water, salt and pepper until blended. In a large nonstick skillet, heat butter over medium-high heat. Pour in egg mixture. Mixture should set immediately at edge. As eggs set, push cooked portions toward the center, letting uncooked eggs flow underneath.
- When eggs are thickened and no liquid egg remains, add cheese, tomato and green onion to 1 side. Fold omelet in half and cut into 2 portions; slide onto plates.

492. Bacon and Spinach Frittata

Ingredients

- 6 duck eggs or 8 hen eggs
- 1 tablespoon grass-fed ghee
- 4 ounces pasture-raised bacon, cut in 1/2-inch pieces
- 1 1/2 cups green beans, cooked and cut in half
- 2 cups of spinach or collard greens, steamed and roughly chopped
- 4 ounces cherry tomatoes, sliced in half (optional)
- 1 rosemary sprig, finely chopped

Instructions

- Preheat convection oven to 350 F
- In an oven-proof wide saucepan (I used a 12-inch pan) over medium heat, add the ghee, bacon and rosemary. Cook for 3 minutes until the bacon is slightly crisp.
- To the same pan, add the green vegetables and tomatoes to heat up and soften.
- Whisk the eggs in a bowl and then add to the pan, making sure they cover and reach all corners of the pan. Leave to cook for 5 minutes to set on the base and sides.
- Transfer the pan to the oven and allow to cook for another 5 minutes until the top of the frittata has set. Remove and allow to cool.
- Slice into 3 portions and serve with salad.

493. Low Carb Beef Stir Fry

Ingredients

- 1/2 cup zucchini, spiralized into 6-inch noodles
- 1 bunch baby bok choy
- 1/4 cup organic broccoli florets
- 8 ounces grass-fed flank or skirt steak, sliced against the grain into thin strips
- One 1-inch knob of ginger, peeled and cut into thin strips
- 2 tablespoons avocado oil or grass-fed ghee, divided
- 2 teaspoons coconut aminos

Instructions

- Chop the end of the stem off your bok choy and discard.
- In a heated pan, add 1 tablespoon of oil or ghee and sear your steak on medium-high heat, 1-2 minutes on each side.
- Reduce heat to medium. Add remaining ghee, broccoli, ginger and coconut aminos to the pan. Cook for one minute, stirring frequently.

- Stir in bok choy and cook for another minute.
- Stir in zucchini and cook until the noodles are at your desired preference. Watch closely, because they cook quick!

494. Zucchini & Gouda Skillet Frittata

Ingredients

- 6 large eggs
- 2 tablespoons 2% milk
- 1 teaspoon chopped fresh oregano
- 1/2 teaspoon salt
- 1/8 teaspoon pepper
- 2 tablespoons butter

- 2 medium zucchini (7 to 8 ounces each), thinly sliced
- 1 medium onion, chopped
- 2 tablespoons olive oil
- 1 medium tomato, diced
- 1 cup shredded Gouda cheese
- 2 tablespoons minced fresh basil

Instructions

- Combine first five Ingredients; set aside. In a large nonstick skillet, melt butter over medium heat. Add zucchini and onion. Cook until tender, 6-8 minutes; remove.
- In same skillet, heat oil over medium heat. Add egg mixture.
- Cook until set, gently lifting edges of cooked egg to allow liquid to run underneath. Top with zucchini mixture, diced tomato and cheese.
- Cover and cook until cheese is melted, 2-3 minutes. Sprinkle basil on top.

495. Steak Cobb Salad with Cilantro-Lime Vinaigrette

Ingredients

- 3 ounces grass-fed hanger steak
- 1 teaspoon avocado oil
- 1 pasture-raised egg
- 1 slice pasture raised bacon
- 1 cup riced cauliflower
- 1/2 avocado
- 1 cup arugula

- 1 cup mixed greens
- 2 tablespoons olive oil
- 1 teaspoon Brain Octane Oil or MCT oil
- ½ teaspoon lime juice
- 1 teaspoon apple cider vinegar
- ¼ teaspoon sea salt
- ¼ cup diced cilantro

Instructions

Bacon Cauliflower Rice

- Add minced bacon to a pan over medium heat, cook until no longer translucent

- Add cauliflower rice to the pan and cook for 4 minutes

Grass-Fed Hanger Steak

- Pat the steak dry and salt both sides generously
- Add avocado oil to pan over medium heat
- Add steak to the pan and cook for 4 minutes a side
- Let the steak rest for 5 minutes and then slice against the grain

Soft-Boiled Egg

- Bring 6 cups of water to rolling boil
- Set eggs into the water, cover and cook for 7 minutes

Cilantro-Lime Dressing

Add lime juice, apple cider vinegar, sea salt, cilantro, brain octane and olive oil in a food processor and blend until there are no more large chunks of cilantro.

Salad

Add mixed greens, arugula and all toppings in a bowl and toss

496. Garlic Butter Baked Salmon in Foil

Ingredients

- 1 ¼ pound sockeye or coho salmon (preferably wild caught)*
- 2 tablespoons lemon juice
- 2 cloves garlic, minced
- 2 tablespoons cold butter, cubed
- 1/2 teaspoon salt
- ¼ teaspoon black pepper
- ¼ teaspoon Italian seasoning
- ¼ teaspoon red pepper flakes
- 1 tablespoon chopped parsley, for garnishing (optional)

Instructions

- Position a rack in the center of the oven and preheat the oven to 375°F.
- In a saucepan over medium heat, combine the lemon juice and minced garlic, allow the lemon juice to reduce to 1 tablespoon. Add in 1 tablespoon of butter, remove pan from heat and swirl so the butter starts to melt. Place back on the heat for a few seconds, removed and continue to swirl until butter completely melts. Repeat with second tablespoon of butter. When butter is completely melted, remove sauce from stove.
- Place the salmon filet in a piece of foil large enough to fold over and seal. Using a brush or spoon, brush the salmon with the garlic butter sauce. Season with salt, pepper, Italian seasoning, and red pepper flakes. Cover with foil so that all sides are properly closed so the sauce does not leak.

- Bake the salmon for 12-14 minutes or until firm. Open the foil and allow the fish to broil under the broiler for 2-3 minutes, keeping an eye on it so the fish does not burn. Remove from oven, top with parsley. Serve immediately.

497. Spinach-Mushroom Scrambled Eggs

Ingredients

- 2 large eggs
- 2 large egg whites
- 1/8 teaspoon salt
- 1/8 teaspoon pepper
- 1 teaspoon butter
- 1/2 cup thinly sliced fresh mushrooms
- 1/2 cup fresh baby spinach, chopped
- 2 tablespoons shredded provolone cheese

Instructions

- In a small bowl, whisk eggs, egg whites, salt and pepper until blended. In a small nonstick skillet, heat butter over medium-high heat. Add mushrooms; cook and stir 3-4 minutes or until tender. Add spinach; cook and stir until wilted. Reduce heat to medium.

- Add egg mixture; cook and stir just until eggs are thickened and no liquid egg remains. Stir in cheese.

498. Tortilla Española (Spanish Omelette)

Ingredients

- 350 ml extra virgin olive oil divided
- 110 g white onion very thinly sliced crosswise
- 700 g medium radishes peeled & very thinly sliced crosswise
- 8 eggs
- kosher salt to taste
- freshly ground black pepper to taste
- fresh parsley to garnish

Instructions

- Heat up olive oil in a 10-inch non-stick pan over medium heat until it begins to simmer.

- Turn your heat down to low and add in the radish and onion slices, seasoning with a bit of salt as you layer them on the pan. Stir occasionally until tender, silky smooth and fully cooked (37-45 minutes, depending on size and thickness).

- Do not let the radishes or onion brown.

- Lightly whisk your eggs with a generous pinch of salt in a medium bowl, while the radishes are cooking. Set aside.

- Drain fully the radishes and onions once cooked, reserving 2-3 tablespoons of the oil. Allow to cool for a couple of minutes (so as to not scramble your eggs). Pour in your eggs.

If using a skillet

- Preheat oven to 350°F/180°C.

- Wipe out skillet and grease with reserved oil. Pour in egg and radish mixture and cook until the sides begin to set (3-5 minutes).

- Remove from heat, sprinkle with toppings (if using any), and bake for 10-12 minutes, or until fully set. Allow the tortilla to rest for 10 minutes before serving.

If using a non-stick pan

- Lightly grease a non-stick pan with reserved oil. Pour in egg and radish mixture and cook, swirling and shaking the pan rapidly until the sides begin to set (3 minutes). Turn off your heat and cover your pan for 5 minutes (your tortilla will continue to cook, without burning).

- Take pan off the heat and over the sink: place a large plate on top of the skillet, set a hand on top, and invert the tortilla onto it.

- Add one or two more tablespoons of olive oil to the pan, and slowly slide the tortilla from the plate back onto the skillet. Cook for 3-4 more minutes, until the second side is lightly browned but the tortilla is still tender.

- Invert the tortilla back onto a clean plate. Allow it to rest for 10 minutes before serving.

499. Slow Cooker Mexican Shredded Beef

Ingredients

- 3 1/2 pounds pastured beef short ribs or beef shank
- 2 teaspoons ground turmeric
- 1 teaspoon salt
- 1/2 teaspoon pepper
- 2 teaspoons ground cumin

- 2 teaspoons ground coriander
- 1/2 cup water
- 1 cup cilantro stems, coarsley chopped
- Optional: 4 cloves of garlic (crushed), 1 teaspoon chipotle powder and 2 teaspoons paprika

Instructions

- In a small bowl, combine dry Ingredients.

- Add short ribs to slow cooker and lightly coat each piece in the spice mix.

- Sprinkle cilantro stems and optional garlic over the ribs. Carefully add water without rinsing spices off the meat.

- Cook on low for 6-7 hours, or until it is falling apart. Check the meat at 6 hours and cook longer if it is not tender enough.

- If desired, drain cooking liquid into a small saucepan and reduce for 10-15 minutes over medium heat.

- Return liquid to the crock pot. Using two forks, pull the meat apart and shred the beef.

- Serve hot with Bulletproof guacamole, silverbeet leaves as a taco, roasted pumpkin, cucumbers, green beans and fresh cilantro.

500. Mediterranean Broccoli & Cheese Omelet

Ingredients

- 2-1/2 cups fresh broccoli florets
- 6 large eggs
- 1/4 cup 2% milk
- 1/2 teaspoon salt
- 1/4 teaspoon pepper

- 1/3 cup grated Romano cheese
- 1/3 cup sliced pitted Greek olives
- 1 tablespoon olive oil
- Shaved Romano cheese and minced fresh parsley

Instructions

- Preheat broiler. In a large saucepan, place steamer basket over 1 in. of water. Place broccoli in basket. Bring water to a boil. Reduce heat to a simmer; steam, covered, 4-6 minutes or until crisp-tender.

- In a large bowl, whisk eggs, milk, salt and pepper. Stir in cooked broccoli, grated cheese and olives. In a 10-in. ovenproof skillet, heat oil over medium heat; pour in egg mixture. Cook, uncovered, 4-6 minutes or until nearly set.

- Broil 3-4 in. from heat 2-4 minutes or until eggs are completely set. Let stand 5 minutes. Cut into wedges. Sprinkle with shaved cheese and parsley.

501. Lemon Balsamic Chicken

Ingredients

- 8 boneless skinless chicken thighs (about 2 lbs)
- 3 tbsp. pastured butter
- 1 cup sliced onion
- 1 cup shredded purple cabbage
- 2 tbsp. minced lemon rind

- 2 bay leaves
- 2 tsp pink Himalayan salt
- 1 tsp dried Italian herb blend
- 1 tsp coarse black pepper
- 1.5 tbsp. balsamic vinegar
- 5 tbsp. olive oil

Instructions

- Heat your electric pressure cooker on sauté mode. Add in 2 tbsp. of butter.

- While it melts, peel and slice your onion. Go ahead and prep your lemon rind and your cabbage, too!

- Add the onion, cabbage and lemon to the pressure. Sauté, stirring often until tender.

- Add in the chicken thighs, seasonings and bay leaves. Stir well and cook, browning the chicken for a 2-3 minutes.

- Pour in the vinegar. Cancel the sauté function. Close the lid, select pressure cook. Set it to poultry or high for 20 minutes.

- Once it has finished, let the pressure releases naturally. Open the lid, stir the chicken to shred. Mix in the last tablespoon of butter.

- Spoon this delicious saucy chicken all over your zoodles, drizzle with olive oil or avocado oil! Enjoy!

502. Poached Cod in Tomato Broth

Ingredients

- 1 pound wild-caught cod fillet, cut into 3-inch squares
- One 28-ounce can organic whole peeled tomatoes (BPA-free), drained
- 1.5 cups pastured chicken stock
- small pinch of saffron (about 15 threads)
- 2 bay leaves
- 3 tablespoons avocado oil
- Sea salt to taste

Instructions

- In a frying pan set to medium heat, add oil. Using your hands, crush the peeled tomatoes into the pan. Add stock, saffron, bay leaves, and salt to taste.
- Bring broth to a simmer over medium heat, then reduce heat to low.
- Add cod fillets and cover, simmering for 5-7 minutes or just until fish begins to flake.
- Serve fish with tomato broth.

503. Crustless Spinach Quiche

Ingredients

- 1 cup chopped onion
- 1 cup sliced fresh mushrooms
- 1 tablespoon vegetable oil
- 1 package (10 ounces) frozen chopped spinach, thawed and well drained
- 2/3 cup finely chopped fully cooked ham
- 5 large eggs
- 3 cups shredded Muenster or Monterey Jack cheese
- 1/8 teaspoon pepper

Instructions

- In a large skillet, saute onion and mushrooms in oil until tender. Add spinach and ham; cook and stir until the excess moisture is evaporated. Cool slightly. Beat eggs; add cheese and mix well. Stir in spinach mixture and pepper; blend well. Spread evenly into a greased 9-in. pie plate or quiche dish. Bake at 350° for 40-45 minutes or until a knife inserted in center comes out clean.

504. Fried Chicken

Ingredients

- 6 boneless chicken thighs
- 4 oz crushed pork rinds
- 2 tsp ground thyme
- 2 tsp salt
- 1 ½ tsp paprika
- 1 tsp garlic powder or 1 tbsp. crushed fresh garlic

- ¼ tsp ground cayenne pepper
- ¼ tsp black pepper
- 1 egg
- ¼ cup mayonnaise
- 2 tbsp hot sauce
- 1 tbsp mustard

Instructions

- Preheat oven to 425 degrees Fahrenheit and line baking sheet with parchment paper or aluminum foil and place baking rack on top.
- Using paper towels, pat each piece of chicken dry. Set aside.
- In a small mixing bowl, combine dry Ingredients. Whisk together until fully incorporated. Transfer half of dry ingredients to a shallow dish.
- In a separate bowl, mix together egg, mayonnaise, hot sauce, and mustard.
- Dip one chicken thigh at a time into egg wash then into dry Ingredients, flipping over multiple times to fully cover chicken in breading mixture.
- Transfer breaded chicken to the baking rack on prepared baking sheet. Continue breading remaining chicken thighs.
- Place chicken on the baking and bake until internal temperature reaches 165 degrees Fahrenheit, about 35-40 minutes, depending on the thickness of the chicken thigh. Allow them to cool slightly before serving.

505. Cauliflower Mac and Cheese Recipe with Cheese Sauce

Ingredients

- 1 head Cauliflower (cut into small florets)
- 3 tbsp Butter (divided into 2 tbsp and 1 tbsp)
- Sea salt
- Black pepper
- 1 cup Cheddar cheese (shredded)
- 1/4 cup Heavy cream
- 1/4 cup Unsweetened almond milk (or any milk of choice)

Instructions

- Preheat the oven to 450 degrees F (232 degrees C). Line a baking sheet with foil or parchment paper.

- Melt 2 tablespoons (28 g) of butter. In a large bowl, toss together the cauliflower florets with the melted butter. Season with sea salt and black pepper.

- Arrange the cauliflower florets on the prepared baking sheet. Roast for about 10-15 minutes, until crisp-tender.

- Heat the cheddar cheese, heavy cream, milk, and remaining tablespoon of butter, stirring frequently. (You can do this on the stove in a double broiler, or in the microwave.) Heat until the cheese mixture is smooth. Be careful not to overheat or burn the cheese.

- Toss cauliflower with cheese sauce right before serving.

506. Asparagus Cream Cheese Omelet

Ingredients

- 4 fresh asparagus spears, trimmed and cut into 1-inch pieces
- 4 large eggs
- 1/4 cup sour cream
- 2 teaspoons dried minced onion
- 1/4 teaspoon salt
- 1/4 teaspoon crushed red pepper flakes
- 2 teaspoons butter
- 2 ounces cream cheese, cubed and softened

Instructions

- Fill a small saucepan three-fourths full with water; bring to a boil. Add asparagus; cook, uncovered, 2-4 minutes or until crisp-tender. Remove and immediately drop into ice water. Drain and pat dry.

- In a small bowl, whisk eggs, sour cream, onion, salt and pepper flakes. In a large nonstick skillet, heat butter over medium-high heat. Pour in egg mixture. Mixture should set immediately at edge. As eggs set, push cooked portions toward the center, letting uncooked eggs flow underneath.

- When eggs are thickened and no liquid egg remains, top one side with cream cheese and asparagus. Fold omelet in half. Reduce heat to low; let stand, covered, 1-2 minutes or until cream cheese is melted. Cut omelet in half before serving.

507. Superfood Meatballs

Ingredients

- 3lbs 85% lean grass fed ground beef
- 1lb pastured chicken livers
- 1 large shallot
- 4 medium carrots
- 3 garlic cloves
- 2 tbsp. grass fed butter
- 1 tsp dried oregano

- 2 tbsp. coconut aminos (separated)
- 3 tsp salt (separated)
- 2 tsp black pepper
- 1 tbsp. dried thyme (dried)
- 1 tbsp. garlic powder
- Olive oil

Instructions

- Heat a large cast iron skillet on medium heat. While it heats, mince the shallots, carrots and garlic until fine. When the skillet comes to temperature add in the vegetables and sauté until aromatic and tender, about 8 minutes, stir often.

- Add in the chicken livers along with 1 tsp salt and dried oregano. Cook, stirring often, until the livers are browned all over. Add in the 1 tbsp. coconut aminos and 1 tbsp. apple cider vinegar and cook until reduced and livers are cooked.

- Remove from heat, and let cool a few minutes. Transfer to a food processor and pulse until it looks like ground beef. Then transfer to a large bowl, to cool to room temp.

- Pre-heat oven to 425F. Add the ground beef to the bowl with the remaining salt and the rest of the seasoning. Mix well. Shape 1 ½ inch balls, will make aprx 30.

- Drizzle olive oil all over the sheet pan. With oiled hands, coat each meatball in a little olive oil and you handle it to place it on the sheet pan. Then lightly drizzle them with the remaining coconut aminos.

- Place in the oven, roast at 425F for 5 minutes. Then turn the temperature down to 350F and roast another 20 minutes before removing from the oven.

- These meatballs are perfect for meal prep or feeding a crowd. Dunk them in ranch, pile on some guac or drizzle with lemon tahini sauce for some extra fats!

508. Shrimp Scampi Recipe

Ingredients

- 2 summer squash
- 2 tbsp butter
- 1/4 cup chicken broth or white wine?
- 2 tbsp lemon juice
- 1/8 tsp red chili flakes
- salt and pepper to taste
- 1 pound shrimp deveined
- 2 tbsp parsley chopped

Instructions

- Cut summer squash into noodle shapes using a spiralizer tool. Spread noodles out on top of paper towels. Sprinkle with salt and set aside for 15-30 minutes. Blot the excess moisture away or lightly wring out with dry paper towels.

- In a saute or frying pan, melt butter over medium heat. Add chicken broth, lemon juice (or wine), and red chili flakes. Bring to a light boil, then add in shrimp. Simmer until shrimp begin to turn pink and reduce heat to low.

- Taste the sauce, then mix in salt and pepper to your liking. Add the summer squash noodles and parsley to the pan and toss to distribute the shrimp and coat the noodles in sauce. Remove from heat and serve.

509. Broccoli Quiche Cups

Ingredients

- 1 cup chopped fresh broccoli
- 1 cup pepper jack cheese
- 6 large eggs, lightly beaten
- 3/4 cup heavy whipping cream
- 1/2 cup bacon bits
- 1 shallot, minced
- 1/4 teaspoon salt
- 1/4 teaspoon pepper

Instructions

- Preheat oven to 350°. Divide broccoli and cheese among 12 greased muffin cups.

- Whisk together remaining ingredients; pour into cups. Bake until set, 15-20 minutes.

- Health Tip: Swap half-and-half for whipped cream and save more than 60 calories and 6g saturated fat per serving.

510. Portobello Bun Cheeseburgers

Ingredients

- 1 lb. grassfed 80/20 ground beef
- 1 tbsp Worcestershire sauce
- 1 tsp pink Himalayan salt
- 1 tsp black pepper
- 1 tbsp avocado oil
- 6 portobello mushroom caps, destemmed, rinsed and dabbed dry
- 6 slices sharp cheddar cheese

Instructions

1. In a bowl, combine ground beef, Worcestershire sauce, salt, and pepper.
2. Form beef into burger patties.
3. In a large pan, heat avocado oil over medium heat. Add portobello mushroom caps and cook for about 3-4 minutes on each side. Remove from heat.
4. In the same pan, cook burger patties for 4 minutes on one side and 5 minutes on the other side, or until desired doneness is achieved. Add cheese to top of burgers and cover with a lid and allow cheese to melt, about 1 minute.
5. Layer one portobello mushroom cap, then cheeseburger, desired garnishes, and top with remaining portobello mushroom cap.

Optional garnishes

1. Sliced dill pickles
2. Romaine
3. Sugar-free barbecue sauce
4. Spicy brown mustard

511. Salmon Gremolata with Roasted Vegetables

Ingredients

- 4 salmon fillets

Gremolata

- 2 cloves garlic
- 1/4 cup parsley leaves
- 1 lemon, zested
- 1 cup almond flour
- 1 tbsp olive oil
- salt
- pepper

Roasted Vegetables (Optional)

- 1 bunch asparagus
- 1 cup cherry tomatoes
- 1 tbsp olive oil
- salt
- pepper

Instructions

- Heat your oven to 350F for a fan oven, 380F for non fan oven.

- Blitz the garlic, parsley and almond meal together in a blender or food processor, then stir in the lemon zest.

- Place the salmon fillets on a greased or parchment lined sheet pan.

- Season the salmon fillets with salt and pepper, brush or spray with a little oil, then carefully press the Gremolata crumb mixture on top.

- If you are using the optional vegetables to roast alongside the salmon, simply toss them in a little oil, place them around the salmon on the sheet pan and season with salt and pepper.

- Bake for 15-20 mins until the fish is cooked through and the tops are golden.

512. Ham & Feta Omelet

Ingredients

- 4 large eggs
- 1 green onion, chopped
- 1 tablespoon 2% milk
- 1/4 teaspoon dried basil
- 1/4 teaspoon dried oregano
- Dash garlic powder
- Dash salt

- Dash pepper
- 1 tablespoon butter
- 1/4 cup crumbled feta cheese
- 3 slices deli ham, chopped
- 1 plum tomato, chopped
- 2 teaspoons balsamic vinaigrette

Instructions

- In a small bowl, whisk eggs, green onion, milk and seasonings until blended. In a large nonstick skillet, heat butter over medium-high heat. Pour in egg mixture. Mixture should set immediately at edge.

- As eggs set, push cooked portions toward the center, letting uncooked eggs flow underneath. When eggs are thickened and no liquid egg remains, top one side with cheese and ham.

- Fold omelet in half; cut into two portions. Slide onto plates; top with tomato. Drizzle with vinaigrette before serving.

513. Loaded Cauliflower Bake

Ingredients

- 1 large head cauliflower, cut into florets
- 2 tbsp. butter
- 1 cup heavy cream
- 2 oz. cream cheese
- Salt and pepper to taste
- 1 1/4 cup shredded sharp cheddar cheese, separated
- 6 slices bacon, cooked and crumbled
- 1/4 cup chopped green onions

Instructions

- Preheat oven to 350 degrees.
- In a large pot of boiling water, blanch cauliflower florets for 2 minutes. Drain cauliflower.
- In a medium pot, melt together butter, heavy cream, cream cheese, 1 cup of shredded cheddar cheese, salt, and pepper until well-combined.
- In a baking dish, add cauliflower florets, cheese sauce, all but 1 tbsp. crumbled bacon, and all but 1 tbsp. green onions. Stir together.
- Top with remaining shredded cheddar cheese, crumbled bacon, and green onions.
- Bake until cheese is bubbly and golden and cauliflower is soft, about 30 minutes.
- Serve immediately and enjoy!

514. Loaded Cauliflower

Ingredients

- 1 pound cauliflower florettes
- 4 ounces sour cream
- 1 cup grated cheddar cheese
- 2 slices cooked bacon crumbled
- 2 tablespoons snipped chives
- 3 tablespoons butter
- 1/4 teaspoon garlic powder
- salt and pepper to taste

Instructions

- Cut the cauliflower into florettes and add them to a microwave safe bowl. Add 2 tablespoons of water and cover with cling film. Microwave for 5-8 minutes, depending on your microwave, until completely cooked and tender. Drain the excess water and let sit uncovered for a minute or two. (Alternately, steam your cauliflower the conventional way. You may need to squeeze a little water out of the cauliflower after cooking.)
- Add the cauliflower to a food processor and process until fluffy. Add the butter, garlic powder, and sour cream and process until it resembles the consistency of mashes potatoes. Remove the

mashed cauliflower to a bowl and add most of the chives, saving some to add to the top later. Add half of the cheddar cheese and mix by hand. Season with salt and pepper.

- Top the loaded cauliflower with the remaining cheese, remaining chives and bacon. Put back into the microwave to melt the cheese or place the cauliflower under the broiler for a few minutes.

- I visually divide the cauliflower into sixths. Serving size is approximately 1/3-1/2 cup.

515. Mascarpone-Mushroom Frittata Stack

Ingredients

- 8 large eggs
- 1/3 cup heavy whipping cream
- 1/2 cup grated Romano cheese, divided
- 1-1/2 teaspoons salt, divided
- 5 tablespoons olive oil, divided
- 3/4 pound sliced fresh mushrooms

- 1 medium onion, halved and thinly sliced
- 2 tablespoons minced fresh basil
- 2 garlic cloves, minced
- 1/8 teaspoon pepper
- 1 carton (8 ounces) Mascarpone cheese

Instructions

- In a large bowl, whisk eggs, cream, 1/4 cup Romano cheese and 1 teaspoon salt.

- In a 10-in. skillet, heat 2 tablespoons oil over medium-high heat. Add mushrooms and onion; cook and stir until tender. Add basil, garlic, pepper and remaining salt; cook and stir 1 minute longer. Transfer to a bowl; stir in mascarpone cheese and remaining Romano cheese.

- In same pan, heat 1 tablespoon oil over medium-high heat. Pour in 2/3 cup egg mixture. Mixture should set immediately at edges. As eggs set, push cooked portions toward the center, letting uncooked eggs flow underneath.

- Let stand, covered, 5-7 minutes or until completely set. Remove to a serving platter; cover and keep warm. Repeat with remaining egg mixture making two additional frittatas, using remaining oil as needed.

- Place one frittata on a serving platter; layer with half of the mushroom mixture. Repeat layers. Top with remaining frittata. Cut into wedges.

516. Low Carb Lasagna

Ingredients

- 1 tablespoon butter, ghee, coconut oil, or lard
- 1/2lb spicy Italian sausage or sweet Italian sausage
- 15oz ricotta cheese
- 2 tablespoons coconut flour
- medium-high large whole egg
- 1 1/2 teaspoon salt
- 1/2 teaspoon pepper
- 1 teaspoon garlic powder
- a large clove garlic (finely chopped)
- 1 1/2 cup mozzarella cheese
- 1/3 cup parmesan cheese
- 4 large zucchini's
- 16oz Rao's marinara sauce
- 1 tablespoon mixed Italian herb seasoning
- 1/4 to 1/2 tsp red pepper flake (depending on how spicy you want this dish)
- 1/4 cup basil

Instructions

- Slice the zucchini then sprinkle generously with sea salt. Place your salted zucchini on a paper towel for 30 minutes. Once 30 minutes is up, wring the zucchini noodles with a paper towel one last time to extract any moisture.

- Heat 1 tablespoon of butter or fat of choice in a large skillet over medium-high heat. Crumble and brown Italian sausage. Remove from heat and let cool.

- Preheat oven to 375 degrees and coat a 9×9 baking dish with cooking spray or butter.

- Add ricotta cheese, 1 cup of mozzarella cheese, 2 tablespoons of parmesan cheese, 1 egg, coconut flour, salt, garlic, garlic powder, and pepper to a small bowl and mix until smooth. Set aside. Add Italian seasoning and red pepper flakes to a jar of marinara, stir well. Set aside.

- Add a layer of sliced zucchini to the bottom of greased dish. Spread 1/4 cup of cheese mixture over zucchini, sprinkle with 1/4 of the Italian sausage and then add a layer of sauce. Repeat process 3-4 times until Ingredients are all gone, ending with a layer of sauce. Add remaining mozzarella cheese and sprinkle with remaining parmesan cheese.

- Cover with foil and bake for 30 minutes. Remove foil and bake for an additional 15 minutes until golden brown. Remove from oven and let sit for 5-10 minutes before serving. Sprinkle with fresh basil if desired.

517. Chinese pork with Brussels sprouts

Ingredients

- 11/3 lbs pork belly
- 2 tbsp tamari soy sauce
- 1 tbsp rice vinegar
- 2 garlic cloves
- 3 oz. butter or coconut oil
- 1 lb Brussels sprouts
- ½ leek
- salt and ground black pepper

Instructions

- Cut the pork belly into bite-sized pieces.
- Rinse and trim the Brussels sprouts. Cut in halves or quarters depending upon their size.
- Add the pork to a pan and place it over medium-high heat. Fry until golden brown.
- Smash the garlic cloves and add them along with the Brussels sprouts and the butter. Fry until the sprouts are starting to turn golden brown.
- Mix soy sauce and rice vinegar in a small bowl and add that to the pan.
- Season with salt and pepper to taste.
- Finally sprinkle on thinly sliced leeks. Give it all a stir and serve.

Tip!

For a gluten-free and soy-free alternative to soy sauce, try coconut aminos; check the label, but expect about one gram net carbs per teaspoon.

If you can't find pork belly you can use bacon instead. If you want to vary this dish you can substitute the Brussels sprouts for green beans or broccoli and there will be little to no change to the amount of carbs.

CONCLUSION

It is important to eat different types of foods as stated by the Dietary Guidelines for Americans. Dialysis patients are not excluded from this guideline. This book provided a lot of information about a nutritious diet that will provide many health benefits and may even save someone's life. It is up to you if you would like to follow it in order to live a healthier lifestyle to prevent chronic illnesses and have a better quality of life.

A lot of the recipes are fast and simple to make with common and relatively affordable ingredients. Appropriate serving suggestions are provided in many of the recipes. A practical information category includes tips to achieve success with this diet and a few ideas for snacks and meals. Also, I'm aware that a lot of people follow a restricted diet, desire to lose weight or maybe even have to gain weight. This is why I have come up with recipes that can be modified to meet your personal requirements.

I would be delighted if you enjoy the dishes in this recipe book and I hope it provides you with the life-sustaining nutrients that are required, but most especially, that you never stop savoring the taste of your meals

Printed in Great Britain
by Amazon